Unborn Human Life and Fundamental Rights

AD FONTES

SCHRIFTEN ZUR PHILOSOPHIE

Herausgegeben von Tadeusz Guz

BAND 15

PETER LANG

Pilar Zambrano, William L. Saunders (eds.)

Unborn Human Life and Fundamental Rights

Leading Constitutional Cases under Scrutiny.

Concluding Reflections by John Finnis

PETER LANG

Bibliografische Information der Deutschen Nationalbibliothek
Die Deutsche Nationalbibliothek verzeichnet diese Publikation
in der Deutschen Nationalbibliografie; detaillierte bibliografische
Daten sind im Internet über http://dnb.d-nb.de abrufbar.

Library of Congress Cataloging-in-Publication Data A CIP catalog
record for this book has been applied for at the Library of Congress

This book is an outcome of the research project PICTO–Austral 2016-0095;
and was made possible, in part, by a grant from the Institute for Human Ecology
at The Catholic University of America.

Gedruckt auf alterungsbeständigem,
säurefreiem Papier.

ISSN 1613-947X
ISBN 978-3-631-77554-7 (Print)
E-ISBN 978-3-631-79387-9 (PDF)
E-ISBN 978-3-631-79388-6 (EPUB)
E-ISBN 978-3-631-79389-3 (MOBI)
DOI 10.3726/ b15804

© Peter Lang GmbH
Internationaler Verlag der Wissenschaften
Berlin 2019
Alle Rechte vorbehalten.

Peter Lang – Berlin · Bern · Bruxelles ·
New York · Oxford · Warszawa · Wien

Das Werk einschließlich aller seiner Teile ist urheberrechtlich
geschützt. Jede Verwertung außerhalb der engen Grenzen des
Urheberrechtsgesetzes ist ohne Zustimmung des Verlages
unzulässig und strafbar. Das gilt insbesondere für
Vervielfältigungen, Übersetzungen, Mikroverfilmungen und die
Einspeicherung und Verarbeitung in elektronischen Systemen.

Diese Publikation wurde begutachtet.

www.peterlang.com

Dedicated with admiration and gratitude to Mary Ann Glendon, Learned Hand Professor, Harvard Law School—valiant defender of the dignity and rights of every member of the human family.

Foreword

This volume, which we hope will be of interest to the educated layman as well as professors and students, is the outcome of a joint effort of planning, coordination, and editing extending over more than five years. It was intended, from the very beginning, to lay the basis for a comparative analysis of the legal and moral reasoning underlying leading cases from constitutional and international courts that define the legal value of unborn human life. With this purpose in mind, the volume collects the work of scholars from twelve different countries, representative of three distinctive legal identities: Latin American Constitutional Courts and the Inter-American Court of Human Rights; European Courts and the European Court of Human Rights; and Common Law jurisdictions.

Far from being random, the selection of these three distinct jurisprudential "communities" is grounded in normative and theoretical reasons. From the normative point of view, while Latin American constitutional courts are bound by the American Convention of Human Rights, which states that the right to life should be protected by law from the moment of conception (Article 4.1), neither European states nor common law jurisdictions are bound by the American Convention, nor by any other international convention explicitly acknowledging the existence of the right to life from the moment of conception (though, of course, it can be argued that many binding international treaties do so implicitly). This disparity provides a particularly enlightening viewpoint for assessing the extent to which international conventions on human rights control domestic constitutional decisions dealing with the most fundamental concepts of any human rights system, such as life, dignity, and person.

The constitutions in the European and common law context involved in the cases studied in chapters one to seven do not—except for Ireland from 1983 until 2018—explicitly recognize legal personhood before birth. This legal fact has been interpreted from *Roe vs. Wade* (1973) onwards as a reason for denying the existence of personhood and the right to life before birth, and asserting that the rights to privacy, reproductive health, equality, or the free development of personality of the mother, among others, include the liberty to terminate pregnancy or to discard embryos. As is also remarked in chapters one to seven, legal and judicial evolution after *Roe vs. Wade* either reinforced or extended this understanding.

On the other hand, the explicit acknowledgment of the right to life from the moment of conception by the American Convention might be considered a good explanation for the fact, discussed in chapters eight to twelve, that all Latin American constitutional decisions included in this volume, saving those from the Mexican Federal Court, asserted that states are obliged to effectively secure the right to life from the moment of conception. Nevertheless from 2012 onwards the trend is steadily towards the European and common law understanding that States are obliged to secure the liberty of women to terminate pregnancy or to discard embryos in the name of privacy, reproductive health, equality or the free development of personality, or even dignity. This interpretative shift is not backed by any amendment to the underlying legal framework; rather it is based upon a novel understanding that goes from overtly neglecting legal personhood at some time before birth (*Artavía Murillo*) to passing over the state´s obligation to protect unborn human life and thus rendering it void (*F.A.L*).

One may very well ask why the absence of an explicit constitutional or conventional recognition of personhood before birth is understood by European and common law courts as a reason for denying it, while the constitutional and conventional silence regarding any right to abortion, or access to reproductive techniques that entail discarding embryos, is no obstacle to the judicial recognition and enforcement of abortion, and/or the discarding of embryos. Similarly, one may very well ask, what are the strictly legal reasons that led one generation of constitutional courts in Latin America to affirm the obligation of states to secure the right to life from the moment of conception, and what are the contrary reasons, also strictly legal, that are now leading the present generation to deny it.

The answer to these questions is indicated by the very need to raise them. If pure legal reasons cannot be easily identified, it is probably because they do not exist. It appears, instead, that, beyond the legal framework conditioning the decisions reviewed in this book, all of them are part of a common moral-political debate that touches the conceptual roots of any constitutional system. And this allows us to pass from the normative to the theoretical reasons behind our choice to scrutinize leading cases dealing with unborn human life in these three different legal contexts.

It is an undiscussed topic in present legal theory that, although constitutional and international human rights decisions are inevitably conditioned by their legal background, they are also founded in moral/political reasoning that is rarely made explicit, but is always present. Among other reasons that explain the mixed moral-legal nature of constitutional and conventional interpretation and adjudication, two are especially relevant to the purposes of this book.

In the first place, there is the abstract nature of human rights´ language, which almost always restricts itself to naming the rights to be secured by the law, without specifying which concrete public policies are fitted to this purpose, leaving this judgment to the courts. In addition to the gap between human rights language and human rights decisions, which by itself might explain the creative nature of constitutional and conventional interpretation, the moral nature of such interpretation follows from the clear moral purpose of constitutions and international conventions, which consists of securing to *all* human beings the respect and consideration that is due to their dignity. Both the abstract language and the moral purpose of constitutions and human rights international conventions require, in short, that judicial interpretation and adjudication in both fields necessarily entail—and not only eventually—a deep immersion into moral and political reasoning.

Coming back to the theoretical reasons behind this book, judicial decisions defining and applying the most fundamental and abstract concepts of person and dignity cannot do otherwise than to bring to light the moral horizon that, perhaps in a less than perfectly clear way, animates constitutional and conventional interpretation generally. The disclosure of this moral horizon is indispensable, in the first place, in any political order that strives for compliance with the *Rule of Law* and more accurately, as Professor Finnis argues in his concluding chapter, with the principle of "separation of judicial from legislative power ... in view of the need for a constitutional organ or institution that is dedicated to upholding and enforcing the law in force at the time (past) when a dispute arose." The disclosure is likewise necessary for anyone committed to the construction of a just and truly humane society. In effect, the more familiar we are with the comprehensive horizon—or, to rephrase Rawls, with the comprehensive conceptions of the world—that, for better or for worse, sustain our constitutional practices, the easier it will be to make our way towards the *just* societies we intend to construct, through the valid legal—and thus legitimate—channels of political action.

As an outcome of the research project PICTO–Austral 2016-0095, this book seeks to serve as a positive contribution to the discussion of the named theoretical concerns in the fields of jurisprudence, human rights theory, and constitutional law. The authors invited to take part in it were selected in view of their academic leadership in these disciplines, in the specific constitutional practice they were requested to study. All of them were asked to complement a descriptive approach with a critical analysis of *both* the legal and moral reasoning underlying the leading decisions under study. We are deeply thankful for their generous acceptance of our invitation in the early stages of this project, for their patience along the (quite long) time it took us to assemble all the contributions that we deemed indispensable for this study. We are grateful for their contributions to the volume that we are now proud to present. We acknowledge the support afforded for editing this book by the Institute for Human Ecology of the Catholic University of America. A special acknowledgment is due to Professor John Finnis for the insightful concluding essay to this volume, drawing together the many threads of the individual chapters into a comprehensive whole.

Pilar Zambrano and William L. Saunders

Contents

List of Contributors 13

William L. Saunders
1 Judicial Interference in the Protection of Human Life in the United States: Actions and Consequences 15

Gerard V. Bradley
2 Whither United States Abortion Law? 29

Dwight Newman
3 Canada's Abortion Jurisprudence: The Creep of Procedural Rights and the Reinterpretation of Liberty 53

Salvatore Amato
4 To Be and Not to Be. The Uncertain Identity of Unborn Children in Italian Case Law 71

Angel J. Gómez Montoro
5 Leading Cases from the Spanish Constitutional Court Concerning the Legal Status of Unborn Human Life 83

Jerzy M. Ferenz and Aleksander Stępkowski
6 The Emergence of the Right to Life in Polish Constitutional Law 115

William Binchy
7 The Unborn Children and the Irish Constitution, Including Analysis of the Role of the European Court of Human Rights 133

Juan Cianciardo
8 The Specification of the Right to Life of the Unborn in the Inter-American Human Rights System: A Study of the *Artavía Murillo* Case 163

Pilar Zambrano
9 A Moral Reading of Argentine Constitutional Case Law on the Right to Life before Birth 185

Alejandro Miranda and Sebastián Contreras
10 Commentary on the Constitutional Court of Chile's Decision
Concerning the So-Called "Morning after Pill" 205

Hugo S. Ramírez García and José María Soberanes Díez
11 The Right to Life in the Context of Mexican Legal
Experience: From the Constitution to the Jurisprudence 223

Luis Castillo Córdova
12 Legal Status of Unborn Human Life: A Case from Peru 233

John Finnis
Unborn Human Life and Fundamental Rights: Concluding Reflections 255

List of Contributors

Salvatore Amato
Full professor of Philosophy of Law and Biolaw in the Department of Law of the University of Catania and member of the Italian National Bioethics Council

William Binchy
Barrister-at-Law; Adjunct Professor of Law, Trinity College Dublin; formerly Regius Professor of Laws, 1992–2012; Commissioner, Irish Human Rights Commission, 2000–2011.

Gerard V. Bradley
Professor of Law, University of Notre Dame.

Luis Castillo Córdova
Professor of Constitutional Law, University of Piura, Law Faculty, (Perú).

Juan Cianciardo
Professor of Philosophy of Law at the University of Navarra, Law Faculty, Spain; research fellow of CONICET, Argentina.

Sebastián Contreras
Professor of Legal Philosophy at the University of Los Andes, Chile.

Jerzy M. Ferenz
PhD in criminal law, Barrister, practicing in Warsaw.

John Finnis
QC, FBA. Professor of Law & Legal Philosophy Emeritus, University of Oxford; Biolchini Family Professor of Law, University of Notre Dame Indiana.

Angel J. Gómez Montoro
Professor of Constitutional Law. University of Navarra, Spain.

Alejandro Miranda
Professor of Legal Philosophy at the University of Los Andes, Chile.

Dwight Newman
Professor of Law and Canada Research Chair in Indigenous Rights in Constitutional and International Law at the University of Saskatchewan.

Hugo S. Ramírez García
Professor of Philosophy of Law, Universidad Panamericana, Law Faculty, México.

William L. Saunders
Law Fellow and Director of the Program in Human Rights, Institute for Human Ecology; Director of the Center for Human Rights, School of Arts & Sciences; and Co-Director, Center for Religious Liberty, Columbus School of Law; The Catholic University of America.

José María Soberanes Díez
Professor of Constitutional Law, Universidad Panamericana, Law Faculty, México.

Aleksander Stępkowski
PhD habillited, Professor of Law at University of Warsaw Faculty of law and Administration, Head of the Sociology of Law Chair. Formerly, he had organized and was the first President of the Ordo Iuris Institute for Legal Culture. He used to serve as the Deputy Minister of Foreign Affairs for legal, treaty issues and human rights. In 2019 he was appointed Judge in the Supreme Court of the Republic of Poland.

Pilar Zambrano
Professor of Human Rights and Political Thought at the University of Navarra, Faculty of Law, Spain; research fellow of CONICET, Argentina.

William L. Saunders

1 Judicial Interference in the Protection of Human Life in the United States: Actions and Consequences

Abstract: Any system of "rights" built upon the denial of the very cornerstone of the entire concept of "human rights"—that is, the right to life of each human being simply because that being is in existence—is built upon a basic falsehood about the human person and about the nature of society. Such a system, in its very roots, denies the possibility of achieving the common good, which is the primary, legitimate aim of political/legal authority. Hence, when political authority fails in its obligation to protect life and, thereby, to create an essential condition for achieving the common good, all of society is imperiled. The unraveling of the rule of law and the undermining of mutual respect among citizens unfolds in myriad ways, some obvious and some subtle. In this chapter, we shall examine these general propositions in the situation in the United States by focusing on rulings of the Supreme Court of the United States in their social and bioethical context.

Keywords: Human rights, Life, Abortion, Judicial review, Stem cell, Embryo

1 Introduction

Any system of "rights" built upon the denial of the very cornerstone of the entire concept of "human rights—that is, the right to life of each human being simply because that being is in existence—is built upon a basic falsehood about the human person and about the nature of society. Such a system, in its very roots, denies the possibility of achieving the common good, which is the primary, legitimate aim of political/legal authority. Hence, when political authority fails in its obligation to protect life and, thereby, to create an essential condition for achieving the common good, all of society is imperiled. The unraveling of the rule of law and the undermining of mutual respect among citizens unfolds in myriad ways, some obvious and some subtle.

In this chapter, I shall examine these general propositions in the situation in the United States by focusing on rulings of the Supreme Court of the United States in their social and bioethical context.

2 Political/Legal System of the United States

I have two points to make and two conclusions to draw from those points. The first is this: to understand the experience in the United States, one must recognize that abortion was imposed upon the country by our Supreme Court. I use the word "imposed" intentionally to indicate that it was all but *ultra vires* manner in which it did so. I will demonstrate this point by a brief review of the America's legal/political system.

The United States is governed by a written constitution. The U.S. Constitution, at least to American eyes, is an old and venerable document. On September 17, 2012, Americans celebrated its 225th anniversary. Unlike national constitutions in many European countries, it has remained relatively unchanged over time, having been amended only 27 times during these 225 years. (Our amendment process is quite exacting, requiring multiple votes by representatives of the people.[1] The process was designed to ensure that changes to our constitutional system have been carefully considered, over a significant time-period, and have gained wide-spread public support.)

However, for the Constitution to win ratification by the states (which at the time were essentially sovereign political units), it was necessary that a series of amendments be added to the Constitution. Called *The Bill of Rights*, these first ten amendments set forth the rights that citizens of the states wished to make certain they were not losing by agreeing to a national compact (i.e., by agreeing to be bound by the Constitution). The Bill of Rights protected many rights that are now commonly protected in constitutional democracies—freedom of press, freedom of speech, freedom of religion,[2] freedom from unreasonable search and seizure,[3] right to a fair trial,[4] as well as other rights perhaps more peculiarly American.[5]

Further, you should be aware that after the American Civil War,[6] during which the southern states were prevented, through a long and terrible war, from leaving (or "seceding") from the national union, a series of amendments were adopted. Collectively called the "Civil War Amendments," these amendments (the 13th, 14th,

---

1 Article V of the Constitution provides for amendment as follows: "The Congress, whenever two-thirds of both Houses shall deem it necessary, shall propose amendments to this Constitution, or, on the application of the legislatures of two-thirds of the several States, shall call a Convention for proposing amendments, which, in either case, shall be valid to all intents and purposes, as part of this Constitution, when ratified by the legislatures of three-fourths of the several states, or by Conventions in three-fourths thereof, as the one or the other mode of ratification may be proposed by the Congress…"
2 First Amendment: "Congress shall make no law respecting an establishment of religion, or prohibiting the free exercise thereof, or abridging the freedom of speech or of the press, or the right of the people peaceably to assemble, and to petition the Government for a redress of grievances."
3 Amendment Four.
4 Amendment Six.
5 Such as the right to bear (own, possess) arms (weapons) in the Second Amendment. ("A well-regulated militia, being necessary to the security of a free state, the right of the people to keep and bear arms, shall not be infringed.")
6 The Civil War began in 1861 and ended in 1865.

and 15th) were aimed at securing the full and equal rights of black Americans,[7] who had once been slaves but were now free.

The plain fact is that nowhere—neither in the original text of the Constitution nor in the Bill of Rights nor in the Civil War Amendments nor in any other amendment—does the word "abortion" appear.

Further, the U.S. system of government is one of what we call "federalism." Europeans might use the term "subsidiarity." Either way, the principle is that all governmental power is not concentrated in the nation-state; rather, it is diffuse throughout a system that includes local and state governments as well as the national government. In other words, it has been the historical assumption in the United States that all matters need not be solved at the national level. Most of the work of "governing"—that is, the resolution of most issues that characteristically arise in a democracy—is left to the state and local levels.

The American system is also characterized by a formal "separation of powers" between the Congress (or parliament), the president (or the executive), and the judiciary.[8] This is true on both the national and state levels. (Each state has its own system of legislature, executive, and judiciary.)

On the national level, as set forth in Article III of our Constitution, the role of the Supreme Court is quite limited. In all but two cases (cases affecting ambassadors and cases in which one of the 50 states is a party), the jurisdiction of the Supreme Court is "appellate . . . and under such regulations as Congress shall make."[9] In other words, Congress has the express power to choose to limit the influence of the Supreme Court by restricting the kinds and numbers of cases it reviews. Thus, to summarize, one familiar with the American system of constitutional democracy would reasonably expect the question whether there should be positive laws providing a right to abortion, as well as the extent of such a right, to be decided by the people, through their elected representatives, probably at the state level.

---

7 The 13th Amendment abolished slavery; the 15th guaranteed the right to vote. The 14th, whose provisions are more extensive than the 13th or the 15th, essentially guaranteed citizenship. However, the 14th also guaranteed equality, and that guarantee will be examined in more detail subsequently in this article.
8 The principles of federalism and separation of power are contained throughout the Constitution.
9 Article III, section 2: "In all cases affecting ambassadors, other public ministers and consuls, and those in which a state shall be a party [or litigant], the Supreme Court shall have original jurisdiction. In all the other cases before mentioned [i.e., in section 1 of Article III
—"all cases and controversies, in law and equity, arising under this Constitution, the laws of the United States, and treaties"], the Supreme Court shall have appellate jurisdiction, both as to law and fact, with such exceptions and under such regulations, as the Congress shall make."

3 First Point and First Lesson

In fact, that is precisely how the issue was being addressed before 1973. Efforts were being made in some states to create non-punishable categories of abortion, or to liberalize laws against abortion more generally. Those efforts were vigorously resisted. The political battles were heated, and the tide surged back and forth, in particular legislatures, depending on particular circumstances. In other words, the democratic process was working.

But that all changed in 1973. In two cases decided the same day, the U.S. Supreme Court announced the Constitution gave a right to abortion (though the Constitutional text does not contain the word). Under the American system, national laws are "the supreme law of the land," displacing inconsistent state laws.[10] Thus, in one stroke of the Justices' pen (to put it poetically), the democratic efforts to deal with abortion in the 50 states were rendered null and void. All restrictions were swept away. America was now (as explained below) a nation of "abortion on demand." Let me be clear what that means: it means that a woman can have an abortion at any time for any reason.

I imagine you will find this shocking. To help to understand how this occurred, let me examine the cases in more detail.

In perhaps the most famous case in American history, *Roe v. Wade*, the Supreme Court purported to "find" or discover a right under the Constitution for a woman to terminate her pregnancy.[11] The Court held that the "right to privacy" (which had itself been discovered or "implied" by the Court a few years earlier[12]) included a right to abortion.

The 14th Amendment (one of the Civil War Amendments) says, *inter alia*, that a state may not "deprive any person of life, liberty or property without due process of law." The Supreme Court held that a "foetus" was not a "person" for purposes of the 14th Amendment's protection for its "life."[13] Thus, any arguments based upon a state's obligation to protect *persons* within its jurisdiction (which would have countered a "privacy" right to abortion) were rejected.[14]

---

10 Article IV, paragraph two: "This Constitution, and the laws of the United States which shall be made in pursuance thereof, and all treaties made, which shall be made, under the authority of the United States, shall be the supreme law of the land…"
11 *Roe v. Wade*, 410 U.S. 113 (1973).
12 *See Griswold v. Connecticut*, 381 U.S. 489 (1965).
13 *Roe v. Wade*, p. 158.
14 However, when the text of the 14th Amendment is examined, one can recognize that there is a plausible argument that a state *does* have such an obligation to protect the unborn. Amendment 14 provides, in pertinent part: "… Nor shall any state deprive any person of life, liberty, or property, without due process of law; nor deny to any person within its jurisdiction the equal protection of the laws."

In *Roe*'s companion case, *Doe v. Bolton*,[15] the Supreme Court extended this new abortion right throughout all nine months of pregnancy. It did so through what is commonly referred to as the "health exception." The Court defined the health of the woman to include any factor "relevant to the well-being of the patient," whether "physical, emotional, psychological, familial, or the age of the woman."[16]

Furthermore, the decision to have an abortion need be reviewed solely with the abortionist.[17] No other doctor or medical personnel need be consulted. Thus, the woman will not benefit from the experience of a family physician or from a personal physician who knows her well. In a rather bizarre twist of legal logic, she is required only to consult the person who has a financial interest in convincing her to have an abortion, the abortionist, and she need only do so once. Evidence suggests that these consultations are brief, and immediately precede the abortion. In practice, any justification qualifies as a "health exception" to any restrictive abortion law. As subsequent Supreme Court decisions have demonstrated,[18] this expansive definition of health means that abortion simply cannot be precluded if the woman wants it.[19] The only abortion she may not have is what is called a "partial-birth abortion," that is, one in which delivery is initiated and the child is killed by crushing its skull before the head has emerged. This has been prohibited by national law, which has been upheld (i.e., held to be permissible under the Constitution) by the Supreme Court in the case, *Gonzales v. Carhart*.[20] However, this does not preclude other methods of abortion *at any time* during pregnancy, as the Supreme Court expressly noted in its decision.[21]

In the next important Supreme Court case, *Planned Parenthood v. Casey*,[22] which was decided in 1992, nineteen years after *Roe* and *Doe*, the Supreme Court affirmed the "abortion right." However, it no longer relied upon the "implied privacy right" as it had in *Roe/Doe*. Rather, it placed the abortion right squarely under the express "liberty" protected under the 14th Amendment.[23] It announced an expansive definition of "liberty"—"At the heart of liberty is the right to define one's own concept

---

15 410 U.S. 179 (1973). The two cases concerned different state restrictions on abortion. (Texas law was reviewed in *Roe*, while Georgia law was reviewed in *Doe*.
16 *Doe v. Bolton*, p. 192.
17 The Supreme Court in *Doe* struck down a requirement that two physicians, including the woman's family doctor, consult, and left the matter to the woman's "attending physician," that is, the abortionist. *See, Doe* at p. 163.
18 530 U.S. 914 (2000).
19 This is not surprising. As *Roe* itself stated: "If the State is interested in protecting fetal life after viability, it may go so far as to proscribe abortion during that period, *except when it is necessary to preserve the life or health of the mother*." *See, Roe* at pp. 163–164 (emphasis added).
20 550 U.S. 124 (2007).
21 At page 157: "Alternatives are available to the prohibited procedure."
22 *Planned Parenthood of Southeastern PA v. Casey*, 505 U.S. 833 (1992).
23 *Planned Parenthood of Southeastern PA v. Casey*, pp. 846–853.

of existence, of meaning, of the universe, and of the mystery of human life. Beliefs about these matters could not define the attributes of personhood were they formed under compulsion of the state."[24] Because the Supreme Court subjects laws to exacting scrutiny when they infringe individual Constitutional rights, such an expansive definition of "liberty" gives the Supreme Court essentially unlimited discretion to "discover" other rights within "liberty," and to strike down laws that place a "substantial burden" upon it.

Since the decision in *Casey* did not change or limit the meaning of the "health exception," the situation remained—and remains to this day—essentially the same as when *Roe* and *Doe* were announced: abortion is available at any time for any reason. Only three or four other nations have such expansive "abortion rights."[25]

Though the Supreme Court in *Casey* called upon those protesting the pro-abortion regime to end their protests and to accept the Court's "resolution" of the abortion question, they have not done so. The issue of abortion remains at the center of American politics and elections. For example, on January 24, 2013, the March for Life brought several hundred thousand Americans to D.C. to protest the Supreme Court decisions I have discussed. This has happened every year since *Roe* and *Doe* were decided, that is, *for 40 consecutive years.*

To repeat, my first point is that abortion was imposed across the United States by the Supreme Court despite the absence of any authorizing language in our fundamental legal document (the Constitution) or in any positive, national law, and despite the U.S. system of federalism and separated powers, which should logically have entailed that the issue be left to the political processes of the 50 individual states for resolution.

The lesson I draw from this point is: in order to protect life, it is not enough that laws do not grant a positive right to abortion. Rather, legal protection for the unborn must be *explicit*. Otherwise, pursuant to a wide-spread rights-creating mentality and to notions of "evolving constitutions," modern judges will find a way to create a right *against* life in the name of expanding "liberty," "human rights," or "women's rights," as happened in the United States. This is richly ironical—in the name of "rights," courts deny the most basic human right; courts, whom many modern people regard as the guarantors of rights, become the deprivers of rights

---

24 *Planned Parenthood of Southeastern PA v. Casey,* p. 851.
25 The United States is one of approximately 10 nations (out of 195) that allows abortion after 14 weeks (North Korea, Netherlands, Singapore, Sweden, Vietnam, United Kingdom, Western Australia (a state of Australia), United States, United Kingdom, Canada, China) and one of only 3 (with Canada and China) that allows abortion for any reason after viability. *See Center for Reprod. Rights, the World's Abortion Laws* (2008), http://www.re-productiverights.org/sites/crr.civicactions.net/files/pub_fac_abortionlaws2008.pdf; *World Abortion Policies 2011. United Nations Department of Economic and Social Affairs Population Division,* March 2011. www.unpopulation.org, http://www.un.org/esa/population/publications/2011abortion/2011wallchart.pdf

for the weakest; constitutions, which do not mention "abortion," and deny the state the power to deprive anyone of "life" arbitrarily, are interpreted by courts to guarantee a "liberty" to abortion.

As noted, all this is illustrated by the experience of the United States. Therefore, the lesson to be drawn, I suggest, is that the fundamental legal/political documents of a nation (a) should preclude such judicial over-reaching by expressly limiting the power of the courts, and (b) should expressly grant legal recognition and protection to the unborn.

4 Can Decisions Such as *Roe* Be Contained within the Context (Only) of Abortion?

Roe-related jurisprudence of "abortion rights" has been defended, or explained, as being about a woman's right to control her body. This is implicit in the Court's holding: "We, therefore, conclude the right to personal privacy includes the abortion decision . . ."[26] Understood on this basis, it was claimed that *Roe* did not have consequences beyond the abortion context; *Roe/Doe* were seen to concern a particular situation—the presence of a fetus in the body of a woman who does not want it there. In situations where there were other facts (i.e., where there was no fetus in the body of a woman who wanted it removed), *Roe/Doe* would not apply. However, as I shall attempt to show in an extensive discussion of Congressional efforts concerning cloning, *Roe*'s "effects" have not been limited to the abortion context. Whatever the hopes of *Roe*'s opponents or the professions of its advocates, *Roe* has not proved, in fact, to be limited to situations involving a woman's "right to choose," or to control her own body. Rather, the legal fictions employed in the *Roe* jurisprudence to deny the protection of the law to one class of human beings have extended far beyond the abortion context to endanger other human beings in very different situations.

The intense public debate about stem cell research and cloning in the United States over the past decade demonstrates the point, as will be discussed in more detail below. In that debate, though the issue had nothing to do with a woman's control of her body, those supporting human embryonic stem cell research even denied the scientific fact that the embryo is a human being[27] (and, thus, is

---

26 *Roe v. Wade*, p. 154.
27 "Human development is a continuous process that begins when an oocyte (ovum) from a female is fertilized by a sperm (or spermatozoon) from a male." Keith L. Moore and T. V. N. Persaud, The Developing Human: Clinically Oriented Embryology, 6th edn., Philadelphia: W.B. Saunders Company, 1998, p. 2. *See* also, T. W. Sadler, *Langman's Medical Embryology*, 7th edn., Baltimore: William & Wilkins 1995, p. 3: "The development of a human being begins with fertilization, a process by which the spermatozoon from the male and the oocyte from the female unite to give rise to a new organism, the zygote."

presumptively entitled to the protection of the law). The task of those advocates was made easier in two important ways by *Roe/Doe*, one obvious and one subtle.

The obvious way is this: since the Supreme Court decided embryos/fetuses were not "persons" under the 14th Amendment, it seemed to follow they were *different from* other human beings in important ways (after all, all *other* human beings are persons and are entitled to the protection of the law). Thus, it seemed obvious (though that conclusion was wrong) that it was "acceptable" or "appropriate" to subject these human beings (embryos and fetuses) to lethal violence based upon the rights, or even claims, of other human beings. Thus, if embryos are not persons and can appropriately be subjected to lethal violence based upon the demands of others, it was appropriate that they be "used" (and destroyed) in embryonic stem cell research, which was designed, after all, to benefit other human beings.

This is, as I say, an obvious effect. The more subtle— indeed, the deeper—way *Roe/Doe* infected (and affected) the stem cell debate is this: it taught the American people that scientific facts can be ignored for policy reasons.

5 Semantic Gymnastics—"De-humanizing" the Embryo/Fetus

In 1970, in what became a famous editorial, *California Medicine*, the journal of the California medical association, candidly noted that in order for a right to abortion to be generally accepted, it would be necessary to undermine traditional Western ethics of respect for, and the equality of, each human life.[28] The aim was to "separate the idea of abortion from the idea of killing."[29] The editorial approved of what it called "semantic gymnastics" whose aim was to deny "the scientific fact, which everyone really knows, that human life begins at conception and is continuous whether intra- or extra-uterine until death."[30]

It is precisely this scientifically established fact that Justice Harry Blackmun, writing for the majority in *Roe v. Wade*, ignored. Justice Blackmun claimed, "[i]t should be sufficient to note briefly the wide divergence of thinking on this most sensitive and difficult question."[31] He then considered various religious, philosophical, and historical views. He also discussed how the law had treated injuries to the fetus in a variety of contexts. He found a lack of unanimity among all these sources. Thus, given this diversity of opinions, he concluded "[the Supreme Court] need not resolve the difficult question of when life begins."[32] This conclusion, in turn, enabled Justice Blackmun to set up his well-known "trimester" system for balancing various interests of the state and the woman in the regulation of abortion.

---

28 *California Medicine: The Western Journal of Medicine,* Editorial, September 1970, p. 67.
29 Ibid.
30 Ibid.
31 *Roe v. Wade,* p. 160.
32 *Roe v. Wade,* p. 159.

However, significantly, Justice Blackmun failed to consider another discipline—that of basic embryology. If he had, it would have been clear that the embryo, from the first day, is a developing human being. If it had been so recognized, Justice Blackmun would have had to consider its status for purposes of personhood protection under the 14th Amendment. By avoiding the scientific facts about the beginning of human life, however, Justice Blackmun was able to avoid the constitutional dilemma presented by that fact. While we cannot know Justice Blackmun's subjective intention, it is clear that, objectively speaking, in the holding in *Roe*, he engaged in precisely the "semantic gymnastics" that had been advocated by *California Medicine* three years earlier.

6 Stem Cell/Cloning Debate in the United States

How did Blackmun's reasoning influence policy debates in non-abortion contexts? Let us consider the example of cloning.

On August 9, 2001, six months after his inauguration, President George W. Bush addressed stem cell research in a nationally televised speech.[33] The President announced that federal funding for human embryonic stem cell research would be subject to significant restrictions[34] and ordered the National Institutes of Health to limit grant-making for such research.[35] Nonetheless, following President Bush's decision cloning, considered an essential part of human embryonic stem cell research, became the focus of a protracted political debate in the United States generally and in the United States Congress in particular.

On February 27, 2003, the House of Representatives (hereafter, the "House") passed the Human Cloning Prohibition Act of 2003 (hereafter, the "Act").[36] The Act provided that "it shall be unlawful for any person or entity, public or private . . . to perform human cloning. . . or to ship or receive . . . an embryo produced by human cloning or any product derived from such an embryo."[37] The Act defined "human cloning" as "human asexual reproduction, accomplished by introducing nuclear material from one or more human somatic cells into a . . . oocyte whose nuclear material has been removed or inactivated so as to produce a living organism . . .

---

33 *See*, White House Fact Sheet, Aug. 9, 2001.
34 The President permitted federal funding for stem cell research derived from an embryo prior, but not after, the date of his speech.
35 The National Institutes of Health issued guidelines incorporating the President's decision on November 7, 2001. "Notice of Criteria for Federal Funding of Research on Existing Human Embryonic Stem Cells and Establishment of NIH Human Embryonic Stem Cell Registry" at http://grants1.nih.gov/grants/guide/notice-files/NOT-OD-02-005.html.
36 H.R. 534.
37 Section 302 (a) (1) & (3).

that is genetically virtually identical[38] to an existing or previously existing human organism."[39]

In the months before the vote on the Act, there was a competing bill for the members of the House to consider. This bill, H.R. 801 (hereafter, the "Bill") was titled the "Cloning Prohibition Act of 2003." Section 2, titled, "Prohibition against Human Cloning," would have amended the Food, Drug and Cosmetic Act (21 U.S.C. 301 et seq.) to make it "unlawful for any person . . . to use human somatic cell nuclear transfer technology, or the product of such technology, to initiate a pregnancy . . . or to ship, mail, transport, or receive the product of such technology knowing the product is intended to be used to initiate a pregnancy."[40] "Human somatic cell nuclear transfer technology" was defined as "transferring the nuclear material of a human somatic cell into an egg cell from which the nuclear material has been removed or rendered inert."[41]

When the Act and the Bill are compared, one notes that each claims to be intended to prohibit human cloning. However, a careful reading of the Bill shows it prohibits cloning ("somatic cell nuclear transfer technology") solely for the purpose of "initiat[ing] a pregnancy." The Bill does not prohibit cloning for any other purpose. The Act, however, is not so limited. Its prohibition is not effected by the *purpose* for which cloning is accomplished. It says: "It shall be unlawful for any person or entity, public or private . . . to perform or attempt to perform human cloning."[42]

It is fair to wonder why the Bill prohibited human cloning solely for the purpose of "initiating a pregnancy." One might well ask for what other purposes might cloning be undertaken. The short answer is, for research. Cloning might be undertaken to create embryos which could be used (and destroyed) in human embryonic stem cell research. Thus, the meaning of the Bill was that if cloning were undertaken to initiate a pregnancy, it was banned, but if it were undertaken to produce an embryo that could be used in research, it was permitted.

When the Act—not the Bill—passed the House and was introduced in the Senate, opponents introduced an alternative, S. 303. Titled "Human Cloning Ban and Stem Cell Research Protection Act of 2003" this alternative bill (hereafter, the

---

38 The Act uses the phrase "virtually identical" for the following reason. Some DNA is contained in the cytoplasm of the ooctye—the mitochondrial DNA. Hence, even when the nucleus—or "genetic material"—of one of the donor's cells is transferred into the ooctye from which its own nucleus has been removed, the resulting organism, retaining the original mitochondrial DNA in the oocyte's cytoplasm, has a genetic composition that is not exactly the same as the donor. However, it is "virtually identical" to the donor.
39 Section 301(1).
40 Section 2(a).
41 Ibid.
42 Section 302.

"Alternative") stated its purpose was "to prohibit human cloning and to protect important areas of medical research, including stem cell research."[43] The Alternative would have amended the U.S. Code to prohibit "any person or other legal entity" from "conduct[ing] . . . human cloning."[44] Human cloning was defined as "implanting or attempting to implant the product of nuclear transplantation into a uterus or functional equivalent of a uterus."[45] "Nuclear transplantation" was defined as "transferring the nucleus of a human somatic cell into an oocyte from which the nucleus . . . ha[s] been . . . removed or rendered inert."[46]

However, the definition of "nuclear transplantation" (i.e., transferring the nucleus of a human somatic cell into an oocyte from which the nucleus has been removed) is the very definition of cloning. In other words, "nuclear transplantation" is a synonym for "cloning." Thus, the Alternative prohibits cloning if, and only if, there is also an attempt to "implant" the cloned human embryo "into a uterus or functional equivalent of a uterus." Otherwise, cloning would not be prohibited under federal law. Thus, if the aim is to clone a human being to use that human being in research, even lethal human embryonic stem cell research, the Alternative establishes no prohibition. The Alternative is similar to the Bill, and directly opposed to the Act, in this regard. It is hard to conclude other than that this was precisely the intention of the drafters of the Alternative since the Alternative's stated purposes include "protect[ing] important areas of medical research, including stem cell research."

7 Second Point and Second Lesson

How, we may ask, is it possible that members of both houses of United States Congress could have seriously considered enacting bills (the Bill in the House and the Alternative in the Senate) which would have permitted research based upon the intentional creation and destruction of a whole class of human beings? The answer, I believe, can be found in *Roe v. Wade*.

Let us recall what *Roe* held. It held that the Court did not need to determine when human life begins, and it so held on the basis of a divergence among religious, philosophical, historical, and legal authorities on the question. Having found this divergence, the Court was able to avoid the acute dilemma that would have been posed if it had relied on basic embryology, that is, the scientific source. For embryology has always been clear that from the first moment of its life the embryo is a human being. Had the Court recognized this, it would have been forced to squarely confront the question of the Constitutional "personhood" of that human

---

43 Sec. 2.
44 Sec. 101.
45 Ibid.
46 Ibid.

being. Obvious parallels to the slavery question, in which certain human beings were denied Constitutional protection as "persons," would have been unavoidable. At a minimum, the Court could not have pretended that since the basic question of the humanity of the foetus was unsettled, it could proceed to a judicial balancing of other interests. However, by ignoring the science, the Court was able to avoid squarely confronting the legal question.

This, it appears, is the legacy of *Roe*—our culture can no longer be honest about the dilemmas we face. With human embryonic stem cell research, we face a dilemma—should we destroy human beings during research that promises cures for a variety of diseases and injuries? To evaluate the question, we must begin by admitting the facts—the embryo is a human being, and our culture has never countenanced the destruction of human beings (without their consent) for research aimed to benefit others. If those who, nonetheless, wish to proceed with that research have an argument, why we should behave differently in this instance, the burden must be upon them to make the argument. However, proponents of embryonic stem cell research and cloning have not had to engage the facts and make the (difficult) argument because *Roe* taught the American people that we can ignore the scientific fact of life's beginning.

Thus, my second point: *Roe* could not be limited to the abortion context, but had a deep and important effect on thinking about other issues (such as stem cell research and cloning). Therefore, the second lesson I would submit is this: failure to protect human life in one area of law will lead to failure elsewhere. Life must either be protected everywhere, or it is at risk everywhere.

Bibliography

Center for Reproductive Rights, the World's Abortion Laws (2008), http://www.reproductiverights.org/sites/crr.civicactions.net/files/pub_fac_abortionlaws2008.pdf.

Keith L. Moore & T.V.N. Persaud, *The Developing Human: Clinically Oriented Embryology*, 6th Edition, Philadelphia: W.B. Saunders Company, 1998.

"Notice of Criteria for Federal Funding of Research on Existing Human Embryonic Stem Cells and Establishment of NIH Human Embryonic Stem Cell Registry" at http://grants1.nih.gov/grants/guide/notice-files/NOT-OD-02-005.html.

T. W. Sadler, *Langman's Medical Embryology*, 7th Edition, Baltimore: William & Wilkins, 1995.

California Medicine: The Western Journal of Medicine, Editorial, September 1970.

White House Fact Sheet, August 9, 2001.

World Abortion Policies 2011. United Nations Department of Economic and Social Affairs Population Division, March 2011. www.unpopulation.org, http://www.un.org/esa/population/ publications/2011abortion/2011wallchart.pdf

Cases:

Roe v. Wade, 410 U.S. 113 (1973).
Griswold v. Connecticut, 381 U.S. 489 (1965).
Doe v. Bolton, 410 U.S. 179 (1973).
Stenberg v. Carhart, 530 U.S. 914 (2000).
Gonzalez v. Carhart, 550 U.S. 124 (2007).
Planned Parenthood of Southeastern PA v. Casey, 505 U.S. 833 (1992).

Gerard V. Bradley

2 Whither United States Abortion Law?

Abstract: In what might still be the most famous moral and philosophical defense of choosing to have an abortion, Judith Jarvis Thomson argued in 1971 that opponents of abortion "commonly spend most of their time establishing that the fetus is a person, and hardly any time explaining the step from there to the impermissibility of abortion." "[W]e need to be shown also that killing the fetus violates its right to life, i.e., that abortion is *unjust* killing of a human person." [Emphasis added.] In this chapter we revisit Thomson's article in light of the latest developments in American constitutional law, with a special focus on the decision of the Supreme Court in *Whole Women's Health*. The chief aim is not, however, to engage her conclusions about the scope of morally justified abortion. Rather the main purpose is to show that Thomson's question—how far is abortion the morally justified killing of one person by another?—is *the* question today in American law.

Keywords: Judith Jarvis Thomson, Abortion, *Whole Woman's Health*, Feticide, Justified killing

1 Introduction

In what might still be the most famous moral philosophical defense of choosing to have an abortion, Judith Jarvis Thomson wrote in 1971 that she was "inclined to think [] that we shall probably have to agree that the foetus has already become a human person well before birth."[1] "By the tenth week," Thomson observed, the fetus "already has a face, arms and legs, fingers, and toes; it has internal organs, and brain activity is detectable."[2] She denied that "the foetus is a person from the moment of conception." But Thomson granted that proposition, too, for the sake of arguing that women have a broad, but not unlimited, right to abortion.[3]

---

1   I *Phil. & Pub. Aff.* 47 (1971).
2   Id.
3   Thomson said very little about the reasons for her denial, save that she rejected what she described as the "most common argument" in favor of fetal personhood. That argument (found on the first page of her essay) surely seems to be a garbled version of what would now be called "the no-substantial-change" argument, which is most cogently developed and defended by Patrick Lee, in *Abortion and Unborn Human Life*. Thomson's reply to it is brief and jejune: she incorrectly describes it as a "slippery slope" argument, and lamely compares the assertion that the person Judith Thomson in 1971 (for example) is substantially the same as that entity which (who) came to be inside her mother at the moment of fertilization, to acorns and trees. Id. At 47. Of this comparison John Finnis wrote in his 1973 critique of Thomson's article: "It is discouraging to see her relying upon so heavily and uncritically on

Thomson wanted to argue against pro-lifers on ethical, not metaphysical, grounds. She saw a tactical opportunity. "Opponents of abortion," Thomson wrote, "commonly spend most of their time establishing that the foetus is a person, and hardly any time explaining the step from there to the impermissibility of abortion." But "it is by no means enough to show that the foetus is a person, and to remind us that all persons have a right to life." "[W]e need to be shown also that killing the foetus violates its right to life, i.e., that abortion is *unjust* killing" of a human person.[4] [Emphasis added.]

It is time to revisit Thomson's article. The chief aim of this visit is not, however, to engage her conclusions about the scope of morally justified abortion. The main purpose is rather to show that Thomson's question—how far is abortion the morally justified killing of one person by another?— is *the* question today in American law.

But how could that be so? There are after all more than a million lawful abortions a year in the United States. The Supreme Court in June 2016 expanded the scope of abortion rights, over against restrictive state regulation, in *Whole Woman's Health v. Hellerstedt*. Freedom to choose abortion seems to be a settled feature of our constitutional jurisprudence, with the rights of the fetus wholly subordinated to it.

Whole Woman's Health actually supplies one reason why Thomson's question is our question. That case will focus anti-abortionists' considerable political energies on the fetus as bearer of a right-not-be-killed similar, if not identical, to that enjoyed by other persons. This has already become a fruitful source of pro-life initiatives. Henceforth, it will likely be the leading front for those seeking to legally limit abortion, notwithstanding that they face a strong judicial headwind. In fact, the constitutional law surrounding abortion, considered as a whole and especially including the Equal Protection Clause, reveals that this resistance is itself unreasoned, an arbitrary stipulation favoring abortion, supported by raw power. So this paper argues. When reason supplants will in the relevant sector of constitutional law, we will discover that Judith Thomson's question lies at its core.

---

this hoary muddle." J. Finnis, "The Rights and Wrongs of Abortion" in III *Collected Essays: Human Rights and the Common Good* 282, 304 (2011).

4   Thomson, *supra* note 1, at 57. Right-to-lifers were hardly the only ones who made the assumption (if that is what it was) that if the fetus is a person then abortion is unjust. Two years after Thomson's essay appeared, the Supreme Court in *Roe v Wade*—whose members were not pro-life—stated that if the unborn counted as " 'persons' within the protection of the Fourteenth Amendment, the case for abortion liberty 'collapses,' because the 'foetus' right to life would be guaranteed specifically by the Amendment." *If* the unborn were recognized as constitutional persons, only abortions to save a pregnant woman's life could be justified killing, and consistent with equal respect for the lives of unborn "persons."

2 *Whole Woman's Health*: Extending the Mother's Right to Choose Abortion

The doctrinal innovation in Whole Woman's Health raised the bar of judicial review for state regulations of abortion grounded in concerns for maternal health (there, hospital admitting privileges for abortionists and the quality of the medical apparatus at abortion clinics). This holding will make sure that such maternal health regulations have crested, especially where they are enacted (as many have been) with a view to not only woman's health but to reducing the overall incidence of abortion. *Whole Woman's Health* appears even to hold that reasonable maternal health laws are unconstitutional, where they substantially impede some women's access to abortion.

The constitutionality of abortion regulations for the sake of informing the woman's consent to abortion—such as notifications of available alternatives and facts about fetal development—was untouched by *Whole Woman's Health*. There is surely space for further refinement of these advices. But these too have reached a plateau as anti-abortion measures; future refinements will not yield dramatic decreases in abortion rates. It has long been settled law; moreover, that grown women have a unilateral right to choose abortion husbands and/or fathers need not consent. Notification to them may be required only in circumstances which do not threaten the woman's independence of decision. Even minors have a right of effective unilateral access to abortion, due to the constitutionally required alternative of judicial "bypass" to parental consent and notification. There is little potential here for creative and effective legislation which could decrease the incidence of abortion.

The future of the American anti-abortion movement lies, then, in restrictions founded upon the fetus's right to life. This is not to say solely that activists need to have *something* to do and that other avenues are blocked. Fetal right to life *should* be anti-abortionists' focus, because the fundamental and unvarying wrong in abortion is not slipshod medical practice or unintelligent assent—troubling as those contingent and common evils are—but *killing*, as Judith Jarvis Thomson well understood

That abortion kills someone with a right to life has become easier to see since *Roe v. Wade*. Progress in scientific research and medical practice has made both birth and "viability" nearly unbelievable grounds for demarcating between "human life" demanding moral respect, and mere "potential life" which has no traction in justice against a mother's desires. (The Eighth Circuit recently criticized "viability" as a litmus line because it "tied a state's interest in unborn children to developments in obstetrics, not to developments in the unborn."[5]) The near-ubiquity of sonograms has probably done more to convince the popular mind that a real baby comes to be by ten weeks into pregnancy than intellectual arguments for fetal personhood

---

5   *MKB Management Corporation v. Stenehjam* (8th Cir. July 15, 2015, at 9).

have. Earlier and earlier prenatal medical interventions for the sake of the unborn patient confirm this impression. DNA indubitably confirms the substantial biological identity of the embryo with the human being whose features Thomson could see at ten weeks. Cogent philosophical argument confirms what common sense operating on all this (and other) data so strongly suggests: not only that a distinct human individual comes to be at fertilization, but that this individual is substantially the same as the individual (with an as-yet undoubted right-not-to-be-killed) who is born nine months later, is brought home from the hospital days after that, and so on throughout that person's earthly life.

Conscientious legislators and citizens will therefore continue to enact abortion restrictions premised upon the personhood of the unborn. They will do so not because they are at a loose end, but because they believe it to be what justice requires. As a matter of fact, they have recently enacted in many American states two types of abortion restrictions for the sake of the unborn as rights-bearers. One type involves prohibitions which recognize (as did Thomson) that the fetus is a person "well before birth," and even before "viability." Examples include bans after the point of "fetal pain" (at about 20 weeks), and "fetal heartbeat" prohibitions after about 8 weeks. Both these sets of laws include exceptions for abortions necessary to preserve the life of the mother or her physical health against severe injury. They all represent attempts to more or less align abortion regulation with the scope of morally justified killing of one person by another.

The second tranche of recent pro-life legislation would ban entirely abortions sought for particularly unworthy reasons, such as the sex or race of the unborn child. These enactments establish a fetal-personhood beachhead (so to speak), by linking the unborn to the wider community of persons protected against unjust discrimination. By prohibiting abortions "solely" for a prohibited reason, these laws also link up with Thomson's amended question, which was (in her words) "the permissibility of abortion in some cases," but in no case for "the right to secure the death of the child."[6]

That is: Thomson defended a woman's decision to evict someone who would occupy uninvited her body for nine months. Her defense of "unplugging" the renowned violinist (without intending to kill him) explored the requirements of justice when a pregnant woman wants to eject a fetal squatter. Thomson asked whether it is morally justified to knowingly cause the death of an unborn "person" by and through an act undertaken for the purpose of *terminating a pregnancy.*

This was essentially the question raised by an Indiana statute recently enjoined by a federal judge. Indiana defended its prohibition on race and sex selection abortions by noting, *inter alia,* that women affected by the ban obviously did not object to being pregnant or to carrying a child to term. The only desire which these laws disrupted was the woman's wish to have a little girl rather than a little boy (or vice versa). Women seeking a sex-selection abortion are obviously not aborting

---

6   *Supra* note 1 at 66.

for the sake of ending a pregnancy. They are seizing the opportunity which pregnancy affords them in a post-*Roe* world to terminate a child who happens to be of the wrong sex.[7]

Judges have so far enjoined the operation of almost all of these fetal-right-to-life abortion restrictions. They have done so—some with apparent regret [8] and some not[9]—largely upon the strength, not of legal or ethical (or scientific or medical) reasoning, but upon a quarter-century old Supreme Court precedent, *Planned Parenthood v. Casey*. *Casey* in turn affirmed what it called the "central holding" of *Roe v. Wade*: women must have the "ultimate" authority to decide about continuing a pregnancy. But neither in *Casey* nor in *Roe* nor in any other case has the Supreme Court taken up the task of arguing—much less showing—that the victim of an abortion is *not* a homicide victim. Nowhere has the Supreme Court taken up the burden of arguing against the proposition that people really come to be at fertilization, notwithstanding the Court's recognition that whether they do decisively affects the constitutionality of abortion rights.

In *Roe* the Court expressly declined to "resolve the difficult question of when life begins."[10] That case was decided upon the curious basis that the state could not deny a pregnant woman all choice about abortion by imposing what the Court called "one theory of life" upon her. The justices for their own part neither affirmed nor denied, in any clear or necessarily presupposed manner, any such "theory." *Casey's* affirmation of *Roe* did not rest upon ratification of *Roe's* reasoning (such as it was), but upon social expectations which the Court's 1973 ruling enabled. For two decades, the subscribers to the *Casey* joint opinion wrote, people "have organized intimate relationships and made choices," relying upon access to abortion in case contraception should fail.[11] The salient fact in *Casey* had nothing to do with the moral status of the fetus, a matter which the Court in that case studiously avoided analyzing. The salient fact had to do with the benefits of abortion for other people.

Since *Casey*, lower courts have done little more than recite the de-personalizing phrase "potential life," when they consider the possibility that the unborn have a right to life which their mothers must respect. Some courts have even reasoned backwards about abortion and fetal rights: first, posit lawful abortion; second,

---

7   *See* Planned Parenthood of Indiana and *Kentucky v. Commissioner* (So. Dist. IN, June 30, 2016) at 12–14.
8   *See* for example, *MKB* ("Although controlling Supreme Court precedent dictates the outcome in this case, good reasons exist for the Court to reevaluate its jurisprudence," insofar as the Court's "viability standard has proven unsatisfactory because it gives too little consideration to the substantial state interest in potential life throughout pregnancy.")
9   *See*, for example, Planned Parenthood of Indiana and *Kentucky v. Commissioner* (So. Dist. IN, June 30, 2016).
10 410 U.S. at 159.
11 533 U.S. 855.

derive from that permission what one would have to say about the unborn to make lawful abortion something which a decent society would countenance. Then Seventh Circuit Chief Judge Richard Posner, for example, wrote in 1998 that the conclusion that the fetus is not a person "follows inevitably from the decision to grant women the right to abort."[12] In other words: *assume* that abortion on demand ordained by *Roe* is just; now, talk about the fetus. Exposure of unborn human beings to maternal violence has evidently become an axiom or a postulate of our constitutional law. It is as if the legal culture has turned Thomson upside-down. She observed that some people say "pro-life" and presume that it means abortion is always wrong. Many people today say "pro-choice" and presume that it means the unborn are not persons. But being "pro-choice" establishes nothing about the true status and rights of the child *in utero*.

The most compelling reason why Thomson's question is our question is also why the prevailing regime of stipulation and avoidance cannot much longer evade evidence and reason. What Thomson granted for sake of argument has become an established fact: the unborn *are* recognized as persons with a right not to be killed in 38 American states as well as in federal law. These statutes—commonly described as "feticide" prohibitions—accord the unborn the same, or substantially the same, right to life as everyone else, with the exception mandated by the Supreme Court in *Roe v. Wade* for lawful abortion.

Some feticide defendants have challenged their convictions upon constitutional grounds, chiefly Equal Protection. They ask: How could it be that the norms of justified killing are never satisfied for the father, while they are never relevant for the mother, even when both act in the same way and for the same reasons? They assert that ambient norms of justification govern everybody, just as they protect everybody. These defendants raise a double-barreled challenge to the *status quo* about abortion. They argue for equal protection of homicide laws for themselves and their interests, insofar as the law permits persons to use lethal force against other persons who threaten them. They say that justified use of force must be available to all on *equal* terms. But this claim depends necessarily upon a second equal protection assertion, namely, that the law cannot constitutionally undermine the first equality by varying the personal status of the one against whom force is used. They say that if the fetus is a person who can be unjustly killed by *them*, then it must be so, for *everyone*, including pregnant women (even if the requirements of justice vary somewhat, due to the female monopoly on pregnancy).

Courts have so far not stepped up to answer these grave questions. It is not clear how they could, without upsetting the current law of abortion.

These constitutional questions are more urgent due to how the *Roe* Court defended *its* minting of abortion rights. Here the Court put aside legal and philosophical reasoning. *They* turned to real-world experiences. But the Justices did not make much out of pregnancy. In fact, *Roe* listed seven types of "detriment" as

---

12   *Coe v. County of Cook,* 162 F. 3d 491, 495 (1998).

reasons for abortions. One of them—the "stigma" of unwed motherhood—has since disappeared. Of the rest, only one had apparently to do with carrying a child in the womb: "medically diagnosable harm" during pregnancy. The other "detriments" which the justices said justified abortion are gender-neutral. They have entirely to do with the anticipated burdens of raising a child, burdens upon which mothers have no monopoly. These burdens of child-rearing included (in *Roe's* words) the prospect that "[m]aternity, or additional offspring, may force upon the woman a distressful life and future." In addition, "[p]sychological harm may be imminent. Mental and physical health may be taxed by child care. There is also the distress, for all concerned, associated with the unwanted child, and there is the problem of bringing a child into a family already unable, psychologically and otherwise, to care for it."[13] These burdens typically affect mothers more than fathers. But not always, and it is surely unreasonable to suppose that they do not often fall very heavily upon expectant fathers."

The challenges of raising children are real enough. But no one maintains that those cited by the Court would be sufficient to justify killing these burdensome children, or anyone else for that matter, other than a fetus (as their concessions on the hypothesis of fetal personhood made clear).[14] Those challenges are not gender-specific; men just the same as women have good reasons—often, the *same* reasons—to delay becoming a parent, perhaps indefinitely. *Roe* thus supplied little material from which a response to feticide defendants' constitutional challenges could be assembled.

The unique physical dependence of a child *in utero* upon his or her mother must be dealt with honestly in any honest account of the morality of abortion. But that does not mean that abortion calls forth a unique set of justificatory norms, or that its morality depends upon *sui generis* evaluative criteria. To the suggestion that it does, the reply would be that *that* claim about the *singularity* of choosing abortion would have to be defended on grounds consistent with Equal Protection of the laws.

Judith Thomson argued for a substantial abortion liberty by appealing to general norms about the justified use of deadly force, and to widespread intuitions and tutored reactions to those norms as applied to life-threatening situations.[15] She cited examples of moral duty and right involving grown-up, physically independent people, such as the Parable of the Good Samaritan, burglars climbing in one's

---

13 410 U.S. 153.
14 *See* note 4, *supra*.
15 Thomson argues specifically about ethics, and did not really engage the matter of legal permission. For sake of this paper, I take the scope of ethically justified killing of unborn persons to be basically symmetrical with legally justified killing of unborn persons. No doubt they are as a general matter. The modest differences between them in some situations—and the question of which if any there should be in the case of abortion--are here left aside.

window, Henry Fonda applying a life-saving touch to the forehead of the author (and more). Thomson reasoned about abortion the way that she (or anyone else) would—and should—reason about the justified killing of A by B: what's fair in light of all the relevant circumstances in which A and B find themselves. For Thomson, abortion presented a unique type of fact pattern. But she sought to illumine the relevant requirements of justice according to general principles governing the ethically appropriate use of deadly force against anyone, albeit applied to the peculiar circumstance of pregnancy.

Thomson's question is finally this: What should be the scope of lawful abortion, where ordinary norms of justification are applied to the woman's decision, based upon difficulties distinctive to her pregnancy, to terminate it knowing that by doing so she will cause the death of another person with a right to life equal to hers?[16]

3 *Roe* and States' Laws against Feticide

Thirty-eight states as well as the national government have since 1973 enacted laws specifically against fetal homicide, or *feticide*: the unjustified killing of an unborn child. These laws identify the unborn child as a victim, wholly distinct in contemplation of law from his or her mother. Injury to the mother by one seeking to harm or destroy a child *in utero* constitutes a separate legal harm, a criminal offense in addition to that against the fetus. These laws must be distinguished, too, from laws which punish unlawful abortions—including self-abortion—for the sake of regular medical practice and maternal safety. These are usually misdemeanors, and never punished so gravely as to make these prohibitions comparable to feticide.[17]

---

16 This whole notion of "terminating a pregnancy" is more conceptually distinguishable from terminating an unborn child than it is practically. No doubt there are some medical interventions which can accurately be described by those who choose them as "terminating a pregnancy," albeit where one certain effect of doing so is to kill the unborn child. Dealing with an ectopic pregnancy is an example, as is removing a cancerous womb. But these procedures might better be described as surgical procedures which are not "abortions." In any event, the vast majority of abortions, including those undertaken for reasons having to do with some unwanted aspect of pregnancy (say, to be rid of intolerable morning sickness) more than with the burdens of raising a child once born, terminate pregnancy precisely by actions—dismemberment, deprivation of nourishment, or (in the old days) by saline injection—intended to destroy the baby *in utero*. Subsequent discharge or removal of fetal remains is not and should not be described as constituting an "abortion," lest (among other reasons) every stillbirth be thus described. Thomson was at least working with an unstable distinction, and perhaps with one with practically no relevance to the choices women make when they have abortions.

17 Compare the case of a mother who was sentenced to 9–18 months in jail for helping her 16-year-old daughter perform a self-abortion, with that of Airman Boies or John

The unborn victim's description in these laws ranges from "child *in utero*" to "human being" to "person." They typically include an explicit immunity for women seeking to terminate their own pregnancies in lawful abortion. The most widely known feticide prosecution in recent years involved Californian Scott Peterson, who was sentenced to two life terms of imprisonment for killing his pregnant wife and their unborn son in 2002. The federal feticide law says that it may also be referred to as "Laci and Conner's Law," in remembrance of Peterson's two victims.

The federal "Unborn Victims of Violence Act"[18] of 2004 is the most prominent example of these laws protecting unborn lives. In pertinent part it says that "whoever" "causes the death of or bodily injury to," a "child who is *in utero*" is guilty of an offense apart from any accompanying offense against the woman carrying the child. This distinct offense is subject to the same punishment as would be the identical misconduct if it were committed against the "unborn child's mother," which would be the same punishment as if the offense were committed against anyone else. A "child *in utero*" is defined as a "member of the species homo sapiens, at any stage of development, who is carried in the womb."

There have been many prosecutions under this law. One of the most recent is that of John Andrew Welden. On May 14, 2013 he was indicted by a federal grand jury for violating the UVVA, in that he "intentionally caused the death of…the unborn child *in utero* of "R.L."[19] The baby was his. "R.L.," who was later publicly identified as Remmee Jo Lee, was Welden's girlfriend.

Welden faced life in prison without possibility of parole for the murder. An educated 28-year-old from a large, prosperous (but broken) family, Welden was steadily employed. When he learned of his girlfriend's pregnancy, he was "shock[ed] and fright[ened]."[20] The prospect of being a father not only scared him. It caused "sadness, guilt, hopelessness, and worthlessness," effects perhaps abetted by his underlying tendency towards depression. Welden was also romantically involved with Tara Fillinger, who said that she and Welden were "discussing marriage."[21] In no recondite or technical sense, Weldon was unprepared and unwilling to assume the obligations of being a parent. Notwithstanding that Remmee Jo Lee assured Welden that she would raise the baby herself "without [making] any demands of" him,[22] he resolved to kill their unborn child.

Weldon, discussed *infra*, who were sentenced to 13 years and life, respectively, for feticide (though Weldon finally pleaded guilty to a lesser charge). On the criminal proceeding against the mother of the 16-year-old, *see The New York Times* Magazine, September 22, 2014 ("A Mother in Jail for Helping Her Daughter Have an Abortion").

18 18 U.S.C. 1841 (2004).
19 *United States v. John Andrew Welden*, filed May 14, 2013, Count Two.
20 P. 14. *Tampa Tribune*, June 14, 2013.
21 *Tampa Tribune*, June 14, 2013.
22 Transcript of Initial Appearance and Bond Hearing, p. 8. Lee never said that she consented to the chemical abortion. She told the court during a March hearing,

Welden did so in a manner that, save for his deception of Lee, would be indistinguishable from a medical (as opposed to surgical) abortion. Welden ordered some Misoprostol from an out-of-state pharmacy. He affixed to the abortion pills a pharmacy label indicating that it was amoxicillin, a common antibiotic. Welden then convinced Lee that she needed to take the pills to treat an infection which he falsely said had been diagnosed by his father, a doctor who specialized in fertility treatments. Lee took the pills that day. Next morning, she miscarried. Welden soon confessed. He was arrested, and eventually pleaded guilty to lesser charges, netting him thirteen years' imprisonment.

A similar scenario played out in the case of Airman First Class Scott Boie, who was charged with intentionally killing his unborn child.[23] Boie married his girlfriend shortly after learning that she carried their child. But he was never happy about the pregnancy and soon asked her to have an abortion. When his wife declined, Boie bought some Misoprostol. He ground the drug into a powder and secretly put some of it into his wife's food and drink on four different occasions. She soon miscarried. Boie confessed, and eventually pleaded guilty under the federal Unborn Victims of Violence Act to the lesser offense of attempting to kill his child. Boie was dishonorably discharged and sentenced to nearly 10 years in prison.

In Boie's and Welden's cases, an unborn child's father effectively performed an abortion by the same means and for the same sorts of reasons that the child's mother could have chosen to abort as a matter of right. Exercising her constitutional right would require professional assistance, since self-abortion is illegal in approximately 40 states. But nothing about the course of the proceedings against either man would have been different if he in fact had been a physician.

This asymmetry of legal treatment requires some reasonable defense. That explanation is not to be found in the phrase "a woman's control over her body," unless constitutional law is going to hold that a mother may take the occasion of being pregnant to terminate another person whose existence will (might?) sometime later become unwelcome to her. Indeed, that phrase ("control over her body") has become a kind of totem in discussions of abortion's justice. When used by apologists for *Roe,* it usually signals that no satisfactory answer is forthcoming, or is going to be attempted, or is felt to be worth the effort.

Consider now the case of a 17-year-old Utah girl, described in court documents due to her age as "J.M.S," and the 24-year-old man whom she hired to abort her unborn child. J.M.S. had no objection to being pregnant or, it appears, to having a child, save that her boyfriend threatened to break up with her if she did not have an abortion. Lawful abortion was not readily available to her, due to the advanced state of her pregnancy and the scarcity of abortion-performing doctors

---

though, that Welden remained her "best friend and that she loved him in spite of what . . . he had done to her," as quoted in *Tampa Tribune, supra* note 8.

23 *See United States v. Boie,* 70 M.J. 585 (2011).

in her vicinity. J.M.S. therefore hired Aaron Harrison after they met at a 7–11 store. She accompanied him to his parents' home, where Harrison kicked her in the stomach five times in an unsuccessful attempt to cause a miscarriage.[24] She paid Harrison $125.

Harrison was convicted and sentenced for attempted murder. Notwithstanding that Utah law exempted women from prosecution for murder in cases of "abortion," J.M.S. too faces criminal penalties. The Utah legislature had amended its criminal homicide statutes in 1983 to include within that crime anyone who "intentionally . . . causes the death of another human being, including an unborn child at any stage of development."[25] "Abortion" was an exception, and in no circumstance could a woman be charged for obtaining an "abortion." But "abortion" was defined as the post-fertilization "procedures" to "kill a live unborn child," which the Utah Supreme Court interpreted to include only *medical* procedures. Kicking a pregnant woman in the stomach did not qualify. The attorney for J.M.S. argued that any assault upon a fetus at the mother's request amounted to an "abortion." The Court disagreed.[26]

The difference between criminal homicide and lawful abortion in this case was not any mental state, for both man and woman wanted to kill the same unborn child. Nor was the difference rooted in the pregnant woman's consent; Aaron Harrison had it. The legally decisive difference was the nature of the "procedure" employed. Because J.M.S. sought an abortion by amateurish means, the state high court concluded that she could be charged with solicitation to commit murder.[27]

---

24 J.M.S. gave birth a few months later. The baby was subsequently adopted by a relative.
25 *Utah v. J.M.S.*, p. 10.
26 An Indiana appellate court recently (July 22, 2016) adopted the contention (pressed by a woman convicted of feticide) that all actions undertaken with the pregnant woman's consent to end a pregnancy constitute "abortions." These abortions could be lawful or unlawful. But in no case may a woman be prosecuted for procuring her own abortion. Nor may a consenting woman be prosecuted under Indiana law, according to this court, for feticide, which the court defined as extending to third party acts against the expectant mother *without* her consent. See *Patel v. Indiana*, Case No. 71A04-1504-CR-166. The court in this court threw out the defendant's convictions for feticide and for the highest grade of criminal neglect of her child, which was, in fact, born alive and died after his mother deposited him in a trash dumpster. The court entered a judgment of conviction for a lesser felony criminal neglect. The court reasoned throughout its opinion about the coherent meaning of the relevant Indiana statutory framework, and did *not* say or imply that any of its conclusions was due to the pull of constitutional considerations, including those found in the Supreme Court's abortion jurisprudence.
27 The case of J.M.S. is one of several in which women have been found liable for killing their unborn child. *But see also* the case of Erica Basoria, who was pregnant with twins by Gerardo Flores. By the time she discovered it and concluded that she wanted an abortion, it was too late: her doctor said that neither he nor any other local doctor could safely perform the abortion. Basoria testified at Flores' trial for capital murder

Thus, for what it is worth, J.M.S. turned out to lack the degree of "control over her body" she desired.

To the skein so far sketched of identity of choice, intention, act, and harm to the unborn should now be added the same norms of justification. Jaclyn Kurr stabbed her boyfriend, Antonio Pena, to death. She was convicted after trial, notwithstanding her contention that she killed Pena after he "punched her two times in the stomach and [after she] warned Pena not to hit her because she was carrying his babies." Evidence at trial indicated that Kurr had recently become pregnant. The trial court nonetheless denied her request that the jury be instructed about justification. Her proposed instruction was the standard one, commonly used in every American jurisdiction.[28]

Kurr asked that the jurors be told that her use of lethal force against Pena was justified if she had a reasonable fear that he was going to kill, or cause serious bodily harm, to her or to unborn baby.[25] Kurr's conviction was overturned on appeal. The higher court held that Michigan's unborn children's protection act law established that deadly force was justified in defense of an unborn child of any age. "Indeed, she may under the appropriate circumstances use deadly force to

---

that she then asked him to terminate her pregnancy by stepping on her abdomen. He did so, but only after—as the appellate court recounted Basoria's testimony—she repeatedly asking him to. Basoria supplemented Flores' efforts with some of her own. The court which affirmed Flores' convictions wrote: "[b]y the last week of her pregnancy, she was striking herself every day" [434]. Basoria subsequently delivered stillborn twins. Flores was sentenced to life in prison.[23]

These facts are taken from *Flores v. State*, 245 S.W. 3d 432 (Ct. Crim. App. 2008).

28 *Justification* "involves conduct which would otherwise be criminal, but which under the circumstances is socially acceptable and which deserves neither criminal liability nor even censure" (LaFave, *Criminal Law,* 471, quoting Paul Robinson). "Thus burning a field in order to create a firebreak preventing a raging fire from reaching nearby homes," conduct which would otherwise be criminal mischief is justified (LaFave, *Criminal Law,* 471). Using lethal force against and even killing—both ordinarily serious crimes—are justified when done in self-defense or in defense of *another. Justification* is very different from *excuse.*

Excuse on the other hand pertains to situations where the misconduct is criminal and morally reprehensible, but where holding a particular person criminally responsible for the misconduct is judged to be inappropriate. Criminal acts are excused, not on the basis of the net value of any act, but due to characteristics of the actor, usually some sort of extraordinary stress or diminished capacity. Paul Robinson explains that " 'justified' conduct is correct behavior that is encouraged or at least tolerated. . . . An excuse represents a legal conclusion that the conduct is wrong, undesirable" but that punishment is inappropriate. "Excuses do not destroy blame" (LaFave, *Criminal Law,* 473). They do, however, reduce or eliminate criminal liability.

Whether pregnant women could properly be excused, *as a class,* for the unjustified killing of their unborn children by abortion is an important question of law and social policy, which I do not consider in this paper.

protect her foetus even if she does not fear for her own life." This holding undoubtedly extends to third parties, too. A friend (or stranger) who happened upon Pena assaulting Kurr could have justifiably killed Pena, based upon a reasonable fear that he was going to kill Kurr or her baby *in utero*. To the obvious challenge that its reasoning would justify anti-abortion protesters using force to interrupt an imminent abortion, the *Kurr* court limply cited *Roe* for the proposition that *that* sort of imminent harm to another's life was "lawful."[29]

These cases are a small sample of available illustrations. It is readily apparent, however, that notwithstanding access to lawful abortion mandated by *Roe*, unborn children from the moment of fertilization are *not* merely "potential life." So far considered, judges (such as Richard Posner) who say that abortion rights imply that the unborn are not and cannot be "persons" are mistaken. The unborn are indeed persons with a right not-to-be-killed, on a par with that of everyone else, save for the anomalous case of "lawful" abortion.

Abortion rights amount to a stipulated exception to the law of justified killing of one person by another. For it surely cannot be the case that the personal status of the fetus (or of anyone else) could vary depending upon whether it is struck by a fist from outside the womb or severed by a scalpel inserted into the womb or killed by Misoprostol taken wittingly or not or taken wittingly but provided by a doctor or a layman. Much less could it be the case that the acts and intentions of other persons could flip the fetus from being a person with an equal right-not-to-be-killed to a non-entity which is utterly invisible to the law.

4 *State v. Holcomb* and the Mother's Exclusive Right — through Abortion — to Permit Destruction of the Unborn Child

Barry Holcomb was convicted of strangling his girlfriend Laura Vaughan to death. Her unborn child perished with her. For the child's death Holcomb was convicted of first-degree murder, just as he was for killing Vaughan. Holcomb knew that Laura was pregnant, and prior to the murders he had threatened to kill both of them. Under Missouri law, the location of a homicide victim *in utero* made absolutely no difference to Holcomb's criminal liability. Holcomb received consecutive life sentences, without possibility of parole.[30]

Barry Holcomb appealed his convictions. He stated the challenge which emerges from these pages plainly: "all intentional and unjustified killings of preborn children must be treated the same."[31] The Missouri appellate court nonetheless upheld his conviction for killing his own unborn child, where the victim was

---

29 These facts are taken from a copy of the slip opinion in *Michigan v. Kurr* (Mi. Ct. App. 2002), a copy of which is in the author's possession.
30 These facts are taken from *State v. Holcomb*, 956 S.W. 2d 286 (Mo. App. W. D. 1997).
31 956 S.W. at 292.

expressly declared to be, simply, a "person" for purposes of the state murder law. The *Holcomb* court observed that "[i]t is basic doctrine of *Roe v. Wade*, and it is understood by persons on all sides of the abortion controversy, that *Roe* limited to the mother the legal right to consent to the destruction of her unborn child."[13] For the rest of the world, "destruction of the unborn child" was criminal homicide.

Yes, that is the prevailing positive law. But *why?* On what critical grounds can it be adequately defended?

Matthew Bullock and Lisa Hargrave were having a baby. Hargrave was 22 to 23 weeks pregnant on New Year's Eve 2002, when she and Bullock consumed some alcohol and cocaine at a party. After returning to their apartment, Hargrave did some more cocaine. Bullock asked her to stop for the baby's sake.[32] When Hargrave ignored his request, they argued and, according to Bullock's later statement to the police, he blacked out. Next thing he knew (according to his testimony) he was on top of Hargrave, strangling her. Because he feared that Hargrave would call the police on him, Bullock bound and gagged her. After she struggled to break free, Bullock returned and strangled her to death. Their unborn child died, too, as a result.[33]

The Pennsylvania Supreme Court affirmed Bullock's multiple convictions, including one for voluntary manslaughter of his (and Hargrave's) unborn child. Bullock appealed. He mounted the same challenge as did Holcomb, and in much the same language The *Bullock* court responded to the challenge by saying that "the mother is not similarly situated to everyone else, as she alone is carrying the unborn child."[34] This is true in an important but limited sense: the presence of a child within the mother's body gives rise to possibilities of justified use of force that arise for no one else. Ordinary principles of justification would thus permit her to terminate her pregnancy, and thus to knowingly end the unborn child's life, if she reasonably feared her own death or her own serious bodily injury. General principles of justification would not go much beyond that, as a glance at any state's criminal provisions governing homicide, and the justified use of deadly force, shows.

The *Bullock* court also asserted that "the statutory language does not purport to define the concept of personhood or establish when life as a human being begins and ends."[35] Pennsylvania's lawmakers had, however, described the manslaughter victim in *Bullock* an "unborn child," which they defined as a member of the "species homo sapiens"; that is (according to any standard dictionary): one of humankind, a human being.

---

32 Several women have been successfully prosecuted for harming or killing their unborn child due to consumption of illegal drugs during pregnancy. Again, for what it is worth, each has turned out to lack the desired "control over her body."
33 These facts are taken from *Commonwealth v. Bullock*, 913 A. 2d 207 (2006).
34 913 A. 2d at 216.
35 913 A. 2d at 212.

The court added (here relying upon language from an earlier feticide appeal) that "whether an embryo is a human being [is] irrelevant to criminal liability under the statute."[36] Quoting next from another feticide case, *Bullock* said that "[t]he statute only requires proof that, whatever the entity within the mother's womb is called, it had life and, because of the acts of the defendant, it no longer does."[37] The Armed Forces appellate court in Airman Boie's case adopted all this language, and concluded that the issue was whether the "embryo" "had the properties of life and whether [Boie] attempted to end that life –or at least to destroy those "properties"—by poisoning" his wife's food. But, leaving aside whatever exactly "properties of life" *in this space* denotes and how a being with those "properties" differs from a person, the question pressed by Bullock (and Holcomb and Boie and others) remains unanswered: how could the father of a child do what his wife could do for the same reason and with the same motives to the same effect (upon "properties of life" (if you wish)) be imprisoned for life, while she is not even questioned by the law?

Justice Baer concurred in the *Bullock* result. He wrote separately to "emphasize certain matters implicit" in the Pennsylvania Court's decision. Baer "emphasized" that, although the conviction was in all respects indistinguishable from that of killing the deceased mother, it "should not, and cannot, be interpreted as an attempt in any way to define, generally, a foetus as a life-in-being or as endorsing the notion that the interruption of the reproductive process is the killing of human life."[38]

How so? We have already seen that this assertion was contrary to the plain language of the Pennsylvania statute. Even if granted, however, it solves nothing, unless Baer was prepared to defend the proposition that the personal status of the unborn as a homicide victim *varies*, depending upon the motives and interests of the one who would do the killing. On this line of thought, one would not ask in the case of *Dudley & Stephens* whether consuming the sickly cabin boy was justified or at least excusable homicide. One would rather ask if the defendants were so hungry that their ailing victim ceased to be a person at all!

Baer concluded that "*Roe* and its progeny remain the law in this nation and any attempt based upon the legislature's choice of language . . . to undermine its constitutional imperative, is unavailing." This bold declaration indicates a steely determination to retain the abortion liberty established by *Roe*. But it surely has no tendency to critically justify the asymmetric abortion regime which that case inaugurated.

Baer's resolve gave slightly larger expression to the curt denial which a U.S. district judge delivered to the attorney for John Welden. Todd Foster asserted

---

36 913 A. 2d at 213, quoting the Minnesota Supreme Court in *State v. Merrill*, 450 N.W. 2d 318, 324 (1990).
37 913 A. 2d at 213, quoting *People v. Ford*, 581 N.E. 2d 1189, 1201 (Ill. App. 3d 1991).
38 913 A. 2d at 219.

at an early hearing that there were "some tensions" between *Roe v. Wade* and prosecuting his client for feticide. Judge Lazzara was—according to the news report of the hearing—"flabbergasted." His reply, in total, was this: "That argument will not fly."[39]

Why not?

One might think these judges should stand by abortion rights because they are members of an inferior court and the Supreme Court has continued to affirm the "central holding" of *Roe v. Wade*. But this thought contradicts the fundamental role of a judge, no matter of what level of court. *Every* judge in America is sworn to uphold the Constitution, and *every* litigant is entitled to judgment according to the Constitution. The Supreme Court has never taken up the dilemma posed by litigants such as John Welden and Airman Boie, Barry Holcomb and Matthew Bullock. Judges are therefore not following the Supreme Court when they decide these men's cases as they have decided them. They are rather improvising an answer by, it seems, declaring their undiluted allegiance to something very much like abortion on demand. But that is a stance, not an argument.

5 Reassessing Thomson's Argument on the Right to Abortion and Unborn Legal Personhood

The most obvious response available to Baer, Lazzara, and other like-minded judges is to roll-back fetal personhood, so that the unborn cannot be murder victims. The alternatives to this response can scarcely be entertained. One alternative would be to admit fetal personhood, but to open up ordinary norms of justification so that distraught fathers, perhaps also ambushed by contraceptive failure or deceit in the matter by the impregnated woman, could lawfully kill their unborn children. Besides the difficulty of lining up such a license with the mother's well-being and choices, any such expansion of justification could not be limited to cases of parents and unborn children. Admitting fetal personhood while stipulating that distress short of a reasonable fear that one's life is imminently threatened could justify killing another person would put everyone in peril. For any attempt to limit the revised justificatory license to, say, mothers and fathers only and for a limited catalogue of specific emotional, psychological, and financial trials would simply raise again the Equal Protection (and justice) questions we have explored throughout this paper.

For example: Why should a severe disability justify killing an unborn person but no other person? Why should the "stigma of unwed motherhood" always be a reason sufficient for a woman to abort the person in her womb, but never for the child's father, or for her—that is, the woman's own—mortified father, who has (for example) lost face in his religious community due to his daughter's sexual sins?

---

39 *Tampa Tribune*, June 14, 2013.

The only practical alternative to reconfiguring abortion law so that it centers upon Judith Thomson's question is to preserve the *status quo* by declaring that the unborn simply are not persons. One prerequisite for doing so or, perhaps, a personal qualification for advocating this path would be that one conscientiously believes, on the strength of evidence and argument, that persons do not come to be until birth, or at least viability (after which point an advocate might agree that abortion should be permitted only where objectively justified). This position is improbable, and in my judgment unreasonable. In any event, good-faith is a precondition because lying about such an important matter would be wrong. The lie would be made worse by its consequences: a whole class of persons whom one silently believes possess a right-to-life would be exposed to being killed with impunity. It is a prerequisite also because the Posnerian option simply restates the arbitrary position which this path is supposed to bypass. *Saying* that the unborn are not persons because that is what one has to say if one is "pro-choice" is exactly the evasion which this alternative to Thomson is meant to overcome.

The judicial heavy-lifting involved in pursuing this depersonalization option would extend way beyond invalidation of all feticide statutes, and beyond reversing the convictions of Scott Peterson and all the other men we have encountered in these pages. An Indiana federal judge invalidated the state's newly enacted requirement that fetal remains be disposed in a humane manner, according to the legal norms governing the treatment of human corpses generally. Not even applying the legal test which the Supreme Court prescribes for this sort of law—the "undue burden" standard of *Casey*, as refashioned in *Whole Woman's Health*—the court concluded that the implied characterization of an unborn child as a human person (or something close enough) was simply excluded from the law by the Court's abortion jurisprudence.[40] This court relied upon the earlier Posner opinion, in which he concluded that the license issued to women by *Roe* had to mean that the Court resolved what it called the "difficult question of when life begins," and that the Court's answer was (at least) viability, and probably at birth.[41] Again, this is no argument against fetal personhood or in favor of the justice of abortion.

This reading of *Roe* suffers in any event from insurmountable difficulties. One is that it flies in the face of that Court's explicit declaration that it did *not* resolve the difficult question of when life begins, a question which the Court rightly recognized was not a narrow or technical question of legal reasoning or usage (like the question about what the Court called "constitutional" personhood), but about reality. That ontological (my word) problem lay, the justices opined, within the provinces of philosophers and scientists. Not only did the Court say that it passed on the question. It said that the judiciary was not competent to answer it. The Court here was at least pitifully naïve, and possibly intentionally evasive.

---

40 See *Planned Parenthood of Indiana and Kentucky v. Commissioner*, 265 F. Supp. 3d 859 (S.D. Ind. 2017).
41 Id. at 870.

Nonetheless this professed incompetence was essential to the holding in *RIdoe*. We should at least presume that the Court meant what it said, and that it understood the nature of implication and entailment.

In *Roe v. Wade* the Supreme Court affirmed three propositions about the status of unborn children as human persons.

① The first proposition was that the unborn are *not* constitutional persons. The Court asserted that the word " 'person' as used in the Fourteenth Amendment does not include the unborn"[42] This conclusion was important because, as the Court plainly stated, the case for abortion liberty would otherwise "collapse", because (the Court recognized, then: the foetus's "right to life would then be guaranteed specifically by the Amendment."[43] The Court concluded that if the unborn were recognized as constitutional persons, only abortions to save a pregnant woman's life could be consistent with equal respect for the life of the unborn.

Writing for the *Roe* Court, Justice Blackmun treated the constitutional-person question as one about past legal usage, as an inquiry about a technical term whose meaning in *Roe* depended upon how it was understood in the nineteenth century. He considered two kinds of historical evidence.[44] Critical to his reasoning were the twenty or so uses of the term "person" in the Constitution (such as that no "person shall be elected President more than twice"). Blackmun concluded that none of these usages indicated "with any assurance, that it has any possible prenatal application." "All this, together with our observation that throughout the major portion of the 19th century prevailing legal abortion practices were far freer than they are today," Blackmun added, "persuades us that the word 'person' as used in the Fourteenth Amendment does not include the unborn."[45]

This first proposition affirmed by the *Roe* Court had no connection to the subject matter of the second and third. These latter two affirmations had to do with whether the unborn really are persons. The common concern of these two

---

42 410 U.S. 156.
43 Id. at 156 –157.
44 Blackmun did not explore the most probative historical evidence available, namely, that stemming from proposal and ratification of the Fourteenth Amendment itself, as that evidence bears upon the relationship between constitutional personhood (if you like) and real personhood. If Blackmun had done so he would have readily discovered abundant confirmation of what the constitutional text and structure itself so strongly suggests: they are the same! The historical record supports the proposition unequivocally rejected by the *Roe* Court, and by every member of that Court since, namely, that "constitutional" "persons" includes everyone who is really a person, every genuine human being, all of God's children. Everyone who in truth is a person is a "constitutional" person. See G. Bradley, "Constitutional and Other Persons," in J. Keown, R. George, eds., *Reason, Morality, and the Law: The Philosophy of John Finnis*, 249–268 (Oxford 2013).
45 Id.

propositions is the question: When do persons truly begin? Do they really begin at conception or at any other time before live birth?[46]

"Texas urges," Blackmun wrote in *Roe,* that apart from the Fourteenth Amendment, "life begins at conception and is present throughout pregnancy."[47] Texas further argued that "[o]nly when the life of the pregnant mother herself is at stake, balanced against the life she carries within her, should the interest of the embryo or foetus not prevail."[48] On this view, the state has a "compelling interest"— indeed, a duty— to "protect[] that life from and after conception." The sources of this "duty" no doubt included Texas's constitutional obligation to accord all persons within its borders the "equal protection of the laws."

The *Roe* Court neither affirmed nor denied the state's proffered answer to the question about when persons begin. The Court instead declared its incompetence in the matter: "We need not resolve the difficult question of when life begins. When those trained in the respective disciplines of medicine, philosophy, and theology are unable to arrive at any consensus, the judiciary, at this point in the development of man's knowledge, is not in a position to speculate as to the answer." This is the second proposition about unborn persons affirmed by the *Roe* Court: persons— or, in the Court's phrase, "life, as we recognize it"[49]—may truly begin at conception or at some later time before birth. But it is not for the judiciary to say that they do or that they do not.

The third proposition affirmed in *Roe* had to do with whether legislators (and other competent political authorities) are similarly disabled from judging authoritatively when persons begin. *Roe* implicitly but surely determined that they are not so incompetent. The evidence that *Roe* affirmed Proposition Three is not limited to the Court's silence; that is, to the fact—and it is a fact—that nowhere in *Roe* does the Court *say* that legislators, for example, may not judge when persons truly begin. The Court also reviewed various areas of law where legislators predicated valuable rights of the unborn child.[50] The Court questioned none of these legal regimes. The majority concluded from this review only that the "unborn have never been recognized in the law as persons *in the whole sense*"; that is, in every respect, or to the extent that adults (for example) are so recognized.[51] [My emphasis.] The Court did not expressly reject the predicate of Texas's contention that it bore a "duty" to ban abortion because persons begin at conception. The Court instead sidestepped the

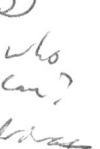

---

46 The Court assumed that the Constitution settles that persons come to be no later than at birth. The justices were mistaken, however, and thus never faced up to the challenge of showing how or why it is that a human individual becomes a person when he or she is born—but not before—or at any other time between fertilization and death.
47 Id. At 159.
48 Id. At 150.
49 Id. At 161.
50 Id. At 161–162.
51 Id.

predicate while denying the conclusion: "Logically," the state's asserted interest in protecting the unborn "need not stand or fall on acceptance of the belief that life begins at conception or at some other point prior to live birth." And a woman's interest in abortion generally outweighed that state interest, whatever exactly it might be.

The stated reasons for the abortion liberty supply further evidence of *Roe's* affirmation of Proposition Three. The Court stated that legislators may affirm what they wish about the unborn, so long as they do not, "by adopting one theory [of when] life [begins], override the rights of the pregnant woman that are at stake."[52] Those "rights" were rooted neither in a judicial conclusion about when persons begin (Proposition Two), nor in the denial of legislative competence in the matter (Proposition Three). The ground of the abortion liberty articulated in *Roe v. Wade* was, instead and unquestionably, the seven "detriments" we considered earlier in this paper, that the state would "impose" (the Court's term) upon the pregnant woman by denying her the abortion option.

Proposition Three was confirmed and more explicitly articulated by the Supreme Court in the 1989 *Webster* decision.[53] Missouri's legislators declared that the "life of each human being begins at conception." They defined "unborn children" to include "all . . . offspring of human beings from the moment of conception until birth at every stage of biological development." They mandated that "the laws of this state shall be interpreted and construed to acknowledge on behalf of the unborn child at every stage of development, all the rights, privileges, and immunities available to other persons, citizens, and residents of the state," subject only to federal constitutional limitations (chiefly, those found in *Roe* and its progeny).

The Supreme Court in *Webster* upheld all these provisions. The Court interpreted its prior cases to mean "only that a state could not justify an abortion regulation *otherwise* invalid under *Roe v. Wade* on the ground that it embodied the state's view" of when people begin. (Emphasis added.)

Proposition Two was essential to *Roe's* legitimacy. The *Roe* majority opinion begins with an argument, not about abortion or about the personhood of the unborn, but about the Court's peculiar competence to resolve—this "sensitive and emotional" question, one plagued by "vigorous opposing views," and to end a debate marred by "the deep and seemingly absolute convictions that the subject inspires." The Court's warrant (so to speak) lay precisely in its capacity "to resolve the issue by constitutional measurement, free of emotion and predilection."[54] Such was the *Roe* Court's self-described "task."

This special competence depended upon the justices' detachment from the "philosophic" issues raised by abortion; that is, the aloofness expressed by Proposition Two. This detachment allowed and equipped them to resolve the divisive

---

52 Id.
53 492 U.S. 490 (1989).
54 410 U.S. at 116.

abortion question in a uniquely credible and authoritative way. That way was free of emotion, partisanship, and of either side's "absolute[ness]." That way was a third way, a distinct path between the warring sides' moral arguments. As the *Casey* justices said in 1992: "Men and women of good conscience can disagree about the profound moral and spiritual implications of terminating a pregnancy." The *Casey* plurality added: "Our obligation is to define the liberty of all, not to mandate our own moral code."

The combined effect of these *Roe* propositions is paradoxical, at least. Propositions One and Two mean that even if the unborn really are human persons (who would obviously benefit from legal protection against being killed), they are still *not* "persons" whose lives are protected by the Constitution. Proposition Three means that legislators may recognize the unborn as real persons with the same right not to be killed as everyone else, save that *Roe* means that what would be unjustified homicide by everyone else requires no articulated justification at all by the unborn person's mother.

This is to say that Richard Posner and those following him are mistaken when they assert that *Roe* implies that fetuses cannot be real persons. Although the *Roe* justices probably did not consciously consider what to do about Barry Holcomb et al., they quite studiously built into the foundation of abortion rights all the conditions and predicates which make their challenges possible, and rationally compelling. It so happens, then, that these men's challenges expose the fact that *Roe* is a house built upon sand. Posner, Baer et al. are legally entitled, in a sense, to take the pro-abortion side in the ensuing debate. They are not morally or juridically entitled to do so by their own *ukase*. They are under a duty, in fact, to critically justify their stance according to the canons of reasoning incumbent upon judges in constitutional cases.

6 Conclusion

Courts have so far denied the feticide defendants' appeals, with little more articulated reason than the obvious fact that granting these claims would rattle the structure of abortion rights in place since 1973. So they might; that is exactly what it would mean to consider Judith Thomson's question. But these muscular judicial refusals to engage the constitutional and moral questions raised by the feticide defendants compound the naiveté and evasiveness of *Roe*. They take the Court's tragic deficiencies to a new level, one where urgent questions about the lawfulness of killing are simply suppressed.

But suppressing the question is risky as a short-term strategy, and in the long run it will not do at all. Even now conscientious legislators easily see the truth that people come to be at fertilization. They just as easily see that courts do not refute the claims of justice which these lawmakers make on behalf of the unborn, so much as the courts ignore them. As the truth about unborn persons lodges itself more securely in our law and culture (by add through, among other mechanisms, feticide prosecutions like those we have explored here), the gravely anomalous character of abortion rights will become more, not less, obvious, and disturbing. Lawful abortion will become more, not less, divisive politically and socially. The alienation of so many pro-life persons from the basic governing structures of their society will increase over time, not decrease. Graver impositions on them will be needed to keep the incumbent abortion regime intact.

Continued suppression of Thomson's question—*the* question about abortion as critically justified killing of a person—could eventually deliver abortion to the status once occupied in American law by slavery: a deeply divisive social practice contrary to natural justice, maintained only by dint of positive law, which elites preserved from criticism by suppressing dissent and protected from constitutional danger by making *it* a master principle of law. Slavery became the sun around which the surrounding legal culture orbited.[55] But at least slavery was arguably countenanced by the Constitution's text, and respectable principles of federalism were mustered to give it a veneer of further constitutional sanction. *Roe* on the other hand claimed no textual or even close precedential support. It abrogated a federalistic approach to abortion.

Such a fateful course for abortion law—a decline into dogma enforced by sheer judicial and political power—should not, however, be presumed, or lightly anticipated.

Bibliography

Bradley, Gerard, «Constitutional and Other Persons», in J. Keown, R. George, eds., *Reason, Morality, and the Law: The Philosophy of John Finnis* 249–268 (Oxford 2013).

Finnis, John, «The Rights and Wrongs of Abortion», in III *Collected Essays: Human Rights and the Common Good*, Oxford University Press, 2011.

LaFave, and Wayne, R., *Criminal Law*, 5th revised Edition, West Academic Press, 2010.

Lee, Patrick, *Abortion and Unborn Human Life*, The Catholic University of America Press, 1984.

Thompson, Judith, «A Defense of Abortion», *Philosophy & Public Affairs*, 47 (1971).

---

55 Supreme Court justices (among many others) commonly lament that abortion has effected a Copernican revolution in constitutional law. (Justice Thomas is the latest in this long line of dissenters, writing in *Whole Woman's Health* about how the Court manipulates doctrine in abortion cases "to achieve its desired result".)

Cases:

MKB Management Corporation v. Stenehjam (8th Cir. July 15, 2015, at 9).

Planned Parenthood of Indiana and Kentucky v. Commissioner, (So. Dist. IN, June 30, 2016).

Roe vs. Wade, 410 U.S. 113 (1973)533 U.S. 855

Coe v. County of Cook, 162 F. 3d 491, 495 (1998)18 U.S.C. 1841 (2004)

United States v. John Andrew Welden, filed May 14, 2013, Count Two.

Tampa Tribune, June 14, 2013.

United States v. Boie, 70 M.J. 585 (2011).

Utah v. J.M.S.

Patel v. Indiana, Case No. 71A04-1504-CR-166.

Flores v. State, 245 S.W. 3d 432 (Ct. Crim. App. 2008).

Michigan v. Kurr (Mi. Ct. App. 2002), a copy of which is in the author's possession.

State v. Holcomb, 956 S.W. 2d 286 (Mo. App. W. D. 1997)956 S.W. at 292.

Commonwealth v. Bullock, 913 A. 2d 207 (2006)913 A. 2d at 216.

State v. Merrill, 450 N.W. 2d 318, 324 (1990).

People v. Ford, 581 N.E. 2d 1189, 1201 (Ill. App. 3d 1991).

Tampa Tribune, June 14, 2013.

Planned Parenthood of Indiana and Kentucky v. Commissioner, 265 F.Supp. 3d 859 (S.D. Ind. 2017).492 U.S. 490 (1989).

Dwight Newman

3 Canada's Abortion Jurisprudence: The Creep of Procedural Rights and the Reinterpretation of Liberty

Abstract: This chapter explains the background to, and key aspects of, Canada's leading abortion decision, the *Morgentaler* case, showing that the case itself concerned certain procedural issues at the time. Second, the chapter describes subsequent political and legal developments, specifically on abortion in Canada, showing why these developments have continued and further entrenched the legacy of *Morgentaler*, albeit with occasional challenges to it. Third, the chapter argues that cases outside the abortion context specifically—notably, on harm reduction-model drug injection sites, on prostitution, and on euthanasia—have furthered the atomized reinterpretation of liberty present in *Morgentaler*. Ultimately the conclusion is that Canada's particular creep of procedural rights combined with an increasingly atomized picture of human identity has resulted in a much transformed jurisprudential landscape, but one that may have opened itself to new challenges that may yet alter some of these outcomes in the decades ahead.

Keywords: R v Morgentaler, [1988] 1 SCR 30, Abortion, Formalistic rights, Ordered liberty, Personal decisions

1 Introduction

Canada's criminal law on abortion is, in some senses, simple to describe: there are no criminal law restrictions on abortion on any ground or at any stage of pregnancy. Late-term abortion is entirely permissible—as is sex-selective abortion, or abortion for any other reason. Although there have been some types of ongoing political efforts to challenge this position, at no point has a political consensus emerged so as to alter this quite unique legal framework of what could be called "abortion on demand" or even to have any widespread political discussion of it. Although there are provincial health-related regulations on some aspects of delivery of abortion,[1] Canada's criminal law has nothing to say on abortion.

This is a relatively recent position for Canadian law. As in the United States, the current position came about not through full-fledged grassroots mobilization for abortion on demand but through a decision of nine judges—or, in Canada's case, seven, since the Court was short-staffed at the time of the leading decision, *R. v. Morgentaler* (1988).[2] However, unlike in the United States, much differently

---

1 See the significant study on this point by Rachel Johnstone & Emmett Macfarlane, "Public Policy, Rights, and Abortion Access in Canada" (2015) 51 *Int'l J. Cdn. Studies* 97.
2 *R. v. Morgentaler* [1988] 1 S.C.R. 30.

than *Roe v. Wade*[3] and *Casey*,[4] Canada's *Morgentaler* decision was based on procedural aspects of the system then in place and did not actually pronounce a constitutional right to abortion, even though it is sometimes mischaracterized as having done so. The absence of any current criminal restriction actually came about more through the challenges of attaining political consensus for any particular framework, with the Court's striking down of Canada's prior abortion law having established a default position that has never been legislatively altered.

That said, Canada's abortion jurisprudence offers a story not just of the creep of procedural rights but of some broader philosophical considerations as well. Reading the related jurisprudence that has built upon *Morgentaler*, the story it presents is one of a rapidly shifting reinterpretation of liberty that unmoors liberty and even the human person from any rootedness in an ordered society. An analysis of liberty focused on atomized individuals leads in some very different directions that ultimately has many far-reaching consequences for the social fabric and human individuals, in ways that may have effects quite different than those anticipated when setting out down such a road.

This chapter seeks to trace these themes. First, it explains the background to and key determinations in Canada's leading abortion decision, the *Morgentaler* case, showing that the case itself concerned certain issues in the procedure of the system at the time. Second, it turns to describe subsequent political and legal developments specifically on abortion in Canada, showing why these developments have effectively continued and further entrenched the legacy of *Morgentaler*, albeit with occasional challenges to it. Third, it turns to an argument that cases outside the abortion context specifically—notably, on harm reduction-model drug injection sites, on prostitution, and on euthanasia—have furthered the atomized reinterpretation of liberty present in some of the *Morgentaler* judgments. The ultimate conclusion is that Canada's particular creep of procedural rights combined with an increasingly atomized picture of human identity has played out in a very much transformed jurisprudential landscape but one that may have effectively opened itself to new challenges that may yet alter some of these outcomes in the decades ahead.

2 The *Morgentaler* (1988) Decision: Background and Consequences

The course of Canadian law on abortion was centrally affected by one individual, Henry Morgentaler, a physician who opened an abortion clinic in the late 1960s. Canadian criminal law originally followed English criminal law, which had made it a criminal offense to perform an abortion.[5] A significant modification was

---

3   *Roe v. Wade*, 410 U.S. 113 (1973).
4   *Planned Parenthood of Southeastern Pennsylvania v. Casey*, 505 U.S. 833 (1992).
5   For a detailed discussion of the historical position of abortion in English law, see generally John Keown, *Abortion, Doctors and the Law: Some Aspects of the Legal*

legislatively effected through Canada's federal Parliament (which has authority over criminal law) as part of omnibus criminal justice reform legislation pursued by then-Justice Minister Pierre Trudeau in 1969.[6] This modification created a system of "therapeutic abortion committees."[7] Abortion would remain a crime, but there would be an exception where a physician in an accredited hospital performed an abortion that was approved by that hospital's therapeutic abortion committee. This committee was authorized to permit abortions where the committee certified in writing that "the continuation of the pregnancy of such female person would or would be likely to endanger her life or health."[8] The committee would consist of at least three physicians appointed by the hospital to consider questions related to pregnancy terminations within the hospital.[9] That it was difficult to have three physicians to serve on such a committee in some locales would become an issue some decades down the road in court.

Around this same time, Henry Morgentaler began performing abortions in his private clinic, in defiance of the statutory rules on provision of abortion through hospitals. After several trials, in some of which juries refused to enforce the law and in one of which he was convicted through an unusual substitution of a guilty verdict for the jury acquittal, Morgentaler pursued one of his cases before the Supreme Court of Canada on several different issues, including federalism grounds, grounds under Canada's statutory *Bill of Rights*, and arguments on the criminal law defense of necessity and the powers of appellate courts to overturn jury acquittals. At the end of the case, though, the law stood.[10] Although enforcement efforts against him were limited for political reasons, Morgentaler's challenges to the law itself would be unsuccessful, at least until he had a new legal tool introduced in the 1980s.

Although it previously had a deep common law tradition of liberties and, later, a statutory bill of rights adopted in the light of this tradition, Canada adopted a written constitutional bill of rights only in 1982, as part of the *Constitution Act, 1982*. That written bill of rights, the *Canadian Charter of Rights and Freedoms*, was part of a larger effort to "patriate" the Canadian Constitution by taking domestic control of future amendments to the Canadian Constitution. Prior to 1982, the power of amendment remained with the United Kingdom Parliament, as it had been at the time of the establishment of Canada through the *British North America Act*, which was renamed the *Constitution Act, 1867*.[11]

Regulation of Abortion in England from 1803 to 1982 (Cambridge: Cambridge University Press, 2002).
6   *Criminal Law Amendment Act*, S.C. 1968–1969, c. 38.
7   *Criminal Code*, R.S.C. 1970, c. C-34, s. 251, as established by ibid.
8   Ibid., s. 251(4).
9   Ibid., s. 251(6).
10 *R. v. Morgentaler* [1976] 1 S.C.R. 616.
11 For a general history of constitutional amendment in Canada, see Guy Régimbald & Dwight Newman, *The Law of the Canadian Constitution* (Toronto: LexisNexis, 2013) at 17–42.

In the course of pursuing the 1982 amendments to patriate the Constitution, Prime Minister Pierre Trudeau included the *Charter of Rights* as a key amendment that would constitutionally entrench rights. The text of the *Charter* was relatively abstract, and it contains no specific text on abortion. During constitutional negotiations leading up to the 1982 amendments, repeated assurances were offered that the *Charter* would have no specific implications on abortion.[12] However, those assurances would turn out not to be correct, given the course the Supreme Court of Canada would take in the subsequent years on the interpretation of *Charter* rights.

Within the *Charter*, the main section that comes into play is s. 7, which states that "[e]veryone has the right to life, liberty and security of the person and the right not to be deprived thereof except in accordance with the principles of fundamental justice." The other provision that might have seemed likely to come into play was s. 1, which permits legislators to impose "reasonable limits" on *Charter* rights, but the application of s. 1 limitations to s. 7 rights long tended not to be permitted by Canadian courts, until a recent change on this point to which the paper will return later.[13] So, the constitutional question that can be put is whether a particular law, like that on abortion, deprives individuals of s. 7 interests like liberty or security of the person in a manner not consistent with the "principles of fundamental justice."

Just three years after the adoption of the *Charter*, the Supreme Court of Canada effectively pronounced that the textual meaning of the *Charter*, and the actual intentions of the drafters, would not be determinative of judicial interpretation. In the landmark 1985 *BC Motor Vehicle Reference* judgment, the Court read expansively s. 7 so as to permit the courts to carry out substantive review of legislation by suggesting that the "principles of fundamental justice" would go beyond procedural principles.[14] This was contrary to specific discussions in the constitutional negotiation process of trying to use language that would limit the s. 7 text to procedural due process.[15] In explaining its tack, the Court pronounced that its

---

12 The topic was raised both in the more formal negotiations and in broader public discussions. In response to a letter from the Canadian Council of Catholic Bishops, Prime Minister Pierre Trudeau—a law professor before his career in politics—indicated that the *Charter* was an inappropriate place to settle the issue of abortion and offered his assurance that no provision of the *Charter* is "reasonably capable of an interpretation that would either enshrine a right to abortion or a right to life for the unborn": "Rights charter worries bishops," *Montreal Gazette* (June 3, 1981) 91.
13 Many case law references suggested that a s. 1 justification for a s. 7 infringement would be rare but possible: Régimbald & Newman, *supra* note 11, at 621–623. A recent Ontario Court of Appeal decision, to be discussed further below, actually found such a s. 1 justification for a s. 7 infringement: *R. v. Michaud*, 2015 ONCA 585, leave to appeal to SCC refused (May 2016).
14 *Re B.C. Motor Vehicle Act* [1985] 2 S.C.R. 486.
15 See ibid. at paras. 36–37 (outlining some key passages of testimony at the 1981 Special Joint Committee of the Senate and House of Commons on the Constitution of Canada).

role was to carry out "purposive" constitutional interpretation that would see the rights in the *Charter* develop in accordance with the Court's reading over time of their underlying purposes.[16] In the criminal law context, the Court thus effectively declared that it could review the reasonableness of criminal law provisions. That claimed jurisdiction has led it to a series of more recent decisions on such topics as prostitution and euthanasia to which we will return later in this chapter.

In the immediate aftermath of the 1985 *BC Motor Vehicle Reference*, though Morgentaler could now clearly pursue a challenge against the s. 251 abortion provision of Canada's *Criminal Code* even in the face of the evidence that the drafters had not understood the 1982 *Charter of Rights* to be making any determination on abortion. His case reached the Supreme Court of Canada in 1988, and the Court struck down s. 251 as unconstitutional.[17]

Interestingly, however, the case drew only on the malleability of constitutional interpretation and not substantive due process *per se*. The reasoning actually hinged on procedural considerations. The majority of justices in *Morgentaler* (1988)—out of three sets of reasons from five majority justices, with two justices dissenting—held only that the therapeutic abortion committee system adopted in the opening up of access to abortion in 1969 was procedurally problematic. For Chief Justice Dickson and Justice Lamer, the primary concern with the system was the violation of a principle of fundamental justice of not creating an illusory defense, being a defense so hard to access that it does not amount to a defense at all.[18] For justices Estey and Beetz, the primary concern was one of the system creating delays in practice, with consequent possible risks to the health or lives of women while awaiting processing through a therapeutic abortion committee.[19] Two dissenting justices, justices McIntyre and LaForest, found no violation at all, even on these procedural issues.[20]

The nature of the procedural reasoning at stake relates to the nature of the *Charter* right infringed. Section 7 of the *Charter* is infringed on the reasoning at issue by an infringement of security of the person through a possible effect on the life or health of the woman—something the very statutory provision at issue raised—where the procedure for protection of life or health is challenging to access or susceptible of delays. And, on the traditional position where a s. 7 infringement cannot be successfully justified through the rights limitation clause in s. 1 of the *Charter*,[21] only these effects matter, as opposed to any other considerations

---

16 Ibid. at para. 21.
17 *Morgentaler* (1988), *supra* note 2.
18 Ibid. at 70 per Dickson J.
19 Ibid. at 91 ff per Beetz J.
20 Ibid. at 132 ff per McIntyre J.
21 Ibid. There is an extensive discussion of Justice Wilson's engagement with the case in Ellen Anderson, *Judging Bertha Wilson: Law as Large as Life* (Toronto: University of Toronto Press, 2002).

Parliament might have been weighing in developing such a system that was obviously set up to provide for careful consideration of the decisions at issue.

Justice Bertha Wilson, the first and then-lone female justice on the Supreme Court of Canada, was the only justice in *Morgentaler* who articulated a right to abortion in her concurring judgment, albeit only in the early stages of pregnancy.[22] In interpreting the right to liberty in s. 7 of the Canadian *Charter,* she drew directly on American privacy rights jurisprudence, notably the line of jurisprudence leading up to and including *Roe v. Wade.*[23] Interestingly, at the same time, in a part of the judgment that often receives less attention, she also accepted that the state interest in fetal life that led to a balancing with the woman's rights as pregnancy went on and would ground restrictions on abortions later in pregnancy—as she put the point, "I think s.1 of the *Charter* authorizes reasonable limits to be put upon the woman's right having regard to the fact of the developing foetus within her body."[24] Justice Wilson indicated that there was no reason to consider the procedural issues until the Court had considered the underlying substantive issue.[25] And she ultimately determined that there was an inherent s. 7 violation in any law on abortion, on the basis that it did not show "respect" for "deeply personal choices" and the "freedom of conscience" of the woman making a decision on abortion.[26]

However, the other majority judgments made no determination on the issue of abortion itself and made constitutional determinations only concerning appropriate procedures in the context of an exception for life or health. Those procedural considerations were sufficient to lead the Court to strike down the law.

From a constitutional standpoint, no standard approach to interpretation of judgments would take Justice Wilson's solo opinion to state the rule adopted by the Court. Considering the two main approaches on this matter, Justice Wilson's opinion represented neither (a) the majority of the Court nor (b) the most narrow approach within those judges needed to make up a majority.[27] Indeed, the majority justices, writing more narrowly, rejected exactly the approach that Justice Wilson's opinion took.[28] Accordingly, Justice Wilson's reasons did not represent the legal

---

22 *Morgentaler* (1988), *supra* note 2.
23 *Roe v. Wade, supra* note 3. See *Morgentaler,* ibid., discussing not just *Roe* but also other cases such as *Skinner v. Oklahoma,* 316 U.S. 535 (1942); *Griswold v. Connecticut,* 381 U.S. 479 (1965); *Eisenstadt v. Baird,* 405 U.S. 438 (1972); *Loving v. Virginia,* 388 U.S. 1 (1967).
24 *Morgentaler,* ibid. at 181.
25 Ibid. at 161. ("A consideration as to whether or not the procedural requirements for obtaining or performing an abortion comport with fundamental justice is purely academic if such requirements cannot as a constitutional matter be imposed at all.")
26 Ibid. at 180.
27 On the Canadian rules on *ratio* in the context of a divided Court, see generally Michelle Biddulph & Dwight Newman, "Equality Rights, Ratio Identification, and the Un/Predictable Judicial Path Not Taken: Quebec (Attorney General) v. A and R. v. Ibanescu" (2015) 48 U.B.C. L. Rev. 1.
28 *See Morgentaler* (1988), *supra* note 2, at 51 per Dickson J.

result of the *Morgentaler* case. When some law professors teach only Justice Wilson's opinion as if it represented the *Morgentaler* case, they do a fundamental injustice to their students and, indeed, to the Canadian Constitution itself.

However, Canada ended up in a position not only *as if* Justice Wilson's opinion had carried the day but going even further on abortion than Justice Wilson's opinion itself. The actual majority reasoning in the case would have permitted Parliament to re-enact a new abortion law applying throughout pregnancy so long as it did not have the same procedural defects as the therapeutic abortion committees system. Indeed, the Court arguably expected that Parliament would enact a new law. Even Justice Wilson's opinion would have permitted Parliament to come back with a set of partial restrictions on abortion grounded in a s. 1 justification. However, in the reality of politics, it proved immensely difficult to find sufficient agreement on any particular replacement legislation, leading to a position of no legislation at all, something arguably not anticipated by any justice on the Court.

Following the federal election that took place in 1988, the government introduced successor legislation in the House of Commons in the form of Bill C-43. This legislation would have eliminated the procedural hurdles of the therapeutic abortion committees system by providing for approval by one physician—who could also be the one performing the abortion—on expanded grounds that included not only physical health but also mental and psychological health.[29]

This new legislation faced opposition from both sides. Those favoring abortion access opposed it as imposing new restrictions compared to the *status quo* that the Supreme Court of Canada had now established. And those seeking to restrict abortions tended to see it as not going far enough. Although the legislation made its way through the House of Commons, a free vote in the Senate ended up defeating the bill through a tie vote on January 31, 1991. Since no government bill has ever been introduced on abortion since, and the few private members' bills to be introduced have failed, an unforeseen result—a system of no legislation at all on abortion—has become the new *status quo*.[30]

There is today no particular momentum for any new criminal bill on the topic. Despite early allegations of a "hidden agenda" on such topics as abortion, the Conservative government of Prime Minister Stephen Harper in place from 2006 to 2015 studiously avoided opening the issue, even to the extent of squashing private members' bills on such topics as sex-selective abortion and as commissioning a study on the beginnings of life. Without hearts and minds prevalently in favor of new abortion legislation, the government did not wish to open divisive social issues. The latest Canadian government, the Liberal government of Prime Minister Justin Trudeau, operates on the assumption that the Supreme Court of Canada decided in 1988 that all abortions must be permitted, and Trudeau effectively

---

29 *See* discussion in Karine Richer, "Abortion in Canada: Twenty Years after *Morgentaler*," 2008 PRB 08-22E, Library of Parliament (2008).
30 See ibid. at 4–5.

prohibited pro-life politicians for running as Liberal candidates unless they would agree to discard the issue.[31] Although this was not what the Supreme Court decided in *Morgentaler*, it is nonetheless what the *Morgentaler* decision effectively institutionalized.

Several years later, the Supreme Court decided another case involving Henry Morgentaler in what is sometimes called *Morgentaler (No. 3)*.[32] In this case, the province of Nova Scotia sought to block Morgentaler from establishing an abortion clinic in Nova Scotia, ostensibly through legislation regulating provision of certain health care procedures through private clinics. However, the factual record showed much evidence that the real aim of the legislation was in fact to limit abortions in Nova Scotia. The Court held that such an aim was outside provincial powers, as having the intent of criminal law legislation that could be enacted solely by the federal government. Thus, even if some provinces were politically willing to act on abortion in some ways, they were effectively precluded from doing so. Some scholars arguing for abortion access have argued that the picture is more complicated when one considers lower court decisions and have claimed that provinces have enacted more regulation on abortion than commonly realized.[33] However, at least at the Supreme Court of Canada level, the subsequent case law further entrenched the result from the 1988 *Morgentaler* decision.

3 Subsequent Developments and the Continuation of the *Morgentaler* Legacy

That the 1988 *Morgentaler* decision has become politically institutionalized, despite the inconsistency with the reasoning of the *Morgentaler* decision itself, is perhaps not as surprising as it might first appear. Politicians have not been alone in entrenching it. Subsequent to the 1988 *Morgentaler* decision, various court cases that could have affected the position it established have all failed on a variety of

---

31 See Jennifer Ditchburn, "Abortion Issues Trail Harper, Trudeau as Each Take Different Positions," *Canadian Press* (July 15, 2014) (reporting that Trudeau said that "[s]ince 1988, the Supreme Court of Canada has affirmed that a woman's right to choose in this matter is part of her fundamental rights and freedoms").
32 *R. v. Morgentaler* [1993] 3 S.C.R. 463.
33 Johnstone & Macfarlane, *supra* note 1. For another survey of some early provincial regulations and lower court challenges, see also Mollie Dunsmuir, "Abortion: Constitutional and Legal Developments," Canadian Parliamentary Research Branch Current Issue Review 89-10E (revised version of 18 August 1998). Notably, one province, Prince Edward Island, has not provided abortions since the *Morgentaler* decision, though it paid for some abortions performed out-of-province. It was the last province holding this position, and it backed down in the face of a legal challenge in early 2016 and committed to provide abortion access in Prince Edward Island by the end of 2016.

different grounds, with some effect of tending to institutionalize the result on abortion itself.

Two of these cases came the next year. In the first, *Borowski*, the Supreme Court of Canada ruled to be moot an attempt to argue that s. 251—the same provision that *Morgentaler* had struck down the prior year—did not provide sufficient protection to the fetus's right to life under s. 7 of the *Charter* or to equality rights of the fetus under s. 15.[34] The trial court and appellate court in the case had ruled against the existence of rights held by the fetus, but the Supreme Court of Canada avoided that issue altogether. Because s. 251 had been struck down, the basis for the case was now gone. The timing of the *Morgentaler* decision in January 1988 thus led to the Court not dealing with *Borowski* even though it had granted leave in *Borowksi* in July 1987 and then had not heard it sufficiently promptly for it no longer to be technically moot by the time it was heard. Technical grounds effectively extended the implications of *Morgentaler*.

The second case also coming the next year, *Tremblay v. Daigle*, concerned an attempt by a father to seek an injunction to prevent his common law partner from aborting their child.[35] Although the trial judge and a majority of the Quebec Court of Appeal held that the fetus did hold rights as a juridical person under Quebec civil law and human rights law, the Supreme Court of Canada overturned this decision and held against the claim by reading differently the Quebec Civil Code provisions at issue. In the context of an unsympathetic case in which an abusive father attempted to restrain the mother from aborting the child, the Court read the textual provisions in such a way as to avoid putting any other woman through a similar "ordeal" as that faced by Ms. Daigle.[36] The broader legal result was to foreclose certain arguments of fetal rights and thus to further institutionalize the *Morgentaler* decision.

Later cases concerning fetal rights claims have extended these conclusions. In considering whether the *parens patriae* authority of the courts would permit them to restrain a pregnant woman from engaging in glue sniffing that would harm her fetus, the majority of the Supreme Court of Canada ruled in the *Winnipeg Child and Family Services* case in 1997 that it could not do so because a fetus was not a juridical person.[37] Although two dissenting justices suggested that such a legal rule was based on outdated medical conceptions,[38] their view did not carry

---

34 *Borowski v. Canada (Attorney General)* [1989] 1 S.C.R. 342.
35 *Tremblay v. Daigle* [1989] 2 S.C.R. 530.
36 Ibid. (referring to domestic abuse and the "ordeal" faced by Daigle through the combination of circumstances from the abuse itself and the judicial process surrounding the abortion). Tremblay has subsequently faced further convictions for various assaults on women and was eventually declared a dangerous offender, so he was never a sympathetic plaintiff for a test case on fetal rights or the role of the father.
37 *Winnipeg Child and Family Services (Northwest Area) v. G. (D.F.)*, [1997] 3 S.C.R. 925.
38 Ibid. at para. 120 per Major J.

the day. A majority was concerned with the incompletely specified "potential ramifications" of the Court exercising its *parens patriae* authority in this context.[39] Well-intended efforts to protect children from the effects of their mothers' drug abuse during pregnancy thus become hostage and ultimately victim to their possible implications for abortion rights.

In the course of the reasoning, the majority judgment of Justice McLachlin (as she then was, prior to her elevation to chief justice) also commented specifically on an appellate-level tort decision, *Dobson*, in which the New Brunswick Court of Appeal had permitted a lawsuit by a child against its mother for prenatal injuries arising from the mother's negligence.[4] Justice McLachlin implied that the decision was wrong, writing that "[t]o permit an unborn child to sue its pregnant mother-to-be would introduce a radically new conception into the law; the unborn child and its mother as separate juristic persons in a mutually separable and antagonistic relation."[41] Although a judgment of Justice Major for two dissenting justices in *Winnipeg Child and Family Services* referred to the *Dobson* decision more favorably,[42] it was nonetheless arguably no surprise when the Supreme Court of Canada two years later overturned the *Dobson* case on which it had already commented unfavorably.[43]

The *Dobson* leave materials were given to the justices sitting on the *Dobson* leave application two weeks before the release of the *Winnipeg Child and Family Services* judgment, and their leave decision came three weeks after, so the two cases had links from the get-go. The justices in *Dobson* carefully refrained from mentioning that their *Winnipeg Child and Family Services* judgment had already commented on the case, but the majority judgment of Justice Cory was nonetheless a relatively straightforward application of its principles.

Where matters get somewhat more interesting is in the decision of Justice McLachlin to write a separate concurring judgment in *Dobson* to comment on the "constitutional values" at play.[44] Here, in a judgment also supported by Justice L'Heureux-Dubé, she specifically evoked the 1988 *Morgentaler* decision as reflecting constitutional values opposed to the development of tort law in ways that might restrain women's liberty, writing that the development of tort actions based on harms to a fetus had "the potential to jeopardize the pregnant woman's fundamental right to control her body and make decisions in her own interest: *R. v. Morgentaler* [1988] 1 S.C.R. 30, *per* Wilson J."[45] She also went on to

---

39 Ibid. at para. 59 per McLachlin J.
40 Ibid. at para. 28, discussing *Dobson (Litigation Guardian of) v. Dobson* (1997), 148 D.L.R. (4th) 332 (N.B.C.A.).
41 *Winnipeg Child and Family Services*, supra note 37 at para. 29.
42 Ibid. at para. 126.
43 *Dobson (Litigation Guardian of) v. Dobson* [1999] 2 S.C.R. 753.
44 Ibid. at paras. 83 ff.
45 Ibid. at para. 85.

reference very briefly the equality rights of women without further case authority on the issue. Where she had written technically in *Winnipeg Child and Family Services* when writing for the majority, Justice McLachlin now wrote more expansively of autonomy and treated the Wilson opinion from the 1988 *Morgentaler* decision as if it had reflected the constitutional determination in the case.

Justice Major, now supported by Justice Bastarache, wrote again in dissent in *Dobson*, noting that his readiness to leave undisturbed the lower courts' conclusions on tort law as something to be modified, if at all, by legislators reflected the technical majority principles in *Winnipeg Child and Family Services*. But he also indirectly questioned the suggestions of Justice McLachlin's concurring judgment. Justice Major noted: "At issue is the relationship between the rights of a pregnant woman and the rights of her born alive child. A one-sided emphasis on either side of this relationship necessarily misses the subject-matter it is attempting to analyze. Such an emphasis simply begs the question."[46] Justice McLachlin was nonetheless content to leave her concurring judgment as a very short judgment of a mere few paragraphs that now sought to explicitly entrench the Wilson judgment from *Morgentaler* while referencing the constitutional values of "liberty" (in the constitutional text) and "autonomy" (not found in the constitutional text).[47]

4 New Section 7 Jurisprudence and the Atomized Reinterpretation of Liberty

The 1988 *Morgentaler* decision has had an interesting new life in an increasingly bold series of decisions from Chief Justice McLachlin on her favored value of "autonomy." This view of "autonomy" ultimately amounts to a significant reinterpretation of liberty, with a textually rooted right now becoming something quite different.

Some years on from *Dobson*, and now a decade ago, in a coauthored judgment with Justice Major, Chief Justice McLachlin and Justice Major cited various judgments from *Morgentaler* numerous times in their judgment in *Chaoulli*, a case concerning the constitutional violation arising from delayed medical treatment worsened by a prohibition on private health insurance within some provinces in Canada's Medicare system of publicly funded health care.[48] The dissenting justices tried to show *Morgentaler* to be inapplicable to this broader context, but Chief Justice McLachlin obviously saw a strong connection.

This was something she expounded upon in a 2011 judgment in *PHS Community Services Society ("Insite")*, a case in which she declared it unconstitutional for the federal government to refuse to permit the operations of a provincially authorized

---

46 Ibid. at para. 125. *See also* ibid. at para. 129 (further referencing the rights of the child).
47 Ibid. at paras. 85–86.
48 *Chaoulli v. Quebec (Attorney General)* [2005] 1 S.C.R. 791, 2005 SCC 35.

safe injection site for those with drug addictions.⁴⁹ There, Chief Justice McLachlin wrote that "[w]here a law creates a risk to health by preventing access to health care, a deprivation of the right to security of the person is made out: *Morgentaler* (1988), at p. 59, per Dickson C. J., and pp. 105–106, per Beetz J. [. . .]."⁵⁰

More than often realized, the *Insite* decision paved the way for Chief Justice McLachlin to render further autonomy-oriented decisions in later cases on major social issues. Although *Insite* could have been decided on simpler federalism grounds, Chief Justice McLachlin chose to make it a case about s. 7 of the *Charter* and to use it to pronounce a number of principles about the creation of risks to individuals amounting to a s. 7 security of the person violation relatively easily, even in the context of broader social considerations behind the policies generating those risks to individuals.⁵¹

Two dramatic recent cases reversing past Supreme Court of Canada precedents on major social issues continue this trend in Chief Justice McLachlin's constitutional jurisprudence. In recent years, she has been able to develop this jurisprudence unopposed, partly owing to the absence of major constitutionalists from the Supreme Court of Canada bench. Such was the case in unanimous decisions to overturn major precedents on prostitution and on euthanasia, with the Supreme Court unanimously striking down legislation against both in the course of the last three years.

In the Supreme Court of Canada's 2013 *Bedford* decision,⁵² Chief Justice McLachlin considered the claims put by a wealthy Toronto dominatrix that laws preventing her from hiring security guards, operating in consort with others, and advertising her business violated her security of the person rights by putting her at more risk in running her sex business than if these laws did not exist. That these claims grounded an assault on laws intended to protect prostitutes from pimps did not change the legal analysis. The legal analysis focused on whether the laws created any risk for any individual compared to that individual's position without those laws, without reference to their broader social context. Where they did put some individual at risk, then a security of the person infringement was made out, and where this was significant for the individual, it was rapidly determined to be overbroad and grossly disproportional and thus in violation of the principles of fundamental justice.

In the Supreme Court of Canada's 2015 *Carter* decision,⁵³ Chief Justice McLachlin considered the claims of individuals enduring suffering who were prevented from

---

49 *Canada (Attorney General) v. PHS Community Services Society* [2011] 3 SCR 134, 2011 SCC 44.
50 Ibid. at para. 93.
51 See Dwight Newman, "The PHS Case and Federalism-Based Alternatives to Charter Activism" (2013) 22 Const. Forum 85.
52 *Canada (Attorney General) v. Bedford*, 2013 SCC 72 [2013] 3 S.C.R. 1101.
53 *Carter v. Canada (Attorney General)*, 2015 SCC 5 [2015[1 S.C.R. 331.

ending their lives by the existence of Criminal Code provisions banning assisted suicide and declaring that no individual may consent to his or her own death. Drawing on *Morgentaler* amongst other cases in seeking to explain why a choice to die was a fundamentally protected right worthy of constitutional respect, Chief Justice McLachlin explained liberty and security of the person as both oriented to individual autonomy and dignity and thus appropriately considered together for purposes of the case.[54] A decision to die, she argued, would come from control over bodily integrity and a "deeply personal response to serious pain and suffering," both rooted in individual dignity and autonomy.[55]

In rendering the *Carter* decision that struck down Canada's prohibitions on physician-assisted suicide in certain circumstances of enduring suffering, Chief Justice McLachlin enacted into law her long-held view on the issue of assisted suicide, which she had previously expressed in dissent in the 1993 *Rodriguez* case,[56] though with something of a new turn. In *Rodriguez*, she focused specifically on an individual's autonomy with respect to disposing of his or her own body and any state constraints on the individual body thus being an infringement of security of the person. In *Carter*, she expresses a shifted conception of "autonomy" that now encompasses more explicitly the more general engagement in "deeply personal response[s]" to the circumstances of life. What is at stake is not just the security of the individual body but a broader conception of liberty as "autonomy" in the sense of being able to make individual decisions outside of social frameworks shaping individual decision-making. The individual is, on this conception, increasingly atomized.

That more atomized view of the individual is inherent in the form of legal reasoning used in this jurisprudence. The question considered across these cases is whether there is an impact on an individual, largely without reference to the social context and impacts on the broader community from an alternative approach to the law. That not only unjustly ignores impacts on others but enmeshes the autonomy-based argument itself in certain performative self-contradictions.

To back up one moment, it is worth noting that Justice Wilson's approach in the 1988 *Morgentaler* opinion, which is tracked by language in various more recent judgments by Chief Justice McLachlin, supposes a broad sphere of autonomy, which the state is bound to respect. As she puts the point, "Liberty in a free and democratic society does not require the state to approve the personal decisions made by its citizens; it does, however, require the state to respect them."[57] Taken on its own, such a statement may seem to express a worthy principle, albeit in somewhat ill-defined terms. State "respect" for "personal decisions" obviously cannot mean that the state is barred from making all laws that affect "personal decisions."

---

54 Ibid. at para. 64.
55 Ibid. at para. 68.
56 *Rodriguez v. British Columbia (Attorney General)* [1993] 3 SCR 519.
57 *Morgentaler* (1988), *supra* note __, at 188.

There is extensive further reasoning needed to establish what is within the scope of so-called "personal decisions" and how far the "respect" for them must extend. The difficulty is that both Justice Wilson and Chief Justice McLachlin uproot these concepts from the broader tradition of which they form a part and render them into terms without the meaning that they could and should have within a proper tradition of respect for liberty within the social order.

That their approach is mired in a philosophical problem applying to the "respect for personal decisions" approach becomes more fully apparent when one realizes that the justices espousing it do not apply it consistently. In considering in the *Bedford* prostitution case whether the claim should fail on the basis that the harms from the law were not caused by the law or the state but by choices made by individuals involved in prostitution, Chief Justice McLachlin referred to constraints on individual choice so as to uphold her preferred outcome for the case. She wrote: "Whether because of financial desperation, drug addictions, mental illness, or compulsion from pimps, they often have little choice but to sell their bodies for money. Realistically, while they may retain some minimal power of choice—what the Attorney General of Canada called 'constrained choice' (transcript, at p. 22)— these are not people who can be said to be truly 'choosing' a risky line of business (*see PHS*, at paras. 97–101)."[58] Although there is much truth in this statement, it simultaneously suggests that Chief Justice McLachlin seeks simultaneously to justify respect for personal decisions on assumptions of individual freedom and its normative force and to justify ignoring certain effects of individual "choices" based on assumptions of a more social scientific model of the person.

What the reasoning leaves out is the traditional realization that individual liberty operates within a social context and the choices made about limits on individual liberty actually shape that context in ways that condition in turn the circumstances for the exercise of individual liberty. Each individual actually has an interest in the quality of the culture in which he or she is to exercise his or her individual liberties.[59] Indeed, without a well-ordered culture, the liberties are, to some degree, not even fully meaningful. Now, there is arguably a nascent realization in Chief Justice McLachlin's comments in *Bedford* that the individual offered "choices" about entry into prostitution does not exercise the same meaningful choices when in certain conditions of victimization in a highly sexualized culture that is fully ready to objectify persons. What she seems to miss is that the presence or absence of legal norms on prostitution and the circumstances surrounding it (such as laws to restrain pimps) profoundly affect those conditions.

On abortion, there are increasingly accepted realizations that legalization of abortion, seemingly out of respect for women's choices, also has constraining effects on women's choices through the changes it effects to the social fabric and

---

58 *Bedford, supra* note 52, at para. 86.
59 *See* generally Robert P. George, *Making Men Moral: Civil Liberties and Public Morality* (Oxford: Clarendon Press, 1995).

the culture surrounding the circumstances leading up to abortion. These changes actually carry with them new constraints, as identified in some of this literature: where abortion is seen as a legally easy option, it becomes increasingly the case that the option not to abort becomes seen as a free choice by a woman that should not receive any particular support from others; a culture of sexualization and sexual pressures on women is supported; and care for the vulnerable is undermined as a basic value to at least some degree.[60] Each of these points could of course be developed at greater length—and has been elsewhere—but the basic point is that an analysis focused simply on "respect" for "personal choices" in some particular current circumstances may have policy effects that actually shift those circumstances in ways that undermine the very values that the decision claimed to be furthering. The form of analysis engaged in within the line of jurisprudence at issue is simply inadequate to the significance of its consequences.

5 Conclusions

The deeper Canadian tradition on liberty is one of ordered liberty within a social fabric, capable of being protected through parliamentary institutions and not just through judicial supremacy. Ideas of liberty were richly present at the 1867 founding.[61] The 1982 constitutional amendments, which implemented a written constitutional bill of rights, ought to be implemented more in accord with these traditions, as the negotiating history would actually support to a meaningful extent. Such traditional approaches offer more scope for consideration of individual liberties within the broad social fabric and within the culture that sustains and nurtures humanity over time. The current trends in Canadian *Charter* analysis have departed from these traditions in a variety of contexts, including that of abortion.

Canada's singular position of having no criminal law on abortion was not legally implied by the 1988 *Morgentaler* judgment, although this situation was the practical effect of the judgment. Going from their judgments, none of the justices voting to strike down the law foresaw a situation of no law whatsoever. The majority, with judgments written by Chief Justice Dickson and by Justice Beetz for a total of four of the seven justices, expected a new law that would correct the procedural shortcomings of the prior law. Justice Wilson expected a new law that struck a balance between the woman's interests and the state's interests in the life of the fetus somewhere within the pregnancy, with such a law to receive a s. 1

---

60 *See* generally Charles C. Camosy, *Beyond the Abortion Wars: A Way Forward for a New Generation* (Grand Rapids: Eerdmans, 2015); Sidney Callahan, "Abortion and the Sexual Agenda: A Case for Prolife Feminism," in M. Therese Lygaught et al., eds., *On Moral Medicine*, 3rd edn. (Grand Rapids: Eerdmans, 2012).
61 *See* generally Janet Ajzenstat, *The Canadian Founding: John Locke and Parliament* (Montreal: McGill-Queen's University Press, 2007).

justification. Various political dynamics, however, took the position of Canadian law to somewhere that none of the justices anticipated.

Some have long read *Morgentaler* more broadly than it was written, and that overly broad reading has a current hold on certain legal imaginations. At the same time, however, certain legal developments have also moved toward a deeper entrenchment of its more radical aspects, those cutting a wider swathe through the law based on certain theories of individual autonomy and individualized accounts of liberty.

Those latter theories have supported a longer line of jurisprudence with which Chief Justice McLachlin has been able to dominate the Court's constitutional jurisprudence in recent years, including on such significant social issues as drug injection sites, prostitution, and euthanasia. And someone could rightly conclude that this larger trend of jurisprudence would lend support, in return, to a broader reading of *Morgentaler*, which later cases have effectively helped to entrench. That these constitutional theories have held such sway speaks, though, to a problematic philosophical trend. The approach adopted has been too individualized and has been missing a broader analysis of impacts on the social fabric and the culture within which liberty is to live. In the process, they frankly risk self-contradiction.

Intriguingly, one recent development in Canadian jurisprudence may have opened room for new arguments. Although often unnoticed, Justice Wilson's solo judgment in *Morgentaler* left clear room for a s. 1 justification for a s. 7 infringement, thus allowing room for the sort of balancing of individual interests and state interests that the progeny of this judgment have assumed away. That sort of justification for a s. 7 infringement has, in subsequent years, often been presumed to verge on the impossible.[62] However, drawing on parts of the *Bedford* decision on prostitution—one of the very cases to be carrying forward the atomized approach that this paper has critiqued—the Ontario Court of Appeal recently concluded that there must be room for a s. 1 justification for a s. 7 infringement and actually found one on the facts of the case, and the Supreme Court of Canada tacitly accepted this by refusing leave to appeal.[63] There can thus be new arguments put for limits on the broad interpretations of s. 7 adopted by the courts.

Were there the political motivation to act, it is not difficult to imagine laws on abortion for which plausible s. 1 justifications could be offered, whether based on timelines within the pregnancy as imagined by Justice Wilson herself or whether constructed as responses to particularly disturbing phenomena like sex-selective abortion. The latter phenomenon—and the resounding defense of it by some of those who want no change from Canada's current singular position—speaks very significantly on some of the unexpected consequences of the Supreme Court of Canada's 1988 decision to strike down Canada's then-existing abortion law. The record is clear that the justices did not envision a scenario of no law whatsoever,

---

62 Régimbald & Newman, *supra* note 11, at 621–623.
63 *R. v. Michaud*, 2015 ONCA 585, leave to appeal to SCC refused (May 2016).

and it is surely tragically ironic that one of the consequences of their decision is to permit a particular discriminatory targeting.

When considering large social questions on the basis of formalistic rights arguments, the justices risk missing the larger implications of their decisions. Though they now verge on lost, Canada has proud traditions of parliamentary engagement with complex questions of trying to reconcile or balance rights that are potentially in conflict. The form of legal argument in the s. 7 jurisprudence under discussion is frankly insufficient to the matters at issue. Canada has reached a certain set of circumstances based on particular applications of judicial power that show themselves to have been insufficiently considered. Though there are no definitive signs of such at this moment, there are nonetheless possibilities that principled applications of legal tradition may yet develop a richer jurisprudence in future.

Bibliography

Anderson, Ellen, *Judging Bertha Wilson: Law as Large as Life* (Toronto: University of Toronto Press, 2002).

Ajzenstat, Janet, *The Canadian Founding: John Locke and Parliament* (Montreal: McGill-Queen's University Press, 2007).

Biddulph, Michelle & Newman, Dwight, "Equality Rights, Ratio Identification, and the Un/Predictable Judicial Path Not Taken: Quebec (Attorney General) v. A and R. v. Ibanescu" (2015) 48 U.B.C. L. Rev. 1.

Callahan, Sidney, "Abortion and the Sexual Agenda: A Case for Prolife Feminism," in M. Therese Lygaught et al., eds., *On Moral Medicine*, 3rd edn. (Grand Rapids: Eerdmans, 2012).

Camosy, Charles C., *Beyond the Abortion Wars: A Way Forward for a New Generation* (Grand Rapids: Eerdmans, 2015).

Ditchburn, Jennifer, "Abortion Issues Trail Harper, Trudeau as Each Take Different Positions," Canadian Press (July 15, 2014)

Dunsmuir, Mollie, "Abortion: Constitutional and Legal Developments," Canadian Parliamentary Research Branch Current Issue Review 89-10E (revised version of August 18, 1998).

George, Robert P., *Making Men Moral: Civil Liberties and Public Morality* (Oxford: Clarendon Press, 1995).

Johnstone, Rachel & Macfarlane, Emmett "Public Policy, Rights, and Abortion Access in Canada" (2015) 51 *Int'l J. Cdn. Studies* 97.

Keown, John, *Abortion, Doctors and the Law: Some Aspects of the Legal Regulation of Abortion in England from 1803 to 1982* (Cambridge: Cambridge University Press, 2002)

Newman, Dwight, "The PHS Case and Federalism-Based Alternatives to Charter Activism" (2013) 22 Const. Forum 85.

Régimbald, Guy & Newman, Dwight, *The Law of the Canadian Constitution* (Toronto: LexisNexis, 2013).

Richer, Karine, "Abortion in Canada: Twenty Years after *Morgentaler*," 2008 PRB 08-22E, Library of Parliament (2008).

Cases:

Criminal Law Amendment Act, S.C. 1968–1969, c. 38.

Criminal Code, R.S.C. 1970, c. C-34, s. 251.

R. v. Morgentaler [1976] 1 S.C.R. 616.

R. v. Michaud, 2015 ONCA 585, leave to appeal to SCC refused (May 2016).

Re B.C. Motor Vehicle Act [1985] 2 S.C.R. 486.

Roe v. Wade, 410, U.S. 113 (1973).

Skinner v. Oklahoma, 316 U.S. 535 (1942).

Griswold v. Connecticut, 381 U.S. 479 (1965).

Eisenstadt v. Baird, 405 U.S. 438 (1972).

Loving v. Virginia, 388 U.S. 1 (1967).

Borowski v. Canada (Attorney General) [1989] 1 S.C.R. 342.

Tremblay v. Daigle [1989] 2 S.C.R. 530.

Winnipeg Child and Family Services (Northwest Area) v. G. (D.F.) [1997] 3 S.C.R. 925.

Dobson (Litigation Guardian of) v. Dobson (1997), 148 D.L.R. (4th) 332 (N.B.C.A.).

Dobson (Litigation Guardian of) v. Dobson [1999] 2 S.C.R. 753.

Chaoulli v. Quebec (Attorney General) [2005] 1 S.C.R. 791, 2005 SCC 35.

Canada (Attorney General) v. PHS Community Services Society [2011] 3 SCR 134, 2011 SCC 44.

Canada (Attorney General) v. Bedford, 2013 SCC 72 [2013] 3 S.C.R. 1101.

Carter v. Canada (Attorney General), 2015 SCC 5 [2015[1 S.C.R. 331.

Rodriguez v. British Columbia (Attorney General) [1993] 3 S.C.R. 519.

R. v. Michaud, 2015 ONCA 585.

Salvatore Amato

4 To Be and Not to Be. The Uncertain Identity of Unborn Children in Italian Case Law

Abstract: In the Italian legal system, the juridical status of the unborn child is not clearly defined. In 1975, the Constitutional Court ruled that the foetus is a human individual, but not a human person. Ever since, the unborn child's rights have sometimes been denied and sometimes affirmed. For instance the Assisted Fertilization Act states that it is necessary to consider the rights of all parties involved «including offspring», but most courts tend to recognize the existence of a right to the child as a right over the child. Such contradictions reflect the difficulties in reaching an optimal balance between the respect for human life from the outset and the values at play in reproductive technologies.

Keywords: Offsprings, Parental figures, Reproductive technologies, Abortion, Values

1 Introduction

Like all civil legal systems, the Italian legal system is essentially built on the requirements of a capitalist society intent on managing its own assets through the free market.[1] The legal person becomes important due to the economic effects of what capacity (s)he has or will have to own and use. The prevalence of this economic aspect over the existential aspect has relegated the unborn human life to the margins of the regulative context. According to Art. 1 of the Italian Civil Code legal capacity is acquired at birth, "the rights given by law to a conceived child are subject to the event of birth," and therefore at the time when patrimonial interests come into effect. The few provisions of the Civil Code, in which specific mention is made to the unborn child (Art. 462, 687, 715, 784), concern the various aspects of the right to acquire assets through succession or gifts. Hence, the lawmaker is only interested in the unborn child if there are assets to preserve or manage.

This vision has changed as a result of the coming into force of the Constitution which does not explicitly mention the unborn child, but sets out a variegated and complex vision of the human being, to whom "inviolable human rights, be it as an individual or in social groups expressing their personality" (Art. 2) must be recognized and guaranteed. The individual becomes part of the legal experience not just for what (s)he has, but for what (s)he is, for what (s)he wishes for and what (s)he aspires to. Art. 3 of the Constitution states that it is the State's responsibility "to remove all economic and social obstacles that, by limiting the freedom and equality of citizens, prevent full individual development..."

---

1 L. Mengoni, *La tutela giuridica della vita materiale nelle varie età dell'uomo*, in "Rivista trimestrale di diritto e procedura civile," 1982-71, p. 1119

This ambitious plan of care and attention towards all the unexpressed potential cannot but include the unborn child, who, perhaps, is unexpressed potential par excellence. The Constitutional Court has interpreted this deep existential valence[2] in the wider sense by extending, as we shall see, without hesitation, the application of Art. 2 and 3 to the legal status of the unborn child. The problem consists in the scope of this protection in the face of other constitutional interests, considered on a par with them, if not of greater prominence.

2 The Social Background: Techno-Science and the Fracture between Procreation and Pregnancy

The use of reproduction technologies and in particular the new perspectives offered by techno-science constitute the other element of change, not only because they force the lawmaker to explicitly intervene on the moral status and the legal availability of embryos, but also because they have broken the dualism between mother and child and between life and life to be. The legal status of the unborn child is based on a number of important decisions issued by the Constitutional Courts of the majority of Western countries on the topic of abortion in the mid-twentieth century.

The protection of privacy, the right to self-determination, and the prohibition of any bodily invasion have offered a sufficiently argumentative model for the judges in order to resolve the dramatic conflict between the will (or even the life) of the mother and her child. "Antiabortion laws violate principles of constitutional privacy ... because the grounds for such laws are non neutral in the constitutionally forbidden way in an area of the core of the fundamental human rights of intimate personal relationships."[3]

The fracture between procreation and pregnancy imposed by the use of reproduction technologies dissolves the exclusive personal intimacy of the dualism between a mother and a child, because it causes a multiplication of parental figures (genetic mother, expectant mother, social mother). If we add to artificial procreation the possibilities and responsibilities resulting from pre-implantation or prenatal diagnosis we realize that the doctor's intervention substitutes the sexual act: "The doctor is the author who controls the whole insemination process: taking both gametes, treating them, fertilizing them ... ascertaining that fertilization has taken place, deciding on the possibility of being able to implant the embryo, and transferring the embryo into the woman's body."[4]

---

2   A. Nicolussi, *Lo sviluppo della persona umana come valore costituzionale e il cosiddetto biodiritto*, in "Europa e diritto private," 2009-1, p. 3.
3   David A-Richards, *Toleration and the Constitution*, Oxford University Press, Oxford, 1986, p. 262.
4   L. Palazzani, *Introduction to the philosophy of biolaw*, Roma, Studium, 2009, pp. 56–57.

From the mother-child relationship which characterizes the traditional view of pregnancy (and which is projected into the issue of abortion), we have moved on to the relationship between mothers-child, mother/mothers-doctor-child. The protection of privacy can only take place within the framework of the right to family planning and therefore a procedure in which various subjects are involved and which depends on different variables. In the extreme case of *designer babies* family planning transgresses into scientific planning (mother/mothers-doctor-science-child).

The embryo is freed not only from its mother, but sometimes from every other vital plan (orphan embryos, excessive embryos, embryos created for scientific purposes, or those donated to science). The changing relationship between procreation and pregnancy also affects the dualism between life and life to be, highlighting a plurality of legally important thresholds concerning the different interests of those involved: oocyte, the activated oocyte, the syngamic oocyte, the ootid or oocyte with two pro-nuclei or pre-zygote, zygote, embryo. The protection of life gets lost in an indistinct zone of "not yet life" (embryo), "not enough life" (foetus), "no longer life" (biological commodities).

3 Two Colliding Horizons: The Embryo as a Person and the Embryo as an Object

Within such a varied horizon the mere patrimonial vision of life to be no longer has any sense. Art. 1 of the Italian Civil Code is surpassed by a series of judicial decisions that offer a more and more intense protection to life before birth, in compliance with the existential push which is present in the Constitution. The right to health and therefore to be born healthy, the right to assistance and diagnosis, the right to a genetic identity, the right to human dignity, the right to not be created only for scientific purposes,[5] and also the right to enjoy and benefit from having two parental figures[6] are recognized to the unborn human life. So we are defining an ever wider constellation of rights which authorizes us to state that "the embryo is one of us."[7]

This subjective push collides with the new mentality imposed by the techniques of artificial insemination, where procreation slides more and more towards creation and planning. What is created and planned are objects: precious, wished for, loved and protected, but they are not subjects, and they do not become so until their creator makes a decision or they become so only because their creator

---

5 F. Brunetta D'Usseaux, *Esistere per il diritto. La tutela giuridica del non nato*, Milano, Giuffrè, 2001.
6 Therefore a child has the right to claim compensation for moral damages if (s)he is born after his/her father's death, when that death occurred during pregnancy due to crimes committed by a third party (Cass Civ. sez. III 3 May 2011 No. 9700).
7 Italian National Bioethics Committee, *Identity and Status of Human Embryo*, 22nd June 1996.

has made a certain decision. The French sociologist Luc Boltanski[8] has written some extremely interesting papers on this purely elective fact of the foetal condition. He demonstrates how *the grammar* of procreation can end up conditioning the *experience* of people, directing their parental plans towards profoundly different outcomes which influence legal perspectives. In the collective imagination the foetus no longer exists. What exists is the "authentic foetus" (which is part of an engendering plan), the "tumoral foetus" (which is destined to be aborted), the "existentialist foetus" (which is considered as such on the basis of religious beliefs), the "barbarous foetus" (which does not feature in any parental plans), the "totalitarian foetus" (that foetus whose birth is conditioned by the policy of the State), the "techno-foetus" (which is discarded by reproduction technologies): each one has a pre-determined destiny which is not established by biology, but by the social circumstances which have directed the will of the "creators" one way or another.

In law both these situations can coexist: the need to attribute greater and greater importance to the rights of the unborn child and the tendency to consider him/her a mere object resulting from the choice of others, "a commodity,"[9] of whom and for whom we have the control and the responsibility. The birth of a child suffering from incurable diseases (*wrongful birth*) becomes the "guilt" for having allowed a *wrongful life*, which can be rejected if discovered through genetic testing or if there has been misinformation (*wrongful conception*) and can also be rejected as long as abortion is possible (*wrongful pregnancy*).

The claims for "damage to procreation" has weaved its way through the legal culture of all Western countries, marked by some historic decisions: in the United States the Curlender case [10]; in France the Perruche case;[11] in Germany a decision of the federal law court in 1986;[12] in Holland the Molenaar case;[13] in Italy the Court of Verona of 4th October 1990. This explains why the forms of protection are often converted into their opposite. The right to health and the right not to suffer can be translated into the expected statement of the right not to be born, because *nothingness* is always preferable to *nothing of death*.[14] Even the lack of a double parental

---

8   L. Boltanski, La condition fœtale. Une sociologie de l'engendrement et de l'avortement, Paris, Gallimard, 2004, cap. V.
9   R. Mackenzie, *From Sanctity to Screening: Genetics Disabilities, Risk and Rhetorical Strategies in Wrongful Birth and Wrongful Conception Cases*, in "Feminist Legal Studies," 1999-7, pp. 175–191.
10 *S. T. Curlender v. Bio-Science Laboratories Court of Appeal of California*, Second Appellate District - 11 June 1980 (106 Cal. App. 3d 811; 1980 Cal. App. LEXIS 1919; 165 Cal. Rptr. 477).
11 Refer to the work of O. Cayla and Y. Thomas, *Du droit de ne pas naître, À propos de l'affaire Perruche*, Paris, Gallimard, 2002.
12 BGHZ 86, 204 in which E. Picker, *Schadenersatz für das unerwünschte eigene Leben "Wrongful Life,"* Tübingen, Mohr, 1995.
13 A. Hendriks, *Wrongful Suits? Suing in the name of Terri Schiavo and Kelly Molenaar* in *European Journal of Health Law*, 2005-12, pp. 97–102.
14 Judge Weintraub's *assenting opinion* in *Gleitman v. Cosgrove* (1967) 227 A. 2d, p. 711.

figure is presented to the Italian judges as an argument in order to deny the right to the implantation of the frozen embryo of a separated couple.[15] An implantation requested by the mother and refused by the father.

Nobody denies that the unborn child must receive greater protection rights that go way beyond mere economic interests, but the doubt still remains whether (s)he is a subject of the law and if it is possible to recognize the first and fundamental prerogative of a subject of the law, the right to life. We are talking about a "non thing," about a "non subject," about "a centre of legal interest." It almost seems that the law, having removed the easily accountable relationship between the commodities and money of patrimonial relations, is not in a position to absorb all the existential implications which lie in the implementation of constitutional values and prefers to put them to one side resorting to the easiest way to avoid suffering: avoiding life. The unborn human life therefore hangs in the balance between being and not being: it deserves to be protected, but it is a variable protection which does not depend on norms, but on the way in which they are interpreted and adapted to the circumstances, often to promote values and life models that have nothing to do with the unborn child.

4 Ruling 27 of the Italian Constitutional Court

The decisions of the Italian Constitutional Court on prenatal life fall within the scope of these particular developments. We must bear in mind that judges are only exposed to reality and values through the mediation of rules and disputes, which they must resolve. Their vision is conditioned by the single issue which is placed before them. The object of ruling No. 27 of the Italian Constitutional Court of 18th February 1975 was the protection of a woman's health, when the continuing pregnancy could endanger her life. The foetus was considered the indirect object of the decision. The court did not have to determine what it was and when human life began, but whether the prenatal life has legal significance and if it was a limit to the right of self-determination of the pregnant woman. Faced with the harsh dualism between the mother's life and the child's life, the court did not hesitate: "there is no equivalence between the right not only to life but also to the health of who is already a person, such as the mother, and the safeguard of the embryo who has yet to become a person." To the credit of the judges, they did not look at this issue on a factual basis, declaring that the foetus is not yet life, but on the basis of values: the value of the actual life of the mother and the value of the potential life of the unborn child, considered both in its biological and existential aspect. This resulted in the strange outcome whereby the constitutional acknowledgement of the unborn child is tied to the legitimization of abortion.

---

15 Court of Bologna, ord. 9 May 2000, in "Famiglia e diritto" 2000-5, pp. 487 and following.

According to Art.1 of the Italian Civil Code the legal protection of an unborn child begins at birth, but now this ruling by the Constitutional Court states that this protection begins at conception: "Art. 2 of the Constitution recognizes and guarantees the inviolable rights of man, among which the situation of the unborn child have to be placed, albeit with its peculiar characteristics." A hybrid situation of being and not being was therefore established in the Italian legal order, which continues to exist today. The unborn child *is* the object of protection and abortion can only take place under medical instruction and "wherever possible any intervention must attempt to save the life of the foetus." It *is not* the object of protection if it constitutes a danger, even "not immediate," for the health of the expectant mother.

Enforcing the decision of the Constitutional Court, the Abortion Act (No. 194 of 22nd May 1978) creates confusion between being and not being again. Article 1 seems to explicitly recognize legal importance to prenatal life: "The State guarantees the right to conscious and responsible procreation, it recognizes the social value of maternity and protects human life from its beginning." It is true that the lawmaker is not clear about what he intends by the beginning of life (conception? syngamy? the formation of the nervous system?), but it is undeniable that the rule that the State "protects human life from its beginning" has an enormous symbolic and ethical value regarding the rule "legal capacity is acquired at birth" in Art. 1 of the Civil Code. Moreover, the law sets down that abortion shall only take place in authorized public structures, after a series of medical consultations and prescriptions, and that, after the first 90 days, it is only possible if the pregnancy or the birth pose "serious risks" to the life of the woman (Art. 6).

This scrupulousness is more apparent than real, because the doctor only has a consultative role, with no tools to protect the life of the unborn child, when he considers the mother's choice to be lacking in foundation. In the first 90 days the interruption of a pregnancy is permitted not only for therapeutic reasons, but also during the continuation of the pregnancy, the delivery or maternity would involve a serious risk to "psychic health," in relation to the unborn child's state of health, to its economic, social or family conditions, to the circumstances in which the conception happened, or to the potential presence of anomalies or malformations" (Art. 4.) Therapeutic abortion, which in the decision of the Constitutional Court appeared indispensable in order to safeguard the life of the mother, has become abortion for several other reasons: psychological, economic, social, family. These are reasons which, if put to the constitutional judge, perhaps would have determined a different trade-off of interests. In the Abortion Act the "serious risk to life" emphasized by the Court has become a risk for the desired or supposed, probable or even hypothetical living conditions of the mother. The effects which the law produces are, therefore, very far from the suffered trade-off of interests and values overshadowed by the Constitutional Court: the woman has unquestionable decision-making power on condition that it respects the established procedures.

5 The Assisted Fertilisation Act

To be or not to be? "To be" from the theoretical point of view. "Not to be" from the practical point of view. This explains why the legal literature, whilst recognizing the constitutional importance of prenatal life, has enormous difficulties in asserting that the unborn child is a legal person. The unborn child has "a sort of right to life" in a descriptive sense, not a formal one, but a strongly felt one . . ."[16] The Constitutional Court has continued, over time, to maintain this situation of uncertainty, refusing to declare the Abortion Act unconstitutional, both when it was criticized as being insufficient protection for the embryo as well as when the restrictions to a woman's right to self-determination were denounced. The Court's decision No. 35 of 10th February 1997 ruled that the proposal for a referendum which leaned towards the complete liberalization of abortion within the first 90 days was inadmissible and with it the annulment of the formulation of Art. 1. The Court asserted that, it is not only the State which cannot renounce the protection of the unborn child, but that this requirement "has been strengthened" as a result of the numerous international declarations on the rights of the child. The Court clarified that "the concept which is inherent in the Italian Constitution has been strengthened, in particular in Art. 2, according to which the right to life, meant in its broadest sense, should be included in the list of inviolable rights, and therefore among those rights which have a so-called privileged position in legislation, in as much as they belong . . . to the essence of the supreme values underpinning the Italian Constitution. According to some legal analysts[17] it is an important development compared to the decision of 1975. In reality, nothing has changed in the interpretation of the Abortion Act: it has only emphasized the difference between the ideal model and its practical implementation.

In regulating medically assisted procreation, the lawmaker attempted to implement the principles affirmed by the Constitutional Court. Faced with the potential conflict between child and childmaker[18] in relation to the creation of an excessive number of embryos, the multiplication of the parental figures, eugenics, scientific experimentation and to cloning, in the Assisted Fertilisation Act No. 40 of 19th February 2004 the child was given a voice: Art. 1 states that "in order to facilitate the resolution of the reductive problems deriving from sterility or human infertility, recourse to medically assisted procreation is consented, in line with the conditions and according to the modalities set out in law, which ensure the rights of all subjects involved, including offspring." In this case the rule does not have a purely theoretical value, as in Art. 1 of the Abortion Act. The protection of the unborn child

---

16 Cosimo M. Mazzoni, *I diritti dell'embrione e del feto nel diritto privato. Rapporto sull'Italia*, in "Nuova giurisprudenza civile commentate," 2002-2, p. 123.
17 V. Possenti, *La vita e l'essere: L'embrione è persona? Il personalismo ontologico in La vita e l'essere. L'embrione grumo di cellule o persona?*, Venezia, Marcianum, 2013, p. 44.
18 Melinda A. Roberts, *Child versus Childmaker. Future Persons and Present Duties in Ethics and in the Law*, Boston, Rowman & Littlefield, 1998.

has been realized in a series of heavy limitations with regard to the techniques to be used (prohibition of the donation of gametes and cloning), the subjects allowed (sterile or infertile, heterosexual couple), the treatment (prohibiting the fertilization of more than three embryos and obligation of implantation of all of them, prohibiting the production of embryos for research purposes, prohibiting any selection with regard to eugenics and any predetermination of genetic characteristics). Moreover Art. 14 prohibits "cryopreservation and the destruction of the embryos, taking into consideration Law No. 194 of 22nd May 1978."

It is hard to find an act of Parliament in the history of the Italian legal system that has received such harsh and repeated criticism as the Assisted Fertilisation Act has. Comments such as a "monstrous legislation" "human (in)civility fuelled by religious fanaticism," "an insult to intelligence," "scientific nonsense" have been made. Without delving into the merits of such opinions, it should be noted that the limitation of the Assisted Fertilisation Act lies in its value: to try and dissolve the tie between being and not being, removing all the potentially prejudicial elements for the unborn child which are inherent in assisted reproduction techniques. "We find ourselves in fact before a statute that cannot be evaluated under a technical profile, if has not previously been evaluated under a bioethical profile."[19] From an ethical point of view the Assisted Fertilisation Act casts a spotlight on the contradictions of the past, on a legal subjectivity which is given to the unborn child yet which is immediately denied by the right to abortion, and on the series of progressive rights given to the unborn child (the right to succession and gift, the right to health, the right to assistance and diagnosis, the right to a genetic identity, the right to human dignity, the right to not be created only for scientific purposes and also the right to enjoy and benefit from having two parental figures, the right to damage to procreation) without ever explicitly recognizing its right to life and on which all these other rights depend.

Casting the spotlight has not helped to cancel the problems. How can Art. 1 be interpreted, for example, when it states that the law ensures the rights of all the subjects involved, including the unborn child? Is it the unquestionable acknowledgement, to the unborn child, of full legal subjectivity with integral recognition of all relevant rights, and in particular, the right to life? Is it a lesser form of legal subjectivity "cut to fit the measure of the new born child," which cannot be evaluated in the same manner as the principle of the equal treatment of adult subjects?[20] It is a legal subjectivity relevant to specific situations (not an object of commerce, not formed only for scientific research) which allows the unborn child to be considered as "the direct holder of protected interests, or indeed one of our kind, as long as no contrasting interests emerge."[21] The Assisted Fertilisation Act repeatedly

---

19 D'Agostino, *Bioetica della riproduzione umana: dibattiti attuali*, in "Notizie di politeia," 2005, XXI, p. 77.
20 D. Busnelli, *Di chi è il corpo che nasce?* in Cosimo M. Mazzoni ed. by *Per uno statuto del corpo umano*, Milano, Giuffrè, 2008, p. 120.
21 P. Zatti, *Maschere del diritto volti della vita*, Milano, Giuffrè, 2009, p. 178.

states that it does not intend to touch upon the aspects which are regulated by the abortion law. But is that possible? Procreation and abortion have a common structural bond. If the embryo becomes a legal person for procreation, it cannot be an object for abortion or vice-versa. And this is the dead end which the Assisted Fertilisation Act faces. If we link Art. 1 to Art. 14 which forbids the cryopreservation of embryos and calls for a "single and contemporaneous implantation" of all the embryos which have been formed, we find ourselves faced with the paradox that the embryo, a life which is about to develop, can never be destroyed, whilst the foetus, a life which is already considerably formed, can be destroyed under certain conditions. Taking this interpretation to the extreme, a woman would be obliged to undergo the implantation of the embryos, even against her will, but could subsequently ask for the authorization to have an abortion. A grotesque situation that highlights how the problem is constituted by the fact that assisted reproduction will always be marked by forms of damage for the unborn child. The cryopreservation of embryos, the donation of gametes, and the selection of embryos does not happen by chance; they are structured choices in "artificial birth."

6 Conclusion

The decision of the Constitutional Court No. 151 of 8th May 2009 took this into consideration. In order to protect the childmaker, the court once again sacrificed the child, stating that "the protection of the embryo is not, however, absolute, but limited by the necessity to identify a correct trade-off with the protection of the requirements of procreation." The creation of embryos in excess, their implantation, and pre-implantation diagnosis are left to the evaluation of the doctor and the will of the patients. The Court rules that, in the absence of any other consideration of the subjective conditions of the woman who undergoes medically assisted procreation procedures, the legal provision that no more than three embryos should be created is in direct contrast with Art. 3 of the Constitution. "In particular when it is reviewed under the twofold profile of the principle of reasonableness and equality, in as much as the lawmaker reserves the same treatment to dissimilar situations; as well as prejudice to the woman's health."

The Court has not taken a backward step on the constitutional importance of the embryo, but in the trade-off of interests it has further removed the values established at the start: firstly it was the psychophysical state of the mother and now it is the "requirements of procreation" which mark the fate of the unborn child. Are the requirements of procreation a constitutional value? It seems so, according to another decision No. 162 by the Constitutional Court of 10th June 2014, whereby forbidding the donation of gametes was declared unconstitutional. Making reference to the decision of 2009, the judges declared that the "just requirements of procreation" are a new constitutional value that imposes the protection of the fundamental freedoms of a couple to form a family with children.

The Constitutional Court's decision No. 229 of 21st October 2015 returned to the problem, stressing the right to not transfer to the woman's uterus those embryos which, from the pre-implantation diagnosis, had genetic diseases. Nevertheless, the judges denied that it is legitimate to suppress the deformed embryos, since "the violation of the protection of the dignity of the (even though) unhealthy embryo, which would result from its suppression *tamquam res*, does not however find justification, in terms of counterweight, in the protection of any other antagonist interest." Thus the decision states that there is a duty to cryoconserve these embryos. "In fact, the embryo, whatever its more or less broad recognisable degree of subjectivity correlated to the genesis of life, certainly cannot be reduced to mere biological material."

Habermas sustains that, in a pluralistic vision of the world, we cannot attribute, a priori, the same absolute protection to the embryo that we attribute to an adult subject, but neither can we consider it an ordinary object, "an asset which is in competition with other assets." Indeed, in a society which is strongly conditioned by market logic, we must find an inviolable entity which is free from the idea of profit and market: even more so if this inviolable entity is at the basis of human identity and is therefore the ideal foundation of freedom. This is why it is important to underline the symbolic function that the protection of human embryos would have for all those "who cannot defend themselves in first person."[22] The Italian Constitutional Court has, at least, affirmed this symbolic defence.

Bibiliography

Boltansky Luc, 2004, *La condition fœtale. Une sociologie de l'engendrement et de l'avortement*, Paris, Gallimard.

Brunetta D'usseaux Francesca, 2001, *Esistere per il diritto. La tutela giuridica del non nato*. Giuffrè, Milano.

Busnelli Francesco D., 2008, *Di chi è il corpo che nasce?*. In C. M. Mazzoni (a cura di), *Per uno statuto del corpo umano*. Giuffrè, Milano.

Cassese Sabino, 2015, *Dentro la Corte. Diario di un giudice costituzionale*. Il Mulino, Bologna.

Cayla Olivier e Thomas Yan, 2002, *Du droit de ne pas naître, À propos de l'affaire Perruche*, Paris, Gallimard.

Comitato Nazionale Per La Bioetica, 22 giugno 1996, *Identità e statuto dell'embrione umano*. In http://bioetica.governo.it/it/documenti/pareri-e-risposte/identita-e-statuto-dellembrione-umano/

D'agostino Francesco, 2005, «Bioetica della riproduzione umana: dibattiti attuali». In *Notizie di politeia*, XXI, 77.

Habermas Jürgen, 2003, *The Future of Human Nature*, trans. Cambridge, Polity.

---

22 J. Habermas, *The Future of Human Nature*, trans. Cambridge, Polity, 2003, p. 98.

Hendriks Aart, 2005, «Wrongful Suits? Suing in the name of Terri Schiavo and Kelly Molenaar». In *European Journal of Health Law*, 2005-12, 97–102.

Mackenzie Robin, 1999, «From Sanctity to Screening: Genetics Disabilities, Risk and Rhetorical Strategies in Wrongful Birth and Wrongful Conception Cases». In *Feminist Legal Studies*, 1999-7, 175–191.

Mazzoni Cosimo M., 2002, «I diritti dell'embrione e del feto nel diritto privato. Rapporto sull'Italia». In *Nuova giurisprudenza civile commentata*, 2002-2. Anno 3 Numero 1 Giugno 2017 ISSN 2421-4302.

Cases:

Cour de Cassation, France, Ruling 99-13701 of 17th November 2000.

Supreme Court of New Jersey, *Gleitman v. Cosgrove* (1967), 49 NJ, 227.

Court of Appeal of California, Second Appellate District, *S. T. Curlender v. Bio-Science Laboratories* of 11th June 1980.

Constitutional Court of Germany, BGHZ 86, 204.

Court of Bologna, Ord. 9, May 2000.

Italian Constitutional Court, Ruling No. 27 of 18th February 1975.

Italian Constitutional Court, Ruling No. 35 of 10th February 1997.

Italian Constitutional Court, Ruling No. 151 of 8th May 2009.

Italian Constitutional Court, Ruling No. 162 of 10th June 2014.

Italian Constitutional Court, Ruling No. 229 of 21st October 2015.

Angel J. Gómez Montoro

5 Leading Cases from the Spanish Constitutional Court Concerning the Legal Status of Unborn Human Life[1]

Abstract: This chapter analyzes the evolution of the protection of unborn human life in Spain since the enactment of the 1978 Constitution. It focuses, in particular, on the study of the laws and the constitutional jurisprudence on two relevant matters: the regulation of abortion and the in vitro fertilization, the use of embryos their tissues and organs. Both the legislator and the Constitutional Court have opted for a gradualist protection of the embryo that leaves many questions open from the perspective of the right to life (Article 15 SC) and human dignity (Article 10.1 SC)

Keywords: The right to life, Unborn human life, Abortion, In vitro fertilization, Embryo

1 The Introduction of Abortion in Spain and the STC 53/1985

1.1 From Criminalization to Decriminalization in Certain Circumstances

When the Constitution of 1978 was enacted, abortion in Spain, as in many other countries, was a crime[2]. The text of the new Constitution included a complete catalogue of rights—among which the right to life figures prominently[3]—without including any explicit statement on the status of the *nasciturus* (the unborn). Nevertheless, the issue of abortion was present during the debates on the drafting of the Constitution regarding the holder of the right to life.[4] Initially, the draft of the

---

1 In this chapter I will use the following abbreviations:
FJ: Legal GroundFFJJ: Legal GroundsLOTC: Spanish Constitutional Court ActSTC: Spanish Constitutional Court DecisionSSTC: Spanish Constitutional Court Decisions
2 Articles 411 to 417 of the Criminal Code of 1944, then in force, punished all abortions with prison for those that carried them out and for the woman who consented to the abortion (though the punishment in the latter case were, sensibly, shorter).
3 According to Article 15, "everyone has the right to life and to physical and moral integrity, and under no circumstances may be subjected to torture or to inhuman or degrading punishment or treatment." The death penalty is hereby abolished "except as provided for by military criminal law in times of war."
4 The evolution of the text in Article 15, including the debates it caused in the chambers, can be found at http://www.congreso.es/est_consti/.

Constitution established that "everyone has the right to life and physical integrity." However, as a result of an amendment, the text was amended thusly: "the right of the person to life and to physical and moral integrity is inviolable." This text was subjected to a new amendment returning to the original phrasing due to the doubts that might arise in relation to the term "person" and, more specifically, to the fact that according to Article 29 of the Civil Code, personhood is linked to birth. The new amendment was passed by a wide margin, but it was clear from the debates that there was a lack of agreement among the political forces regarding the constitutionality of abortion, a problem that would be necessary to face later on.[5]

The approval of the Constitution did not change the legal treatment of abortion, which basically remained a crime. Over the course that followed the adoption of the Constitution, the question was present both in the debates on the reform of the Criminal Code and in some decisions of the Constitutional Court which dealt with the issue tangentially. In September 1979 the Council of Ministers approved a bill, which, though maintaining the crime of abortion, considerably reduced the punishments. Nevertheless, the bill was not passed.[6] In 1981 the Communist Parliamentary Group proposed a decriminalization bill that also failed to be approved.[7]

Four years later, in its decisions STC 75/1984 and STC 70/1985, the Constitutional Court of Spain ruled in favor of the protection of the unborn. In the first case, the Constitutional Court overruled a judicial decision that had condemned a woman and her accomplice for having an abortion in England. Strictly speaking, the question was not the constitutionality of the crime of abortion but the court's decision to convict the appellants. The Constitutional Court considered that the conviction had been made through an analogical extension contrary to the principle of legality of Article 25.1 of the Spanish Constitution; therefore, the Court granted the appeal. Nevertheless, two aspects of this decision are interesting. First, the Court's statement that, in accordance with Article 15 of the Spanish Constitution, "prenatal human life is worthy of constitutional protection" (FJ 6). This argument became a touchstone in the subsequent STC 53/1985, a case in which the protection of the embryo was derived from the idea of a constitutional value and not from the existence of a subjective right to life recognized in law. Second, it is

---

5   On the parliamentary debate and the differing opinions see G. Rodríguez Mourullo, "Comentario al art. 15 de la Constitución," in O. Alzaga (ed.), *Comentarios a la Constitución Española de 1978*, volume II, Edersa, Madrid 1997, pp. 270 and ff.
6   The bill was published in the *Boletín Oficial de las Cortes Generales. Congreso de los Diputados*, on January 17th, 1980. The original draft, prepared by a group of experts in the General Codification Commission, decriminalized abortion in case of risk to the life and health of the mother, rape and fetal abnormalities. However, this bill was not followed by the Government (*see* J. Cerezo Mir, "La regulación del aborto en el proyecto de nuevo Código penal español," *Anuario de Derecho Penal y Ciencias Penales*, 1982, volume 35, pp. 564 and ff.).
7   Bill to regulate the voluntary termination of pregnancy, in *Boletín Oficial de las Cortes Generales. Congreso de los Diputados*, 14th of July 1981, pp. 529–535.

also worth noting the separate concurring opinion of Magistrate Tomás y Valiente, whose perspective was much more radical. In his view, a systematic interpretation of the Constitution showed that "the human person holds the fundamental rights contained in Article 15 of the Spanish Constitution. The fetus and, before, the embryo, are not human persons, but mere *spes hominis*." Given that, according to Article 29 of the Civil Code, birth determines personhood, "that which is not a person is not and cannot be a holder of rights."

In similar terms, but even more categorically, the same magistrate filed a dissenting opinion in the decision STC 70/1985—which was issued after STC 53/1985. This decision examined the constitutionality of the law decriminalizing abortion before the law came into force. According to the dissenting magistrate, the Criminal Code's regulation of abortion was contrary to the Constitution "because it does not take into account those rights of the pregnant woman arising from Articles 15 and 10 of the Spanish Constitution", rights which "in certain hypotheses, must prevail" against the constitutional value embodied by the *unborn*[8].

In 1982—some years before the above-mentioned judgments were handed down—the Spanish Socialist Workers Party (PSOE) came into power after making an electoral promise to decriminalize abortion. In February 1983, it put a bill before the Parliament in order to reform the Criminal Code. The bill—which was approved by the Parliament—maintained the crime of abortion, but made it non-punishable if the following circumstances were found: 1. "Grave danger to the life or the health of the pregnant woman"; 2. Pregnancy due to a rape; 3. "where it is probable that the fetus shall be born with serious physical or psychological defects."

Against the new Act, and before it was enacted and published, an appeal of unconstitutionality with automatic suspensive effects on its enactment was filed before the Constitutional Court.[9] The Court delivered its decision through STC 53/1985, of 11 April.

1.2 STC 53/1985

As was expected, the appeal generated an intense debate both in the legal scholars— and in society in general—as well as within the Constitutional Court itself. In fact, the Court was divided into two blocks of six magistrates in favor and against the

---

8   It was, however, a minority opinion and the regulation of abortion was never questioned before the Constitutional Court prior to decriminalization.
9   The possibility to challenge the constitutionality of laws before their final approval by the Parliament was not included in the Constitution, but introduced by the LOTC for the "Autonomous Statutes" and other organic laws. This "prior appeal" was particularly controversial and, in fact, it was abolished in 1985. In 2015 it was reintroduced but only for the Statutes of Autonomy (Organic Act 12/2015). *See* A. J. Gómez Montoro, "El control previo de constitucionalidad de Estatutos de Autonomía y demás leyes orgánicas," *Revista Española de Derecho Constitucional*, no. 22, 1988, pp. 123–174.

constitutionality of the Act, a situation in which the president's casting vote turned out to be decisive.[10] The decision accepted the constitutionality of the "indication system"—the three above-mentioned circumstances—but it declared the act unconstitutional for not establishing sufficient guarantees to ensure that abortion would only be performed in the legally defined circumstances and to prevent potential fraud. This was severely criticized by the dissenting opinions.

1.2.1 Right to Life and Prenatal Life

The starting point of the judgment is the consideration that the right to life guaranteed by Article 15 of the Constitution is "the projection of a higher value of the constitutional legal system—human life—and constitutes the essential and principal fundamental right (. . .) without which the remaining rights would have no possible existence." A right, moreover, that is inextricably linked to the "basic legal value of personal dignity acknowledged in art. 10" (FJ 3).

With regard to prenatal life or "life in formation," the Court makes certain important points in its FJ 5. Specifically, it holds that "human life is an evolution, a process that begins with gestation (. . .) and ends with death," and that gestation generates a "*tertium* existentially distinct from the mother." Given that life is a process, there are qualitative changes relevant to law, especially birth and, prior to that, the moment from which the *unborn* becomes capable of life independent from the mother.

From the points made by the Court, it may be assumed that if the Constitution protects life with the emphasis mentioned, "it cannot fail to protect it" in a "stage of its process" which is (. . .) "a moment in the development of life itself" (FJ 5).

1.2.2 The Life of the Unborn as a Constitutional Interest

Once the constitutional obligation to protect the life of the *unborn* has been admitted, the question arises as to its proper scope. More specifically, the question arises as to whether the protection deserved by the *unborn* derives from a subjective right or from the fact that it is a constitutionally protected good or value. It has become widely accepted that the Constitutional Court solved the controversy by excluding the unborn from the right to life of Article 15 of the Constitution. This opinion has been held in part due to the fact that, in subsequent pronouncements, the Court itself considered that it had already followed that thesis in this leading case.[11] However, a detailed reading of this decision reveals that the Court does not give any reason for such lack of rights (which is not categorically rejected either)

---

10 In accordance with Article 90.1 LOTC, "Unless otherwise stated by Law, the decisions shall be adopted by the majority of the members of the Plenum, Chamber or Section participating in the deliberation. In the event of a tie, the President shall have the casting vote."

11 In STC 212/1996 and STC116/1999, which we shall analyze later, the Court reiterates that "Article 15 of the Constitution, in effect, recognizes the right to life as a

but it just analyzes and rejects the arguments of the plaintiffs. Certainly, these had claimed that according to an interpretation of Article 15 of the Constitution in the light of the parliamentary debates, the whole text of the Constitution and the international treaties, the subjective right of the *unborn* should be recognized.[12]

The Court rejected the first of their arguments since the term "everyone"— though introduced as a replacement for the term "person" in order to protect the *unborn*—has an ambiguity that was never cleared up in the constitutional debates. The debates demand the protection of the *unborn*, but they do not imply that the *unborn* holds a subjective right to life (FJ 5). The same conclusion would be reached from a systematic interpretation of the Constitution. According to the Court, the term "all"—which is employed by other constitutional provisions regarding fundamental rights (Articles 9.2, 17.4, 18.1 y 4, 20.3, 27)—constitutes a well-defined reference to all persons that are born. Finally, the mention to the international treaties is also not a conclusive one. Both the French and the Spanish version of Article 6 of the International Covenant on Civil and Political Rights (ICCPR) and of Article 2 of the European Convention on Human Rights use the term "person," but the ECHR has never derived from this term a subjective right of the unborn (FJ 7).

For the reasons above, the Court concludes "the arguments put forward by the appellants cannot be accepted in support of the thesis that the *unborn* is entitled with the right to life." The decision, however, does not analyze whether other reasons justify such an entitlement. Moreover, it does not go so far as to expressly reject the right, but it plainly states that "in any case—and this is decisive for the issue examined in this appeal—we must state that the life of the *unborn*, (. . .) is a legal good constitutionally protected by Article 15 of our fundamental norm" (FJ 7). This protection includes two obligations for the State: a duty to abstain from interrupting or hindering the process of gestation, and a duty to establish a legal system that effectively protects life—which implies in turn the criminal guarantee.[13]

---

fundamental right which (. . .) in accordance with STC 53/1985, is held by born persons, without this entitlement being extended to *nascituri*" (*cfr.* FFJJ 3 and 4).

12 By virtue of Article 10.2 of the Constitution, the Spanish bill of rights has to be interpreted in the light of the international treaties on human rights (for a detailed analysis, see A. Saiz Arnaiz, *La apertura constitucional al derecho internacional y europeo de los derechos humanos: el artículo 10.2 de la Constitución Española*, Consejo General del Poder Judicial, Madrid 1999).

13 In his argument, however, the Court makes no reference to the question whether the *nasciturus* is or is not a person, perhaps to avoid any confusion with the concept of the person for private law purposes—which, as has been said before, is linked in our tradition with birth—or perhaps to avoid a conclusion that would lead to the unlawfulness of abortion. "Insofar as it is legal to abort (. . .)—categorically states G. Jakobs—the fetus cannot be considered a person" ["Does the unlawful abortion of persons exist?" *Poder Judicial*, no. 60, 2000 (IV), p. 168]. Starting from Jakobs's distinction, J. M. Silva warns about the revival of the doctrine of the "Criminal law of the enemy." In his view, there is a "Criminal law of citizens" and a "Criminal law

In the Court's reasoning there is a relevant logical leap, since "the decisive" point is not just whether there is an obligation to protect the unborn, but also what the fundamental nature of that protection is. In this respect, it is not the same to hold a fundamental right as to be a constitutionally protected "interest."[14] Over all these years, the Court has never provided further reasons to exclude the *unborn* from the right to life perspective beyond those deployed to refute the arguments of the plaintiffs in the STC 53/85. It seems insufficient, given its position and its supreme function of interpreting the Constitution. In addition, it must be noted that the Court is not bound by the arguments of the parties when it comes to determining who the right-holder is or what constitutional contents are protected by the right.

In my view, the conclusion that the *unborn* is not a holder of the right to life is far from being clear. The unborn is certainly engaged in a special relationship of dependency with respect to the mother. Yet, article 15 of the Constitution does not

---

of enemies," that is, of "outlawed human beings," human beings excluded from the protection of the law (*see* "Los indeseados como enemigos. La exclusión de seres humanos del *status personae*" *Revista Electrónica de Ciencia Penal y Criminología*, 09-01, 2007, pp. 1–18). For this reason, some authors have insisted on the need for a constitutionally adequate concept of the person: *see* the work of A. Ollero, "Todos tienen derecho a la vida. ¿Hacia un concepto constitucional de persona?" published in the volume *Bioderecho. Entre la vida y la muerte*, Thomson-Aranzadi, Cizur Menor 2006, pp. 75 and ff.; especially pp. 100 and ff.; and P. Sánchez-Ostiz, "¿Tienen todos derecho a la vida? Bases para un concepto constitucional de persona", *Revista Electrónica de Ciencia Política y Criminología*, 11-11, 2009.

14 As stated by J. M. Silva Sánchez, "no state of necessity can justify depriving another of their life, to which he/she has a right. Therefore, the admission of abortion as a legal act cannot but start with the rejection of the right to life of the conceived" (*see* "Los indeseados como enemigos. La exclusión de seres humanos del *status personae*," cit., p. 7). Although some authors are opposed to this view (and the German Constitutional Court has itself admitted the constitutionality of abortion despite recognizing that the fetus holds the right to life), most of the authors who defend the constitutionality of abortion consider that the existence of a subjective right to life would make abortion unlawful. Significant here, for example, are the words of Magistrate Tomás y Valiente in his separate opinion to STC 53/1985: "I understand, although do not share, the opposition to the non-punishment of abortion in defense of the supposed fundamental right to life of the *nasciturus*. It is a classic line of reasoning from which one could arrive, with undeniable internal coherence, to a ruling against the legalization of abortion in certain circumstances." In a similar vein, *see* E. Peñaranda Ramos, "Fases en el desarrollo de la vida y grados de su protección. A propósito del tratamiento jurídico-penal del tratamiento preimplantatorio," in *Homenaje al Prof. Rodrigo González Mourullo*, Thomson-Civitas, Cizur Menor, 2005, and C. Tomás-Valiente, "La jurisprudencia constitucional española sobre el aborto," in Ian Shapiro, Pablo de Lora Deltoro, and Carmen Tomás-Valiente, *La Suprema Corte de Estados Unidos y el aborto*, Fundación Coloquio Jurídico Europeo, Madrid, 2009, pp. 102–103.

protect an abstract notion of life, but the "right to life" of each single human being, and the Court categorically stated that human life begins with gestation, and that gestation generates "a *tertium* existentially distinct from the mother" (STC 53/1985, FJ 5), that is to say, a new human being.[15]

On the other hand, it is surprising how the Court infers from Article 15 of the Constitution the conclusion that the fetus is a constitutionally protected interest. In FJ 4, the Constitutional Court appeals to the so-called "objective dimension of fundamental rights," whereby these rights include not only subjective rights against public interferences, but also the positive obligation of the State to protect them against private interferences. But still, what the judgment appears to ignore is that this objective dimension is nothing but a consequence of a subjective right. In the case of the unborn child, however, the Court invokes the "duty to protect" not as an additional guarantee but as an alternative route to the recognition of the fundamental right. As far as I know, the Court has never done this with any other fundamental right.[16] Normally, the recourse to the objective dimension of fundamental rights is justified to strengthen the protection provided by the subjective right and not, as is the case here, to substitute it.[17]

Finally, the solution adopted here contrasts too with the expansive interpretation held by the Constitutional Court in hard cases concerning the entitlement of

---

15 A critical analysis of this separation between the protection of the fetus and the capacity to hold the right to life in A. Ollero, "Todos tienen derecho a la vida. ¿Hacia un concepto constitucional de persona?" published in the volume *Bioderecho. Entre la vida y la muerte*, cit., pp. 81 and ff.). This author criticizes "the attempt to seek refuge in values in order to—ignoring the inhumane consequences—undo the link between *legal protection and personhood* (p. 83), and to reduce the unborn to the status of a "*valuable object*" by not recognizing its status as a person (p. 87, italics in the original).

16 As I have written elsewhere, "from the dogmatic fundamental rights point of view, it is not understandable that the legally protected interest—the human life or, rather, the life of a human being—be unfolded into two distinct contents: one true subjective right in the case of human life after birth, and a constitutionally protected interest—with no subjective dimension-, when it is the life of the *nasciturus*" (A. J. Gómez Montoro, "Respuestas al cuestionario," in S. Huerta Tocildo y M. Pérez Manzano (ed.), *Cuestiones actuales de la Protección de la Vida y la Integridad Física y Moral*, Aranzadi, Cizur Menor, 2012, p. 83).

17 The situation is different when a constitutionally protected asset has no subjective element. In these cases (environment, culture, artistic heritage, etc.), it is difficult to speak of subjective rights. With regard to the positive obligations to protect arising from fundamental rights, *see*, for all, F. Simón Yarza, *Medio ambiente y derechos fundamentales*, Centro de Estudios Políticos y Constitucionales, Madrid, 2012, especially pp. 99 and ff.

rights,[18] that is, with regard to aliens,[19] legal persons,[20] and (in some cases) even entities without personhood.[21]

1.2.3 The Constitutionality of the Indication System

The Constitutional Court insists upon the protection afforded to prenatal life by Article 15 of the Constitution. The right of the mother cannot unconditionally prevail against the child. On the contrary, following the line drawn by the German Constitutional Court in its 1975 ruling,[22] the Court considers that there is a positive obligation to protect the unborn life, a duty which includes the provision of criminal guarantees which can only be exceptionally superseded at the face of conflicting fundamental rights or constitutional assets. To sum up: neither the life of the *unborn* nor the freedom of the woman can prevail unconditionally upon each other. Thus, the Court concludes, "the constitutional interpreter is required to consider the rights on the basis of the question raised, attempting to harmonize them if possible" or to specify "the conditions and requirements in which the prevalence of one upon the others may be admitted" (FJ 9).

With regard to the circumstances of decriminalization foreseen by the legislator, the Court reaches the conclusion that an adequate balance among the interests involved has been struck, so the Act is upheld. Nevertheless, the scant detail with which the Court has dealt with such consideration is again surprising. The Court does not analyze each circumstance in detail, following the three steps that, according to consolidated case law doctrine, require full consideration of all the assets and rights at play.[23] Far from that, it validates each circumstance with more or less generic categorical statements. Thus, for example, it assumes that the exception of "serious danger" to the health of the pregnant woman implies that "her right to life and physical integrity" is at stake. Therefore, "the fact that the mother's health should prevail is not unconstitutional" (FJ 11). Strangely enough, the Constitutional Court offers no single condition whereby the concurrence of a

---

18 See A. J. Gómez Montoro, "Titularidad de Derechos," in M. Aragón Reyes and C. Aguado Renedo (ed.), *Derechos fundamentales y su protección. Temas básicos de Derecho Constitucional. Volume III*, Civitas, Madrid, 2011, pp. 42–58.
19 See among others, STC 117/1985, STC 95/2003, and STC 236/2007.
20 STC 23/1989 and STC 139/1995 among many others. See A. J. Gómez Montoro, "Los derechos fundamentales de las personas jurídicas. Un intento de fundamentación," en *Revista Española de Derecho Constitucional*, núm. 65, 2002, pp. 49–105.
21 STC 214/1991.
22 Ruling of 25 February 1975 (BVerfGE 39, 1).
23 See, for all, R. Alexy, *Theorie der Grundrechte*, Sshurkamp, 3ª ed., Frankfurt a.M., 1996. And among Spanish scholars, J. M. Rodríguez de Santiago, *La ponderación de bienes e intereses en el Derecho Administrativo*, Marcial Pons, Madrid, 2000, especially pp. 118 and ff.

"serious danger" might be appreciated, or whether the danger must be physical or psychological or either of them.

In a similar way, regarding eugenic abortion the judgment holds that "the use of a criminal penalty would entail the imposition of a conduct which exceeds what is normally required of a mother and of the family" (FJ 11). Certainly, the important sacrifices involved in caring for a child with serious physical or psychological deficiencies cannot be disregarded. Nevertheless, the mere reference to the fact that in such situations obligations arise that exceed those normally required is not by itself sufficient to decide the constitutionality of such provision. A more detailed and proportional consideration of the serious obligation to protect the unborn child would be expected from the Court.[24]

The scant weight afforded by the judgment to women's rights has been criticized, even in some of the dissenting opinions.[25] In particular, the scarce importance given to the free development of the personality (Article 10 of the Constitution) and to the right to privacy (Article 18 of the Constitution) has been censured. It is true that women's rights barely appear in the reasoning of the Court. Perhaps this is due to the fact that the free development of the personality is not a right under our Constitution (in contrast with Article 2.1 of the German Constitution), and that Article 18 of the Spanish Constitution—which, literally enshrines the "right to intimacy"—has never been understood (neither in 1985 nor now) as a right to privacy in the North American sense or in the manner in which the European Court of Human Rights interprets the right to private life of Article 8 of the Convention.[26] Furthermore, the lack of deliberation upon the potential rights of the woman makes the sacrifice of the life of the *unborn* in all cases even more paradoxical.[27]

---

24 As part of its argument, the Court also points to the insufficient nature of State and social provisions for such situations, and affirms that "insofar as progress is made" in "enforcing preventive policy" and in "the health care in a Social State" this progress will decisively contribute "to preventing the situation on which decriminalization is based" (FJ 11). However, reality has disproved this prediction, since the undeniable improvement of public health care does not seem to have led to a decrease of the number of abortions. Besides, the Court allows abortion with total independence of the health care resources available in each moment.

25 Especially in the opinion formulated by Magistrate Rubio Llorente. Similarly, Magistrate Tomás y Valiente denounces, in his dissenting opinion, the absence of considerations for "the first" the "higher values" mentioned by the Constitution: "liberty."

26 On the rather expansive interpretation of this provision by the ECHR, see A. J. Gómez Montoro, *Vida privada y autonomía personal o una interpretación* passe-partout *del artículo 8 CEDH*, in VV.AA., *La Constitución política de España. Estudios en homenaje a Manuel Aragón Reyes*, Centro de Estudios Políticos y Constitucionales, Madrid, 2016, pp. 617–650.

27 Hitherto, the Court has not admitted a general right to free self-determination, yet it is progressively inclined to do so, perhaps due to the influence of the Strasbourg

1.2.4 The Conditions for the Constitutionality of Decriminalization

Therefore, the Court accepts the indication system that excludes the unborn from legal protection in such cases "based on protection of constitutional rights of women and the circumstances arising in specific situations." Its judgment does not end there, but declares that Article 15 of the Spanish Constitution requires the legislator to establish a system guaranteeing that the protection of the fetus does not diminish "the efficacy of the system" beyond "that required by the purpose of the new precept" (FJ 12) Here, the Court concludes that those guarantees are not given: specifically, it considers that, in the cases of therapeutic and eugenic abortion, in addition to the participation of the doctor, it must be ensured that the intervention is carried out in medical centers authorized to this effect. In the case of rape, the Court considers that due to the objective difficulties for assuring in advance the legality of such abortions, prior reporting of the offense is necessary.

In response to some possible criticism, the Court says that the conditions imposed fall within the scope of its constitutional function, and do not entail "legislation from the bench." The Court considers itself enabled by the law (*cfr.* Art. 79.4 b LOTC) to "indicate the amendments which in its opinion, and without excluding other possible changes, would permit the approval of the law by the competent body" (FJ 12).[28]

2 The New Regulation

Notwithstanding the debates that followed in the wake of this case, the fact is that only three months later, the legislature approved a new Organic Law (LO 9/1985, of 5 July) through which a new Article 417 bis of the Criminal Code was introduced, making abortion non-punishable in the aforementioned circumstances, and introducing the guarantees that the Court had indicated in its decision. This new Act was not challenged and remained in force for more than 25 years, until the approval of LO 2/2010.[29]

Court (*see* C. Tomás-Valiente, "La jurisprudencia constitucional española sobre el aborto", cit., pp. 95 and ff.).

28 Despite these explanations, the Court's decisions were harshly criticized in dissenting opinions, in particular those of magistrates Tomás y Valiente and Rubio Llorente, who considered the Court to have overstepped the limits of its jurisdiction to occupy the position of legislator.

29 In fact, Article 417 bis of the Criminal Case was one of the few norms that remained in force when a new Code was approved through LO 10/1995 of 23 November.

2.1 From the "Indication System" to the "System of Deadlines": Organic Law 2/2010 of 3 March on Sexual and Reproductive Health and Voluntary Termination of Pregnancy

2.1.1 The Evolution of Abortion in Spain under the 1985 Act

Since the entry into force of the new Act, and as was predicted, the number of abortions in Spain rose steadily, from 411 in 1986 to 16,206 in the following year and reaching its peak in 2011 with 118,359 abortions (a rate of 11.49 per 1,000 women between the ages of 15 and 55).[30] As for the conditions invoked, roughly

---

30 According to the data published by the Spanish Ministry of Health, the evolution of abortions up to 2014 (the last year available) was the following:

Year	Number of VIPs (induced abortions)	Rate per 1,000 women	Year	Number of VIPs (induced abortions)	Rate per 1,000 women
1986	411	0.05	2001	69,857	7.66
1987	16,206	1.96	2002	77,125	8.46
1988	26,069	3.11	2003	79,788	8.77
1989	30,552	3.61	2004	84,985	8.94
1990	37,231	4.35	2005	91,664	9.60
1991	41,910	4.79	2006	101,592	10.62
1992	44,962	5.10	2007	112,138	11.49
1993	45,503	5.15	2008	115,812	11.78
1994	47,832	5.38	2009	111,482	11.41
1995	49,367	5.53	2010	113,031	11.71
1996	51,002	5.69	2011	118,359	12.47
1997	49,578	5.52	2012	112,390	12.12
1998	53,847	6.00	2013	108,690	11.74
1999	58,399	6.52	2014	94,796	10.46
2000	63,756	7.14			

Proponents of the new abortion regulation, approved in 2010, credit it with the decrease in recent years. However, and although no conclusive data are available to the respect, it may be related to other factors, such as the correlative decrease in the number of births (www.ine.es/jaxi/menu.do?type=pcaxis&path=/t20/e304/&file=inebase):

Year	Number of births
2010	486,575
2011	471,999
2012	454,684
2013	425,715
2014	427,595

97% of the abortions were justified on the basis of the health of the mother; circa 3% for fetal abnormalities; and less than 0.05% were rape cases.[31] There is no evidence of any case where the request was rejected, and it is also noteworthy the scant number of preliminary investigations aimed at considering a possible infringement of the Act (less than 0.1% of abortions).[32] All this suggests that, in spite of being an indication system, in practice it worked like a system with hardly any restrictions.[33]

2.2 The Arguments for the Reform and the Context of the New Regulation

Despite that, and after the 2004 elections, the Socialist Party Government led by President Rodríguez Zapatero put forward, as had been outlined in their electoral manifesto, a new regulation introducing a deadline-based system. The new regulation was not approved through reform of the Criminal Code but it was included in the Organic Law 2/2010, of 3 March, on Sexual and Reproductive Health and Voluntary Termination of Pregnancy.

In the extensive preamble to the Act, the reasons for its approval and the ideological proposals that inspire it are clearly set out. The starting point is very different from the previous regulation, which was framed within the scope of the criminal protection of life. The focus is no more placed in the duty of the State, arising from Article 15 of the Spanish Constitution, to protect life in formation, but in the free self-determination of the mother and her sexual and reproductive

---

This, in turn, suggests other reasons such as easy access to contraception methods, such as the so-called "morning-after pill" which can now be bought in drug stores without prescription. Also pointed out has been the drop in the numbers of immigrants as a result of the economic crisis.

31 Data from 2001 to 2010—that is, before the new Act was enacted—can be seen at www.msssi.gob.es/profesionales/saludPublica/prevPromocion/embarazo/docs/IVE_2010.pdf, p. 19. After the introduction of the new Act, the first cause of abortion is the mere request of the woman, followed at far away by the serious risk to the health or the life of the pregnant woman, and fetal abnormalities (for example, in 2013 the figures were 89.9% for the first case and 6.9% for the second and 3.1% for the third).

32 *Vid.* P. Sánchez-Ostiz, "¿Tienen todos derecho a la vida? Bases para un concepto constitucional de persona," cit., p. 3.

33 As J. M. Silva Sánchez wrote in 2007, "twenty years after the decriminalization of abortion through an indication system enforced in an extremely relaxed manner, we observe the absolute lack of legal (and extra-legal) protection of the unborn life" ("Los indeseados como enemigos. La exclusión de seres humanos del *status personae*," cit., p. 5).

rights,[34] among which is "the decision to have children and when to have them."[35] The protection of this personal autonomy is linked with the need to fight discrimination against women, "for whom pregnancy and motherhood are facts that deeply affect their lives in every sense." Some international documents are invoked—the United Nations Convention on the Elimination of All Forms of Discrimination against Women (1979), the Beijing Platform for Action agreed at the Fourth United Nations Conference on Women (1995), the Convention on the Rights of Persons with Disabilities (2006) and the 2001/2128 European Parliament Resolution on Sexual and Reproductive Health and Rights. There is also a reference to the necessity of adapting the Spanish legislation to the "consensus of the international community on the matter."

In addition, the new Act was justified in a number of somewhat dogmatic statements, to say the least. On the one hand, it was claimed that there was a need to provide certainty and security, since the enforcement of the previous regulation had led to "uncertainty and practices detrimental to legal security, with serious consequences to both the safety of women's rights and the effective protection of the concerned legal interest." However, for more than three decades of enforcement of the previous Act, there does not seem to have been any uncertainty but the one required to protect the life of the *unborn*, and to make sure that it was not destroyed but in the legally provided circumstances. Hence, it is hard to imagine how the greater legal protection offered by the "deadline-based" law might ensure greater protection for the alleged "legal interest."[36]

On the other hand, the Act attempts to show respect for the Constitutional Court's doctrine issued by the STC 53/1985, but it affirms that, "based on expert opinion and comparative law, legislators considered it reasonable to allow a period of fourteen weeks guaranteeing the right of women to make an informed decision about termination of pregnancy, free from interference from third parties." Furthermore, it is claimed "experience shows that prenatal life is best protected by policies that actively support motherhood and pregnant women." Regarding the

---

34 This new focus is specifically evident in the rest of the Act. According to Article 12, for example, the conditions for access to termination of pregnancy "shall be interpreted in the manner most favorable to the protection and effectiveness of the fundamental rights of the woman requesting the intervention."

35 Of course, there is no objection to this statement. But it is obvious that the legal problems are not the same before pregnancy than when a prenatal life protected by Article 15 of the Constitution exists.

36 Several authors have also insisted on the argument of legal certainty and equality, insofar as police and legal investigations may be initiated in some cases in accordance with the law, and not in others (*see*, for example, A. Ruiz Miguel, *El aborto: Problemas constitucionales*, Centro de Estudios Constitucionales, Madrid, 1990, pp. 13 ff.). The reasoning remains striking, since the very same can be said of any crime and, in fact, the alleged inequality would not disappear with the deadline-based regulation unless abortion was legalized throughout the entire pregnancy.

first point, it is clear that the "deadline-system" implies a profound change with respect to the previous indication system; regarding the second, not a single piece of evidence is provided in support of the idea that countries with a deadline-based system have a lower number of abortions.

2.3 The New Regulation

In accordance with the new Act, abortion is possible on the basis of the sole decision of the woman during the first 14 weeks, provided that she has been informed of her rights and of the available public maternity support services and assistance, and that three days have elapsed from the delivery of this information (Article 14).

After the 14-week term has elapsed, and provided that the 22nd week of the pregnancy has not expired, abortion is possible on medical grounds. Specifically: a) if the woman's life or health is at serious risk [Article 15a)]; and b) if there is a risk of serious fetal anomalies [Article 15b)].

Finally, abortion is possible at any stage of the pregnancy if the fetus suffers from a disease that is extremely serious or incurable [Article 15c)]. In this final case, it is necessary that the decision be confirmed by a medical committee composed of two experts in gynecology or prenatal diagnosis, plus one pediatrician (Article 16).

One of the most controversial aspects of the Act was the regulation of abortion for minors: 16- to 18-year-old girls. According to Section 4 of Article 13, they do not need further consent for the abortion; they are only required to inform one or two of their legal representatives, father, or mother. Even this duty may be dispensed whenever the minor alleges that such notification would lead to clear and present danger of domestic violence, threats, mistreatment, or distress.

Article 19.2 treats the conscientious objection in considerably strict terms: it may only be invoked by health professionals directly involved and provided that the health care provision (having the abortion) is not undermined. Finally, the Act requires that the training of health professionals be gender-sensitive, and requires that medical and health science curricular programs include training in the clinical practice of abortions (Article 8).

2.4 An Open Debate

2.4.1 The Conditions for the Constitutionality of Decriminalization

Despite attempts to present the Act as respectful of the doctrine of the STC 53/1985, and although several authors had no doubts as to its constitutionality,[37]

---

37 See, for example, A. Ruiz Miguel, *El aborto: Problemas constitucionales*, cit., pp. 89 ff.; M. Pérez Manzano and C. Tomás-Valiente, "Comentario al art. 15" in M.E Casas Baamonde and M. Rodríguez-Piñero y Bravo-Ferrer, *Comentarios a la Constitución Española*, Wolters-Kluwer, Madrid, 2008, p. 314; J. C. Martorell Mateu, "La regulación involuntaria del embarazo," in S. Huerta Tocildo and M. Pérez Manzano (ed.), *Cuestiones actuales de la Protección de la Vida y la Integridad Física y Moral*, cit.,

I think that it is difficult to reconcile the new regulation with the Court's jurisprudence. As we have seen, STC 53/1985 starts by declaring the constitutional obligation of the legislator to protect life, an obligation that must include criminal protection. According to the Court, such a protection can only be excluded when there are specific, serious reasons to justify doing so, and provided that guarantees are established to ensure that there shall be no legal abortions outside of those circumstances. In the new regulation, the legislator adopts a very different perspective, giving absolute preference to the free choice of the woman in the first 14 weeks, even if the reasons for the decision to abort are not relevant, and without requiring much in terms of guarantees.

While, in an indication system, it is the legislator that ponders the conditions under which decriminalization is possible, in the new regulation the legislator decides that the life of the *unborn* shall cede, at all times, to the will of the mother (disregarding the circumstances that led her to the decision to abort). This implies a total abdication of the duty to protect to the woman's right to decide, which has no express support in the Constitution but has been built up on the basis of certain rights that used to have a very different content (privacy, right to motherhood . . .), and of the principle—which is not a right in our Constitution—of the free development of the personality. Both categories are employed in order to justify a nearly absolute right to abortion in the first 14 weeks.[38]

The only limit to the will of the mother is a procedural one: the information she must receive before her consent. But even this information is far from the kind of advice provided for, v. gr., in German legislation. On the one hand, Article 17.1 establishes an unqualified obligation to receive advice on the different methods of termination of pregnancy, as well as on other circumstances such as the legal conditions to have the abortion and the legal conditions that medical centers have

---

pp. 63–64) or M. L. Cuerda Arnau (id., pp. 70–71). The same opinion is shared by P. de Lora Deltoro in his work "Abortar y dar vida. ¿Es constitucional la Ley 2/2010?" published in the same volume (pp. 92–109), although De Lora recognizes the strength of some of the arguments deployed by STC 53/1985 to declare unconstitutional the system introduced by the new Act. Nevertheless, De Lora develops an additional argument, in his opinion not sufficiently considered by STC 53/1985, that is, "the 'equality' dimension of the termination of pregnancy" (pp. 93 ff.).

38 As G. Rodríguez Mourullo says, the deadline-based system is incompatible with the recognition to the unborn of a right to life. The termination of pregnancy is left to the woman's free choice without requiring her to state any reason for her decision ("Comentario al art. 15 de la Constitución," cit., pp. 278 ff.). For L. M. Díez-Picazo, the deadline-based system is hardly reconcilable with the principles settled by STC 53/1985, and it would require appealing to constitutional values distinct from those taken into account in this case. Ultimately, it would lead to the configuration of the voluntary interruption of pregnancy as a right, something that "supposes a radical change in the solution to the constitutional problem of abortion" (*Sistema de derechos fundamentales*, Civitas, 4ª ed., Madrid, 2013, 208 ff.

to meet in order to practice abortions. By contrast, according to Section 2, information on alternatives to abortion shall be provided in a written, sealed envelope (i.e., not even a conversation is required nor is there a guarantee assuring that the woman knows the contents of the envelope). Furthermore, such information does not include any reference to the value of human life and its status as a constitutional interest.

Any reference to the value of human life is absent throughout the whole regulation. It is highly significant that among the public policies and educational measures that appear in Title I of the Act, there is not a single reference to the importance of human life nor a single measure aimed at educating on the seriousness of abortion and the existence of alternatives once a pregnancy has taken place.

Some of these objections to the validity of the new Act were expressed in an appeal of unconstitutionality lodged by 71 deputies of the Popular Party. Submitted to the Constitutional Court on June 1st, 2010, the appeal challenged several articles of the Act. Despite the time passed since then, the Court has not issued its decision, so the uncertainty remains.

2.4.2 The Failed Reform of the Act

Perhaps one of the reasons behind the Court's delay is the fact that, in the 2011 elections, the Popular Party obtained an absolute majority that allowed it to reform the Act, as it had promised in its electoral manifesto. Consequently, soon after the government was formed, the minister of justice announced a reform that would repeal the Act enacted by the previous government and would reestablish the old indication system, even with some further restrictions. The draft was presented not just as a piece of "legislation on abortion," but as a law for "the protection of the life of the unborn and of the rights of the pregnant woman." It was approved by the government on December 20th, 2013, and submitted to the advisory opinion of the general council of the judiciary.[39] However, on September 23rd, 2014, on the face of the wave of criticism voiced by pro-choice advocates, the prime minister announced that the project would be abandoned and that only the provision regarding the consent of minors between 16 and 18 years old would be modified. In his view, this was one of the most problematic aspects of the Act.[40] Therefore, on

---

39 The scant emphasis placed on the type of measures that help a woman overcome the conflict that leads her to an abortion remains noteworthy in both the legislation and in the party manifestos. Although many of the proponents of abortion consider it an evil, there is often an adverse reaction to such proposals. An exception in the Spanish context was the Act of the Cortes Valencianas 6/2009, of June 30th, on the Protection of Motherhood, which established measures to assist the pregnant woman to continue with her pregnancy. Yet, the Act was politically contested and derogated as soon as there was a change in the composition of the Cortes Valencianas.
40 This decision was followed by the resignation of the Minister of Justice Alberto Ruiz Gallardón, who had sponsored the project.

September 21st the Organic Law 11/2015 was passed to repeal the legal provisions on minor consent introduced by Act 2/2012. Under an explicit reference to the general legislation on the autonomy of the patient, the new regulation establishes that both minors and incapable persons shall require the express consent of their legal representatives in order to have an abortion. The conflicts that may arise will be solved in accordance with the general rules on minor consent of the Civil Code.

3 The Weak Protection of the Embryo in the Legislation on In Vitro Fertilization and the Use of Embryonic Organs and Tissues and the SSTC 212/1996 and 116/1999

3.1 Act 35/1988 on Assisted Reproduction Techniques and Act 42/1988 on Donation and Use of Human Embryos and Fetuses and Their Cells, Tissues, and Organs

Along with STC 53/1985, the other two leading cases on the status of prenatal life are SSTC 212/1996 and 116/1999. These Acts do not relate to abortion, but to the problems arising from in vitro fertilization and the subsequent generation of embryos, as well as to the eventual use of organs and tissues of the so-called "non-viable" embryos for therapeutic and research purposes. Although these decisions are two-and-a-half years apart, in reality they both concern laws which were passed almost at the same time and which, to a great extent, pose common problems:[41] Act 35/1988, of 22 November, on Assisted Reproduction Techniques (whose constitutionality was examined in STC 116/1999) and Act 42/1988 of 28 December on the donation and use of embryos and human fetuses or their cells, tissues, and organs (covered by STC 212/1996).[42]

The first of these Acts regulated assisted reproduction techniques for the first time in Spain. Specifically regulated were artificial insemination and in vitro

---

41 In the origin of the new legislation is a report prepared by the Special Commission for the Study of In Vitro Fertilization and Artificial Human Insemination, created by the Congress and presided over by the deputy and physician Marcelo Palacios (the so-called Palacios Report). See an analysis of this report, from a different point of view, in A. Calvo Meijide, "El permisivismo en la FIV: b) El informe Palacios, fundamento de la legislación española" in J. Ballesteros (ed.), *La humanidad* in vitro, Comares, Granada 2002, pp. 63 ff., and J. A. Souto Paz, "El informe Palacios y la ley de reproducción asistida," in A. Díaz Martínez (ed.), *Régimen jurídico-privado de la reproducción asistida en España: el proceso legal de reformas*, Dykinson, Madrid, 2006, pp. 187–196.
42 Despite the importance of such matters, once more, the Constitutional Court took an excessive period of time to resolve the appeals (almost 8–11 years). In addition, the Spanish Constitution does not provide for the suspension of a law while a constitutional appeal is pending, thus allowing the situation to be consolidated by the time.

fertilization with transfer of embryos and gamete intra-fallopian transfer. Among the general principles (Chapter II) are the prohibition of the fertilization of human eggs for any purposes other than human reproduction (Article 3), the provision that only the number of pre-embryos considered scientifically most appropriate will be transferred into the uterus (Article 4), and the possibility given to the woman to demand the interruption of the process at any stage (Article 2.4).

The donation of sperm is also regulated. It shall be anonymous at all times (Article 5.5) and under no circumstances shall be lucrative or commercial (Article 5.3). Regarding the receptors, any adult woman with full capacity to work (Article 6.1) can use the sperm. However, married women need the consent of their husband (Article 6.3). The Act also contains provisions concerning the parenthood of children born using these techniques (Articles 7 to 10).

For the purposes of this article, the rules on cryopreservation deserve special attention (in particular, the provision that the surplus embryos should be kept in authorized banks for a maximum of five years [Article 11, Section 3]), on diagnosis and treatment (Articles 12 and 13), and on research and experimentation (Articles 14 to 17). In addition, the Act contains provisions on the requisites that health care centers and biomedical equipment have to meet in order to carry out such techniques (Articles 18 and 19), and on the creation of the National Commission on Assisted Human Reproduction (Art. 21). An administrative (non-criminal) system of violations and punishments is also established (Article 20).

The Act 42/1988, on the donation and use of embryos and their organs and tissues, is much briefer. It bans any use of embryos, organs, or human tissues with a lucrative or commercial nature [Article 2d)]. As for the donation of embryos or fetuses, only those that are "clinically non-viable or dead" can be donated [Article 2e)]. The law prohibits abortions purely aimed at the donation of embryos or fetuses, as well as their subsequent use (Article 3.2). It also establishes the criteria to act upon them (Article 6), and to use them for research and experimentation (Articles 7–8). Finally, Article 9 establishes a purely administrative system of violations and punishments.

Deputies of the Popular Party challenged both Acts at the Constitutional Court, and the appeals were resolved by STC 212/1996 and STC 116/1999. Notwithstanding their singularities, these decisions present some common problems, so they will be considered together.[43] In both cases, the Court basically upholds the

---

43 Even though the judgment is focused on the *status* of prenatal life, there are yet other interesting questions posed that exceed the aims of this work and, therefore, we shall not deal with. Specifically, STC 212/1999 includes important considerations on the constitutional concept of the family (FJ 15) and on the problems posed by the anonymous nature of donation with regard to the possibility of the investigation of paternity guaranteed by Article 39.2 of the Spanish Constitution (FJ 16). Both judgments refer to the scope of the "reserve of Law" and the possibility of a regulation on the part of the government, an issue which, though indirectly related to the protection of the embryo, is not significant enough for the purposes of this work.

laws as constitutional. There is just one declaration of unconstitutionality in each of them for violating the principle of legality,[44] as well as an interpretive ruling of another two precepts.[45] Regardless of their final result, it is worth noting the lack of depth with which many of the problems involved are dealt with, some of which pose enormous legal and ethical problems. As I shall attempt to demonstrate here, on several occasions the Court resolves the question with categorical but non-evident statements, leaving the reader with the impression that he is faced with willed decision rather than a legally reasoned one.

3.2 Negation of the Right to Life of the Embryo and Consequences for Its Consideration as a Constitutionally Protected Legal Interest

3.2.1 *The Embryo Does Not Hold the Right to Life*

Both appeals alleged the unconstitutionality of the Act as a whole due to its infringement of the "organic law reserve" that Article 81 of the Spanish Constitution establishes for fundamental rights.[46] The Court rejects the allegation, taking the opinion that the right to life "as such and in accordance with STC 53/1985 is held by those that are born, without such entitlement being extended to *nascituri (unborn)*." Therefore, the fundamental right to life "is not deemed to be relevant" (STC 212/1996, FJ 3; the statements are reiterated in FFJJ 4 and 5 of STC 116/1999).[47] Consequently, to resolve the appeals the Court has to take in account not the right

---

44 With regard to the system of violations and punishments, Articles 9.1 of Act 42/1988 and 20.1 of Act 35/1988 referred to the General Health Act with the adjustments required. The Court understands that the later subsection leaves the system wholly undefined and is therefore contrary to Article 25.1 of the Spanish Constitution.
45 Articles 5.1 of Act 42/1988 and 12.2 of Act 35/1988, which declare that only diagnostic actions benefitting the *nasciturus* or in accordance with the applicable legislation can be performed on embryos. As has just been indicated, in both cases the Court points out that the stated applicable legislation can be none other than that which regulates the conditions for the decriminalization of abortion (FJ 12 of STC 212/1996 and STC 116/1999).
46 This is a specific source of law of the Spanish legal system, inspired by the French one. It is a law that regulates particularly important matters, and its singularity lies on its being approved by an absolute majority in the Congress of Deputies.
47 As we have already seen, STC 53/1985 does not justify—at least not sufficiently in my opinion—the exclusion of *nascituri* as holders of the right to life. Instead, it places the emphasis on the fact that, in any case, they are protected under Article 15 of the Spanish Constitution. These new decisions show up the crucial differences derived from the choice of either of those options.

to life, but the obligation to protect arising from Article 15 of the Spanish Constitution.[48]

3.2.2 Two New Categories: Pre-embryos and Non-viable Embryos and Their Legal Relevance

Regarding the Act on donation of embryos and their tissue, the Court resolves its possible conflict with Article 15 of the Spanish Constitution by creating a new category, the "non-viable embryo." The Act is constitutional—STC 212/1996 says in its FJ 5—since it assumes "the non-viable character of embryos and human fetuses." Accordingly, they lack the quality that would afford them the status of a legal interest whose protection is required by Article 15 of the Spanish Constitution: "they cannot be given the character of *nascituri* at all, since this is what the expression non-viable means, that is, that they will never be 'born.'"

STC 116/1999 employs the same notion of non-viability in order to confirm the constitutionality of Articles 15 and 16 of the Assisted Fertilization Act, which regulates the research and experimentation with the so-called "pre-embryos."[49] This concept is explicitly used by the law, whose Preamble says: "it is generally accepted that the term pre-embryo, also referred to as pre-implantation embryo corresponding to the pre-organogenesis phase, designates the group of cells resulting from the progressive division of the egg from fertilization up to approximately fourteen days later, when it attaches stably to the interior of the uterus, completing the process of implantation."[50] This statement is considered by the

---

48 Besides, human dignity (Article 10.1 of the Spanish Constitution) might also be affected, as has been pointed out correctly. There is no obstacle whatsoever to understanding that the Constitution protects not only the life of the unborn but also its integrity and health, guaranteed under the same Article 15 of the Spanish Constitution. The question should be raised whether this protection has to be extended to the in-vitro produced embryo, something that was not even considered by the judgments (cfr. P. J. Femenía López, Status *jurídico del Embrión humano, con especial consideración al concebido* in vitro, cit., pp. 225 ff.).

49 As L. M. Díez-Picazo points out, "this legal regulation raises several problems. Apart from the fact that it is not always easy to determine if an embryo is viable, there is a high risk of fraud both in terms of the possibility of masking illegal abortions and of producing more embryos than necessary for assisted reproduction" (*Sistema de derechos fundamentales*, cit., p. 215).

50 For a comprehensive critique of the concept, *see* P. J. Femenía López, Status *jurídico del Embrión humano, con especial consideración al concebido* in vitro, cit., pp. 12–15 and 259. This author decries the attempt to extract legal consequences from changes that, in reality, cannot conceal "a process of life marked by continuity": "the term pre-embryo" serves as a linguistic limitation of the break intended to be created in the representation of the different phases of prenatal development. A different denomination is deemed to correspond to a different reality (pp. 12–13). *See* also, among others, the critiques of A Ollero, *Bioderecho. Entre la vida y la muerte*, cit.,

Constitutional Court to exclude experimentation with viable pre-embryos.[51] Thus, it applies the jurisprudence established by STC 212/1996, according to which non-viable embryos are not protected by Article 15 of the Constitution, and it maintains that the provisions of the Act cannot "raise doubts from the perspective of their adequacy in relation to the constitutionally required system for the protection of human life" [FJ 9C].

In his dissenting opinion to STC 212/1996, Magistrate Gabaldón López (who rejects the construction that negates the right to life of the *unborn*) criticized this new category of "non-viable embryos." In his opinion, the relevant distinction is the one between the dead embryos and the live ones. All live embryos must be protected in the terms established in STC 53/1985. "If life must be protected," he states, "then the only term of exclusion shall be the case where there is no life in the organism. As long as there is life, that is, as long as life does not cease and they are therefore dead, non-viable embryos have life even when they do not have a reasonable chance of surviving" (FJ 4).

It is difficult to deny that both the legislator and the Constitutional Court have introduced a new concept, or if one prefers, a new status of the human being that generates significant questions. At the very least, it constitutes a step beyond the one set out in STC 53/1985, a judgment that demands protection—even criminal protection—of human life in all its stages. We are not before a human life which, either for natural reasons or because it has been generated artificially, without the will to make it viable through implantation in the uterus of the woman, cannot survive or even be born.[52] As highlighted in an early comment on STC 212/1996,[53] the

---

pp. 164 ff. and V. Bellver, "El estatuto jurídico del embrión," in J. Ballesteros (ed.), *La humanidad in vitro*, cit., pp. 255 ff.

51 In Article 15 of the Act, a reference is made to the conditions for authorization of "research with viable embryo." The Court says that "even if the text of the provision is not desirable from a technical legal perspective, an adequate understanding, in accordance with the context in which the text has been regulated, allows for the conclusion that pre-embryos obtained through in vitro fertilization can only be used for scientific experimentation purposes if they are non-viable and provided that (...) the animal model is not suitable for the intended objectives, and so it is authorized by the competent administrative authority..." (STC 116/1999 FJ 8).

52 As indicated by A. Ollero, in the case of in vitro fertilization there is a significant change: in the past, the embryo was viable unless a natural incurable obstacle happened to make it inviable; now, we can speak of a dependent *viability*, since only the will of other persons, through implantation, can make it viable (*Bioderecho. Entre la vida y la muerte*, cit., pp. 26). Regarding the difficulties arising from the concept of viability, *vid.* P. J. Femenía López, Status *jurídico del Embrión humano, con especial consideración al concebido* in vitro, cit., pp. 264 ff.

53 J. Pardo Falcón, "A vueltas con el artículo 15 CE y otras cuestiones más o menos recurrentes de nuestro Derecho Constitucional (un comentario a la STC 212/1996 de 19 de diciembre)," *Revista Española de Derecho Constitucional*, no. 51, 1997, pp. 257–258).

Court ought to have analyzed whether the protection of life provided by Article 15 of the Spanish Constitution is extended or not to these living (although non-viable) embryos. If the answer is affirmative, the Court should have considered whether the harm posed by the legal measures could be justified through other rights or principles of the same kind. On the other hand, as pointed out by C. M. Romeo Casabona, the decision does not clarify whether viability is a strictly biological term (incapacity to continue the process of cell division), or is also extended to other sort of conditions (i.e., the withdrawal or inability of the progenitors to continue).[54]

Another step towards the removal of protection is taken in the case of in vitro fertilized, but not transferred embryos. STC 116/1999 states "in vitro pre-embryos do not enjoy a level of protection comparable to those already transferred to the maternal uterus" (FJ 12). This thesis allows the Court to declare the constitutionality of the so-called pre-implantation diagnosis (Article 12). However, given that both are living human beings, the different treatment based on viability (constitutional protection in one case, and the possibility of destruction for the purpose of experimentation in the other) does not really depend on a biological feature or other external factor, but simply on the decision of the progenitors not to proceed with implantation.[55] And, since this is a technique that may consequently lead to the "selection" of embryos and the non-transference of those that present illnesses, consideration of the dignity of the person is necessary.

3.2.3 Surplus Embryos

One particular problem arises from the legislator's decision to allow the generation of extra embryos that are to be transferred to the woman's uterus in order to be fertilized. This gives rise to what Article 11.3 of the Act calls "surplus pre-embryos" which, as set out, "are cryoconserved in authorized banks, for a maximum of five

---

54 "El derecho a la vida: aspectos constitucionales de las nuevas biotecnologías," in *El derecho a la vida. Actas de las VIII Jornadas de la Asociación de Letrados del Tribunal Constitucional*, CEPC, Madrid, 2003, pp. 35 ff. This author attempts to solve the question by understanding the non-viability on strictly biological terms. This opinion is shared by F. J. Díaz Revorio, "Bioética y valores constitucionales en el comienzo de la vida humana," in M. Gascón Abellán, M.C González Carrasco and J. Cantero Martínez (ed.), *Derecho sanitario y bioética*, Tirant lo Blanch, Valencia, 2011, pp. 809.
55 Moreover, and as has been highlighted, important contradictions remain in the Act: if, according to it, the embryos not transplanted to the uterus are not worthy of protection, it is difficult to understand why experimentation is permitted once the 14-day term has elapsed; if, by contrast, the Act considers that life begins with fertilization, it is hardly understandable how its destruction can be permitted. In any case, "nothing happens to the embryo on the fourteenth day so as to change its status." (P. J. Femenía López, Status *jurídico del Embrión humano, con especial consideración al concebido* in vitro, cit., pp. 259–260).

years."[56] The Court considers that we are before an "inevitable consequence of these techniques," and it justifies it constitutionally because "the Constitution does not render impossible obtaining a sufficient number of pre-embryos to ensure, with modern biomedical knowledge, the probable success of the assisted reproduction technique, so it has to be admitted, as a scientifically inevitable fact, the eventual existence of surplus pre-embryos (FJ 11). In addition, the judgment says that these new pre-embryos are not "human persons": "consequently, the fact that they remain available to the banks after the fixed period of time has elapsed can hardly contradict the right to life (Article 15 of the Spanish Constitution) or human dignity (Article 10.1 of the Spanish Constitution)" (id.).

Once again, the scant argumentative effort of the court is evident: As far as the generation of embryos that are not to be implanted is concerned, the argument is reduced to the efficiency of fertilization, which makes such generation "scientifically inevitable." Such an appeal to science is unconvincing when other countries have not permitted the generation of more embryos than those that are to be transferred and, in any case, the decision does not contain the slightest consideration on the dignity of the embryos, at least from the perspective of the proportionality principle. There is a total prevalence of the efficiency criteria and remains the question if the success of the technique—that anyway gets very low incomes—is a sufficient reason to justify the generation of an unlimited number of embryos.

Perhaps the explanation is implicit in the second of the paragraphs transcribed: for the Court, the protection of the pre-embryo does not seem to affect the right to life or dignity. Nor does it even attempt to offer any argument from the point of view of the duty to protect derived from Article 15 of the Spanish Constitution, which, according to STC 53/1985 extends to human life throughout its course, from gestation to death. The Court uses for the first time the concept *human person*, and does so in order to discard any protection and, in practice, to equate these embryos with gametes. As signaled previously, in its judgment on abortion, the Court explicitly avoided the issue of when personhood begins; now, however, without the slightest justification as to what should be considered a person for constitutional effects, it just affirms that the pre-embryo is not a person. Perhaps this is related with the aim to deny any projection of dignity, which in Article 10.1 of the Spanish Constitution is linked to the concept of the person; we shall return to this point.

The inevitable consequence of the existence of surplus embryos is no less inevitable than the fact that there are banks for their cryoconservation:[57] the Court

---

56 A. Ollero has drawn attention to the implications derived from referring to certain pre-embryos as "surplus." This is something that falls apart from the scientific discourse, and entails a "notably important ethical evaluation" (*Bioderecho. Entre la vida y la muerte*, cit., p. 170).
57 The Court will say that cryoconservation not only does not constitute an attack on human dignity but that it is the only way to optimize the use of already existing embryos (FJ 11). But as V. Bellver correctly points out, the question is not whether

does not find it necessary to explain whether it is compatible with the value of life and the dignity of the human being to generate embryos whose purpose shall not be life,[58] nor to justify the 5-year legal term for their conservation without any further legal provision regarding the destiny of the embryos once the deadline has expired, nor to indicate the constitutional consequences of this omission. The inevitable outcome is that the banks have accumulated dozens of thousands of pre-embryos and, up to 2003, that is to say, 15 years after the entry into force of the Act, no one has made a decision of what to do once this five-year period had elapsed.

3.2.4 *The Absence of Any Criminal Protection*

Another aspect of the regulation subject to constitutional challenge was the absence of any kind of criminal protection of the embryos. The allegation on the part of the plaintiffs does not, a priori, appear to be ungrounded, taking into account that STC 53/1985 has emphatically extended the protection of life provided by Article 15 to prenatal life, and that such protection has to include criminal punishment—which should only be dispensable "in specific cases" (FJ 7). In support of this statement, the Court considers that it is one thing to say that the absence of such criminal protection might justify an appeal of unconstitutionality, and a very different thing that each of the possible violations must, as a consequence, result in punishment (STC 212/1996, FJ 10 and 116/1999, FJ 16). However, the fact is that neither of the two Acts established any criminal sanction whatsoever. The decisions of the Court upholding the Acts are perhaps justified by the fact, highlighted in both decisions, that the new Criminal Code of 1995 had already typified some of these violations as crimes.[59] It could be argued that a decision concerning this issue was no longer necessary. Nevertheless, the criminal norm approved in 1995 by the legislator reinforces the idea that embryos should be criminally protected.

---

it is less of an attack on human dignity to freeze embryos than to destroy them. The issue is whether we should care for the rise of "banks of frozen embryos which, in the medium term, no one knows what to do with" ("El estatuto jurídico del embrión," cit., p. 262).

58 As A. Ollero states in strong, graphic terms, "in vitro fertilization gives rise to the new category of the *moriturus*: a human being manufactured to die, once the merely instrumental function it is destined for has been fulfilled" (*Bioderecho. Entre la vida y la muerte*, cit., p. 160).

59 Title V of the Book II of the new Code typifies various crimes relating to genetic manipulation, especially the alteration of the genotype (Article 159), the fertilization of eggs for purposes other than procreation (Article 160.2), cloning (Article 160.3), as well as in vitro fertilization of the woman without her consent (Article 161).

3.2.5 A Weak Concept of Dignity

Perhaps one of the most striking aspects of these two decisions is the scant presence of the concept of dignity in the Court's reasoning. Unlike what occurs, for example, in the German Constitution, Article 10 of the Spanish Constitution does not define dignity as a fundamental right, but considers it—together with "inviolable rights which are inherent"—as "the foundation of political order and social peace."

With regard to STC 212/1996, and in relation to embryos and human fetuses, the Court admits that the dignity of the person "may have a certain projection on certain aspects of the regulation" (FJ 5), and it points out that patrimonial appropriation of human organs or even the human corpse would be, as the appellants noted, "incompatible with their dignity" (FJ 8). Nevertheless, it takes no heed of such statements and arrives at the conclusion that "the aborted embryo is not but the cellular structure with the possibility of ulterior development" (FJ 6).

The statements included in STC 116/1999 are more relevant, in part due to the fact that the Assisted Reproduction Act had some provisions with a greater impact on human dignity.[60] In some passages, the Court seems to question the value of embryos as such, at least prior to their implantation in the uterus. Thus, referring to non-viable pre-embryos, the Court affirms that this expression refers "to the incapacity to develop and give rise to a human being, a 'person' in the fundamental sense of Article 10.1 of the Spanish Constitution" (FJ 9). Even more clearly, in relation to cryoconservation, it states that "neither un-implanted pre-embryos nor, with greater reason, simple gametes are, to these effects, 'human persons,' and therefore it is difficult to conclude that the fact that they remain available to the banks after a certain period of time is an attack on life (Article 15 of the Spanish Constitution) or on human dignity (Article 10.1 of the Spanish Constitution) (FJ 11)."[61]

---

60 This important issue is what brings magistrates Jiménez de Parga and Garrido Falla to formulate dissenting opinions, albeit their reasoning is not based on substantive aspects but on the organic nature that the Act should have had.

61 However, the Court had previously stated that cryoconservation "not only does not result in an attack, but on the contrary and attending to the current state of the techniques, it seems to us more as a remedy to make better use of the already existing pre-embryos, thus avoiding unnecessary fertilization" (FJ 11). This statement, and the statement—transcribed above—that the patrimonial appropriation of pre-embryos would be contrary to dignity, leads F. J. Díaz Revorio to say that the Court's jurisprudence might be understood as the embryos being covered by the constitutional protection of human dignity, something that he considers to be based on the Constitution and which I evidently share ("Bioética y valores constitucionales en el comienzo de la vida humana," cit., p. 809); but the other citations of the judgment that we have transcribed seem to leave little room for doubt.

This exclusion of dignity in the first stages of prenatal human life, as well as the scant weight afforded it by the Court throughout its judgments, is even more striking considering the importance of this value in the field of Biolaw.[62] If dignity is a value so closely tied in with the condition of being human, it is difficult to deny this value in the first stages of life. As E. W. Böckenförde has clearly stated, dignity cannot be linked to determined properties, signs, or capacities, but it corresponds to all human beings independently of their stage of development, and it must be protected from arbitrary whims and discretion since the first moment of life, and not after a period of time has elapsed.[63]

4 Legislative Evolution

As has been said, the enforcement of the Act gave rise to the storage of thousands of cryoconserved embryos. This fact, together with the technical developments that make it possible to use them for research purposes—in particular for obtaining stem cells—led to the approval of a new law in 2003. Following the advice of the National Commission for Assisted Reproduction, Act 45/2003, of November 21st, amended in some relevant aspects the 1988 regulation.

The legislator considers that the large number of frozen pre-embryos suggests that it is not necessary to obtain so many and, therefore, establishes that a maximum of three ovocytes be fertilized that can be transferred to the mother in each cycle (Article 4.3). Moreover, in order to reduce the number of multiple births, a maximum limit of three pre-embryos per cycle may be transferred to the woman (Article 4.2).

In addition, Article 11 of the Act is amended so that, despite the new restrictions, surplus embryos may be generated in exceptional cases. These embryos shall be conserved for a period equivalent to the fertile life of the mother, and the progenitors are obliged to sign a commitment whereby they consent that, if not transferred, the embryos shall be donated with reproduction purposes as the only alternative (Section 3).

Finally, in order to provide an outlet for the thousands of pre-embryos already frozen, the 1st Additional Provision of the Law establishes that progenitors must choose between the cryoconservation of the embryos until a future transference, the donation to another couple, or their use for research purposes.[64]

---

62 *See*, for example, A. Aparisi Miralles, "En torno al principio de la dignidad humana. A propósito de la investigación con células troncales embrionarias," *Cuadernos de Bioética*, no. 54, 2004, 257–282.
63 Cfr. E. W. Böckenförde, "Menschenwürde als normatives Prinzip. Die Grundrechte in der bioethischen Debatte," *Juristen Zeitung*, 2003, pp. 809–815.
64 The linguistic variations with which the Act refers to unfrozen pre-embryos are striking: in the Preamble speaks of "biological material," and in the First Final Provision calls them "biological structures."

Despite the moderation of the restrictions introduced by the Act—which were in line with other European legislation[65] and which, moreover, authorized the use of embryos for research purposes—it received numerous criticisms from proponents of unrestricted in vitro fertilization. And in fact, the reforms did not last very long, since in 2006 a new Act (Act 14/2006, of May 26th on Assisted Human Reproduction Techniques) was approved. The new legislation repealed the previous one, and it is currently in force.[66] It removed the limit of three ovocytes on the ground that "it creates a difficulty in the ordinary practice of assisted reproduction techniques by imposing the means of achieving greater success with the least possible risk to the health of mother" (Preamble). The Act also removes the separate treatment given to pre-embryos that had been frozen before the 2003 Act came into force. By contrast, it authorizes that all may be used for research purposes with the consent of the progenitors (Article 11), whenever the following requirements are met: that they have been developed for more than 14 days; and that the research be authorized by accredited centers and based on a project duly authorized by the health authorities (Article 15). As a novel element, the Act defines, for the first time, the pre-embryo, which is understood as "the embryo in vitro, constituting of a group of cells resulting from the progressive division of the oocyte from its fertilization up to 14 days later."[67]

With the new legislation,[68] Spain is one of the countries with the fewest restrictions on assisted reproduction: treatment for single women, donation of semen and of eggs, anonymous donation, pre-implantation diagnostics, post-mortem fertilization and sex selection in the event of hereditary sex-linked illness are allowed. There is no shortage of those who celebrate such "advanced" legislation, advanced also in the lack of protection for embryonic life.

---

65 See a summary of the German and Italian regulations in E. Peñaranda Ramos, "Bioética y Derecho Penal en el comienzo de la vida: algunas implicaciones jurídico-penales de las nuevas biotecnologías," cit., pp. 79 ff. In both legislations there is greater protection of the embryo, something the author criticizes but that—for the reasons outlined throughout this text—I believe that responds better to an appropriate balance of the rights and interests at stake.
66 An extensive analysis of the new Act is contained in J. A. Cobacho Gómez (ed.) J. J. Iniesta Delgado (ed.), *Comentarios a la Ley 14/2006, de 26 de mayo, de Reproducción Humana Asistida*, Thomson Aranzadi, Cizur Menor, 2007.
67 It is significant that the pre-embryo is defined as an "embryo," something that seems to confirm that the distinction is, after all, somewhat artificial, albeit loaded with important practical consequences.
68 Neither this Act nor its predecessor was appealed to the Constitutional Court. Nor was Act 14/2007, of July 3rd, on Biomedical Research, which repealed Act 42/1988 on Donation and use of Embryos and Human Fetuses or their Cells, Tissues and Organs, whose Title IV regulated the obtaining and use of embryonic cells and tissue.

5 A Model for the Gradual (Dis)Protection of Life in Formation

As a consequence of the constitutional jurisprudence, we now face a situation of gradual protection of the prenatal human life, as some authors explain. Perhaps the clearest formulation of this progression is the one of C. M. Romeo Casabona[69] a scale which, going from the greatest to the least protection, includes:

1. The fetus capable of continuing its vital process without the concurrence of the mother (extra-uterine viability).
2. The embryo attached or implanted in the maternal endometrium.
3. The viable embryo, capable to continue the biological development process in a natural way.
4. The embryo in vitro before being transferred to the mother.

5. The embryo that is non-viable due to "anomalies incompatible with life": protection would range from the maximum to the minimum based on a) the embryo *in utero*, b) the embryo *ex utero* and c) the embryo *in vitro*.

In accordance with the doctrine of the Constitutional Court, no embryo shall have the right to life, although it will benefit from protection derived from Article 15 of the Spanish Constitution. Thus, this protection will never be the same as the one owned by the born child, nor shall its specific scope be so clear. *De facto*, it can depend on the technological advances and on the perception of society.[70] According to the Constitutional Court, the embryo in utero is constitutionally protected unless certain circumstances concur—those described by the indication system approved in 1985—however, the law has forsaken it to the free will of the mother during the first 14 weeks. With regards to the embryo generated in vitro, it is protected by Article 15 of the Spanish Constitution once it is viable and

---

69 "El derecho a la vida: aspectos constitucionales de las nuevas biotecnologías," en El derecho a la vida. 40 ss. A gradual explanation of the protection of life is also made by F. J. Díaz Revorio ("Bioética y valores constitucionales en el comienzo de la vida humana," cit., pp. 805 ff.), albeit he considers this gradual protection admissible in the case of the right to life but not with regards to dignity (p. 810). Díaz Revorio calls for a clearer definition of the pre-embryo, a definition that would not consider it a person but belonging to human species, and therefore covered by the protection of dignity (p. 812). Another proponent of gradual protection, who also includes human dignity, is E. Peñaranda Ramos, "Bioética y Derecho Penal en el comienzo de la vida: algunas implicaciones jurídico-penales de las nuevas biotecnologías," cit., pp. 99 ff.
70 This is what happened, as we can see, with embryos referred to as "viable": initially, interventions were only allowed for therapeutic purposes (STC 212/1996, FJ 5). Subsequently, when technical advances opened the way to embryonic cells research, the destruction of frozen cells, which would be viable if they were implanted (biologically "viable" in the sense already explained), became constitutionally allowed.

transferred to the uterus of a mother. If it is not viable, even though it is a human being, it does not appear to benefit from any protection in Article 15 of the Spanish Constitution nor from the dignity of the person (Article 10 of the Spanish Constitution). And even if being viable, if it has not been transferred it shall remain frozen and its constitutional protection shall also be frozen until the progenitors decide whether to implant it or donate it to another couple (in which case it shall continue to benefit from constitutional protection) or use it for research purposes (in which case protection is removed altogether).

This division seems to undermine the consideration of life as a "continuum," as stated by STC 53/1985 and repeatedly confirmed by the science.[71] It is true that STC 53/1985 also affirms that life "is a continuous process subject through the effects of time to qualitative changes of a somatic and psychological nature which are reflected in the public and private legal status of the vital subject" (FJ 6). But the true question is whether those prenatal changes are so relevant as to permit the free elimination of life with no legal consequence. It is not so after birth, despite the fact that very relevant changes do occur (self-consciousness, adulthood, etc.), and regardless of the further development of severe disabilities. In my view, nor should it be during gestation.[72]

Bibliography

R. Alexy, *Theorie der Grundrechte*, Shurkamp, 3ª ed., Frankfurt a.M. 1996

Aparisi Miralles, "En torno al principio de la dignidad humana. A propósito de la investigación con células troncales embrionarias," *Cuadernos de Bioética*, no. 54, 2004, pp. 257–282.

J. Ballesteros (coord.), *La humanidad in vitro*, Comares, Granada 2002.

---

71 However, Peñaranda Ramos points out that "the continuation of the vital process in reality depends on the intervention of third parties, firstly on the doctor who performs the implantation, but above all on the women, who must decide" on the basis of her right to privacy ("Bioética y Derecho Penal en el comienzo de la vida: algunas implicaciones jurídico-penales de las nuevas biotecnologías," cit., pp. 105–106). The reasoning, however, is based on the following assumption, that is, the lawfulness of generating embryos in vitro which are not aimed at implantation. For the reasons already outlined, I do not consider such a production compatible with the dignity of the human being (Article 10 of the Spanish Constitution) or with the protection derived from Article 15.

72 An interesting summary of reasons that have led many German criminal experts to consider unacceptable any evaluative difference based on the stage at which life can be found in E. Peñaranda Ramos, "Bioética y Derecho Penal en el comienzo de la vida: algunas implicaciones jurídico-penales de las nuevas biotecnologías," cit., pp. 87 ff. The reasons are nevertheless not shared by Peñaranda, who proposes a model of gradual protection of human life (pp. 99 ff.).

V. Bellver, "El estatuto jurídico del embrión," en J. Ballesteros (coord.), *La humanidad in vitro*, Comares, Granada, 2002.

E. W. Böckenförde, "Menschenwürde als normatives Prinzip. Die Grundrechte in der bioethischen Debatte," *Juristen Zeitung*, 58. Nr. 17 (5. September 2003), pp. 809-815

Calvo Meijide, "El permisivismo en la FIV: b) El informe Palacios, fundamento de la legislación española" en J. Ballesteros (coord.), *La humanidad* in vitro, Comares, Granada 2002.

J. Cerezo Mir, "La regulación del aborto en el proyecto de nuevo Código penal español," *Anuario de Derecho Penal y Ciencias Penales*, 1982, volume 35, págs. 564 ff.

J. A. Cobacho Gómez (Dir.) y J.J. Iniesta Delgado (coord.), *Comentarios a la Ley 14/2006, de 26 de mayo, de Reproducción Humana Asistida*, Thomson Aranzadi, Cizur Menor, 2007.

M. L. Cuerda Arnau, in S. Huerta Tocildo y M. Pérez Manzano (dir.), *Cuestiones actuales de la Protección de la Vida y la Integridad Física y Moral*, Aranzadi, Cizur Menor, 2012.

F. J. Díaz Revorio, "Bioética y valores constitucionales en el comienzo de la vida humana," in M. Gascón Abellán, M.C González Carrasco y J. Cantero Martínez (coord.), *Derecho sanitario y bioética*, Tirant lo Blanch, Valencia, 2011.

L. M. Díez-Picazo, *Sistema de derechos fundamentales*, Civitas, 4ª ed., Madrid, 2013.

P. J. Femenía López, Status *jurídico del Embrión humano, con especial consideración al concebido* in vitro, McGraw-Hill, Madrid, 1999.

A. J. Gómez Montoro, "El control previo de constitucionalidad de Estatutos de Autonomía y demás leyes orgánicas," *Revista Española de Derecho Constitucional*, núm. 22, 1988, pp. 123-174.

A. J. Gómez Montoro, "Los derechos fundamentales de las personas jurídicas. Un intento de fundamentación," en *Revista Española de Derecho Constitucional*, núm. 65, 2002, pp. 49-105.

A. J Gómez Montoro, "Respuestas al cuestionario," en S. Huerta Tocildo y M. Pérez Manzano (dir.), *Cuestiones actuales de la Protección de la Vida y la Integridad Física y Moral*, Aranzadi, Cizur Menor, 2012.

A. J. Gómez Montoro, *Vida privada y autonomía personal o una interpretación* passe-partout *del artículo 8 CEDH*, in VV.AA., *La Constitución política de España. Estudios en homenaje a Manuel Aragón Reyes*, Centro de Estudios Políticos y Constitucionales, Madrid, 2016.

S. Huerta Tocildo y M. Pérez Manzano (dir.), *Cuestiones actuales de la Protección de la Vida y la Integridad Física y Moral*, Aranzadi, Cizur Menor, 2012.

G. Jakobs, "¿Existe un aborto lícito de personas?" *Poder Judicial*, núm. 60, 2000, pp. 159-168.

P. de Lora Deltoro, "Abortar y dar vida. ¿Es constitucional la Ley 2/2010?" in S. Huerta Tocildo y M. Pérez Manzano (dir.), *Cuestiones actuales de la Protección de la Vida y la Integridad Física y Moral*, Aranzadi, Cizur Menor, 2012, pp. 92–109.

J. C. Martorell Mateu, "La regulación involuntaria del embarazo," in S. Huerta Tocildo y M. Pérez Manzano (dir.), *Cuestiones actuales de la Protección de la Vida y la Integridad Física y Moral*, Aranzadi, Cizur Menor, 2012, pp. 63–69.

A. Ollero, *Bioderecho. Entre la vida y la muerte*, Thomson-Aranzadi, Cizur Menor 2006.

J. Pardo Falcón, "A vueltas con el artículo 15 CE y otras cuestiones más o menos recurrentes de nuestro Derecho Constitucional (un comentario a la STC 212/1996 de 19 de diciembre)," *Revista Española de Derecho Constitucional*, núm. 51, 1997, pp. 249–272.

E. Peñaranda Ramos, "Bioética y Derecho Penal en el comienzo de la vida: algunas implicaciones jurídico- penales de las nuevas biotecnologías," *Anuario de la Facultad de Derecho de la Universidad Autónoma de Madrid*, 2006, pp. 75–106.

M. Pérez Manzano y C. Tomás-Valiente, "Comentario al art. 15" in M.E Casas Baamonde y M. Rodríguez-Piñero y Bravo-Ferrer, *Comentarios a la Constitución Española*, Wolters-Kluwer, Madrid, 2008, pp. 311–339.

G. Rodríguez Mourullo, "Comentario al art. 15 de la Constitución," en O. Alzaga (dir.), *Comentarios a la Constitución Española de 1978*, Tomo II, Edersa, Madrid, 1997, pp. 270 ff.

J. M. Rodríguez de Santiago, *La ponderación de bienes e intereses en el Derecho Administrativo*, Marcial Pons, Madrid, 2000.

C. M. Romeo Casabona, "El derecho a la vida: aspectos constitucionales de las nuevas biotecnologías," in *El derecho a la vida. Actas de las VIII Jornadas de la Asociación de Letrados del Tribunal Constitucional*, CEPC, Madrid, 2003, pp. 35 ff.

Ruiz Miguel, *El aborto: Problemas constitucionales*, Centro de Estudios Constitucionales, Madrid, 1990.

Saiz Arnaiz, *La apertura constitucional al derecho internacional y europeo de los derechos humanos: el artículo 10.2 de la Constitución Española*, Consejo General del Poder Judicial, Madrid, 1999.

P. Sánchez-Ostiz, "¿Tienen todos derecho a la vida? Bases para un concepto constitucional de persona", *Revista Electrónica de Ciencia Política y Criminología*, 11-11, 2009.

Ian Shapiro, Pablo de Lora Deltoro, and Carmen Tomás-Valiente, *La Suprema Corte de Estados Unidos y el aborto*, Fundación Coloquio Jurídico Europeo, Madrid, 2009.

J. M. Silva, "Los indeseados como enemigos. La exclusión de seres humanos del *status personae*," *Revista Electrónica de Ciencia Penal y Criminología, 09-01*, 2007, pp. 1–18.

F. Simón Yarza, *Medio ambiente y derechos fundamentales*, Centro de Estudios Políticos y Constitucionales, Madrid, 2012.

J. A. Souto Paz, "El informe Palacios y la ley de reproducción asistida," in A. Díaz Martínez (coord.), *Régimen jurídico-privado de la reproducción asistida en España: el proceso legal de reformas*, Dykinson, Madrid, 2006.

Tomás-Valiente, "La jurisprudencia constitucional española sobre el aborto," in Ian Shapiro, Pablo de Lora Deltoro y Carmen Tomás-Valiente, *La Suprema Corte de Estados Unidos y el aborto*, Fundación Coloquio Jurídico Europeo, Madrid, 2009.

Cases:

Constitutional Court of Spain, STC 53/1985; STC 117/1985; STC 23/1989; STC 214/1991; STC 139/1995; STC 212/1996; STC116/1999, STC 95/2003 and STC 236/2007.

Constitutional Court of Germany: Ruling of 25 February 1975 (BVerfGE 39,1).

Jerzy M. Ferenz and Aleksander Stępkowski

6 The Emergence of the Right to Life in Polish Constitutional Law

Abstract: This chapter examines the emergence of the right to life in Polish constitutional law that took place in the end of 20th century. The first part of the chapter illustrates the development of law relating to abortion in Poland since 1930. Characteristic feature of Polish law in this respect was that totalitarian regimes were always imposing on Poland regulations granting impunity of abortion. Both, German Nazis during the Second World War as well as the communist regime imposed by Soviet Russia after the War, granted wide access to abortion and promoted it among Polish women. Special attention is given to the last decade of 20th century when new legislation was adopted and amended after the collapse of the totalitarian communist regime. The chapter analyses those changes in the wider perspective of the constitutional process that had been taking place during that time. The second part of the text examines the leading constitutional case K 26/96 that has determined the content of Polish law protecting human life at its prenatal stage, given the absence of written constitutional provisions in this respect. Particular attention is given to creative construction of the *Rechtsstaat* principle as well as to application of the principle of proportionality. The first of those principles has allowed the Polish Constitutional Court to declare the right to life as a constitutional principle extending also to prenatal stage of human life development.

Keywords: Right to life, Abortion, Rights of unborn children, Constitutional review in Poland, Rule of law

1 Setting the Context

1.1 Abortion in Polish Law—A Brief Historical Outline

Poland was one of the champions in making abortion legal. Under huge pressure of some intellectuals, who were also promoting (unsuccessfully) eugenics in 1930s, in a Polish Criminal Code enacted in 1932, articles 232–234 decriminalized abortion (expulsion of foetus) if performed in the case of endangerment of the woman's as well as when pregnancy resulted from rape, incest or paedophilia.[1] At that time, it was one of the most liberal laws worldwide[2]. Afterwards, during the Second World

---

1 For more information *see*: M. Gałązka, *Polish Penal Law on the Human Being in Prenatal Stage*, [in:] A. Stępkowski (ed.), *Protection of Human Life in It's Prenatal Stage*, Peter Lang Edition 2014, p. 169; E. Zielińska, *Przerywanie ciąży. Warunki legalności w Polsce i na świecie*, Warszawa 1990, p. 52.
2 For broader context *see*: J. C. Mohr, *Abortion in America: The Origins and Evolution of National Policy*, Oxford University Press, 1978, pp. 34–36; A. E. Doan, *Opposition and Intimidation: The Abortion Wars and Strategies of Political Harassment*, University

War, German Nazi occupiers allowed abortion on demand for Polish women only, as a part of their actions aimed at the extinction of the Polish nation. This law was abolished after the Nazi occupation, restoring the 1932 criminal regulation.[3]

The most substantial change, having certain effects still today, was introduced to Polish law in 1956.[4] As demanded by the Soviet Union, the dependent communist Parliament in Warsaw introduced abortion because of "difficult living conditions of pregnant women" (*de facto* on demand), widely known under the label of "abortion for social reasons." As could be expected, the result was that the unborn child lost all direct legal protection, being protected only indirectly as an element of pregnancy. Also a Soviet law principle was introduced that women are never to be prosecuted for abortion, regardless of the stage of development of the child, the mother's motives, or any other circumstances. The unborn child became absolutely unprotected against the mother, and the principle is still in force, being one of the darkest relics of communist rule in democratic Poland. Despite strong social opposition to abortion, it was strongly promoted by communists and performed on a massive scale, even in workplace abortuaries. Statistics and estimations show there were up to 250,000 abortions per year in the 1980s.

During political change in 1989, a bill was introduced before Parliament aiming to add a provision for full protection of unborn children. It was however not adopted due to the ending of the parliamentary term. Then a strong political and social dispute began, which resulted, finally, in partial protection of the child, as provided by the Act of 7 January 1993 on family planning, protection of human foetus and conditions allowing termination of the pregnancy[5] ("1993 Act"). This statutory enactment introduced full protection of human life including unborn children as a matter of principle, subject to certain exceptions. It provided for full illegality of abortion in criminal law, preserving, however, absolute impunity for the mother, as provided by communists in 1956. Moreover, as a consequence of political compromise, the 1993 Act provided three exceptions in criminal law (eugenic, criminal, mother's life and health). Abortion was still a criminal offence and fully illegal; however it was not prosecuted in those three exceptional cases.

---

of Michigan 2007, p. 46; *Abort i Sverige: Betänkande av Utredningen om utländska aborter*, Edita Sverige AB 2005, pp. 37–38.

3   For broader context see: J. Hunt, "Out of Respect for Life: Nazi Abortion Policy in the Eastern Occupied Territories," *Journal of Genocide Research*, 1999, 1(3), pp. 379–385.

4   *Journal of Acts of 1956*, No. 12, item 61 as amended; for broader context see: M. Lipczyńska, *Ochrona płodu w ustawie z 27 kwietnia 1956 r. i projekcie kodeksu karnego*, Nauka i Prawo 1957, n. 1, p. 23; K. Żmudziński, *Luka w przepisach karnych dotyczących ochrony ciąży*, Nauka i Prawo 1958, n 3, p. 100–102; E. Zielińska, *Przerywanie...*, p. 56.

5   The Journal of Acts of 1993, No. 17, item 78; for broader context see: E. Zielińska, *Przerywanie...*, pp. 69–71; Z. Jędrzejewski, M. Królikowski, R. Kubiak, J. Kulesza, J. Lachowski [in:] L. Paprzycki (ed.), *Nauka o przestępstwie. Wyłączenie i ograniczenie odpowiedzialności karnej. System Prawa Karnego. Tom 4.*, Warszawa, 2016, p. 514–516.

Subsequently in 1996, when post-communist parties came back to power, the parliament passed an Act of 30 August 1996 amending the 1993 Act[6] (1996 Act), which diminished considerably the life-protecting measures. The most important change consisted of the reintroducing of the so-called "social reasons" premise for legal abortion ("abortion because of harsh living conditions or difficult personal situation"). It was *de facto* abortion on demand. The 1996 Act was challenged by a group of MPs who initiated constitutional review.

The Constitutional Tribunal issued on 28 May 1997 the famous judgement K 26/96[7] (K 26/96 judgement). The judgement is of crucial importance to the whole Polish law protecting human life. Its importance has three principal dimensions: 1) introduced the right to life to Polish fundamental rights catalogue and provided its proper understanding as encompassing also prenatal phase of human development; 2) extended constitutional protection of health to the unborn; 3) prohibited abortion for, so-called, social reasons, being *de facto* abortion for demand; thus, the abortion premise was declared to be unconstitutional.

The K 26/96 judgement is truly a landmark case of great importance to Polish constitutional law in general as well as for the law protecting the life of children before birth. Therefore, the argumentation used in this case will be presented below. In order to better understand these arguments, it is important to present a brief outline of constitutional law in the last decade of 20th century, which was a transitory period in Polish constitutionalism after the communist party gave up its political power, giving place to the establishment of democratic rule.

1.2 Polish Constitutional Law in the Last Decade of the 20th Century

Political developments of 1989 in Poland, which triggered further developments in the remaining countries of the Communist bloc, launched a long spell of gradual transformation of the political and legal realities in those countries, making them compatible with the standards of a liberal democracy. In Poland however, the process of gradual institutional change had started earlier, with the reestablishment of the Chief Administrative Court in 1980, followed by the institutionalization of constitutional liability of its ministers before the Tribunal of the State (1983), then the introduction of constitutional review and the establishment of the Constitutional Tribunal (1986), and finally introduction of the Ombudsman (1987).

The famous year 1989 witnessed spectacular political transgressions, which however were not as significant in the legal dimension, as one might expect.[8]

---

6 The Journal of Acts of 1996, No. 139, item 646.
7 Case law of the constitutional court (2) 1997, p. 159.
8 For broader context *see*: A. Lijphart, "Democratization and Constitutional Choices in Czecho-Slovakia, Hungary and Poland 1989–91," *Journal of Theoretical Politics*, 1992, vol. 4, issue 2, pp. 207–223.

Nevertheless, at the end of 1989, one profound change of the communist constitution took place and determined the development of Polish constitutional law, initiating a seven-year-long waiting period for the adoption of a new Constitution of the Republic of Poland in 1997—that is now in force[9]. This crucial change consisted on the change of Article 1 of the communist constitution of 1952,[10] which since then was describing the Republic of Poland as a "democratic state under the rule of law."[11] Subsequently on 17 October 1992, a new Constitutional Act (in contrast to the Constitution itself) was established, which had, however, only an *interim* character and very limited scope of application. It was regulating only political matters of mutual relations between the legislative power and the executive power of the Republic of Poland and the local self-government.[12] Therefore, a vast bulk of old provisions from the communistic constitution of 1952 was maintained.

In effect, between December 1989 and April 1997, Poland has experienced a long transitional period which often is described as "constitutional provisionary."[13] The period was marked by a deficit of constitutional provisions guaranteeing fundamental rights. This meant that the extent of the discretion open to the Polish legislature was very broad. However, the Constitutional Court embarked on narrowing this down, chiefly on the grounds of the *Rechtsstaat* principle (*the state under the rule of law*), as declared in Article 1 as amended in December 1989. In a series of far-reaching rulings, the Court reduced the substantive scope of the discretion open to the legislature by declaring a set of constitutional principles—the "substantive content of the principle of *the state under the rule of law*"—and making them mandatory. For this reason, *the state under the rule of law* is sometimes in Polish constitutional doctrine named as a "meta-principle," being the source of subsequent general, constitutional principles.[14] The list of deduced principles started with the principle of the protection of human dignity, then privacy, followed by

---

9 For broader context *see*: A. Stępkowski, *Zasada proporcjonalności w europejskiej kulturze prawnej. Kontrola władzy dyskrecjonalnej w nowoczesnej Europie*, Warszawa, 2010, pp. 327–331.
10 The Journal of Acts of 1952, No. 33, item 232.
11 For broader context see: A. Wołek, "Lustration/Decomunisation as an Instrument to Enhance Legitimacy: The Influences of the Past on the Present Rules of Politics" [in:] A. M. Blasko, D. Januauskiene, *Political Transformation and Changing Identities in Central and Eastern Europe*, Council for Research in Values & Philosophy 2008, pp. 244–249.
12 The Journal of Acts of 1992, No. 84, item 426.
13 L. Garlicki, *Polskie prawo konstytucyjne. Zarys wykładu*, Warszawa, 2004, p. 61. For similar situation which took place in Hungary, *see*: M. Granat, *Sądowa kontrola konstytucyjności prawa w państwach Europy Środkowej i Wschodniej (na tle niektórych zasad ustrojowych)*, Warszawa, 2003, pp. 237–238.
14 For more detailed examination of this issue *see*: E. Morawska, *Klauzula państwa prawnego w Konstytucji RP na tle orzecznictwa Trybunału Konstytucyjnego*, Toruń, 2003.

the procedural guarantee of the right to a fair trial, and finally the right to life.[15] The right to life was declared in the K 26/96 constitutional judgement, which is presented below. It is worth mentioning however, that the case was determined when the new, regular Constitution of the Republic of Poland of 2 April 1997[16] was already enacted and waiting for entry into force on October 1997, containing constitutional provisions protecting human life in its Article 38.[17]

1.3 Statutory Context of the K 26/96 Judgement

The 1993 Act in its Article 1 introduced a general rule that provided for general protection of all human beings at every stage of their lives. According to Article 1 of the Act, "every human being has an inherent right to life from conception." It was however modified in 1996 so that human life in the prenatal stage of development would be protected only as far as statutory regulations expressly provided for it. By means of the new provision, unborn children appeared to be excluded in principle from legal protection, and granted protection only as a matter of exception if expressly stated by statute.

The 1993 Act introduced also a new provision protecting the health of the unborn. It was Article 23b, with the corresponding amendment of the criminal code, Article 156a. By virtue of Article 23b section 1, subjection of an unborn baby to actions other than those directed towards preserving the life or health of the baby or its mother was prohibited. In Article 23b section 2, the legislation allowed prenatal screening only if it did not increase the risk of miscarriage and there was a reasonable suspicion of either treatable genetic disease or serious impairment of the foetus. As concerns new article 156a introduced to the criminal code, it provided for the penalty of causing harm to the unborn baby's body or health leading to death, unless the prohibited action had a therapeutic purpose benefiting the woman or the child. The 1996 Act overruled articles 23b of the 1993 Act as well as Article 156a of the Criminal Code which denied protection of the health of the unborn.

Apart from the general rule protecting human life in its prenatal stage, the 1993 Act also inserted a new article 149a into the criminal code. This new provision introduced some exceptions to the general rule protecting human life from conception. It provided for impunity from causing death to the unborn child 1) if pregnancy endangered the mother's life or health; 2) if the unborn child died in the course of action directed towards saving the mother's life; 3) if the prenatal screening disclosed severe and irreversible defects of foetus; 4) if there was a reasonable suspicion that pregnancy was a result of a criminal offence.

---

15 Ibidem, s. 271–183, 290–337.
16 The Journal of Acts of 1997, No. 78, item 483.
17 According to article 38 of the Constitution 1997 "the Republic of Poland shall ensure the legal protection of the life of every human being."

The 1996 Act concurrently introduced those abortive premises (subject to some alterations in wording, which will not to be discussed here) into the Act itself as a new article, 4 a. This changed considerably the legal character of the abortive premises. By that time, as a matter of principle, abortion was a criminal offence, which was, however, in certain circumstances not prosecuted. Moreover, Article 4a contained one additional abortive premise, allowing abortion because of "harsh living conditions or difficult personal situation" up to the 12th week of pregnancy (Article 4a section 1 point 4). The "hard life conditions or challenging circumstances," known commonly as "social reasons," is such a vague term that it amounted functionally to abortion on demand.[18]

2 The Constitutional Case K 26/96 and Its Argument

2.1 Arguments by Applicants for Constitutional Review[19]

The applicants substantiated their request with a number of well-constructed arguments against the constitutionality of the Act 1996 and the penal code provisions as introduced by the statute. In the absence of the express constitutional proclamation of the right to life, the applicants appealed to the principles of a democratic state under the rule of law. They pointed out that legal provisions should respect inherent and inviolable human rights, especially the right to life of every human being. According to applicants, regulations as introduced by the Amending Act did not meet that requirement. Especially Article 1 section 2 of the 1996 Act had conditioned protection of the unborn child upon the decisions of the ordinary legislature, which amounted in practice to denial of such protection as a principle, making it exceptional.

Regarding the provision that had introduced *de facto* abortion on demand (harsh living conditions and difficult personal situation), the applicants asserted that it was unconstitutional due to the fact that such a regulation was in breach of the principle of solidarity. The legislature had given priority to any interest of the mother (her material living conditions and her personal situation) over the most fundamental, existential interest of her unborn child in the continuation of his/her life. Thus, the legislature had decided to protect a legal good of lower value to the detriment of a fundamental good (human life).

Applicants pointed out that regulations arbitrarily differentiated among the situations of human beings according to the phase of their development. They considered such a differentiation as completely contrary to the constitutional principle of justice and lacking any objective, persuasive criteria. In effect, such a

---

18 For broader context *see*: Z. Jędrzejewski, M. Królikowski, R. Kubiak, J. Kulesza, J. Lachowski [in:] L. Paprzycki (ed.), *Nauka . . .*, pp. 514–515.
19 K 26/96 judgement, at. 1.1.

differentiation was always arbitrary and thus unjust in light of the right to life of every human being. For the same reason, the 1996 Act, in the opinion of applicants, violated the principle of equality with reference to unborn and already born children. The applicants asserted that the criterion of birth was not relevant regarding the protection of life, and as such, it should be considered arbitrary and thus discriminatory.

Finally, the applicants pointed out that the amended provisions violated constitutional guarantees protecting motherhood and family. Motherhood implies a mother-child relationship and—being a protected constitutional value—protects also the unborn child. Similarly, the family category should be understood as including also the unborn child as a necessary personal and structural element of it, and thus the child should benefit from family protection as well.

2.2 Counter-Argument by the Prosecutor General[20]

The prosecutor general argued that there were neither constitutional regulations nor criminal law provisions containing norms which explicitly protected human life in its prenatal phase. Therefore, the prosecutor argued, there were no grounds for such protection. He raised as an example the Irish Constitutional provision protecting unborn life as an argument for his position. Basically, the argument was based on presumption of the lack of protection for unborn babies except in the case it was provided by express written legislative statements. Likewise, a similar construction of Article 2 of the Convention for the Protection of Human Rights and Fundamental Freedoms and Article 6 paragraph 1 of the International Covenant on Civil and Political Rights was presented.

The prosecutor general was arguing that the scope of the protection of human life could be different depending on the preferences of current social opinion. Another argument was that the 1993 Act provided regulations that would be inefficient if plaintiffs prevailed and would result in expanding illegal abortion, as well as abortion tourism. Regretfully, this opinion was not supported with studies or empirical data.

Referring to the "social reasons" abortive premise, the prosecutor general asserted that it corresponds to social expectations and should be considered as an alternative way of decreasing the number of abortions, which allegedly would otherwise be performed illegally. The prosecutor general also argued that the protection of motherhood referred only to the relation of the mother with her already born child and not with the child she was carrying in her womb. The argumentation concluded with some "classical" pro-choice *topics*, rising doubts and uncertainties as to the human status of the foetus, who was presented as a prospective person in comparison to the mother being already an actual person.

---

20 Ibidem, at. 1.2.

3 Constitutional Review of Pro-Abortion Statutory Provisions

The Constitutional Tribunal ruled some provisions of 1996 Act were unconstitutional, due to incompatibility with the principle of democratic state under the rule of law. In effect it was partially re-establishing some of the 1993 Act provisions. As was already stated, the judgement in K 26/96 case has three principal effects. Firstly, it declared the constitutional principle of protection of human life regardless of its stage of development[21]; secondly, it provided constitutional protection for the health of the unborn children[22]; thirdly, it prohibited abortion for so-called social causes, being *de facto* abortion on demand.[23]

3.1 Protection of Human Life and Its Extent

As was already mentioned, there was no explicit right to life in Polish constitutional provisions then in force. Accordingly, the tribunal was applying to a large extent a proactive interpretation, referring most often to the principle of the democratic state under the rule of law.[24] Further, the Constitutional Tribunal might have been encouraged to make its proactive interpretation because it knew of the already enacted, although still in its *vacatio legis* period, new Constitution of 1997, which provided for the protection of life for everyone in Article 38. This however was of psychological importance, not legal.

At the very beginning of the discussion, the Constitutional Tribunal asked the general question: whether and to what extent existing constitutional provisions were providing protection for life and health of the foetus. The question was not easy to answer, as there was virtually no constitutional provision protecting human life at that time. The search for a textual basis for constitutional protection of human life was therefore directed towards Article 1 of the temporarily upheld constitutional provisions of the 1952 Constitution, as amended in 1989, declaring the Republic of Poland to be a democratic state under the rule of law.[25]

---

21 Ibidem, at. 3.
22 Ibidem.
23 Ibidem, at. 4.3.
24 For broader context *see*: A. Miętek, *Zasada demokratycznego państwa prawnego w orzecznictwie Trybunału Konstytucyjnego*, Dialogi Polityczne (11) 2009, p. 75–84; L. Morawski, *Wstęp do prawoznawstwa*, Toruń, 2006, pp. 61–62; E. Morawska, *Klauzula państwa prawnego w Konstytucji RP na tle orzecznictwa Trybunału Konstytucyjnego*, Toruń, 2003, s. 53.
25 K 26/96 judgement, at. 4.3.

3.2 Democratic State under the Rule of Law

In the absence of directly protective constitutional measures, the Constitutional Tribunal held that in its very nature the principle of a democratic state requires constitutional protection of human life. Therefore, constitutional protection of human life is a necessary element of the principle of the democratic state under the rule of law as declared in amended Article 1 of the constitutional provisions in force in from 1952, that were upheld.[26] The Constitutional Tribunal emphasized that human life is essential and necessary for any form of community life and therefore it must be protected as a basic requirement for the very existence of society. Moreover, the Constitutional Tribunal expressly stated that the said rule requires that protection of human life starts from the very moment of its conception, as there is neither precise nor justified criteria to make any differentiation otherwise. Therefore, there is no doubt that the life conceived from man and woman must be considered as human life.[27]

However, the Tribunal also stated that the fact that human life in every phase of its development is of constitutional value does not mean that the intensity of this protection at any stage of life and in all circumstances should always be the same. The intensity and the type of legal protection depend on several factors of various nature, which must be taken into account by the ordinary legislator determining the appropriate type of legal protection and its intensity. However, the Constitutional Tribunal underlined that the level of protection must always be sufficient. The Tribunal did not specify whether it meant that the intensity of the protection of the unborn could be lower than for those already born.[28] Rational analysis suggests, rather, the opposite solution, as the unborn children, being much more vulnerable, deserve more and not less intensive protection. The Constitutional Tribunal also specified that protection of human life cannot be understood solely as a protection of minimum biological functions which are necessary for the basic existence. It must be understood in a way that supports proper development, including protection of mental and physical health.[29]

The Constitutional principle of the democratic state under the rule of law was not, however, the only one which grounded constitutional protection of human life.

---

26 For broader context *see*: L. Bosek [in:] M. Safjan, *Prawo wobec medycyny i biotechnologii: Zbiór orzeczeń z komentarzami*, Warszawa, 2011, pp. 38–41.
27 K 26/96 judgement, at. 4.3; see also: Constitutional Tribunal judgement on 7 January 2004, K 14/03, Case law of the constitutional court A (1) 2004, p. 1.
28 K 26/96 judgement.
29 Ibidem.

3.3 Motherhood and Family

According to Article 79 section 1 of the constitutional provisions,[30] matrimony, motherhood and family enjoy the assistance and protection of the Republic of Poland. The Constitutional Tribunal referred to this provision as declaring constitutional values that must be protected in a democratic state.[31]

It was stressed that the scope of the motherhood protection covers not only interests of the mother (including during the period of pregnancy) but also interests of her child.[32] Most important, however, is that the aforesaid guarantee points to a specific relationship between a woman and her child, including the unborn one. Similarly, protection of the family should be understood as encompassing the bundle of interpersonal relations, particularly those between parents and children. In this context, the Tribunal emphasized the importance of the procreative function of the family. Therefore, life of the conceived child must enjoy protection as provided by the constitutional provisions protecting motherhood and the family. Moreover, that protection must not be limited to the relationship between parents and their already born children. It must be extended to children in the prenatal stage of their life.[33] Therefore, constitutional protection of family and motherhood must cover development of parents and their children at every stage of their life.[34]

3.4 International Law

The Constitutional Tribunal focused its attention on the context of the whole legal system, providing clear affirmation of the existence of human life before birth as well as the necessity for its protection. The most persuasive argument in this respect was the prohibition of imposition of the death penalty on a pregnant woman. There is no other reason for such a position than the recognition of the value of conceived life.[35] This position was also reflected in the content of international standards,[36] which require protection for children before they are born.

---

30 These are the provisions of the communist Constitution 1952 upheld in force by the Art. 77 of the *interim* Constitutional Act 1992 which were continuing their legal existence until entry into force of the new Constitution 1997.
31 K 26/96 judgement, at. 3.
32 Ibidem.
33 For broader context *see*: L. Garlicki [in:] L. Garlicki, *Konstytucja Rzeczypospolitej Polskiej. Komentarz. Tom III*, Warszawa, 2003, comment to Art. 18, p. 4
34 K 26/96 judgement, at. 3.
35 Ibidem.
36 This particular law provision is direct transposition of the Art. 6 section 5 of International Covenant on Civil and Political Rights providing that capital punishment "shall not be carried out on pregnant women." This UN treaty was however not referred to by the Polish Constitutional Tribunal.

Much attention was focused on the UN Convention on the Rights of the Child (CRC) of 20 November 1989, as ratified by the Republic of Poland.[37] This UN convention provided for useful *locum argumentationis* in this case, particularly the 10th paragraph of CRC's preamble declaring that "the child, because of his physical and mental immaturity, needs special safeguards and care, including appropriate legal protection, before as well as after birth." Also Article 24 section 1 of the CRC indicates the recognition of the right of the child to enjoy the best possible state of health. In the subsequent section 2, it is emphasized that there is a need for efforts to ensure the full realization of this right, including in particular (point d) "appropriate pre-natal and post-natal health care for mothers." This is a clear indication that right to "enjoyment of the highest attainable standard of health" must be attributed to children in the prenatal phase of their development and must be extended not only to the life but also to health of the unborn child.

3.5 Unconstitutionality of Provisions Disabling Protection of Unborn Child's Health

Continuing the argument about constitutional protection of unborn life, the Tribunal declared unconstitutional the deleting of article 23b of the 1993 Act.[38] The 1996 Act introduced in that way significant uncertainty whether the physical integrity of the foetus, as well as the process of its development were still protected by the law. Such a doubt is however unacceptable, as the above-mentioned goods are subject to constitutional protection extending to unborn children. The Tribunal decided the repeal effectuated by the 1996 Act drastically reduced the minimum standards of protection due to the unborn as required by the constitutional regulations. The same conclusion pertained to the repeal of Article 156a of the criminal code. The Constitutional Tribunal asserted that the health and undisturbed development of the human being at the prenatal stage are to be directly derived from the constitutional value of human life, which is to be protected also in its prenatal stage.[39]

According to the Tribunal, causing health problems or injury amounts to breach of a particularly important legal interest as it can result in the future permanent disability of a child. There are also no circumstances that might justify causing such a health problem or injury to the foetus, since it affects a completely defenseless and vulnerable human being. Such behavior can often be qualified as "cruel and inhuman" treatment, which is absolutely prohibited in international law.[40]

---

37 The Republic of Poland ratified the Convention on 30 September 1991 (Journal of Acts of 1991, No. 120, item 526).
38 K 26/96 judgement, at. 4.6.
39 Ibidem.
40 *See*: Art. 5 of Universal Declaration of Human Rights (1948); Art. 7 of International Covenant on Civil and Political Rights (1976); Art. 1 para. 1 of Convention against Torture and Other Cruel, Inhuman or Degrading Treatment or Punishment (1984).

Similarly, affording protection to unborn life and health by means only of the civil law is manifestly insufficient, especially since the child is obviously unable to pursue a personal action and the representation by its mother often would be inefficient. The Tribunal also stated there are good reasons for protection of the unborn child against intentional actions by his mother (or father with the consent of the mother) that would result in deterioration of its health, and that is not effectively compensated by means of a civil action.[41]

The answer was obvious: if the health impairment of the foetus is not penalized, then the constitutional value recognizing human health has no adequate protection in the prenatal phase. Thus, statutory provisions repealing such criminal protection infringe the constitutional requirement of "sufficient protection" to the life and health of unborn. Therefore, both those derogations (respectively Article 3 sect. 2 and 4 of the 1996 Act) were found to be unconstitutional by the Constitutional Tribunal, as they were limiting legal protection of the foetus' health. It was clarified, therefore, that Polish constitutional law contains specific requirements granting some minimum protection to unborn child in respect to its health.[42]

3.6 Abortion for Social Reasons

From the perspective of the whole legal system, the declaration that human life, including its prenatal phase, is to be constitutionally protected was of primary importance. However, in the practical dimension, there was an even more important issue. Therefore, Constitutional Tribunal paid much attention to the issue of the newly introduced abortive premise of "harsh living conditions or difficult personal situation" of mother, if the pregnancy had not exceeded 12 weeks. This abortive premise is commonly described as "abortion for social reasons" and due to the vagueness of this premise is considered as allowing *de facto* abortion on demand.

Basically, constitutional review was focused on the admissibility of imposing restrictions on certain values. Therefore, the Constitutional Tribunal followed a scheme of reasoning consisting of three questions: 1) whether the value to be restricted by statute is constitutionally protected; 2) whether the statutory restriction is motivated by the protection of other constitutional values; 3) whether the legislator complied with the constitutional criteria for solving such collisions, particularly the requirement of proportionality.[43] The said proportionality was understood as proportionality *sensu stricto*, as the first two questions constitute stages for the proportionality review in the broader sense.[44]

---

41 K 26/96 judgement, at. 4.6.
42 *Ibidem*; for broader context see: P. Sarnecki [in:] L. Garlicki, *Konstytucja*..., comment to Art. 38, pp. 7–8.
43 K 26/96 judgement, at. 4.3.
44 It is worth mentioning, that the judgement was issued in the period of formation of proportionality principle in Polish constitutional law. For more details about this

The Constitutional Tribunal reiterated its former conclusion about constitutional protection of human life including its prenatal stage. This imposed important restrictions upon the legislature, which has to set a proper balance between conflicting goods, using an adequate criteria of balancing.[45]

Then the Tribunal clarified the terms "harsh living conditions" and "difficult personal situation" in order to assess the constitutionality of the abortive premises. According to that construction, the expression "harsh living conditions" should be attributed to mother's material situation, which, due to gradual development of pregnancy and child delivery, may deteriorate or prevent its improvement.[46] Regarding the "difficult personal situation," the Constitutional Tribunal stated that it should be understood as a certain psychological state of a woman due to the fact of becoming pregnant. It can reflect relationships with others or limitations the woman is facing during the pregnancy. In this context, the Tribunal gave several reasons why such premises do not justify restrictions on the protection of human life in the prenatal stage of its development.[47]

First of all, neither of those reasons ("harsh living conditions" nor "difficult personal situation"), even if possibly rooted in some constitutional values, is sufficient to justify destruction of innocent human life before birth. Secondly, both premises are very vague in their meaning. Therefore, it is unacceptable to restrict (actually, deny) protection of the fundamental right to life with such vague reasons. Thirdly, constitutional protection of motherhood and family assume that parental responsibilities emerging from the fact of conception could not be considered as a reason for limiting protection of life of the unborn child.[48] These parental obligations are inherent to motherhood and family life, which are constitutionally protected. Therefore, destruction of an unborn child would amount to destruction of another constitutional value—motherhood. Therefore, such destruction is not consistent with the Constitution.[49]

The Constitutional Tribunal also emphasized that the threshold of 12 weeks of pregnancy, which would allow performance of allowed abortion for social reasons, is arbitrary. Moreover, the argument that "social reasons" justify abortion up to 12 weeks is self-contradictory. If the reasons should be constitutionally accepted before the 12th week, they should be also accepted later. The reasons do not cease to exist after the 12th week—to the contrary, the intensity of difficulties for pregnant women after 12th week could be much greater than in earlier stages

---

process: A. Stępkowski, *Zasada proporcjonalności w europejskiej kulturze prawnej. Kontrola władzy dyskrecjonalnej w nowoczesnej Europie*, Warszawa, 2010, pp. 331–345.
45 K 26/96 judgement, at. 4.3.
46 Ibidem.
47 Ibidem.
48 Ibidem.
49 For broader context *see*: D. Dudek [in:] D. Dudek (ed.), *Zasady Ustroju III Rzeczypospolitej Polskiej*, Warszawa, 2009, pp. 82–86.

of pregnancy. Moreover, all the difficulties arising for mother and father from the conception of their new child do not end with the child's delivery. To the contrary, the difficulties become increasingly complex. If such difficulties could be reasonably believed as justifying abortion, the same reasons would justify infanticide (killing babies already born).

The Constitutional Tribunal referred also to the argument about freedom to decide whether to have a baby or not. This argument was carefully considered and the conclusion was the following: the right to make responsible decisions about having children pertains not only to the mother but to both parents, and can be exercised only before the child is conceived.[50] When the child is developing in the prenatal stage, it is too late for a decision whether "to have a baby." Therefore, it is constitutionally impermissible to legalize abortion for social reasons. Constitutional values, which might allegedly justify abortion, by no means have preference over the fundamental value of human life.

3.7 Important *obiter dicta*

As was already mentioned, the judgement was delivered during the *vacatio legis* period of the new (regular) Constitution of Poland. The Constitutional Tribunal emphasized, therefore, that the Constitution of 1997, which was about to enter into force, provided for legal protection of everyone's life in its Article 38. The constitutional basis on which the judgement K 26/96 was based found its clear articulation in article 38 of the Constitution of 1997. Therefore, the Tribunal clarified that the way the right to life was construed in the judgement must be also applied in the future for the construction of the Article 38[51].

4 Conclusion

Despite lack of clear constitutional provisions protecting right to life, constitutional judges were able to establish, by means of intensive interpretation, the constitutional principle of the protection of life at every stage of its development, including the prenatal phase. The Constitutional Tribunal was unable to find objective, scientifically based, non-arbitrary criterion that would justify a different constitutional approach. The Tribunal also rejected the argument that other constitutional values, including personal freedom, prevail over human life. This precedent setting interpretation was based first of all upon the principle of the democratic state under the rule of law; however, an additional rationale was provided by constitutional protection of family and motherhood.

The judgement K 26/96 did not repeal the entire 1996 Act but only its most significant elements. Therefore, Polish law still is protecting unborn human life in a

---

50 Ibidem.
51 Ibidem, at. 4.9.

far from perfect way. There are some contradictions within statutory enactments,[52] which introduce much inconsistency into the existing law. Different public authorities are adopting different approaches to this issue and some are even contrary to the constitutional construction provided by the Tribunal in the case K 26/96.[53]

The judgement has, however, allowed concurrent social action, as undertaken by civil society and the Catholic Church, for considerable change in Polish culture. The change resulted in the great reduction of the number of legal abortions to a few hundred per year. Since 2011, civic legislative initiatives repeatedly are being launched, aiming at provision of better, or complete,[54] protection of children before delivery. So far they are unsuccessful and the statutory enactments concerning protection of life in its prenatal stage, as determined in K 26/96 judgement, remains in force. However, new civic initiatives are still launched as well as a new motion for constitutional review of the eugenic premise for abortion that was filed in the Constitutional Tribunal on 27 of October 2017. The Tribunal will have the opportunity to revisit the issue of the protection of human life in the prenatal stage, 20 years after the K 26/96 judgement. Finally, it is worth emphasizing that K 26/96 judgement had a huge impact on Constitutional Tribunal case-law. It was cited many times in other tribunals, Supreme Courts and Supreme Administrative Court judgements.[55]

---

52 The most apparent contradictions concern absolute impunity of the mother killing her baby before delivery, as well as Article 4b as introduced by the 1996 Act which is declaring that a person having health insurance has right to abortion performed free of charge in public hospitals. There are good arguments to say that "the right" is to be referred to have abortion unpaid and not to abortion itself; however, considerable inconsistency within the legal system remains. For presentation of complicated complexity of regulations protecting human life in the prenatal stage of development *see*: T. Chauvin, *Homo Iuridicus. Człowieka jako podmiot prawa publicznego*, Warszawa, 2014, pp. 325–340.

53 Apparently unconstitutional position has been presenting Patients' Rights Ombudsman who insisted that the removal (by the 1996 Act) of the § 2 in Article 8 of the Civil Code amounting to denial of acquiring civil (private law) rights by *nasciturus* prevents considering the unborn child from being subject to patient's rights. This apparently unconstitutional interpretation was for a long time official position of the Patients Ombudsman. It should be hoped that current change in this position would allow removing this unconstitutionality.

54 For detailed account of the civic initiative supported by 458,000 of citizens in 2016, *see*: K. Jusińska, J. Kwaśniewski, K. Pawłowska, O. Szczypiński, K. Walinowicz, T. Zych, *Równa ochrona prawna dla każdego dziecka zarówno przed, jak i po urodzeniu*, Warszawa, 2016.

55 *See*: Supreme Court judgement on 30 November 2016, III PK 17/16, C. H. Beck, Legalis Legal System; Supreme Administrative Court judgement on 22 September 2016, II GSK 695/15, C. H. Beck, Legalis Legal System; Supreme Administrative Court judgement on 19 May 2016, II OSK 2190/14, C. H. Beck, Legalis Legal System; Constitutional Tribunal judgement on 7 October 2015, K 12/14, Case law of the constitutional court A (9) 2015, p. 143; Supreme Court judgement on 13 May 2015, III

From the universal perspective, judicial activism is considered as profound endangerment for the protection of human life in the prenatal stage of its development. Polish judgement K 26/96 shows it might be also very much protective in respect to the weakest and defenseless. This demonstrates that the issue of the protection of the unborn is to be understood primarily as a culture issue and not a legal one. Law is an important culture-setting factor; however, law is also determined by the overall culture, both when the statutes are drafted and when they are interpreted and applied. Polish legislation concerning abortion is very similar to Germany's or to the Spanish law before President Zapatero. However, it is applied in a very much different way. In effect, all legal abortions performed in Poland represent less than 1% of abortions performed in Germany with the similar legal conditions for abortion. Therefore, efficient protection of the youngest and the weakest children has to combine legal action with social engagement changing contemporary culture in a life-friendly way.

Bibliography

Abort i Sverige: Betänkande av Utredningen om utländska aborter, Edita Sverige AB 2005.

Bosek L. [in:] M. Safjan, *Prawo wobec medycyny i biotechnologii: Zbiór orzeczeń z komentarzami*, Warszawa, 2011.

Chauvin T., *Homo Iuridicus. Człowieka jako podmiot prawa publicznego*, Warszawa, 2014.

Doan A. E., *Opposition and Intimidation: The Abortion Wars and Strategies of Political Harassment*, University of Michigan, 2007.

Dudek D. [in:] Dudek D. (ed.), *Zasady Ustroju III Rzeczypospolitej Polskiej*, Warszawa 2009.

Gałązka M., "Polish Penal Law on the Human Being in Prenatal Stage" [in:] Stępkowski A. (ed.), *Protection of Human Life in It's Prenatal Stage*, Peter Lang Edition 2014.

Garlicki L. [in:] L. Garlicki, *Konstytucja Rzeczypospolitej Polskiej. Komentarz. Tom III*, Warszawa 2003, comment to Art. 18.

CSK 286/14, *Supreme Court Bulletin* (9) 2015; Constitutional Tribunal Judgement on 9 October 2012, P 27/11, Case law of the constitutional court A (9) 2012, p. 104; Constitutional Tribunal Judgement on 22 July 2008, K 24/07, Case law of the constitutional court A (6) 2008, p. 110; Supreme Court resolution on 26 October 2006, I KZP 18/06, *Supreme Court Bulletin* (10) 2006; Supreme Court resolution on 22 February 2006, III CZP 8/06, *Supreme Court Bulletin* (2) 2006; Constitutional Tribunal judgement on 9 October 2001, SK 8/00, Case law of the constitutional court (7) 2001, p. 211.

Garlicki L., *Polskie prawo konstytucyjne. Zarys wykładu*, Warszawa, 2004.

Granat M., *Sądowa kontrola konstytucyjności prawa w państwach Europy Środkowej i Wschodniej (na tle niektórych zasad ustrojowych)*, Warszawa, 2003.

Hunt J., "Out of Respect for Life: Nazi Abortion Policy in the Eastern Occupied Territories," *Journal of Genocide Research*, 1999, n. 1(3).

Jędrzejewski Z., Królikowski M., Kubiak R., Kulesza J., Lachowski J. [in:] Paprzycki L. (ed.), *Nauka o przestępstwie. Wyłączenie i ograniczenie odpowiedzialności karnej. System Prawa Karnego. Tom 4.*, Warszawa, 2016.

Jusińska K., Kwaśniewski J., Pawłowska K., Szczypiński O., Walinowicz K., Zych T., *Równa ochrona prawna dla każdego dziecka zarówno przed, jak i po urodzeniu*, Warszawa, 2016.

Lijphart A., "Democratization and Constitutional Choices in CzechoSlovakia, Hungary and Poland 1989-91," *Journal of Theoretical Politics*, 1992, vol. 4, issue 2.

Lipczyńska M., *Ochrona płodu w ustawie z 27 kwietnia 1956 r. i projekcie kodeksu karnego*, Nauka i Prawo 1957, n. 1.

Miętek A., *Zasada demokratycznego państwa prawnego w orzecznictwie Trybunału Konstytucyjnego*, Dialogi Polityczne (11) 2009.

Mohr J.C., *Abortion in America: The Origins and Evolution of National Policy*, Oxford University Press, 1978.

Morawska E., *Klauzula państwa prawnego w Konstytucji RP na tle orzecznictwa Trybunału Konstytucyjnego*, Toruń 2003.

Morawski L., *Wstęp do prawoznawstwa*, Toruń 2006.

Stępkowski A., *Zasada proporcjonalności w europejskiej kulturze prawnej. Kontrola władzy dyskrecjonalnej w nowoczesnej Europie*, Warszawa 2010.

Wołek A., "Lustration/Decomunisation as an Instrument to Enhance Legitimacy: The Influences of the Past on the Present Rules of Politics" [in:] Blasko A.M., Januauskiene D., *Political Transformation and Changing Identities in Central and Eastern Europe*, Council for Research in Values & Philosophy 2008.

Zielińska E., *Przerywanie ciąży. Warunki legalności w Polsce i na świecie*, Warszawa 1990.

Żmudziński K., *Luka w przepisach karnych dotyczących ochrony ciąży*, Nauka i Prawo 1958, n. 3.

Cases:

Constitutional Tribunal judgement of 28 May 1997, K 26/96, Orzecznictwo Trybunału Konstytucyjnego (2) 1997.

Constitutional Tribunal judgement of 9 October 2001, SK 8/00, Orzecznictwo Trybunału Konstytucyjnego (7) 2001.

Constitutional Tribunal judgement of 7 January 2004, K 14/03, Orzecznictwo Trybunału Konstytucyjnego A (1) 2004.

Constitutional Tribunal judgement of 22 July 2008, K 24/07, Orzecznictwo Trybunału Konstytucyjnego A (6) 2008.

Constitutional Tribunal judgement of 9 October 2012, P 27/11, Orzecznictwo Trybunału Konstytucyjnego A (9) 2012.

Constitutional Tribunal judgement of 7 October 2015, K 12/14, Orzecznictwo Trybunału Konstytucyjnego A (9) 2015.

Supreme Administrative Court judgement of 19 May 2016, II OSK 2190/14.

Supreme Administrative Court judgement of 22 September 2016, II GSK 695/15.

Supreme Court judgement of 30 November 2016, III PK 17/16.

Supreme Court judgement of 13 May 2015, III CSK 286/14, Biuletyn Sądu Najwyższego (9) 2015.

Supreme Court resolution of 26 October 2006, I KZP 18/06, Biuletyn Sądu Najwyższego (10) 2006.

Supreme Court resolution of 22 February 2006, III CZP 8/06, Biuletyn Sądu Najwyższego (2) 2006.

William Binchy

7 The Unborn Children and the Irish Constitution, Including Analysis of the Role of the European Court of Human Rights

Abstract: In 1983 the Eighth Amendment added explicit protection to the life of unborn children in the Irish Constitution. In this chapter, I review the difficulties to affording this protection presented by a number of decisions and determinations of courts and international agencies, and I assess their influence in the recent referendum, in May 2018, which resulted in the removal of constitutional protection for unborn children. I argue that the Irish people have been strongly affected by international influences that represent access to abortion as a right. The future presents great challenges; yet, when one reviews the past, one finds that it too presented formidable difficulties for those seeking to protect unborn lives.

Keywords: Eighth Amendment, X case, *Roche vs. Roche*, *A, B and C V Ireland*, *Mellet vs. Ireland*

1 Introduction

The recent referendum in Ireland, in May 2018, which resulted in the removal of constitutional protection for unborn children, creates huge new challenges for those who value the lives of unborn human beings. There is good reason to hope that this massive reverse is not permanent and that it will be possible over time to rekindle a strong social pro-life culture. Irish people have undoubtedly been strongly affected by international influences that represent access to abortion as a right, but they have scarcely abandoned wholesale their deeper responses to the profound philosophical questions that we all have to confront. The future presents great challenges; yet, when one reviews the past, one finds that it too presented formidable difficulties for those seeking to protect unborn lives.

In this chapter, I review the past, examining the difficulties that have confronted the pro-life cause in Ireland.

2 The Historical Background

Ireland, the object of political and military intervention by Britain for centuries, gained independence for 26 of its 32 counties in 1922.[1] The other six counties, in the northern part of the country, remained part of the United Kingdom, and that

---

1   *See* Binchy, "The Supreme Court of Ireland," Chapter 5 of B Dickson, ed., *Judicial Activism in Common Law Supreme Courts*, at 169–170 (2007).

situation continues to the present day. In both parts of Ireland, the common law system of England continues to apply. The common law tradition, which has many virtues, finds difficulties in the context of human rights protection that it tends to eschew deep philosophical and normative analysis in favour of more casuistic, pragmatic resolutions of individual cases.

In 1937, in the independent part of Ireland, a Constitution[2] was promulgated, which included what we would now call human rights provisions, based on the premise that human beings have inherent worth, dignity and equality and a range of inherent rights and duties that are not the gift of legislators but rather are anterior to positive law.[3] Its anticipation of the Universal Declaration of Universal Rights, formulated 11 years later, is striking. The Constitution embraced, without apology, a natural law philosophy, which allows courts to assess whether enactments of the legislature or acts of the executive comply with the requirements of true law, in their respect for the human rights of those who fall within their limit.

It has to be acknowledged that this approach to law found little support among the Irish judiciary, schooled in the tradition of the common law and echoing an Anglocentric embrace of parliamentary sovereignty. It took the efforts of two judges, Brian Walsh and Chief Justice Cearbhaill O Dalaigh, to drive forward the judicial implementation of the Constitution's philosophy.[4] Walsh J, in particular, was an intellectual force towering over the Irish legal system.[5] With his retirement in 1990, it can be said that the Irish Constitution lost its true champion

---

2   See Kelly, *The Irish Constitution* (4th edn., by Hogan & Whyte, 2004), Doyle, *Constitutional Law: Texts, Cases and Materials* (2008).
3   See Binchy, "Dignity as a Constitutional Concept," in Carolan & Doyle, eds., *The Irish Constitution: Governance and Values*, 308 (2008).
4   Cf Hogan, "Mr Justice Brian Walsh: The Legacy of Experiment and the Triumph of Judicial Imagination" 57 Ir Jur (ns) 1, at 3 (2017): "It is hard to overestimate the task faced by Walsh and Ó Dálaigh. The idea of a written constitution with fundamental rights still seemed unreal to a generation of judges and lawyers immersed in the rigid orthodoxies of the common law, even though this had been the promise of both 1922 and 1937. Given that Walsh was starting from—almost—a blank sheet, some element of trial and error was necessary. In many ways, it is remarkable not only that so much of the jurisprudence of this era has stood the test of time, but that so much of the case law from this period is regarded as the foundational cement of the entire edifice of the modern legal system."
5   Gearty, "Book Review" 28 Ir Jur (ns) 620, at 620 (1993), observed that Walsh J was "rightly regarded as one of the finest defenders of civil liberties ever to have held judicial office in western Europe." See also Hogan, "The Early Judgments of Mr. Justice Brian Walsh" in O'Reilly (ed.), *Human Rights and Constitutional Law: Essays in Honour of Brian Walsh* (1992), 37.

and that its philosophy has found few judges[6] with such a strong sympathy for it.[7]

The Constitution, as originally promulgated, said nothing explicit about abortion. The general assumption, so deeply accepted as not to merit express articulation, was that unborn children fell well within the umbrella of protection afforded to all human beings by the Constitution.

It was only when courts in other jurisdictions rapidly developed a constitutional jurisprudence favouring the right to abortion that the question came to be considered whether the Irish Constitution had been drafted in a way that would ensure effective protection for the right to life of unborn children should that right come under attack in the courts or the legislature. Some commentators [8] took the view that the Constitution did indeed protect the unborn against abortion; there were some judicial *dicta*, of varying degrees of force and specificity, which lent weight to this view.

Other commentators were less sure that the Constitution afforded adequate protection to the unborn against abortion, since it expressly limited its guarantee of the right to life to "every citizen" (a term which did not include the unborn) and since a constitutional right of privacy might be invoked as a basis for legalised abortion.[9] International experience suggested that, in the absence of explicit protection of the right to life of the unborn, constitutions might prove vulnerable to arguments in favour of legalised abortion.[10]

---

6   Costello J was a noted exception. President of the High Court and a former Attorney General, Costello J had the intellectual stature and commitment to the Constitution's values equal to those of Walsh J. Examples of these qualities are his article "The Natural Law and the Irish Constitution" (1956) Studies 403 and his paper "Natural Law, the Constitution and the Courts" in Lynch and Meenan, eds., *Essays in Memory of Alexis Fitzgerald* (1987), 105.
7   Cf Hogan, *op cit* fn 4, *supra*, at 10–12: "[S]ubsequent generations of judges have not always fulfilled the promise held out by Walsh that the Constitution could and would be interpreted to ensure that th[e] highest standards of constitutional protections appropriate to a well-functioning free and democratic society would be secured... . Like Augustus of old, Walsh found a city of brick and left behind a city of marble, even if ... this marble city has itself fallen somewhat into decay over the last 25 years or so since his retirement from the Supreme Court in March 1990."
8   Notably O'Reilly, "Marital Privacy and Family Law" 65 Studies 8 (1977).
9   *See* Binchy, "Marital Privacy and Family Law: A Reply to Mr O'Reilly" 65 Studies 33 (1977).
10 *See* Michael, ' "Abortion and International Law: The Status and Possible Extension of Women's Rights to Privacy" 20 J of Family Law L 241 (1981); Glenn, "The Constitutional Validity of Abortion Legislation: A Comparative Note" 21 McGill LJ 673 (1975); Binchy, "The Need for a Constitutional Amendment," in Flannery ed., *Abortion and the Law* (1983), Chapter 11.

3 The Eighth Amendment

In 1983, after extended public debate, a national referendum passed the Eighth Amendment to the Constitution adding a new subsection to section 3 of Article 40. The subsection read as follows:

> The State acknowledges the right to life of the unborn and, with due regard to the equal right to life of the mother, guarantees in its laws to respect and, so far as practicable, by its laws to defend and vindicate that right.[11]

What is striking about the terms of this provision is that nowhere in it was there any reference to abortion. Instead, the provision articulated an acknowledgement by the State that unborn children have a right to life, no less valuable than that of their mothers, and a guarantee by the State to respect and, so far as practicable, defend and vindicate that right. Philosophically and normatively, Article 40.3.3 cohered completely with the philosophy and norms of the Constitution as originally promulgated. Article 40.3.3 made it plain that there is no hierarchy of entitlement to be protected from a direct attack on one's life. It is clear that the law does not distinguish between the lives of born people, so as to authorise the direct taking of the life of a born person, even where considerable relief to others would flow from such a termination. There is no calculus whereby a court is required to weigh the totality of the constitutional rights and obligations of other persons against the constitutional protection of a born person's life from direct extinction.

There is, however, a clear distinction of principle between directly taking a person's life and acting in a way that is directed to some other purpose which has the indirect result of leading to the death of that person, or of another, as an unintended side-effect. The most obvious example is in the area of the treatment of sick or terminally ill patients. If the purpose of a particular treatment is curative or

---

11 For a comprehensive analysis of the historical background to the amendment campaign and to the public debate surrounding it, see T. Hesketh, *The Second Partitioning of Ireland?* (1990). See also Quinlan, "The Right to Life of the Unborn—An Assessment of the Eighth Amendment to the Irish Constitution" [1984] Brigham Young LL L Rev 371; Hogan, "Law and Religion: Church-State Relations from Independence to the Present Day" (1988) 35 *Am J of Compar L* 47, at 74–83; Charleton, "Judicial Discretion in Abortion: The Irish Perspective" (1992) 6 *Internat J of L & the Family* 349, at 350–362; O'Leary & Hesketh, "The Irish Abortion and Divorce Amendment Campaigns" (1988) 3 Ir Political Studies 43, at 43–55, 58–59; Basil Chubb, *The Politics of the Irish Constitution* (1991), 52–55; Randall, "The Politics of Abortion in Ireland" ch. 5 of J. Lovenduski & J. Dutshoorn, eds., *The New Politics of Abortion* (1986); Girvin, "Social Change and Moral Politics: The Irish Constitutional Referendum 1983" (1986) 31 *Political Studies* 61; Speed, "The Struggle for Reproductive Rights: A Brief History in Its Political Context," in A Smyth, ed., *The Abortion Papers* (1992), 85; Barry, "Movement, Change and Reaction: The Struggle Over Reproductive Rights in Ireland," ibid., 107.

palliative and death results indirectly as an unintended side-effect, the treatment will be consistent with the protection that Article 40.3.3 afforded the patient.

In the context of the medical treatment of pregnant women, this distinction is of very considerable relevance since certain treatments and interventions can impact indirectly on the foetus, at times fatally. In this regard, as with the care of a terminally ill patient, intentionality is key. The purpose, and effect, of the Amendment was to preserve this vital distinction. That is why the Amendment contained the requirement *of due regard* for the equal right to life of the mother and a guarantee to defend and vindicate the right to life of the unborn *as far as practicable*. This distinction between an intentional attack on the life of the unborn, where the purpose is to end the life of the unborn child, and treatment for the mother that results in the unintended, though fully foreseen, death of the unborn child governed medical practice in the State both before and during the period of operation of the Amendment.[12]

3 The X Case

The Supreme Court was first called on to provide a definitive interpretation of Article 40.3.3 in *Attorney General v X*.[13] A 14-year-old girl became pregnant as a result of sexual abuse by a man in his forties, a friend of her family. The girl and her parents decided that she should go to England for an abortion. The parents made it known to the police in Ireland that they were considering this course and raised with them the possibility that someone could be present in England for the purpose of carrying out DNA tests on the aborted foetus by which it was thought that the identity of the father could be ascertained. Legal opinion was sought from the office of the director of Public Prosecutions. The director informed the attorney general, who sought an injunction restraining the first defendant from leaving the jurisdiction and from having an abortion.

---

12 In this context, one may note the statement of Peter Charleton (now a judge of the Supreme Court) that:

in all the cases where the courts have found a breach of the criminal law the primary purpose ... was itself unlawful.

Cases of oblique intention necessarily involve a wrongful act as the accused's primary purpose.... It is not inconsistent to argue that where the primary purpose of the accused is, in itself, lawful, an undesired but foreseen consequence does not come within the scope of an unlawful intention: "Judicial Discretion in Abortion: The Irish Perspective" (1992) 6 Internat J of L & the Family 349 at 360.

Mr Charleton's analysis was pertinent to section 58 of the Offences against the Person Act 1861, but it may be considered to assist one's understanding of Article 40.3.3.

13 [1992] 1 IR 1.

The High Court judge, Costello J, granted an injunction. He considered that the court had a duty to protect the girl's life "not just from the actions of others but from actions she may herself perform." What the court was therefore required to do was to assess by reference to the evidence the danger to the lives of the child and the mother. He was quite satisfied that there was a real and imminent danger to the life of the unborn and that, if the court did not step in to protect it by means of the injunction sought, its life would be terminated.

The Supreme Court lifted the injunction. By a majority of four [14] to one[15], it held that Article 40.3.3 permitted abortion where there is a real and substantial risk to the life, as distinct from the health, of the mother which can be avoided only by an abortion. The majority held, further, that this ground was established in the instant case.[16]

---

14 Finlay CJ, McCarthy, O'Flaherty and Egan JJ.
15 Hederman J.
16 On the question whether it was permissible, in other cases, to grant injunctions against travelling abroad to have an abortion, the Court divided somewhat differently. Finlay CJ, Hederman and Egan JJ considered that it was; McCarthy and O'Flaherty J took the opposite view. This aspect of the law was addressed later in 1992 by further referenda, which resulted in provisions protecting the right to travel, thus removing the possibility of an injunction of this kind being granted in the future, and the provision of information about the identity and locations of places abroad where abortions are carried out. The latter amendment to the Constitution was in due course followed by legislation giving statutory effect to its provisions. In a preliminary examination by the Supreme Court of its constitutional validity, under Article 26 of the Constitution (*Re Article 26 of the Constitution and the Regulation of Information (Services outside the State for Termination of Pregnancies) Bill 1995* [1995] 1 IR 1), counsel for the unborn argued that (as in the Indian Constitution, for example) there are implicit limits on the amendability of the Constitution, consistently with its fundamental norms. The natural law, the counsel said, was one such fundamental norm. This argument was unceremoniously dispatched by the Court in an intellectually primitive manner that provoked the stringent criticism of Constitutional Law expert, Gerry Whyte, "Natural Law and the Constitution" 14 Ir L Times (ns) 8 (1996):

   Essential premises are not properly established; judicial precedents and constitutional provisions which appear to endorse natural law theory are not properly engaged . . . ; and there is a failure to address obvious questions raised by the judgment, such as whether there is any residual role for natural law theory under the Constitution and if so, for which variants of that theory. Ultimately, it must be said, the Supreme Court's reasoning is somewhat simplistic and lacking in sophistication.

   In similar terms, another Constitutional Law expert, Dr. Gerard Quinn, in a paper delivered on 6 July 2000 at the University of San Sebastian Summer School, entitled *Judicial Activism Under the Irish Constitution: Issues and Perspectives: From Natural Law to Popular Sovereignty*, stated:

The role of counsel for the attorney general in this matter was crucial. He conceded without argument that Article 40.3.3 envisaged cases in which abortion would be lawful. He submitted that the phrases "due regard" and "as far as practicable" made it necessary, when interpreting Article 40.3.3, to take into account the mother's other constitutional rights and duties, "as a mother, or a sister, as a daughter, as a parent perhaps," as well as the rights of the mother's parents where the mother was of the age of the first defendant. He submitted that these principles translated into a right to an abortion where the continuation of the life of the unborn constituted a risk of immediate or inevitable death to the mother. He argued that, in the circumstances of the instant case, the evidence had not established a risk of that magnitude.

Finlay CJ accepted all of these submissions, save that relating to the scope of permissible abortion. The chief justice recorded his specific endorsement of the submission that the doctrine of harmonious interpretation of the Constitution involved a consideration of the interrelation of the constitutional rights and obligations of the mother with those of other people "and, of course, with the right to life of the unborn child as well." Such a harmonious interpretation, carried out in accordance with the concepts of prudence, justice and charity, led Finlay CJ to the conclusion that the court was obliged to:

> concern itself with the position of the mother within a family group, with persons on whom she is dependent, with, in other instances, persons who are dependent upon her and her interaction with other citizens and members of society in the areas in which her activities occur.

The chief justice stated that "[h]aving regard to that conclusion" he was satisfied that the test proposed on behalf of the attorney general insufficiently vindicated the mother's right to life and that the proper test was that, if it was established as a matter of probability that there was a real and substantial risk to the life, as distinct from the health, of the mother, which could be avoided only by the termination of her pregnancy, such termination was permissible.

There are passages in the judgements of two other members of the majority of the Court that gave rise to even greater concern to those of a pro-life perspective. McCarthy J contrasted the mother's right to life "a right to a life in being";

No matter how much one might applaud the unceremonious abandonment of a clearly undemocratic portion of jurisprudence one is still uneasy with the result. First of all, the Court gives the impression that natural law thinking had not achieved an elevated status in Irish constitutional in the past. In fact it had and the Court's reasoning in this regard fails to convince. Secondly, the outcome is reminiscent of the situation pertaining under the 1922 Constitution. What would the courts do if the people undemocratically voted to abolish democracy and to purge human rights from the Constitution especially as regards foreigners? Would the court really take the view of "Gesetz als Gesetz" (the law as the law)?

that of the child as a "right . . . to a life contingent; contingent on survival in the womb until successful delivery." He considered that the purpose of the Eighth Amendment could "be clearly identified—it was to enshrine in the Constitution the protection of the right to life of the unborn thus precluding the legislature from an *unqualified* repeal of s. 58 of the Act of 1861 or otherwise, in general, legalising abortion."[17] Similarly, O'Flaherty J observed that the effect of Article 40.3.3 was that "[a]bortion, as such, *certainly abortion on demand*, is not something that can be legalised in this jurisdiction."

In its authorisation of abortion on the ground of suicidal ideation, the majority of the Supreme Court in *Attorney General v X* made no reference to time limits during pregnancy. If the Supreme Court considered that practicability justified the direct taking of the life of an unborn child on the ground of suicidal ideation before the child was viable, in circumstances where the child's location in its mother's womb caused no medical danger to her, it is hard to identify a principled reason why the majority should take a different position in circumstances where the child was viable. In either case, the child's continuing existence would be the source of the suicidal ideation. One can envisage cases where such ideation would be no less if the child were to be delivered alive after having attained viability.

Why did the majority produce such an interpretation of Article 40.3.3? Although it is far from the complete answer, one may examine the influence of the arguments, and concessions, of counsel for the attorney general.[18]

The extent to which counsel's brief had included a full account of current medical obstetric practice is not clear.[19]

---

17 Emphasis added.
18 Undoubtedly the most eminent judicial analyst of the majority's interpretation of the Eighth Amendment in *X* was Mr. Justice Brian Walsh, of the European Court of Human Rights and a judge of the Supreme Court from 1962 to 1991. In a lecture on *Justice and the Constitution* delivered at University College Galway on 11 November 1992. Walsh J observed that the Eighth Amendment

 confers no immunity for taking life and its stated objective is the preservation of and respect for life. It is perfectly consonant with the idea of the safeguarding of the mother's life without intentional and direct intervention to terminate the life of the foetus. The claim that it admits of direct termination has never been fully argued. In the *X* case it was conceded. There was no *legitimus contradictor* to argue against such a construction and therefore the court's decision can only bind the particular case as it was based on a conceded and unargued construction. It is well established that neither a constitutional provision nor even a statutory provision can be construed on the basis of a concession if it were to be binding *in rem*.

19 Counsel made no attempt to distinguish between the intentional taking of unborn life and the death of an unborn child as an unintended result of necessary medical treatment for the mother. Indeed, such limited discussion of the issue of medical treatment by counsel for the attorney general as is reported in the summary of the legal argument in the Supreme Court proceedings appears to involve a conflation of

In reaction to counsel's argument that the Court should take account specifically of the defendant's "rights and duties as a mother, as a sister, as a daughter, as a parent perhaps." Finlay CJ responded by enquiring whether the rights of the girl's parents should be "weighed when favouring the [her] life over the life of the unborn." Counsel for the attorney general replied:

Yes I do say that is so. *The mother's right may be superior to the right to life of the unborn because of the other constitutional rights and duties. But we must look at the circumstances in which it calls for determination.*[20]

It seems impossible to interpret these words as meaning other than that, in the light of a mother's other constitutional rights and duties, her right to life, in some circumstances, might be *superior* to the right to life of her unborn child. Yet, Article 40.3.3 expressly provided that the mother and her unborn had an *equal* right to life.

The judgments of the majority were to the effect that the words "due regard" and "as far as practicable," in conjunction with an assessment of the totality of constitutional rights and duties of the mother and of others, led to the conclusion that it was permissible to extinguish directly the life of the unborn child. That conclusion is consistent only with an *inequality* between the mother's right to life and that of the unborn child.

Could it be argued that the mother and the unborn were not similarly situated in that the mother had a wider repertoire of constitutional rights and obligations, apart from the right to life, than did the unborn? The majority accepted this argument, but if it is tested in another context it may be shown to be false. It is clear, or at all events prior to this decision seemed clear, that a one-year-old baby

---

indirect and direct, without regard to any difference in principle between the two. Witness the following reported interchange:

McCarthy J: Are you saying that there is only one answer: the child must be aborted if the mother is in immediate danger of death? If this is so, where does 'as far as practicable' enter the equation? Do you accept that the Eighth Amendment envisages a 'lawful abortion' in Ireland?

[Counsel for the Attorney General]: Yes, I accept that. For example, a mother suffering from a cancerous condition which requires chemotherapy has the right to have her pregnancy terminated. The pregnancy may be terminated if, but only if, there is an inevitable danger to the right to life of the mother.

The expression "termination of pregnancy" is ambiguous, since it could mean either an abortion, where the child is abstracted from the mother's womb, or, alternatively, medical treatment of the mother, such as chemotherapy, which risks injuring the foetus and which in some instances can result indirectly in the death of the foetus. It is not clear from the argument of counsel for the attorney general which of these processes is envisaged. From the medical standpoint, there is no need in such cases to carry out an abortion, with inevitably fatal consequences for the unborn.

20 [1992] 1 IR, at 35. Emphasis added.

girl's right to life, equal to that of her mother, may not be sacrificed even if the mother's constitutional rights and obligations, which are likely to range vastly more widely than those of her infant daughter, would be greatly facilitated by directly terminating the daughter's life. The equality of the right to life here gives the daughter effective protection; it is not capable of being defeated by other constitutional rights and obligations. If a one-year-old infant's rights to life cannot thus be swept away, it is hard to see how an unborn child's right to life could be destroyed by reference to such considerations unless the mother's right to life was characterised as superior. The Eighth Amendment expressly denied any such superiority. Just as considerations relating to "practicability" do not justify the direct taking of a one-year-old infant's life, they do not permit it in respect of the life of an unborn child.

4 *Roche v Roche*

In *Roche v Roche*,[21] the Supreme Court gave a further indication of its interpretation of Article 40.3.3. The context was not that of abortion but rather of assisted human reproduction. The case involved a dispute between spouses, separated at the time the matter came before the courts, as to whether embryos they had frozen should be implanted in the wife against her husband's refusal. To determine this family law dispute, it was necessary for the Court to address the constitutional status and rights of the embryos.

The Supreme Court, affirming McGovern J, held that Article 40.3.3 afforded the embryos no protection. In the view of four members of the Court, the voters when approving of the Eighth Amendment, had focused on abortion and had not sought to extend its protection to unimplanted embryos. The reference in Article 40.3.3 to the position of the mother added strength to this interpretation, in their view.

This interpretation of the Amendment cannot easily be reconciled with the actual debate at the time the Amendment was before the people or with the philosophical and normative dimensions of Article 40.3.3, which were impossible to reconcile with the denial of protection to human beings at the embryonic stage of their lives. The reference to the mother in Article 40.3.3, which was essential in order to clarify the position of her welfare during pregnancy, did not limit the remit of the provision to cases involving her relationship with her unborn child. Article 40.3.3, on any plausible reading, protected the life of the unborn against being killed by a hostile third party. (At least this proposition seemed clear before *Roche v Roche*.) To restrict its protection to the context of pregnancy seemed unwarranted by its language and contrary to any philosophical or normative coherence.

---

21 [2010] 2 IR 321. For analysis of the decision, *see* Mulligan, "*Roche v Roche*: Some Guidance for Frozen Embryo Disputes" 13 Trinity College L Rev 168 (2010), Binchy, "Courts, Legislators and Human Embryo Research: Lessons from Ireland" 17 *Human Reproduction & Genetic Ethics* 7 (2011).

Murray CJ [22] adopted a strikingly different approach than that favoured by his colleagues. He did not consider that Article 40.3.3 was simply an anti-abortion measure. In his view, that provision in the Constitution "was intended to embrace human life before birth without exception and to extend to it, in express positive terms, the constitutional protections available to life after birth already provided for in Article 40.3.1." Again in contrast to his colleagues, Murray CJ did not conclude from the reference to the mother that Article 40.3.3 necessarily restricted the remit of its protection to unborn lives within the womb. The proviso concerning the equal right to life of the mother was included "to ensure respect and protection for her rights in certain circumstances." If frozen embryos were considered as having the qualities of human life then, "inevitably," in the chief justice's view, they would fall under the rubric of the constitutional provision. Outside the womb, they had the "same qualities as they would have in the womb."

Murray CJ then went on to provide an analysis which went to the very core of the philosophical and normative character of the Constitution. His first major observation was to stress the absence of consensus on the moral status of the embryo:

> The status of the embryo, that is to say its moral status, and specifically the issue as to when human life begins, continues to be debated and discussed as part of a virtually world wide discourse in diverse fora including the most prestigious universities and halls of learning. The many facets of the various sides to that debate, and there are cogent arguments from every perspective, is manifest from the evidence given by the expert witnesses in the High Court. The range of views expressed or referred to in that evidence underscore the absence of any broad multidisciplinary consensus as to precisely when life begins and in particular as to whether it should be considered as beginning at conception or implantation, which are the two reference points with which we are concerned for present purposes.

Turning to "the fundamental issue" in the case, namely, whether the Court should consider that the frozen embryo was human life within the meaning of Article 40.3.3, Murray CJ stated that he did:

> not consider that it is for a court of law, faced with the most divergent if most learned views in the discourses available to it from the disciplines referred to, to pronounce on the truth of when human life begins. Absent a broad consensus or understanding on that truth, it is for legislatures in the exercise of their dispositive powers to resolve such issues on the basis of policy choices.

Against the background of the absence of a consensus as to when human life begins, Murray CJ considered that:

---

22 Murray CJ was the author of the text of the Eighth Amendment, when he was attorney general in 1982.

> [t]he choice as to how life before birth can be best protected, and therefore the point which in law that protection should be deemed to commence, is a policy choice for [Parliament] having due regard to the provisions of the Constitution. It is one which falls to be made having taken into account all the factors and strands of thought which it considers material and relevant.

It was "not a justiciable issue" for the Court to decide that the frozen embryos constitute "the life of the unborn" within the meaning of Article 40.3.3.

This analysis provokes a number of observations. First, the idea that the existence of a lack of consensus, globally or nationally, on the question when human life begins should render its determination beyond the judicial pale seems entirely mistaken. There is no *scientific* controversy about the fact that the human embryo is alive and that it is an entity completely distinct from the parents who generated it. The controversy is not of the empirical order, but rather of the philosophical and normative orders. What does it mean to be human? And how should the notion of being human relate to the framework of rights? Murray CJ was therefore mistaken in using empirical language.

In the world of philosophy as opposed to empirical fact, there is not, contrary to Murray CJ's confident assertion, universal acceptance that a foetus of three months is human life. Charles Hartshorne's observation [23] in regard to children far older than this is worth noting:

> Of course an infant is not fully human. No one thinks it can, while an infant, be taught to speak, reason or judge right and wrong. But it is much closer to that stage than is a three-month foetus.

Somewhat more moderately, but noteworthy nonetheless, another professor in one of those "prestigious universities and halls of learning," Peter Singer of Princeton, has argued [24] that:

> [i]f we compare a severely defective human infant with a nonhuman animal, a dog or a pig, for example, we will often find the nonhuman to have superior capacities, both actual and potential, for rationality, selfconsciousness, communication and anything else that can plausibly be considered morally significant.

He and Helga Kuhse suggest [25] that a period of 28 days after birth might be allowed before an infant is accepted as having the same right to life as others.

In the context of the right to life of people with severe restrictions on brain capacity or with other significant disabilities, yet again there is no global or national consensus on the value to be ascribed to the lives in question. Some have gone so far as to argue that people in a deep coma, in a permanent vegetative state,

---

23 Hartshorne, "Concerning Abortion: An Attempt at a Rational View" *The Christian Century* 42 (January 21, 1981).
24 Singer, *Practical Ethics* (1st ed, 1979), 122–123.
25 Singer & Kuhse, *Should the Baby Live? The Problem of Handicapped Infants* (1985).

are not alive; others have argued that, though alive, they lack sufficient interests to protect them from having their lives terminated. Professor Julian Savulescu, of yet another prestigious hall of learning, Oxford, has commented[26] that

> [s]ince I believe we die when our meaningful mental life ceases, organs should be available from that point, which may signficantly predate brain death.

Murray CJ's invocation of the "political question doctrine" from the jurisprudence of the United States Supreme Court seems hard to explain. That doctrine does not extend to the kind of normative issue that arose in *Roche v Roche*. Most, if not all, normative issues involve debate in society. If the lack of consensus on crucial normative issues were to place them beyond the adjudicative competence of courts, the heart of constitutional jurisprudence would be destroyed.[27]

Although Murray CJ made an unqualified claim to nonjusticiability twice in the passage quoted earlier, he qualified this twice by indicating that it was the Parliament that had "at least initial responsibility" for the matter and that "[t]he onus rests in Parliament, to make the initial policy determination so as to define by law when 'the life of the unborn' acquires protection." The chief justice made no attempt to explain how these qualified statements were capable of reconciliation with his unqualified assertions of nonjusticiability; nor did he indicate how the courts were to engage with what apparently was to become a justiciable issue once the legislature had acted. Ought they concede to the Parliament the entitlement to delay constitutional protection to human beings after conception for such period as it might choose? Was the legislature entitled to delay affording constitutional protection up to the point where there was a consensus, global or natural, that human life existed? If the latter was the position, then it is noteworthy that the chief justice's careful use of language did not commit him to the proposition that

---

26 Savulescu, "Death, Us and Our Bodies: Personal Reflections" 29 *Journal of Med Ethics* 127 (2005).

27 Cf Doyle, Constitutional Law Chapter, in Byrne & Binchy, eds., *Annual Review of Irish Law 2009*, 188, at 251 (2010):

> The import of the Chief Justice's comments is that where people disagree on fundamental moral and philosophical questions, the courts are not entitled to determine the issue, even where that issue arises from the document that judges are sworn to uphold. In Murray C.J.'s view, the decision is a "policy choice" for the Oireachtas which the Oireachtas must make "taking into account all the factors and strands of thought which it considers material and relevant." However, it does not seem right to characterise this question as one of "policy," nor to suggest that the answer is to be reached having taken into account different factors. Moreover, if the status of the embryo is a contested question of philosophy and politics, so too must be the meaning of equality, all personal rights and the separation of powers. Once the Constitution explicitly or implicitly adopts a position on these issues—however indeterminate—it surely falls to the courts to articulate their best interpretation of the contested concept.

implantation represented that point in life's journey at which such a consensus existed. He noted that conception and implantation were the two reference points with which the court was concerned "for present purposes." He observed that he supposed "it could be said that there was a broad consensus among all disciplines that human life begins at implantation of the embryo in the womb or at least not long thereafter." Yet the only point which the chief justice definitively identified as being that where human life existed beyond argument was three months' gestational age. This is not, of course, to interpret the chief justice's remarks as suggesting that legislation delaying legal protection to close to that age would be constitutional; it is, however, noteworthy that he specifically disdained implantation as the latest point at which the legislature was entitled to delay protection and that his use of the absence of consensus as a justification for affording legislative entitlement to delay protection opened the possibility of further delay in the light of increasing international divergence on the value of unborn life.

The primary weakness of Murray CJ's approach was its failure to interpret the Constitution in a coherent philosophical and normative way. Some constitutions limit themselves to normatively neutral provisions relating to such matters as the separation of powers and the respective roles of executive, legislative and judiciary. Other constitutions—of which the Irish Constitution, at all events, up to the recent referendum, has been a striking example—contain a discernable philosophical and normative perspective. They may be based on the theory of human rights that is premised on an understanding of certain rights—including the right to life – as being inherent in human beings, not the mere product of legislation, but prior to positive law. The notion of dignity—the inherent equal worth of every human being—underlies these constitutions.[28] The Supreme Court was called on to interpret Article 40.3.3 in the light of the philosophical and normative framework of the Constitution at that time. The Court's task was greatly eased by the fact that the clear intent of the Amendment had been to clarify what was already implicit in the Constitution rather than to insert a set of values inconsistent with those underlying that framework. The lack of international consensus which Murray CJ identified as a reason for the Court's disentitlement to engage in this process was in fact the very inspiration of the Amendment: to ensure that, in times of normative controversy and debate, the unborn would be protected in accordance with the identifiable human rights philosophy of the Constitution as originally promulgated until the people at some future date might choose to remove that protection by way of a further constitutional amendment. While concerns were concentrated on the dangers of judicial developments which might have these negative effects, the intent was not to surrender to the legislature the power to restrict or remove constitutional protection from unborn human beings.

---

28 The chief justice did refer to human dignity in the international context but failed to develop a substantial analysis of the concept and its implications for human beings and the protection of their rights.

The effect of the Supreme Court decision in *Roche v Roche* was to deny constitutional protection under Article 40.3.3 to embryos *in vitro*. If that constitutional provision afforded them no protection, were they simply devoid of any constitutional rights? The answer was not entirely clear. Hardiman, Geoghegan and Fennelly JJ all spoke of the need to treat the embryo with "respect." Hardiman J regarded the legislature as the body falling under such a duty of respect. He considered that the legislature should address the matter in legislation, observing that:

> [t]he issue is all the more urgent because, of course, scientific developments in the area of embryology and the culturing of stem cells will not stand still. It has been very recently suggested that it may shortly be possible to develop human sperm from such cells. If the legislature does not address such issues, Ireland may become by default an unregulated environment for practices which may prove controversial or, at least, to give rise to a need for regulation.

Fennelly J joined Hardiman J in expressing concern at the absence of any form of statutory regulation of *in vitro* fertilization in Ireland. He noted that counsel for the attorney general had argued that there was "no law or public policy regarding the protection of frozen embryos, in short that they have no legal status." While acknowledging the controversy and sensitivity attaching to the subject matter, Fennelly J went on to say:

> Nonetheless, it cannot be denied that the fertilisation of the ovum brings into existence, outside the womb, the essential unique components of a potential new individual human person. I agree with the judgments of Hardiman J. and Geoghegan J. that the frozen embryo is entitled to respect. This is the least that can be said. Arguably there may be a constitutional obligation on the State to give concrete form to that respect. In default of any action by the executive and legislative organs of the State, it may be open to the courts in a future case to consider whether an embryo enjoys constitutional protection under other provisions of the Constitution.

This raised interesting, and uncertain, questions as to what kind of constitutional protection that might be. It is possible that Fennelly J envisaged that human embryos might invoke protection of their right to life under Article 40.3.2.[29] Perhaps the right to dignity, which found a faint echo in Murray CJ's judgement was in Fennelly J's mind.

5 The Impact of the European Court of Human Rights

The protection of unborn children under Irish law was detrimentally affected by judgements of the European Court of Human Rights [30] in its interpretation of the

---

29 Hardiman J sought to head off any line of thinking in this broad direction, concentrating on Article 40.3.1.
30 The Court was established in 1959: *see* Robertson, "The European Court of Human Rights" 9 *Am J of Comp L* 1 (1960).

European Convention on Human Rights[31]. It may seem curious that an international human rights measure should have injured rather than enhanced the human rights of a group of human beings. The explanation lay in the political role played by the Court.[32]

The promulgation of the European Convention on Human Rights in 1950 was a valiant response to the horrors that had occurred in Europe in the previous two decades. The need for an effective protection of fundamental rights to life, liberty, family and private life, expression and fair trial from state interference seemed obvious in the light of the recent experience of such profound violations of human rights, often perpetrated entirely in accordance with the formal requirements of positive law.

Article 2(1) of the Convention protects the right to life in clear terms:

> Everyone's right to life shall be protected by law. No one shall be deprived of his life intentionally save in the execution of a sentence of a court following his conviction of a crime for which this penalty is provided by law.

It might be considered that this provision afforded protection to unborn children, yet, when it came under scrutiny, first by the European Commission on Human Rights[33] and later by the European Court of Human Rights, it proved ineffective. With Article 2 largely neutralised and providing at best slim, tentative protection, Articles 3 (on inhuman treatment), 8 (on family and private life) and 14 (on non-discrimination) have been used to chip away at effective state barriers to abortion.

Before examining the Court's judgements, it may be helpful to identify the political challenge facing the Court. Europe is not a cultural and normative monolith. There are significant differences between states that have ratified the Convention. These include differences in legal protection of unborn children. Many states have removed any effective legal protection. Others, now a tiny minority, still retain protection. The court was not placed in an easy political situation. If it were to hold that Article 2 protects the right to life of unborn children, it will run into direct and bruising political conflict with the very many states that deny such protection. If, on the other hand, it holds that Article 2 has no application to unborn children, the laws of states such as Ireland will be in breach of the Convention.

In the face of this dilemma, the Court until relatively recently adopted a neutral stance, declining to take a definitive position on the right to life of unborn children

---

31 European Convention for the Protection of Human Rights and Fundamental Freedoms (European Treaty Series, No 5.).
32 The Court has from its inception, inevitably, operated in the political realm, with political goals. *See* Madsen, "From Cold War to Supreme European Court: The European Court of Human Rights at the Crossroads of International and National Law and Politics" 32 *L & Soc Inquiry* 137 (2007).
33 *Bruggemann and Scheuten v Germany* App No 6959/75, 3 EHRR 244 (1981), *Paton v United Kingdom* App No 8416/78, 3 EHRR 401 (1981).

under the Convention and leaving it to the states to fashion their legal policy in accordance with their values. The Court had resort to its "margin of appreciation" doctrine, a device to accommodate pluralism in values as between states.[34]

From the beginning, this strategy appears to have been more strategic than driven by principle. Under the guise of deference to the lack of consensus in Europe as to the moral status of unborn children Thus, in *Vo v France* (35)[35], the Court stated:

> At European level, the Court observes that there is no consensus on the nature and status of the embryo and/or foetus . . ., although they are beginning to receive some protection in the light of scientific progress and the potential consequences of research into genetic engineering, medically assisted procreation or embryo experimentation. At best, it may be regarded as common ground between States that the embryo/foetus belongs to the human race...
>
> [T]he Court is convinced that it is neither desirable, nor even possible as matters stand, to answer in the abstract the question whether the unborn child is a person for the purposes of Article 2 of the Convention ("*personne*" in the French text).

In adopting this approach, the Court effectively drained Article 2 of any capacity to be a barrier to wide-ranging abortion, opened the door to its possible future adoption of the "personhood" strategy that found favour in the United States Supreme Court decision of *Roe v Wade* [36], and enabled other values, protected by the Convention, to trump the right to life of unborn children.

As more states extended legal access to abortion, the Court became emboldened. At present, while not formally abandoning its deference to the margin of appreciation, it is closely interrogating the scope and application of any grounds for abortion that may be part of a state's law and insisting that the ground be interpreted

---

34 In *Open Door v Ireland* 246 Eur Ct H R (ser. A) (1992), the Court held that the margin of appreciation did not prevent Ireland from breaching Article 10 of the Convention where the Supreme Court, in *Attorney General (at the relation of The Society for the Protection of Unborn Children Ireland Ltd) v Open Door Counselling Ltd* [1989] IR 593, had injuncted the provision of specific information as to the identity and location of abortion clinics in England. Finlay CJ had stated (at 625):

> The performing of an abortion on a pregnant woman terminates the unborn life which she is carrying. Within the terms of Article 40, s. 3, sub-s. 3 it is a direct destruction of the constitutionally guaranteed right to life of that unborn child. It must follow from this that there could not be an implied and unenumerated constitutional right to information about the availability of a service of abortion outside the State which, if availed of, would have the direct consequence of destroying the expressly guaranteed constitutional right to life of the unborn.

35 App No 53924/00. July 8, 2004, analysed by Plomer, "A Foetal Right to Life? The Case of *Vo v France*" 5 *Human Rts L Rev* 311 (2005).

36 410 US 113 (1973).

maximally in the interests of expanded access to abortion, with no obvious concern for the rights and interests of the unborn child.

The Court's judgement in *Tysiack v Poland*[37] demonstrates this radical shift in its approach. Condemning what it regarded as an inadequate procedural framework for accessing abortion on a ground specified in Polish law, the Court observed:

> Once the legislature decides to allow abortion, it must not structure its legal framework in a way which would limit real possibilities to obtain it.

This concern is entirely tilted towards expanding access to abortion. The process is all pointing in one direction. No one believes that there is any prospect that the Court would heed an argument that since the formal grounds for abortion in several European states amount in practice to abortion on demand, the unborn children in these states should be protected under the Convention from this failure to keep the practice in line with the formal grounds. The political winds must prevail against it.

In *A, B and C v Ireland, the European Court of Human Rights*,[38] the Court examined the Irish law and held it deficient in its lack of clarity. The third applicant, C., had been in remission from "a rare form of cancer" (unidentified in the proceedings) when she became pregnant. She claimed that she consulted her general practitioner as well as several medical consultants but that, as a result of the chilling effect of the Irish legal framework, she received insufficient information as to the

---

37 App No 5410/03, 45 EHRR 42 (2007).
38 App No 25579/05, [2010] ECHR 2032. For analysis, see Weinstein, "Comment. Reproductive Choice in the Hands of the State: The Right to Abortion under the European Convention on Human Rights in Light of *A, B & C v Ireland*" 27 *Am U Int'l L Rev* 391 (2012), Staunton, "As Easy as A, B and C: Will *A, B and C v. Ireland* Be Ireland's Wake-up Call for Abortion Rights?" 18 *Eur J of Health L* 205 (2011), Ryan, "The Margin of Appreciation in *A, B and C v Ireland*: A Disproportionate Response to the Violation of Women's Reproductive Freedom" 3 UCL *J of L & Jurisprudence* 237 (2014), Ronchi, "Comment, *A, B and C v Ireland*: Europe's *Roe v Wade* Still Has to Wait" 127 L Q Rev 365 (2011), Wicks, "*A, B C v Ireland*: Abortion Law under the European Convention on Human Rights" 11 *Human Rts L Rev* 556 (2011), Daly, "Access to Abortion Services: The Impact of the European Convention on Human Rights in Ireland" 30 *Med L* 257 (2011), de Londras, & Dzehtsiarou, "II. Grand Chamber of the European Court of Human Rights, *A, B & C v Ireland*, Decision of 17 December 2010" 62 *Int & Comp L Q* 250 (2013), McGuinness, "A, B and C Leads to D (for Delegation!): *A, B and C v Ireland* [2010] ECHR 2032" 19 *Med L Rev* 476 (2011), Rhinehart, "Comment, Abortions in Ireland: Reconciling a History of Restrictive Abortion Practices with the European Court of Human Rights' Ruling in *A., B. & C. v. Ireland*" 117 Penn State L Rev 959 (2103). For a compelling analysis of why none of the three claims should have been successful, written before the Grand Chamber handed down its judgment, see Finney, "Shifting towards a European *Roe v. Wade*: Should Judicial Activism Create an International Right to Abortion with *A., B. and C. v. Ireland*?" 72 *U Pitt L Rev* 389 (2010).

impact of the pregnancy on her health and life. She had travelled to England for an abortion.[39]

The Court held that Ireland was in breach of Article 8 of the Convention. It considered that the absence of legislation and the "lack of effective and accessible procedures to establish a right to an abortion" under Article 40.3.3 of the Constitution had resulted in "a striking discordance between the theoretical right to a lawful abortion in Ireland on grounds of a relevant risk to a woman's life and the reality of its practical implementation." It is difficult to reconcile this conclusion with the realities of medical care in Ireland when the Eighth Amendment was in place, where there were no legal restraints on the provision of relevant information about medical risks and health care of the mother and where information about the law on abortion was equally available for the asking.[40]

The Court rejected the claims of the other two claimants, A and B, who had had abortions in England against a background of poverty and alcoholism. These claimants also invoked Article 8, but they were not asserting that they suffered from a medical condition that would warrant an abortion under Irish law. The Court stated:

---

39 No court received evidence in the case. Neither C nor the other claimants had taken any proceedings in an Irish court. In *D v Ireland* [2006] ECHR 1210 (June 22, 2006), the European Court of Human Rights had held admissible a claim that Ireland had breached Article 8 of the Convention in denying abortion to a mother whose child had a life-limiting condition (Trisomy 18). The Court held that the claimant had failed to exhaust domestic remedies. It stated (para 85):

[I]n a legal system providing constitutional protection for fundamental rights, it is incumbent on the aggrieved individual to test the extent of that protection and, in a common law system, to allow the domestic courts to develop those rights by way of interpretation.

The outcome of this case should not necessarily be regarded as one in aid of unborn children. One should heed the observation of Erdman, "The Politics of Global Abortion Rights" 22 *Brown J of World Affairs* 39, at 44 (2015):

This is the empirical reality of all international human rights law: it is ultimately a national project. Read this way, the European Court uses its anti-political doctrines, such as the margin of appreciation, to embed abortion rights within the democratic institutions of the state and thus to generate democratic engagement on abortion, not quiet it. The Court uses international human rights law to call on the Irish state to return to, reconsider, and deliberate on the reform of its abortion law.

For analysis of the issue, see Simon, "'Incompatible with Life': Does Article 40.3.3 Permit Abortion for 'Fatal Foetal Abnormality'?" 21 *Medico-Legal J of Ireland* 21 (2015).

40 *Advocating* that a mother have an abortion was unlawful. Such advocacy was designed to breach the constitutional rights of the particular unborn child. Not dissimilarly, advocating murder and advocating suicide are criminal offences.

> [T]he impugned restrictions [on A and B's Article 8 rights] pursued the legitimate aim of the protection of morals of which the protection in Ireland of the right to life of the unborn was one aspect. The Court does not therefore consider it necessary to determine whether these are moral views stemming from religious or other beliefs or whether the term "others" in Article 8 § 2 extends to the unborn....

This mode of analysis offered little relief to unborn children. The Court refused to give Article 2 any meaningful interpretation, reducing it to an aspect of "the protection of morals," a phrase no longer connoting the premise of an objective moral order protecting the inherent rights of human beings, but instead a contingent and ever-changing cultural phenomenon, where moral perspectives have no objective grounding.

The Court went on to hold that the "consensus" doctrine that it had been developing in earlier cases could not be "a decisive factor" in the Court's examination of whether the impugned prohibition on abortion in Ireland for health and well-being reasons struck a "fair balance" between A and B's privacy rights, on the one hand, and, on the other hand, the "profound moral values of the Irish people as to the nature of life and consequently as to the need to protect the life of the unborn." The fact that, as a result of the "travel amendment" to the Constitution in 1992, pregnant women could travel abroad for abortions was a factor, in the Court's view, contributing to rendering the legal situation in Ireland, as a whole, compliant with the requirements of Article 8. Liberal critics deprecated this aspect of the Court's judgment, arguing that too much deference was afforded to the margin of appreciation, to the neglect of the consensus doctrine. One suspects that, far from indicating a disposition in any way sympathetic to the Irish approach, the Court was simply biding its time, anticipating the change that ultimately occurred with the repeal of the Eighth Amendment.

The government was under no obligation, in Irish law or under the Convention, to introduce legislation providing for abortion based on suicidal ideation, as *Attorney General v X* [41] had decreed. *A, B and C v Ireland* only required clarity in the law and a review procedure. This clarity could have been provided through detailed codes of practice and a transparent review procedure. The Supreme Court's decision in *Attorney General v X*, based on a misapplication of Article 40.3.3 and bad science, was the very antithesis of a model for good legislation.

For reasons of political calculation rather than legal necessity, the government chose to enact the Protection of Life during Pregnancy Act 2013, giving legislative effect to *Attorney General v X*. It did so in the face of the evidence of psychiatrists attending the Parliamentary Committee examining the matter earlier that year, as well as the overwhelming evidence of international research. The legislation set out procedures for obtaining an abortion, requiring the endorsement of psychiatrists in cases of suicidal ideation.

---

41 [1992] 1 IR 1.

Consultant psychiatrist, Patricia Casey, professor of psychiatry at University College, Dublin, gave a coruscating critique of the legislation[42], culminating with the following observations:

> In going through the process of assessment specified under the 2013 Act, psychiatrists are ... being asked to breach Medical Council guidelines in respect of the practice of evidence-based medicine and collaboration with G[eneral] P[ractitioner]s, especially when a person's life may be at risk. Under the current law, psychiatrists are being asked to formally approve an intervention that has no evidential basis in the scientific literature (i.e. abortion) in order to prevent an extremely rare outcome (i.e. suicide) that cannot even be predicted in the manner required under the X case test. Moreover, the law asks them to do this even though for some women an abortion may be associated with subsequent mental health problems, including the very behaviour it was meant to prevent (suicide).

6 The International Covenant on Civil and Political Rights

Still greater danger to the unborn child became apparent in the interpretation given to the International Convention on Human Rights by its monitoring body, the Human Rights Committee. The Convention says nothing directly on abortion but Article 6(1) provides that

> [e]very human being has the inherent right to life. This right shall be protected by law. No one shall be arbitrarily deprived of his life.

In regard to the death penalty, Article 6(5) provides that sentence of death is not to be carried out on pregnant women. The question whether Article 6 protects the unborn child is a matter of debate. Certainly, the text of Article 6(1) lends itself strongly to that interpretation, since manifestly the unborn child is a human being and the protection afforded by the provision extends to every human being. The normative premise underlying Article 6(5) is that the unborn child has a right to life which requires protection. The drafting history of Article 6 allows a range of interpretations. The most recent comprehensive analysis[43] supports the conclusion that an intent to protect the unborn child is consistent with that history.

The idea that the Covenant should become an instrument of attack on the lives of unborn children may seem monstrous, but this is what occurred. In *Mellet v Ireland*,[44] the author of the complaint had been informed, during her pregnancy, that

---

42 Casey, "The Protection of Life during Pregnancy Act: Lacking an Evidential Base and Compromising Psychiatrists" 20 *Medico-Legal J of Ireland* 97, at 102 (2014).
43 Finegan, "International Human Rights Law and the 'Unborn': Texts and *Travaux Preparatoires*" 25 *Tulane J of Int'l & Comp L* 89, at 100–111 (2016).
44 Communication No 2324/2015, June 9, 2016. For analysis of the case, see de Londras, "Fatal Foetal Abnormality, Irish Constitutional Law, and *Mellet v Ireland*" 24 *Med L Rev* 591 (2016).

the child she was carrying had Trisomy 18 and was expected to die either before birth or shortly afterwards. She went to England for an abortion. She claimed, *inter alia*, that the absence of a legal entitlement to have an abortion in those circumstances constituted cruel, inhuman and degrading treatment, in breach of Article 7, breach of her right to privacy under Article 17 and discrimination, in breach of Article 26.

The Irish representatives invoked Article 6 and argued that it had the potential to afford the unborn child a right to life, which was deserving of protection. It could not be definitively concluded that no measure of protection in relation to the right to life was afforded to the foetus, as otherwise Article 6 (5) "would lack sufficiency of meaning, reason and substance." This argument found no purchase with the Committee.

With regard to the claim under Article 7, Ms Mellet had claimed that, as a result of the legal prohibition of abortion, she had been denied the health care and bereavement support she needed in Ireland; compelled to choose between continuing to carry a dying foetus and terminating her pregnancy abroad; and subjected to intense stigma. The Irish representatives argued in reply that the prohibition sought to achieve a balance of competing rights between the unborn child and the mother and that no arbitrary decision-making processes or acts of "infliction" by any person or State agent had caused or contributed to cruel, inhuman or degrading treatment.

Holding that there had been a breach of Article 7, the Committee stated that it considered that:

> the fact that a particular conduct or action is legal under domestic law does not mean that it cannot infringe article 7 of the Covenant. By virtue of the existing legislative framework, the State party subjected the author [of the complaint] to conditions of intense physical and mental suffering. The author, as a pregnant woman in a highly vulnerable position after learning that her much-wanted pregnancy was not viable, ... had her physical and mental anguish exacerbated by not being able to continue receiving medical care and health insurance coverage for her treatment from the Irish health-care system (45)[45]; the need to choose between continuing her non-viable pregnancy or travelling to another country while carrying a dying fetus (46)[46], at her personal expense and separated from the support of her family, and returning while not fully recovered; the shame and stigma associated with the criminalization of abortion of a fatally ill fetus; the fact of having to leave the baby's remains behind and later having them unexpectedly delivered to her by courier; and the State party's refusal to provide her with the necessary and appropriate post-abortion and bereavement care. Many of the negative experiences described that she went through could have

---

45 Translated, this means that the Irish health care system did not fund abortions of children with life-limiting conditions.
46 The unborn child, prior to the abortion, was not dying.

been avoided if the author had not been prohibited from terminating her pregnancy in the familiar environment of her own country and under the care of the health professionals whom she knew and trusted, and if she had been afforded the health benefits she needed that were available in Ireland, were enjoyed by others, and could have been enjoyed by her, had she continued her non-viable pregnancy to deliver a stillborn child in Ireland....

The absence of reference by the Committee to the fate of the unborn child whose life is terminated intentionally is striking.

The Committee held that Ireland had also breached Ms Mellet's privacy rights under Article 17, on the basis that the legal prohibition on abortion of children with life-limiting conditions was arbitrary and disproportionate. Again, the fact that this was part of the Irish Constitution did not save it.

The Committee held that there had been a breach of Article 26, identifying a discrimination between those mothers who aborted their children with life-limiting conditions and those who did not and a further discrimination among those mothers disposed to abort their child as between those who could afford the journey to England and those who could not. The Committee noted Ms Mellet's claim that Ireland's criminalization of abortion had subjected her to a gender-based stereotype of the reproductive role of women primarily as mothers, and that stereotyping her as a reproductive instrument subjected her to discrimination. The Committee did not elaborate on this argument[47], but a number of the members of the Committee fully embraced it in their concurring opinions. Sarah Cleveland observed:

> The author ... articulates an alternative basis for a finding of gender discrimination—that Ireland's legal regime is based on traditional stereotypes regarding the reproductive role of women, by placing the woman's reproductive function above her physical and mental health and autonomy. The fact that the State party may have pointed to a facially nondiscriminatory purpose for its legal regime does not mean that its laws may not also be informed by such stereotypes. Indeed, the State's laws appear to take such stereotypes to an extreme degree where, as here, the author's pregnancy was nonviable and any claimed purpose of protecting a foetus could have no purchase. Requiring the author to carry a fatally impaired pregnancy to term only underscores the extent to which the State party has prioritized (whether intentionally or unintentionally) the reproductive role of women as mothers, and exposes its claimed justification in this context as a reductio ad absurdum."

This approach would appear to open the door to a right to abortion, of as yet undefined but manifestly broad scope, based on the premise that the denial of a pregnant mother's entitlement to terminate her unborn child's life constitutes sex discrimination and that to contradict that premise itself constitutes stereotyping.

---

47 The unborn child, prior to the abortion, was not dying.

The Committee held that, in the light of the breaches of the Covenant that it had found against Ireland under Articles 7, 17 and 26 of the Covenant, Ireland was under an obligation, not only to compensate the complainant and to make available to her any psychological treatment she needed, but also to take steps to prevent similar violations in the future. The Committee stated:

> To that end, [Ireland] should amend its law on the voluntary termination of pregnancy, including if necessary its Constitution, to ensure compliance with the Covenant, ensuring effective, timely and accessible procedures for pregnancy termination in Ireland.

7 Repeal of the Eighth Amendment

The protection afforded by the Eighth Amendment, battered as it was by decisions and determinations of courts and international agencies, had still a profound value. Unquestionably, it saved the lives of thousands of children whose parents would have gone through with the decision to abort them, had the facilities been available to hand. Nonetheless, there was strong political pressure to repeal the Eighth Amendment, led, sadly, by Amnesty International, which received a substantial payment from the Open Society Foundation.[48] The government established

---

48 It is worth noting the sharp criticism of the Committee's approach by one of its members, Anja Seibert-Fohr, in her partial dissent (paras 8–10) in respect of Article 26:

> The author claims that the prohibition is based on a gender-based stereotype which considers women's "primary role . . . to be mothers and self-sacrificing caregivers" and stereotypes the author "as a reproductive instrument'. . . "She also claims that the abortion regime was "reinforcing women's . . . inferior social status" . . . But these allegations which are contested by the State party are not supported by any relevant facts. According to the State party the legal framework is the result of a balancing of the right to life of the unborn and the rights of the woman. Though the Committee disagrees in its findings under article 17 with the outcome of the balancing in the case of a fatally-ill foetus, this finding does not warrant the conclusion that the prohibition on abortion is based on gender stereotypes. It is rather grounded on moral views on the nature of life which are held by the Irish population.
>
> I appreciate that the Committee does not rely on the allegation of gender stereotypes in its finding under article 26. Instead it refers only to "differential treatment to which the author was subjected *in relation to other similarly situated women.*" Nevertheless, the Committee has failed to specify on which other status the distinction is grounded.
>
> Unless the Committee wants to find a violation of Article 26 every time it finds a violation of one of the rights and freedoms protected under the Covenant and deprive this provision of any autonomous meaning and value, the Committee would be well advised to engage with such claims in a more meaningful way giving due account to the notion of discrimination and the prohibited grounds in the future.

a "Citizen's Assembly" composed of 100 randomly chosen people, to address the issue of repeal of the Eighth Amendment. The terms of reference were not so framed but it quickly became clear that the Amendment was indeed on trial. Little enough evidence in its defence was heard. The outcome, predicted by pro-life organisations from a very early stage, was stark: the vote for extending the grounds for abortion was impressive in its extravagance, embracing abortion for disability ("a significant foetal anomaly that is not likely to result in death before or shortly after birth"), supported by 80% [49] and going as far as abortion "on request [no restriction as to reasons]," supported by 64%[50]

The government passed the matter to a parliamentary committee, which also proposed repeal of the Eighth Amendment. In due course, the government put before the people a proposal to repeal the Amendment, replacing it by a statement in the Constitution that "provision may be made by law for the regulation of termination of pregnancy." On 25 May 2018, 66.4% of the electorate who voted in the referendum favoured repeal. The outcome was not unexpected, as opinion polls had indicated consistently that the proposal would succeed, but the margin surprised almost everyone, supporters and opponents alike. Before the Referendum, the Government published a scheme of legislation that it intended to introduce if the Eighth Amendment was no longer part of the Constitution. This would authorise abortion without legal restraint within the first 12 weeks of pregnancy, as well as abortions after that stage, up to viability on a health ground, with an entitlement to abort babies with life-limiting conditions at any time up to birth. Subsequent to the repeal, the government has reiterated the intention to legislate on these lines, with only a limited scope for conscientious objection by health personnel, who would be required, in essence, to refer women for abortions.

Looking back over the recent history of protecting unborn children through the law in Ireland, one is struck by a number of aspects of the stance of those who successfully advocated the removal of that protection: the invisibility of unborn children; the reluctance to acknowledge their very existence; the failure to address their humanity. No one can doubt the sincerity of these advocates, but one must lament their failure to engage fully with the reality and the rights of unborn children, who have no voice that can be heard. Irish society, in allowing the taking of the lives of these innocent children, is sadly implicated in a terrible injustice, in breach of our common humanity. Those who are pro-life have already committed themselves to the challenge of righting this wrong and restoring full protection for the lives of our unborn sisters and brothers.

---

49 *First Report and Recommendations of the Citizen's Assembly: The Eighth Amendment of the Constitution*, 35 (June 29, 2017).
50 Ibid., 36.

Bibliography

Barry, "Movement, Change and Reaction: The Struggle Over Reproductive Rights in Ireland," in A Smyth, ed., *The Abortion Papers* (1992), 107.

Binchy, "Marital Privacy and Family Law: A Reply to Mr O'Reilly" 65 Studies 33 (1977).

Binchy, "The Need for a Constitutional Amendment," in chapter 11 of Flannery, ed., *Abortion and the Law* (1983).

Binchy, "The Supreme Court of Ireland," in chapter 5 of B Dickson, ed., *Judicial Activism in Common Law Supreme Courts* (2007).

Binchy, "Dignity as a Constitutional Concept," in Carolan & Doyle, eds., *The Irish Constitution: Governance and Values*, 308 (2008).

Binchy, "Courts, Legislators and Human Embryo Research: Lessons from Ireland" 17 *Human Reproduction & Genetic Ethics* 7 (2011).

Casey, "The Protection of Life during Pregnancy Act: Lacking an Evidential Base and Compromising Psychiatrists" 20 *Medico-Legal J of Ireland* 97 (2014).

Charleton, "Judicial Discretion in Abortion: The Irish Perspective," (1992) 6 *Internat J of L & the Family* 349 (1992).

Chubb, B. *The Politics of the Irish Constitution* (1991).

Costello, J., "Natural Law, the Constitution and the Courts" in Lynch and Meenan, eds., *Essays in Memory of Alexis Fitzgerald* (1987), 105.

Costello, J., "The Natural Law and the Irish Constitution" *Studies* 403 (1956).

Daly, "Access to Abortion Services: The Impact of the European Convention on Human Rights in Ireland" 30 *Med L* 257 (2011).

de Londras, & Dzehtsiarou, "II. Grand Chamber of the European Court of Human Rights, *A, B & C v Ireland*, Decision of 17 December 2010" 62 *Int & Comp L Q* 250 (2013).

de Londras, "Fatal Foetal Abnormality, Irish Constitutional Law, and *Mellet v Ireland*" 24 *Med L Rev* 591 (2016).

Doyle, O., *Constitutional Law: Texts, Cases and Materials* (2008).

Doyle, Constitutional Law Chapter, in Byrne & Binchy, eds., *Annual Review of Irish Law 2009*, 188 (2010).

Erdman, "The Politics of Global Abortion Rights" 22 *Brown J of World Affairs* 39 (2015).

Finegan, "International Human Rights Law and the 'Unborn': Texts and *Travaux Preparatoires*" 25 *Tulane J of Int'l & Comp L* 89 (2016).

Finney, "Shifting towards a European *Roe v. Wade*: Should Judicial Activism Create an International Right to Abortion with *A., B. and C. v. Ireland*?" 72 U *Pitt L Rev* 389 (2010).

First Report and Recommendations of the Citizen's Assembly: The Eighth Amendment of the Constitution, 35 (June 29, 2017).

Gearty, "Book Review" 28 Ir Jur (ns) 620 (1993).

Gerry Whyte, "Natural Law and the Constitution" 14 *Ir L Times* (ns) 8 (1996).

Girvin, "Social Change and Moral Politics: The Irish Constitutional Referendum 1983," 31 *Political Studies* 61 (1986).

Glenn, "The Constitutional Validity of Abortion Legislation: A Comparative Note" 21 *McGill LJ* 673 (1975).

Hartshorne, "Concerning Abortion: An Attempt at a Rational View" *The Christian Century* 42 (January 21, 1981).

Hesketh, T., *The Second Partitioning of Ireland?* (1990).

Hogan, "Law and Religion: Church-State Relations from Independence to the Present Day" 35 *Am J of Comp L* 47 (1988).

Hogan, "Mr Justice Brian Walsh: The Legacy of Experiment and the Triumph of Judicial Imagination" 57 *Ir Jur* (ns) 1, at 3 (2017).

Hogan, "The Early Judgments of Mr. Justice Brian Walsh" in O'Reilly (ed.), *Human Rights and Constitutional Law: Essays in Honour of Brian Walsh* (1992), 37.

Kelly, *The Irish Constitution* (4th edn, by Hogan & Whyte, 2004).

Madsen, "From Cold War to Supreme European Court: The European Court of Human Rights at the Crossroads of International and National Law and Politics" 32 *L & Soc Inquiry* 137 (2007).

McGuinness, "A,B and C Leads to D (for Delegation!): *A, B and C v Ireland* [2010] ECHR 2032" 19 *Med L Rev* 476 (2011).

Michael, "Abortion and International Law: The Status and Possible Extension of Women's Rights to Privacy" 20 *J of Family Law L* 241 (1981).

Mulligan, "*Roche v Roche*: Some Guidance for Frozen Embryo Disputes" 13 *Trinity College L Rev* 168 (2010).

O'Reilly, "Marital Privacy and Family Law" 65 *Studies* 8 (1977).

O'Leary & Hesketh, "The Irish Abortion and Divorce Amendment Campaigns," 3 Irish Political Studies 43 (1988).

Phelan, "Billionaire Soros Funding Groups Fighting to Repeal Irish Abortion Ban," Irish Independent, 20 August 2016.

Plomer, "A Foetal Right to Life? The Case of *Vo v France*" 5 *Human Rts L Rev* 311 (2005).

Quinlan, "The Right to Life of the Unborn—An Assessment of the Eighth Amendment to the Irish Constitution" [1984] *Brigham Young U L Rev* 371.

Quinn, Gerard, *Judicial Activism Under the Irish Constitution: Issues and Perspectives: From Natural Law to Popular Sovereignty*, paper delivered on 6 July 2000 at the University of San Sebastian Summer School.

Randall, "The Politics of Abortion in Ireland," in ch. 5 of J. Lovenduski & J. Dutshoorn, eds, *The New Politics of Abortion* (1986).

Rhinehart, "Comment, Abortions in Ireland: Reconciling a History of Restrictive Abortion Practices with the European Court of Human Rights' Ruling in *A., B. & C. v. Ireland*" 117 *Penn State L Rev* 959 (2103).

Robertson, "The European Court of Human Rights" 9 *Am J of Comp L* 1 (1960).

Ronchi, "Comment, *A, B and C v Ireland*: Europe's *Roe v Wade* Still Has to Wait" 127 *L Q Rev* 365 (2011).

Ryan, "The Margin of Appreciation in *A, B and C v Ireland*: A Disproportionate Response to the Violation of Women's Reproductive Freedom" 3 UCL *J of L & Jurisprudence* 237 (2014).

Savulescu, "Death, Us and Our Bodies: Personal Reflections" 29 *J of Med Ethics* 127 (2005).

Simon, "'Incompatible with Life': Does Article 40.3.3 Permit Abortion for 'Fatal Foetal Abnormality'?" 21 *Medico-Legal J of Ireland* 21 (2015).

Singer & Kuhse, *Should the Baby Live?: The Problem of Handicapped Infants* (1985)

Singer, P., *Practical Ethics* (1st edn., 1979).

Speed, "The Struggle for Reproductive Rights: A Brief History in its Political Context," in A Smyth, ed., *The Abortion Papers* (1992), 85.

Staunton, "As Easy as A, B and C: Will *A, B and C v. Ireland* Be Ireland's Wake-up Call for Abortion Rights?" 18 *Eur J of Health L* 205 (2011).

Walsh, J., lecture on *Justice and the Constitution* delivered at University College Galway on 11 November 1992.

Weinstein, "Comment. Reproductive Choice in the Hands of the State: The Right to Abortion under the European Convention on Human Rights in Light of *A, B & C v Ireland*" 27 *Am U Int'l L Rev* 391 (2012).

Cases:

Wicks, "*A, B C v Ireland*: Abortion Law under the European Convention on Human Rights" 11 *Human Rts L Rev* 556 (2011).

Mellet v Ireland Communication No 2324/2013, June 9 2016.

Roe v Wade 410 US 113 (1973).

Bruggemann and Scheuten v Germany App No 6959/75, 3 EHRR 244 (1981).

Paton v United Kingdom App No 8416/78, 3 EHRR 401 (1981).

Open Door v Ireland 246 Eur Ct H R (ser. A) (1992).

Vo v France App No 53924/00. July 8, 2004.
D v Ireland [2006] ECHR 1210 (June 22, 2006).
Tyziac v Poland App No 5410/03, 45 EHRR 42 (2007).
A, B & C v Ireland App No 25579/05, [2010] ECHR 2032.

Juan Cianciardo

8 The Specification of the Right to Life of the Unborn in the Inter-American Human Rights System
A Study of the *Artavía Murillo* Case

Abstract: The purpose of this chapter is to examine the position on the right to life taken by the Inter-American Court of Human Rights, based on an analysis of *Artavia Murillo et al. (in vitro fertilization) v. Costa Rica*. The case was decided on November 28, 2012 when the Court found that the State had violated the American Convention on Human Rights by prohibiting assisted fertilization techniques, and obliged the State to include them "in its infertility programs and treatments as part of health care." We maintain that the normative framework used by the Court to solve the case gave rise to a number of logically valid alternative solutions, and we challenge the reasoning afforded by Court to impose one of these. Among other arguments, we sustain that the fact of scientific disagreement concerning the value of unborn life doesn't allow to conclude, as the Court does, that the Convention obliges its signatory parties to legalize and even promote *in vitro* fertilization.

Keywords: Right to life, Human rights, Basis of the right, Principle of reasonableness

1 Introduction

The purpose of this chapter is to study the position of the Inter-American Court of Human Rights with respect to the right to life. I will focus on the analysis of the case of *Artavía Murillo et al. ("In Vitro Fertilization") v. Costa Rica,*" decided on November 28, 2012, in which the Court declared that the prohibition of assisted fertilization techniques applicable in Costa Rica was contrary to the American Convention on Human Rights, and obliged the State to include these techniques "within its healthcare programs and treatments for infertility" (X.4). The judgment of the Court shall be disputed. According to the judgment, scientific disagreements in relation to the value of unborn human life, paradoxically, impose upon States subject to the Convention, the obligation to authorize in vitro fertilization practices, and even include them within reproductive health care public services. The case gained attention again recently after petitions were submitted against Costa Rica for failing to comply with the ruling of the Inter-American Court, giving rise to a new ruling, this time in relation to monitoring of compliance with the judgment, on February 26, 2016.[1] One of the criticisms that will be argued below is that in the 2012 judgment, the Court exceeded its jurisdiction. As Hamilton warned, among the most delicate functions of a court of justice is not to exceed its scope of action,[2] among other reasons because, when this occurs, the risk of noncompliance arises. This, perhaps, is what has occurred in this case.

The analysis shall start with the pressing issue of how to specify the content of human rights, if they are intended to make an effective contribution to legal discourse. As has been affirmed, what is important when it comes to establishing the scope of human rights, what their limits are, and how they relate to other rights and to the public good— is not so much what abstract powers are held by potential holders (in this case, the petitioners), but rather identifying at what point they give way to permitted, due or prohibited behavior.[3] On this conceptual basis, the description of the case and its critical analysis will be addressed successively. The criticisms shall be divided into two parts. In the first part, five reasons will be provided as to why the Inter-American Court erroneously interpreted the applicable regulations; in the second part, a diagnosis shall be made of the reasons that underlie this interpretation.

2 The Case

2.1 The Facts of the Case

The case poses no great difficulties in relation to the facts, beyond their duration in time and the various procedural issues surrounding them. The Inter-American Commission on Human Rights asked the Inter-American Court to declare the international responsibility of Costa Rica regarding the general prohibition of the practice of in vitro fertilization (hereinafter IVF), a prohibition in place in the country since the year 2000. According to the Court's own description of the judgment,

> It was alleged that this absolute prohibition constituted arbitrary interference in the right to private life and the right to found a family. It further alleged that the prohibition violated the right to equality of the plaintiffs, in as much as the State had denied them access to a treatment that would have enabled them to overcome

---

1   See Inter-American Court of Human Rights, "*Artavía Murillo y otros («fecundación in vitro») vs. Costa Rica. Supervisión de cumplimiento de sentencia,*" decided on February 26, 2016.
2   See HAMILTON, A., J. MADISON y J. JAY, *El Federalista,* México, Fondo de Cultura Económica, 1994, LXXVIII; and OYHANARTE, Julio, «Historia del Poder Judicial», *Todo es Historia* 61 (mayo de 1972), p. 90.
3   See ORREGO SÁNCHEZ, Cristóbal, "Supuestos conflictos de derechos humanos y la especificación de la acción moral," *Revista Chilena de Derecho* 37 (2010), 311–342.

their disadvantage with regard to the possibility of having biological children. It also argued that this ban had a disproportionate impact on women.

In order to understand the prohibition to which the petitioners refer, it is necessary to go back in time. Executive Decree No. 24029-S of February 3, 1995, issued by the Ministry of Health of Costa Rica, authorized the practice of IVF for married couples and regulated its practice. "In Section 1, the Executive Decree regulated the performance of assisted reproduction techniques between married couples, and established rules for it to be carried out. In Section 2, assisted reproduction techniques are defined as "all those artificial techniques in which the joining of an egg and spermatozoid is achieved through the direct manipulation of germinal cells in the laboratory."[4] In the remaining Sections of the Decree, among other things, the following is established:

> Section 9. In cases of in vitro fertilization, the fertilization of more than six eggs per patient per cycle of treatment is absolutely prohibited.
> Section 10. All fertilized eggs in a treatment cycle must be transferred to the uterine cavity of the patient. It is absolutely prohibited to discard or remove embryos, or to preserve them for transference in subsequent cycles with the same patient or with other patients.
> Section 11. It is absolutely prohibited to perform maneuvers that manipulate the genetic code of the embryo, along with all forms of experimentation upon same.
> Section 12. It is absolutely prohibited to trade in germinal cells - eggs and spermatozoids - in order for them to be destined for patient treatment in assisted reproduction techniques, whether homologous or heterologous.
> Section 13. Failure to comply with the dispositions herein established shall result in the Ministry of Health having the power to revoke the operating health license and accreditation awarded to the establishment where such breaches have been committed, with the issue being forwarded immediately to the Public Ministry and Professional Association respectively, in order to establish the corresponding sanctions.

IVF was practiced in Costa Rica between 1995 and 2000 by the Costa Rican Infertility Institute. During this period, 15 Costa Ricans were born. The technique was declared unconstitutional by the Constitutional Chamber of Costa Rica on March 15, 2000.[5] This Court based its decision on the following reasons:

a) "violation of the principle of legal reserve," according to which, "only by formal law emanating from the legislative branch through the procedure provided for in the Constitution for the introduction of laws, is it possible to regulate and, where necessary, restrict rights and fundamental liberties." In accordance with the above, the Court concluded that the Executive Decree regulated the "right

---

4   "*Artavía Murillo y otros («fecundación in vitro») vs. Costa Rica*," decided on Noviembre 28 2012, 68.
5   Idem, 69.

to life and dignity of the human being," a reason for which "[t]he regulation of these rights by the Executive Branch [was] incompatible with Constitutional law."
b) Upon considering the application of Section 4.1 of the American Convention, the Constitutional Chamber indicated the following: The question of when human life begins is of transcendental importance in the matter under discussion here, since it is necessary to determine the moment from which the human being is subject to protection under our legal system. There are differing views among specialists. Some consider that human embryos are entities at a stage of development where they have nothing more than a simple potential for life. [. . .] They point out that prior to its attachment, the pre-embryo is composed of undifferentiated cells, and that cellular differentiation does not occur until after it has attached to the lining of the uterus and after the appearance of the primitive cell line—the first outline of the nervous system; from that moment the organ systems and the organs are formed. [. . .] Others, on the contrary, maintain that every human being has a unique beginning that occurs at the very moment of fertilization. They define the embryo as the original form of a being, or as the earliest form of a being and consider that the term pre-embryo does not exist, since prior to the embryo, at the preceding stage, there is a spermatozoid and an egg. When the spermatozoid fertilizes the egg, that entity becomes a zygote and therefore an embryo. The most important feature of this cell is that everything that will allow it to evolve into an individual is already in place; all the necessary and sufficient information to determine the characteristics of a new human being appear to come together in the union of the 23 chromosomes of the spermatozoid and the 23 chromosomes of the oocyte. [. . .] In describing the segmentation of the cells that occurs immediately after fertilization, this view holds that at the three-cell stage a minuscule human being exists and from that stage every individual is unique, rigorously different from any other. In short, as soon as conception occurs, a person is a person and we are in the presence of a living being, with the right to be protected by the legal system."
c) According to the Constitutional Chamber, IVF practices "clearly jeopardizes the life and dignity of the human being" given that " i) "[h]uman beings have the right not to be deprived of their life or to suffer unlawful attacks by the State or by private individuals, and furthermore: public authorities and civil society must help them defend themselves from the dangers to their life," ii) "once conceived, a person is a person, and we are dealing with a living being, with the right to be protected by the law," and iii) "since the right [to life] is declared for everyone, with no exception, it must be protected for both the individual who has been born, and also for the unborn child."
d) Different international standards "impose the obligation to protect the embryo from the abuse that it could be subject to in a laboratory and, especially, the most severe of all, the one that can eliminate its existence." Among these standards is Section 4 of the American Convention: "[t]his international instrument takes a

decisive step, given that it protects the right [to life] from the moment of conception. [In addition] it emphatically prohibits imposing capital punishment on pregnant women, which constitutes direct protection and, therefore, full recognition of the legal and real personality of the unborn child and its rights."
e) Considering the above, the Constitutional Chamber concluded that:

> The human embryo is a person from the moment of conception; hence it cannot be treated as an object for investigative purposes, be submitted to selection processes, [be] kept frozen and, the most essential point for the Chamber, it is not constitutionally legitimate to expose it to a disproportionate risk of death. [. . .] The main objection of the Chamber is that the application of the technique entails a high loss of embryos, which cannot be justified by the fact that it is intended to create a human being, providing a child to a couple who would otherwise be unable to have one. The key point is that the embryos whose life is first sought and then violated are human beings, and constitutional law does not allow any distinction among them. The argument that in natural circumstances there are embryos that are not implanted, or that even if they are implanted they do not develop until birth, is not admissible either, simply because the application of [IVF] entails a conscious and voluntary manipulation of the female and male reproductive cells in order to produce a new human life, which leads to a situation where it is known in advance that the human life, in a considerable percentage of the cases, has no possibility to continue. As the Chamber has been able to verify, the application of the technique of in vitro fertilization and embryo transfer, as it is currently performed, jeopardizes human life. This Court knows that advances in science and biotechnology are so dramatic that the technique could be improved so that the reservations included herein disappear. However, the conditions in which it is currently applied lead to the conclusion that any elimination or destruction of embryos – whether voluntary or derived from the negligence of the person executing the technique or its inaccuracy – violates the right to life, hence the technique is not in keeping with constitutional law and, consequently, the regulation under consideration is unconstitutional as it violates Section 21 of the Constitution and Section 4 of the American Convention on Human Rights. Since the technique violates the right to life, it shall be expressly stated on the record that its use cannot be authorized even based on a norm with legal status, at least while its scientific development remains at the current state and entails certain damage to human life.

Against this decision of the Constitutional Chamber, an international appeal was brought before the Inter-American Court of Justice, which gave rise to the case we are studying. The applicable standards, whose violation was claimed, were Sections 11.2, 17.2, and 24 of the American Convention, in relation to Sections 1.1 and 2 of this international instrument. Also applicable was Section 4.1 on the right to life. One of the axes of the discussion generated in the case was precisely the marginal role played by this last right in the court's judgment.

The Inter-American Court, by a majority, decided to grant the request of the Commission. Judge Diego García-Sayán provided a concurrent opinion, and was joined by Judge Rhadys Abreu Blondet. Judge Eduardo Vio Grossi issued a dissenting opinion. In the analysis of the case, we will focus on the arguments provided by the majority of the court, and we shall avoid procedural aspects.

2.2 The Arguments of the Majority of the Court

It is appropriate here to present below a brief description of the arguments put forward by the Inter-American Court in its judgment.

2.2.1 The Central Issue in the Case: The Right to Private Life

The court considered that: "this case addresses a particular combination of different aspects of private life that are related to the right to found a family, the right to physical and mental integrity and, specifically, the reproductive rights of the individual."[6] How should this web of rights be approached? According to the Court, using the principal of proportionality: "the purpose of this case focuses on establishing whether the Constitutional Chamber's judgment resulted in a disproportionate restriction of the rights of the presumed victims."[7]

2.2.2 The Prohibition of IVF Constituted an Unjustified Interference in Rights Protected by the Convention

a) The judgment of the Constitutional Chamber Interfered with the Right to Private Life and Family of the Petitioners.
   The Court said: "the judgment of the Constitutional Chamber implied that IVF would no longer be practiced in Costa Rica. In addition, the judgment led to the interruption of the medical treatment that some of the presumed victims in this case had begun, while others were forced to travel to other countries to be able to have access to IVF. These facts constitute an interference with the private and family life of the presumed victims, who had to modify or change their possibilities of having access to IVF, which involved a decision of the couples regarding the methods or practices that they wished to try in order to have biological children. The said judgment meant that the couples had to change their course of action with respect to a decision that they had already taken: to try to have children by means of IVF."[8]
b) The Interference Was Unjustified
   The Inter-American Court considered that the restriction of the right to private life and family lacked justification. It based its opinion on two orders of reasons.

---

6 Idem, 144.
7 Idem, 171.
8 Idem, 161.

Firstly, the Court understood that the right to life recognized in Section 4.1 of the American Convention does not require absolute protection of the embryo.

Secondly, the Court found that the restriction lacked justification. In this regard, it recalled that in its own prior judgments, "the Court has established that a right may be restricted by the States provided that the inferences are not abusive or arbitrary; consequently, they must be substantively and formally established by law, pursue a legitimate aim, and comply with the requirements of suitability, necessity and proportionality." In addition, it stated that "the Court has stated previously that the 'absolute right to life of the embryo' as grounds for the restriction of the rights involved is not supported by the American Convention (. . .); thus, it is not necessary to make a detailed analysis of each of these requirements, or to assess the disputes regarding the declaration of unconstitutionality in the formal sense based on the presumed violation of the principle of legality of enacted laws."[9] Notwithstanding this assertion, "the Court considers it appropriate to indicate the way in which the sacrifice of the rights involved in this case was excessive in comparison to the benefits referred to with the protection of the embryo."[10] For this reason its deliberation considered: "(i) the level of harm to one of the rights at stake, determining whether this level of harm was serious, intermediate or moderate; (ii) the importance of ensuring the contrary right, and (iii) whether ensuring the latter justifies restricting the former."[11] The result was favorable to the interests of the petitioners.

3 Analysis of the Judgment

3.1 A Range of Logically Possible Alternatives

The court confronted the need to establish if, in the Inter-American System for Human Rights, a) the "conception" referred to in Section 4.1. of the American Convention is produced upon fertilization, and therefore the embryo is entitled to the right to life from this moment, or if it appears later, with implantation; b) the petitioners have a right to assisted reproduction techniques, or if this is a forbidden conduct, or a merely tolerated one (and therefore susceptible to prohibition by the State). In the event that there is a right to assisted reproduction, the Court should further determine if: c) the expression "general" used in Section 4.1. of the American Convention on Human Rights; c') allows the State to introduce exceptions to the protection of life; c'') forbids the State to introduce exceptions; c''') obliges the State to introduce exceptions.

The Inter-American Court considered that:

a) conception does not occur upon fertilization but upon implantation;

---

9   Idem, 273.
10 Ibidem.
11 Idem, 274.

b) there is a human right to employ assisted reproduction techniques;
c) without the embryo being implanted, no right to life corresponds in the application of Section 4.1;
d) consequently, the prohibition of assisted reproduction techniques constitutes a violation of the Inter-American System of Human Rights.

The Court argued further:

e) the unborn is not a person under the terms of the American Convention on Human Rights;
f) the Convention obliges the introduction of exceptions to the protection of life.

The path chosen was not the only way of reaching the final decision, although it was the one which most restricted the political choices of the State. The possible logical answers to the above questions are at least the following twelve. The Court chose the 12th alternative:

	Conception occurs upon fertilization	Access to in vitro reproduction techniques	The expression "general" in Section 4.1	Result
1	Yes, and therefore the embryo has a right to life from fertilization	It is a human right	It allows the State to introduce exceptions	Reject the petition, because the State has not introduced exceptions
2	No, and therefore the right to life is not recognized until implantation	It is not a human right	Does not apply (permitted)	Reject the petition, because there is no right to change the State's policy on the matter
3	Yes, and therefore the embryo has a right to life from fertilization	It is not a right	It allows the State to introduce exceptions	Reject the petition, because there is no right to change the State's policy on the matter
4	No, and therefore the right to life is not recognized until implantation	It is a human right	Does not apply (permitted)	Grant the petition, because despite the State having failed to introduce exceptions, they ought to have
5	Yes, and therefore the embryo has a right to life from fertilization	It is a human right	It does not allow the State to introduce exceptions	Reject the petition, because the State has not introduced exceptions

	Conception occurs upon fertilization	Access to in vitro reproduction techniques	The expression "general" in Section 4.1	Result
6	No	It is not a right	Does not apply (not permitted)	Reject the petition, because there is no right to change the State's policy on the matter
7	Yes, and therefore the embryo has a right to life from fertilization	It is not a right	It does not allow the State to introduce exceptions	Reject the petition, because there is no right to change the State's policy on the matter
8	No, and therefore the right to life is not recognized until implantation	It is a human right	Does not apply (not permitted)	Grant the petition
9	Yes, and therefore the embryo has a right to life from fertilization	It is a human right	It obliges the State to introduce exceptions	Grant the petition or reject it, depending on the scope assigned to the State's obligation to establish exceptions
10	No, and therefore the right to life is not recognized until implantation	It is not a right	Does not apply (obliged)	Reject the petition, because there is no right to change the State's policy on the matter
11	Yes, and therefore the embryo has a right to life from fertilization	It is not a right	It obliges the State to introduce exceptions	Grant the petition or reject it, depending on the scope assigned to the State's obligation to establish exceptions
12	No, and therefore the right to life is not recognized until implantation	It is a human right	Does not apply (permitted)	Grant the petition, because despite the State having failed to introduce exceptions, they ought to have

Observing the table, we can see that hypotheses 4, 8, and 12 are practically identical, with a slight difference. By identifying conception with implantation, the un-implanted embryo has no right to life and, therefore, the question whether the State could have prohibited, had prohibited, or was obliged to introduce the exceptions alluded to in Section 4.1 of the Convention became abstract. Where, in this alternative, no right is afforded to the embryo and a right is afforded to those that wish access to assisted reproduction techniques, the State must guarantee this right and, therefore, the Court is obliged to grant the petition. The same conclusion is also reached in hypotheses 9 and 11. In the former, the embryo has a right to life from conception that arises upon fertilization, but the petitioners have a right to access to assisted reproduction techniques and the State is obliged to introduce exceptions by Section 4.1 of the Convention. In the latter, the embryo has a right to life, the petitioners have no right to the techniques, and the State is obliged to introduce exceptions by Section 4.1. In both cases, the result of the petition would depend on the extent of the obligation of the State to introduce exceptions established by Section 4.1. If the exception to be introduced by the State consisted in the right to choose assisted reproduction techniques, then the petition would have to be granted. In the first case, such an exception would be less difficult to justify than in the second, given that the existence of a "right" to reproduction techniques would have been previously recognized.

The rest of the possible hypotheses would have led to the rejection of the petition.

3.2 An Unjustified Decision

There existed, in short, a range of logical possible alternatives. The Court chose one of them and attempted to justify its choice. It did so conspicuously poorly. There are two very clear deficiencies: a) the Court did not take into account that each one of the reasons it gave is ambivalent, that is to say, it could have chosen the contrary argument without even considering that there were other possible interpretations, according to elementary legal logic and theory of interpretation; and b) many of the reasons offered by the Court are only apparently so, because the contrary alternative was a better or more attractively supported argument.

The Court should have provided in-depth reasoning for its decision. The reasons, however, remain implicit, hidden. The second criticism reveals that many of the arguments put forward in "*Artavia*" do not pass the test of reasonablesness. In the two following sections, we contend that a better use of the available sources (3.2.1) was possible, or even better justified, and that these are the implicit or hidden reasons that the Court did not reveal (3.2.2).

3.2.1 *Specific Shortcomings of the Judgment of the Inter-American Court*

In his valuable recent work, Santiago Altieri identified five fundamental points that I shall use as a starting point for the ideas expressed in this section.[12] These

---

12 ALTIERI, Santiago, *El comienzo de la personalidad del ser humano en el Derecho uruguayo*, tesis doctoral, Universidad de Zaragoza, 2015, 379–439.

criticisms are based on a different interpretation of the Inter-American sources than the one made by the Court, and bring to light the existence of better alternative interpretations on the one hand, and the ambivalence of Court's interpretation, on the other.[13]

a) A Restrictive Interpretation of Section 4.1 and, Therefore Contrary to the American Convention

Altieri points out, reasonably, that the Inter-American Court's interpretation of Section 4.1 of the Convention does not take into account Sections 29 and 27 of the text. The former rules out any interpretation that restricts the content of rights; the latter excludes the right to life from the list of rights which may be suspended in the event of extraordinary circumstances. The Court did not take into account either of these two standards, in particular the first, although it is evident that the interpretation it afforded of the right recognized in Section 4.1 restricted its scope.

It may be added that the interpretation made in "Artavía" is contrary to other interpretations of the Court itself in previous cases. As has been stated correctly, "the Court had referred to unborn children, using different terms that recognized their status as persons holding human rights. Effectively, in its jurisprudence the Court had referred to unborn persons as "children," "minors," "sons," and "babies" in at least three cases: the case of the *Gómez-Paquiyauri Brothers v. Peru*, the case of the *Miguel Castro-Castro Prison v. Peru*, and the case of *Goiburú et al. v. Paraguay*. The Court also referred to induced abortions as "barbaric acts" in the case of the *Las Dos Erres Massacre v. Guatemala*. Moreover, in the case of the *Sawhoyamaxa Indigenous Community v. Paraguay*, the Court observed the "right to life of children [...] cannot be separated from the likewise vulnerable situation of the pregnant women of the Community" and reiterated the obligation of the States parties to the Convention to guarantee access to parental health."[14]

b) A Partial Reverse of the Recognition of the Right to Life of the Unborn, Which Remains in the Shadows.

The Court recognizes the existence of a right to life of the unborn but, as pointed out by Altieri,[15] it then holds that this right is subject to exceptions (paragraph 188), and that its protection "is gradual and incremental according to its development, since it is not an absolute and unconditional obligation" (paragraph

---

13 This last conclusion is mine. It doesn't appear in Altieri's paper and might not been shared by him.
14 *See* DE JESÚS, Ligia, Jorge A. OVIEDO ÁLVAREZ, AND PIERO A. TOZZI, "El caso Artavia Murillo y otros vs. Corta Rica (Fecundación in Vitro): la redefinición del derecho a la vida desde la concepción, reconocido en la Convención Americana," *Prudentia Iuris*, 2013, 135–164 http://bibliotecadigital.uca.edu.ar/repositorio/revistas/caso-artavia-murillo-costa-rica.pdf.
15 See ALTIERI, Santiago, *El comienzo de la personalidad del ser humano (...)*, 410.

264). The exceptions include the possible legalization of abortion, which in some circumstances would be a right. Whether it is an option or an obligation of the States to legalize abortion according to this interpretation remains unrevealed.

The Court's argument, where it refers directly to this matter, is one of the weakest the entire judgment. The Court even stated that the embryo ought not to be considered a person based on the colorful argument that, under the terms of the Convention, a person is defined as someone who can perform the actions that constitute the objects of the human rights recognized therein, to whom the text usually refers as "all." For example, Section 5 states that "1. Every person has the right to a hearing, with due guarantees and within a reasonable time, by a competent, independent, and impartial tribunal (...)." As the embryo cannot perform any of these actions, for example, it could be alleged that it cannot be "heard"; therefore it is not a person. The argument is erroneous for two reasons. Firstly, it is fallacious. It is an example of the well-known fallacy of hasty generalization. The fact that the embryo cannot yet enjoy some of the rights does not mean that it cannot hold all of them. Secondly, it is inconsistent with how the Court has decided other cases. As Altieri affirms, "the same reasoning applied to children or the disabled would lead us to the conclusion that they are not entitled to such rights either because they cannot—at least at present—exercise some of those rights enshrined in the American Convention of Human Rights, such as, for example, political rights."[16]

c) Excess of Jurisdiction, Aggravated in the Monitoring of Compliance with the Judgment

Thirdly, the ruling bypasses the limits of its own jurisdiction. In the words of Altieri,

> "in this judgment the Court has gone beyond its function of interpreting the ACHR and has assumed the role of generator of legal criteria, beyond that agreed by Signatory States. In effect, in this judgment the Court has used the standard not according to what it means, but to what the Court would like it to mean (...). With its interpretation the Court has virtually abolished all reference to the right to life of the unborn from conception in itself, reducing it to a mere interest, despite its clear statement by the letter of Section 4.1 of the ACHR and has disregarded the legal personality of 'nasciturus' in clear violation of the principle of equality."[17]

These excesses are accentuated in the judgment of monitoring compliance on February 26, 2016.[18] The Court intervened based on the disagreements with regard to the 2012 ruling within the Costa Rican government. The Executive Branch had

---

16 Idem, 411.
17 Idem, 432–433.
18 Inter-American Court of Human Rights, Case "*Artavía Murillo y otros («fecundación in vitro») vs. Costa Rica. Supervisión de cumplimiento de sentencia,*" decided on February 26, 2016.

complied with the judgment launching three legislative initiatives that were ultimately derailed; for this reason, a decree was issued which the Constitutional Chamber declared unconstitutional, because it was deemed contrary to the principle of legality. At this juncture, the Court intervened, declaring that Costa Rica had not complied fully with the 2012 resolution and, among other things, directly declared the validity of the decree authorizing the practice of assisted reproduction techniques in Costa Rica, with or without state intervention in this respect. Judge Eduardo Vio Grossi issued a dissenting opinion in which he pointed out, with reason, that the 2012 ruling had not been ignored.

> with regard to how the Judgment is complied with and the state body responsible for assuming the responsibility to do so. Thus, all these matters are left to the ambit of what is defined in International Law as internal or domestic jurisdiction or that which is exclusive to the State, in which it is the State's responsibility to regulate for itself and, therefore, is not found to be subject to International Law. That is equivalent or similar to what is known as the margin of discretion of the State recognized by International Law.[19]

In any case, the resolution of the majority of the Court in the 2016 ruling modified, unreasonably, the decision of 2012. In the words of Vio Grossi:

> the Resolution modifies the Judgment, based on how it expressly establishes two new obligations, neither of which had been foreseen in the Judgment. Moreover, the Resolution takes two improper procedural steps in the procedure of monitoring compliance with judgments.[20]

These two "new" obligations arising were, firstly, to immediately allow access to IVF and, secondly, to maintain the validity of the Executive Branch decree which had been declared unconstitutional by the Constitutional Chamber. Furthermore, as noted by Vio Grossi, the object of monitoring the compliance with the judgment of 2012 was altered. The State had been ordered to adopt "appropriate measures to ensure that the prohibition of the practice of IVF is annulled," and to regulate "those aspects it considers necessary for the implementation of IVF." In 2016, on the other hand, it was established that the Court would lead "the procedure of monitoring compliance in respect of the corrective measures related to ensuring [. . .] that prohibition of IVF cannot have any legal effect in Costa Rica nor constitute an impediment to the exercise of the right to decide to have biological children through the said reproduction technique, in accordance with. . . (Resolution two of the Judgment)." According to Vio Grossi, "evidently, the said resolution differs radically from that laid down in the Judgment, which as expressed above, orders the State to adopt "appropriate measures" . . . to the effects indicated, and regulates the " necessary aspects" for the implementation of IVF. Therefore, the Court will monitor whether

---

19 Idem, 25.
20 Idem, 26.

or not these aforementioned "appropriate measures" have been adopted and if the alluded "necessary aspects" have been regulated so that "prohibition of the practice of IVF is annulled," and that it does not "constitute an impediment to the exercise of the right to have biological children through access to said reproduction technique." It is worth concluding that the 2016 judgment substantially alters, insofar as it pertains to this case, the procedure for monitoring of compliance with judgments."[21]

d) Omission of all consideration of the Feasibility of the Implementation of the Resolution and Defective Application of the Guarantees of Non-repetition

The Court established, within these conclusions, that the State:

> must make IVF available within its healthcare infertility treatments and programs, in accordance with the obligation to respect and guarantee the principle of non-discrimination. The State must provide information every six months on the measures adopted to make these services available gradually to those who require them and on the plans made to this end, in accordance with paragraph 338 of this Judgment.[22]

In the same paragraph it states that:

> the Costa Rica Social Security Institute must make IVF available within its health care infertility treatments and programs, in accordance with the obligation to respect and guarantee the principle of non-discrimination. The State must provide information every six months on the measures adopted in order to make these services available gradually to those who require them and on the plans that it draws up to this end.[23]

Three observations can be made. The first is that this conclusion follows from two premises, one correct and one incorrect, respectively: a) all fundamental rights possess a double dimension, positive and negative. The former imposes an obligation of abstention or non-violation on the part of the State and individuals; the latter requires the State to ensure the conditions that make the effective validity of the right possible; b) access to assisted fertilization treatment is a fundamental right. The second assertion is the fruit of the imagination of the Court and is not acknowledged anywhere in the text of the American Convention.[24] It consists of nothing more and nothing less than the transformation of a desire into a right. When this is done, the inevitable consequence is the weakening of the concept of rights. If any desire is a right, all rights are weakened and those responsible for protecting them are delegitimized. It could even be said that operations such as

---

21 Idem, 38, 29, and 40.
22 Case "*Artavía Murillo y otros («fecundación in vitro») vs. Costa Rica*," decided on November 28, 2012, 381.4.
23 Idem, 338.
24 *See* Zambrano, Pilar y Sacristán, Estela, "¿Hay límites para la creatividad interpretativa? A propósito del caso «F. A. L.» y la relativización de los derechos fundamentales," Jurisprudencia Argentina 2012-II (AP/DOC/2258/2012).

these dissolve rights completely, because the point of legal interpretation is precisely to distinguish between mere desires, and desires grounded in true rights.

The second observation refers to a serious omission: the Court omitted all consideration of the factual possibilities Costa Rica had of implementing what it was ordered to do. In this regard, Altieri maintains that "bearing in mind the economic resources available to the healthcare systems of Latin American countries and identifying the satisfaction of much more basic health necessities, it should be considered whether the Court has gone too far in imposing this onerous obligation. It appears clear that the State of Costa Rica, when it comes to complying with this part of the Judgment, must distinguish between different situations and evaluate to what extent it ought to comply with this obligation, apparently disproportionate to its (economic) possibilities and to the detriment of other, more compelling necessities. The Judgment argues that "some countries, such as Argentina, Chile and Uruguay, are already attempting to take measures to ensure that assisted reproduction treatment be covered by public healthcare programs and policies" (paragraph 255). However, it seems wholly excessive to burden the health care system of Costa Rica with such provisions under the pretext that three of the richest countries (of Latin America) are beginning to make this possibility "viable."[25]

The third observation refers to the introduction by the Court of a guarantee of non-repetition.[26] Specifically, the Court stated the following:

> The Court observes that the State did not specify the existing mechanisms to raise awareness on reproductive health. Therefore, it orders the State to implement permanent education and training programs and courses in human rights, reproductive rights and non-discrimination for judicial employees in all areas and at all echelons of the Judiciary. These programs and training courses should make special mention of this Judgment and the different precedents in the *corpus iuris* of human rights relating to reproductive rights and the principle of non-discrimination.[27]

A little later in the conclusions section, it added:

> "The State must implement permanent education and training programs and courses on human rights, reproductive rights and non-discrimination for judicial officials in

---

25 Altieri, Santiago, *El comienzo de la personalidad del ser humano (. . .)*, 434, following B. RAMOS CABANELLAS, "El derecho a la vida, el concepto de concepción, y las técnicas de reproducción humana asistida en la interpretación de la Inter-American Court of Human Rights: Caso "Artavia Murillo y otros (Fecundación in vitro) vs. Costa Rica," in *Doctrina y Jurisprudencia de Derechos Civil (Uruguay)*, Año II, Tomo II (2014), 166–167.
26 See LONDOÑO LÁZARO, María Carmelina, *Las garantías de no repetición en la jurisprudencia interamericana. Derecho internacional y cambios estructurales del Estado*, México, Tirant Lo Blanch-Universidad de La Sabana, 2014.
27 "*Artavía Murillo y otros («fecundación in vitro») vs. Costa Rica*," 28 of November 2012, 341.

all areas and at all echelons of the Judiciary, as established in paragraph 341 of this Judgment."[28]

The discussion in relation to the legitimacy of the guarantees of non-repetition (GNR) considered in and of itself is significant. In my opinion, there are compelling reasons that justify their legitimacy in general, although their application must be subject to limits. In other words, although the institution is valued for its recognition, guardianship, and promotion of rights, its exercise may or may not be legitimate, depending on whether certain limits are respected or are exceeded. Londoño Lázaro has proposed a test according to which the legitimacy of a GNR depends on its necessity, its appropriateness, and its deontic status.[29] According to this author, "only in the context of a special type of judgment, referred to as 'ruling with reflex effects,'" is it possible to justify a GNR.

Furthermore, it is understood that reflex effects can only be produced by those judgments that apply the principles of primacy of the human person, coherence, and reasonableness when it comes to interpreting the letter and spirit of the American Convention, and that clearly identify in their content two issues: a structural State failure that results in the violation of a Convention right, and a corresponding international standard that allows overcoming the deficiency in question, partially or totally.

Therefore, reflex effects are excluded from decisions that "either don't deal with structural problems of the States, or where the Court makes interpretations of the Convention which are obscure or unfounded, giving precedence to a certain ideology without adhering to the true spirit that inspires the Convention, or any decision that arbitrarily chooses the primacy of one right over another."[30] Secondly, "the legitimacy of GNRs is conditioned upon it being indispensable— the only way— to implement an international standard obligatory for the State."[31] Finally, " (...) on the basis offered by the formula of the margin of discretion, the judge is called to distinguish the nature of the obligations imposed on the State by the Convention and, considering this issue, must define the corresponding legal standards. (...) Negative obligations reduce the margin of discretion of the State, while positive obligations can ordinarily be satisfied in different ways. (...). Regarding the latter, the international court can, at best, illustrate or make recommendations to the State regarding the alternatives considered more appropriate to prevent future violations, but must abstain from ordering specific measures, unless this be the only or an indispensable way of reaching the proposed end."[32]

---

28 Idem, 381.7.
29 See LONDOÑO LÁZARO, María Carmelina, *Las garantías de no repetición en la jurisprudencia interamericana (...)*, chap. 4.
30 Idem, 310.
31 Idem, 311.
32 Ibidem.

The guarantee of non-repetition ordered by the Court in the case does not comply with the first part of the test for two reasons. Firstly, because it lacks reflex effects as no "consistent constitutional standard" regarding the way to comply with the claimed international obligation can be identified. Secondly, because it involves an obscure and unfounded interpretation of the Convention, arbitrarily awarding primacy to one right over another. This alone would be enough to justify the illegitimacy or unreasonable nature of the judgment to which I refer, but there is more: even under the hypothesis that these two objections were not valid, still the Court failed to pass the third condition of the proposed test, for the Court placed a positive obligation on the State and imposed upon it a course of action, thus violating the national margin of discretion, which is fundamental to the principle of subsidiarity.[33]

e) Unreasonableness of the Factual Findings

The facts of a case must be proven. The factual findings are the fruit of series of choices: one must choose, successively, the relevant facts, the convincing means of evidence, and which of these have the greatest power of conviction. The judge is obliged to take into account the reasons which ground each choice. If no reasons are given, or if reasons given are weak compared to other reasons, the decision would violate the principle of reasonableness (or the preclusion of arbitrariness).[34]

Something similar to this occurred in the "*Artavia Murillo*" case, given that the Inter-American Court based its affirmations in respect to the facts on some expert testimonies, disregarding the rest of the evidence produced in the case. In this respect, Altieri points out that the expert, Zegers, was called to testify over 20 times, without explaining why this opinion was privileged over that of other qualified experts. Moreover, he adds that "even more striking is that Zegers has dedicated his life to the application of reproductive techniques on humans: he is a promoter and booster of in vitro fertilization which is precisely the technique in question in this case. Evidently, his professional competence is not in question. What is reproachable here is that the unfounded decision of the Court to afford such relevance to an interested and therefore not impartial expert. It should have given reasons for admitting an expert with a clear interest, and for privileging this report in respect of others".[35] The Court also failed to consider the application and, ultimately, the extension of the *pro homine* principle.[36]

---

33 Idem, 217–229.
34 See CIANCIARDO, J., "Los fundamentos de la exigencia de razonabilidad," in CIANCIARDO, J. (coord.), *La interpretación en la era del Neoconstitucionalismo. Una aproximación interdisciplinar*, Buenos Aires, Ábaco de Rodolfo Depalma, 2006, 21–36.
35 ALTIERI, Santiago, *El comienzo de la personalidad del ser humano (. . .)*, 438–439, following A. PAÚL DÍAZ, La Corte Interamericana in vitro: comentarios sobre su proceso de toma de decisiones a propósito del caso Artavia, in *Derecho Público Iberoamericano*, N° 2 (2013), p. 329 and footnote 115.
36 See ZAMBRANO, Pilar, "Una lectura transparente de la Constitución," *La Ley* 2008-D-296.

3.2.2 The Background: The Real Reasons of the Court's Decisions

On this final point, I intend to answer the question why the Inter-American Court made the decision that it did. What were the substantive reasons the led the Court to such an unjustified decision from all the logical alternatives available? What lies behind it, in the words of Zambrano and Sacristán, is a semantic-anthropological debate, "which not infrequently 'disguises,' itself behind the authority of law and science to impose one or other of the contested alternatives. The anthropological debate concerns (. . .) the radical legal conceptual distinction between things and persons. The question at hand is whom we recognize the dignity of person or subject of law, and why. But this question cannot be resolved without previously defining a more abstract and thus more fundamental, semantic debate: how are things classified in general in the world and, in particular, in the legal world? Are conceptual classifications the result of a thoughtful, yet somehow explicit, social debate that the law is required to incorporate, at least as long as there is sufficient agreement on it? Are they an interested imposition of a social group to which the law affords its supportive force? Or are they something similar to a representation of reality, which emerges before us already classified, if not in full, at least in part?[37]

In the case of *"Artavía"* the Court has been asked to decide a) from what moment a being is a human being; and b) from what moment a human being is a person. For the Court, embryos are not human beings until implantation, and are not persons at any moment over the course of their existence as embryos. What, definitively, does this mean? It means that, for the Court, embryos are not worthy beings, deserving an unconditional respect. The result is that they are lowered to the status of an object of the physical universe, and are therefore usable, susceptible of being treated as means for purposes other than themselves. The Court segments the life path of the human being into sections or watertight compartments: man is not a man in the initial phase of his existence, despite possessing the same and identical information or genetic material that he will possess the rest of his life. It is not someone, but something. Not a subject, but an object of legal relations (that may be implanted, un-implanted, frozen, or used for experimentation).

This contestable metaphysical concept of the person, laden with highly debatable assumptions, was stated by the Court immediately after declaring solemnly that it would not do so. How was this point reached? By making poor choices. By deciding, without reasons upholding the decision. It assumed a metaphysical concept of a person centered on the idea of autonomy, a quality that is transitory in the life of man and which, therefore, is not coherent with the unconditioned nature of human rights. This assumption was introduced through the back door, almost unintentionally: if it weren't so tragic it would be funny how in only a couple

---

37 See ZAMBRANO, Pilar y Estela SACRISTÁN, "El valor de la vida del embrión en la jurisprudencia estadounidense y argentina," *Boletín Mexicano de Derecho Comparado*, nueva serie, año XLV, núm. 134, mayo-agosto de 2012, 715–759, 754–755.

of paragraphs the Court leaps forward from explicitly declaring itself opposed to any kind of metaphysical argument, to adopting a metaphysical conception of the person, in the most genuine sense of "metaphysical." It consists of a stunning leap in logic: from ethical relativism to "legal absolutism."[38] (In this regard, paragraphs 185, 186, and 187 are very significant).

This self-assignment of competency by the Court is deeply inconsistent with the core thesis of any general theory of human rights. As has been correctly pointed out,[39] if human rights mean anything at all, it is precisely that none of the branches of the State, nor any International Organization of States, can violate the very same thing they are required to protect; on the contrary, they must protect and promote it. If States are required not to violate human rights, even more so are States deprived of the power to determine who is a subject of rights or, what is the same thing, to decide when a being may be considered a human being, and which human beings are (or are not) persons. If States does not hold the power to ignore rights, all the more do they not hold the power to decide who is a holder of rights and who is not.

The Court ignored the indivisible nature of the questions relating to the concept of dignity. It did not take into account that the concept of dignity is transcendental,[40] and therefore a starting point, not a point to be reached or a concept that can be segmented for analysis. To put it in simpler terms, the question "where does dignity start?" cannot be disassociated from the question "does a dignified person deserve absolute respect (in the following sense: it must always be treated as an end and never as a means)?" If the answer to the last question is affirmative, then the moment from which and until when this dignity is possessed cannot be subject to conditions.[41] Subjecting the recognition of dignity to conditions necessarily implies subjecting dignity to conditions. This conditioning turns the absolute obligation of respect for those who possess dignity into a matter of subtle and perverse manipulation, based on the negation of the most simple and fundamental quality of the subject.

---

38 See ALBERT, María, "Relativismo ético, ¿absolutismo jurídico?" *Persona y Derecho* 61 (2009), 33–52.
39 See Pedro SERNA BERMÚDEZ, "El derecho a la vida en el horizonte cultural europeo de fin de siglo," in MASSINI, C. I. y SERNA, P. (eds.), *El derecho a la vida*, EUNSA, Pamplona, 1998, 23–79, 44–45, following Robert SPAEMANN, "La naturaleza como instancia moral de apelación," *El hombre, inmanencia y trascendencia. Actas de las XXV Reuniones Filosóficas*, Pamplona, Universidad de Navarra, 1991, vol. I, 65–66. This same argument is shared by HERVADA, J. in "Problemas que una nota esencial de los derechos humanos plantea a la filosofía del derecho," *Persona y derecho: Revista de fundamentación de las Instituciones Jurídicas y de Derechos Humanos*, ISSN 0211-4526, N°. 9, 1982, 243–256.
40 See Ana Marta GONZÁLEZ, *Naturaleza y dignidad. Un estudio desde Robert Spaemann*, Pamplona, Eunsa, 1996, 45–63.
41 See Robert SPAEMANN, *Lo natural y lo racional. Ensayos de antropología*, trad. D. Innerarity y J. Olmo, prólogo de R. Alvira, Madrid, Rialp, 1989, 89–123.

Once on this path, it becomes very difficult not to weaken or directly eliminate two of the conceptual features of human rights: universality and absolute weight. Human rights are universal because their entitlement does not depend on any condition other than belonging to the human species. In the case of civil rights, for example, entitlement to them depends upon the existence of a positive entitlement, that is, a law or a contract. Without such entitlement, there is no right, despite holding the status of a person. In the case of human rights, on the other hand, their entitlement springs from the sole condition of being a human being. For this reason, human rights are recognized to all human beings. The declarations of human rights echo this by referring to holders by the constant use of the word "all." This universal scope is also entailed in the use of another expression which appears in multiple texts referring to rights: "recognition." Rights are recognized, they are not created.[42] Without universality, there is no possibility of distinguishing a human right from other kinds of rights, nor is there true "recognition" of rights.[43]

Rights whose entitlement lies in the mere condition of being a human being, which are "recognized" and not created or instituted are, moreover, absolute. They are so, not because they demand a conditional protection, but because once their content has been specified (that is to say, related to the rest of the rights and to the just demands of the common good), what results from this specification, their "essential content" or "the sphere of reasonable function" of the right, should be absolutely granted: it cannot be sacrificed for the sake of anything else. To put it another way, their absolute nature entails that neither the State nor any other person, regardless of the power they may hold, can legitimately jettison human rights. Each time a right is neglected, be it the right to life, intimacy, privacy, freedom of expression, etc., the right to act according to our nature as persons is also neglected. Therefore, there is no greater act of manipulation over another person than that of self-assigning the power to decide if she is, indeed, a person: not another *thing*, but "another *one*."[44]

It is contradictory to claim the universal and absolute character of human rights while at the same time rejecting their application to all human beings. These inconsistencies are there in plain view: what has occurred in Guantánamo (the virtual removal of the status of person from a group of adult human beings) is much more closely related to decisions in cases such as *Roe v. Wade*" or "*Artavia*" than might appear at first sight.[45]

---

42 *See* HERVADA, "Problemas que una nota esencial de los derechos humanos plantea a la filosofía del derecho," *Persona y derecho: Revista de fundamentación de las Instituciones Jurídicas y de Derechos Humanos,* ISSN 0211-4526, N°. 9, 1982, 243–256.
43 *See* Jesús BALLESTEROS, "El individualismo como obstáculo a la universalidad de los derechos humanos," *Persona y Derecho* 41 (1999), 15–27.
44 *See* Pedro SERNA BERMÚDEZ, "El derecho a la vida en el horizonte cultural europeo de fin de siglo", op. cit., 44.
45 410 US 113.

Bibliography

Albert, María, "Relativismo ético, ¿absolutismo jurídico?" en Persona y Derecho (61) (2009), pp. 33–52.

Altieri, Santiago, El comienzo de la personalidad del ser humano en el Derecho uruguayo, thesis doctoral, Universidad de Zaragoza, 2015, pp. 379–439.

Bellver Capella, V., "La dimensión prestacional del derecho a la libertad religiosa," en Humana Iura (6) (1996), pp. 257–267.

Camps, V., Guariglia, O., Salmerón, F. (coords.), Concepciones de la ética, Madrid, Trotta S.A., 2013, p. 133.

Cianciardo, J., "Los fundamentos de la exigencia de razonabilidad," en Cianciardo, J. (coord.), La interpretación en la era del Neoconstitucionalismo. Una aproximación interdisciplinar, Buenos Aires, Ábaco de Rodolfo Depalma, 2006, pp. 21–36.

De Jesús, Ligia, "El individualismo como obstáculo a la universalidad de los derechos humanos," en Persona y Derecho (41) (1999), pp. 15–27.

De Jesús, Ligia, Oviedo Álvarez, Jorge A., Tozzi, Piero A., "El caso Artavia Murillo y otros vs. Corta Rica (Fecundación in Vitro): la redefinición del derecho a la vida desde la concepción, reconocido en la Convención Americana," en PrudentiaIuris 2013, pp. 135–164, en http://bibliotecadigital.uca.edu.ar/repositorio/revistas/caso-artavia-murillo-costa-rica.pdf

Díaz, Paúl A., "La Corte Interamericana in vitro: comentarios sobre su proceso de toma de decisiones a propósito del caso Artavia," en Derecho Público Iberoamericano, (2) (2013), en https://www.academia.edu/3754483/LaCorte_interamericana_in_Vitro_Comentarios_sobre_su_Proceso_de_Toma_de_Decisiones_a_Prop%C3%B3sito_del_Caso_Artavi_Murillo, fecha de consulta: 18 de mayo de 2015.

González, Ana Marta, Naturaleza y dignidad. Un estudio desde Robert Spaemann, Pamplona, Eunsa, 1996, pp. 45–63.

Hamilton, A., Madison, J., Jay, J., El Federalista, México, Fondo de Cultura Económica, 1994, LXXVIII. asimismo.

Hervada, Javier, "Problemas que una nota esencial de los derechos humanos plantea a la filosofía del derecho," en Persona y derecho: Revista de fundamentación de las Instituciones Jurídicas y de Derechos Humanos, (9) (1982), pp. 243–256.

Lichtblau, E., *Bush's Law: The Remaking of American Justice*, New York Pantheon, 2008.

Londoño Lázaro, María Carmelina, Las garantías de no repetición en la jurisprudencia interamericana. Derecho internacional y cambios estructurales del Estado, México, Tirant Lo Blanch-Universidad de La Sabana, 2014.

Orrego Sánchez, Cristóbal, "Supuestos conflictos de derechos humanos y la especificación de la acción moral," en Revista Chilena de Derecho (37) (2010), pp. 311-342.

Ruiz Serna Bermúdez, Pedro, "El derecho a la vida en el horizonte cultural europeo de fin de siglo," en Massini, C. I. y Serna, P. (eds.), El derecho a la vida, EUNSA, Pamplona, 1998, pp. 23-79, 44-45.

Spaemann, Robert, "La naturaleza como instancia moral de apelación," en El hombre, inmanencia y trascendencia. Actas de las XXV Reuniones Filosóficas, Pamplona, Universidad de Navarra, 1991, vol. I, pp. 65-66.

Spaemann, Robert, Lo natural y lo racional. Ensayos de antropología, Madrid, Rialp, trad. D. Innerarity y J. Olmo, prólogo de R. Alvira, 1989, pp. 89-123.

Weber, G., "Proportionality, Balancing, and the Cult of Constitutional Rights Scholarship," Can. J. L. & Jurisprudence 23(1), pp. 179-202.

Zambrano, Pilar, "Una lectura transparente de la Constitución," La Ley 2008-D-296.

Zambrano, Pilar, Sacristán, Estela, "¿Hay límites para la creatividad interpretativa? A propósito del caso 'F. A. L.' y la relativización de los derechos fundamentals," en Jurisprudencia Argentina 2012-II (AP/DOC/2258/2012).

Zambrano, Pilar, Sacristán, Estela, "El valor de la vida del embrión en la jurisprudencia estadounidense y argentina," en Boletín Mexicano de Derecho Comparado, nueva serie, año XLV, 134, mayo-agosto de 2012.

Zúñiga Fajuri, M. A., "Derecho a la vida y Constitución: consecuencias de la sentencia de la Corte Interamericana de Derechos Humanos Artavia Murillo v. Costa Rica," en Estudios Constitucionales: Revista del Centro de Estudios Constitucionales 2014, pp. 71-104.

Pilar Zambrano

9 A Moral Reading of Argentine Constitutional Case Law on the Right to Life before Birth

Abstract: This chapter describes, compares, and assesses the argumentative reasoning underlying the three leading cases of the Argentine Constitutional Court that define the legal value of unborn human life: *Tanus* (2001); *Portal de Belén* (2002); and *F.A.L.*, *(2012)*. After a brief description of the "one-step moral reading" interpretative methodology that sustains our own interpretation of these decisions (Section I), three strands of study are deployed in the next paragraphs. First, we review the abstract interpretative arguments issued by the Court regarding the acceptance or rejection of prenatal legal personhood in Argentine Constitutional Law (Sections II and III). Second, we focus on the semantic margin of interpretation that either explicitly or implicitly underlies these abstract interpretative arguments (Sections IV and V). At this stage, our analysis shows that the one-step moral reading interpretative model explained in Section I, has more explanatory power than the alternative two-step one. Third, we focus on the justificatory horizon of interpretation entailed in the interpretative arguments previously identified (Section VI). Finally, we assess the coherence between the categorical nature of fundamental rights, on the one hand, and the semantic and justificatory tenets assumed by the different compositions of the Court, when defining the legal *status* of unborn human life (Section VII).

Keywords: Moral reading, Semantics and interpretation, Abortion, F.A.L., Portal de belén-tanus

1 Introduction[1]

Argentine constitutional case law in regards to the legal *status* of unborn human life may be divided in two distinct eras. The first era was initiated by the leading cases *Tanus* (2001) and *Portal de Belén* (2002), when courts held that constitutional and international human rights Covenants that are binding in Argentina recognize a personal quality in each and every human being from the time of conception, which was, in turn, placed at the moment of fertilization[2]. On this basis, it was understood that these same norms proscribe making the legal term of human

---

1 Sections 3, 8, and 9 of this chapter include a revised and adapted version of some sections of my co-authored article, ZAMBRANO, P., SACRISTÁN, E., «Semantics and Legal Interpretation. A Comparative Study of the Value of Embryonic life under Argentine and U.S. Constitutional Case law», *Journal of Civil Law Studies*, Vol 6, N.1 (2013), 97–140.
2 T., S. c/ Gobierno de la Ciudad de Buenos Aires s/ amparo, Fallos: 324: 5 (2001); *Portal de Belén - Asociación Civil sin Fines de Lucro c/ Ministerio de Salud y Acción Social de la Nación s/amparo*, Fallos: 325: 292 (2002).

life –which is always the life of a person—dependent on its stage of development or on its (chances of) viability inside or outside the womb. Subsequently, the second era commenced with the more recent case *F.A.L.* (2012)[3]. Even though this decision did not explicitly overturn *Tanus´* and *Portal´s* interpretative judgments, it strongly revised Argentina's constitutional and international legal obligations to protect unborn human life, almost to the point of overturning the former interpretative premises.

After a brief description of the "one-step moral reading" interpretative methodology that sustains our own reading of Argentine constitutional case law (Section I), three strands of study will be deployed in the next paragraphs. First, a review of Argentine constitutional case law will be carried out in order to identify the abstract interpretative arguments regarding the acceptance or rejection of prenatal legal personhood in Argentine Law that have been explicitly stated in the three leading cases (Sections II and III). Second, analysis will be focused on the semantic margin of interpretation that either explicitly or implicitly underlies those abstract interpretative arguments (Sections IV and V). At this stage, our analysis shows that the one-step moral reading interpretative model explained in Section I has more explanatory power than the alternative two-step one. Third, the study will be directed towards the justificatory horizon of interpretation entailed in the interpretative arguments previously identified (Section VI). In the final stage, we aim to test the coherence between the categorical nature of fundamental rights, on the one hand, and the semantic and justificatory tenets assumed by the different compositions of the Court, when defining the legal *status* of unborn human life (Section VII).

2 A One-Step Moral Reading of the Constitution

As has been previously remarked by various legal-philosophical schools of thought, the abstract nature of constitutional language remains an open door to political, ethical, and philosophical assessments. In Rawlsian terms, this "open door" incorporates to legal practice, the "comprehensive conceptions" of those who interpret and adjudicate Law.[4] Such an inevitable combination of legal and moral reasoning is the object of an intense, ongoing discussion concerning Law´s ability to check the interpreter´s moral pre-conceptions.

Some authors take a negative stance either out of systematic distrust about the actual intention of legal operators to stick to the law, as is the case of Duncan Kennedy; or out of semantic skepticism, as is the case of Stanley Fish.[5] On the other

---

3   Case F. 259. XLVI. "*F., A. L.* s/ medida autosatisfactiva," 13/3/2012.
4   See RAWLS, JOHN (2005): xvi.
5   Stanley Fish has settled his skeptical position mainly in opposition of Dworkin´s claim that interpretation may and should "fit" with legal practice, among other works, in FISH, STANLEY (1982): 551; and (1983): 299. A good synthesis of the discussion may be found in SADOWSKI, M (2001):1099 ss.

extreme, Andrei Marmor argues, just as Hart had done some time before, that legal adjudication involves moral reasoning only on the rare occasions where the semantic meaning of legal discourse is under-determined.[6] Accordingly, Dennis Patterson distinguishes between understanding and interpretation. For Patterson, while understanding amounts to a neutral identification of the abstract *given* meaning of legal sources and of their applicability to concrete cases, interpretation "depends upon understanding (. . .) already being in place". Interpretation would thus be a "therapeutic" activity, consisting of filling in the gaps left open by a "breakdown or failure in understanding".[7]

Against this two-steps description, Ronald Dworkin has insistently maintained that the creative, moral, and teleological dimension of legal interpretation is neither exceptional nor separable from a neutral understanding of legal sources. In the first place, legal interpretation is always intermingled with moral reasoning because it is also necessarily "justificatory," and therefore always teleological. In the second place, moral reasoning involves all the partial judgments or stages of interpretation, including those which Patterson would call "understanding[s]." Notwithstanding the holistic, moral nature of interpretation, he also maintains that it is possible to objectively distinguish between valid and invalid "moral readings" of the law, both in the case of dogmatic or scientific analysis and in the case of judicial adjudication.[8] In his view, so long as the moral reading "fits" both the general purpose of Law and the concrete way in which each legal practice has actualized its general purpose along its respective historical development, the practice does not amount to sheer construction.[9]

Under this double-fit condition, the moral reading of a constitution remains legal if, and only if, it is coherent with the final values that all legal practices claim to instantiate, and with the way in which each legal practice determines, concretizes, or specifies those common values. The former condition is intended to adjust legal interpretations to the goals that distinguish the law not only from other kinds of social practices, but also and mainly from sheer violence. The latter, instead, proposes to adjust legal interpretations to the specific legal practices *within which* each interpretation takes place.[10]

---

6 See HART, HERBERT, L., (1994): 124; and MARMOR, ANDREI (1995): 23, where he distinguishes (neutral) understanding and (creative) interpretation from a general point of view; and idem: 122, applying this same distinction to the law.
7 See PATTERSON, DENNIS, (2005): 692.
8 The term "moral reading" is taken from DWORKIN, RONALD, (1996): 17.
9 See DWORKIN, RONALD, (1977): chaps. I–IV; (1985): chaps I–VI, specially, 17 and 143–145; (1986): 65–68-, 411–413; (1996): 10; (2006), 18–21; (2011): 130 et sq.
10 The idea that Law substitutes violence as a way of solving social conflicts entails the logical conclusion that the *claim* to replace violence is a necessary element of any legal system. At this level of abstraction, this idea does not yet involve any answer to the question "how should sheer violence be replaced?" and it is partaken by the analytical tradition in the work of authors such as HART, HERBERT, L., (1994): 172;

Focusing our analysis on the substantive content of these two conditions, they may be restated in a *frame* that confines the moral reading of constitutions within two margins: a justificatory-teleological "horizon," and a semantic foundation. The justificatory horizon of interpretation encompasses the values, goods, and ends that justify the existence of legal practices generally, and the anthropological and semantic (epistemic) tenets entailed in the assertion of these values.[11] The semantic ground is composed, on its part, of the textual (in a lexicographic sense), grammatical, and discursive rules that govern the specific texts under interpretation.[12]

Discursive rules allow the reader to pass from a static to a "dynamic" understanding of the texts, by contextualizing the texts' lexicographical and grammatical meanings, both in the general field of law and in the specific legal practice wherein the interpretation takes place. Given the fact that this contextualization can only be performed under the light of the very ends, values, or goods that justify legal practices generally, discursive rules should neither be conflated with, nor reduced to, the interpretative directives that govern each legal practice or each field of law therein. Discursive rules are the outcome of interpreting interpretative directives, but only under the light of the named, final justificatory values.[13]

Three key conclusions should be made at this point. In the first place, as this brief incursion into the nature of discursive rules proves, the two margins of interpretation do not function separately but in a check and balance manner, both limiting and guiding each other. Thus, the identification of the *relevant* legal texts that make up the "semantic margin" of interpretation is the outcome of a preliminary, interpretative judgment (referred to by Ronald Dworkin as the "pre-interpretative judgment"), concerning the nature of both legal sources and the legal system to

---

or RAZ, JOSEPH, (2003): 13 and, most famously, by "non-positivist" authors such as ALEXY, ROBERT, (2002): 47. For an updated analysis of the current discussions around the conceptual relationship between Law and violence, see WEINRIB, JAKUB (2016): 78 et sq.

11 See ZAMBRANO, PILAR (2015): 323–324.
12 It might be argued, as we do, that the semantic ground is never enough a reason for justifying an interpretative statement. Nevertheless, it is hardly discussable that it is always a necessary element of any justified act of interpretation. *See*, WRÒBLESKI, JERZY, AND MAC CORMICK, NEIL (1994): 260; ZAMBRANO (2009): 65 et sq.
13 In a very similar vein, Jerzy WROBLEWSKI argues that contextualization is a necessary condition of every act of interpretation, and that it engenders problems of fuzziness that should not be confused with semantic fuzziness, WROBLEWSKI, JERZY (1985): 242. Focused on the field of international public law, Daniel Peat and Matthew Windsor notice that "a range of issues pertaining to the meaning of the Vienna Convention on the Law of Treaties rules continues to be debated, which is hardly surprising given that the rules on interpretation themselves require interpretation," in PEAT, DANIEL, and WINDSOR, MATTHEW (2015): 6. Against, finding that discursive rules are capable of being neutrally identified, see PATTERSON, DENNISON, (2005): 687.

which the sources pertain.¹⁴ The semantic frame of interpretation is therefore not somewhere "out there," already made up, waiting to be discovered. It is, instead, the outcome of a preliminary interpretative act that involves giving prevalence to certain legal sources over others. So long as this act entails choice, it is either blindly (and hence arbitrarily) made, or else it is grounded in the values, ends, or goods that justify legal practices. If the latter is true, then the teleological frame of interpretation is at stake from the very beginning, when the semantic "ground" is set up by the interpreter. These considerations explain why the one-step moral reading model has more explanatory power than the two-step picture of legal interpretation, stuck in the distinction between understanding and interpretation.

The second conclusion is that the justificatory margin may be studied from either a general or concrete perspective. In the first case, the question is which values, ends, or goods justify general legal practices, and which are the anthropological and semantic (epistemic) theories encompassed by these values. From a concrete perspective, the question is which values, ends, or goods justify a certain legal practice as a matter of fact, according to the interpretative judgments historically entrenched in it. The answer to this question is that which Ronald Dworkin names "inclusive integrity"¹⁵

Finally, asserting that the teleological margin of interpretation controls the whole of legal interpretation does not make legal interpreters as Herculean philosophers, as has so frequently been understood following Dworkin's interpretative theory.¹⁶ It only means that each time a legal text is interpreted and applied, the identified justificatory tenets are put at stake both at a general and at a concrete level, whether or not the interpreter is aware of it. In the face of the inevitable margin of choice that always remains open by the semantic margin of interpretation, any interpreter who sincerely aims at "playing the game of law" should choose the answer that he believes best realizes the concrete values entrenched in the concrete practice wherein the interpretation takes place. However, given that the "entrenched" values may be understood and combined in different ways, all of them feasible from a semantic point of view, the teleological values that justify legal practices from a general perspective are also at stake on this second level of decision.¹⁷ Moreover, the fact that interpreters generally remain unaware of the justificatory or philosophical implications of their reasoning is a good reason for analyzing judicial decisions.

---

14 Ronald Dworkin sustains that, even though the "pre-interpretative" judgment is inseparable from the justificatory one, he also notices that it is the less constructive dimension of interpretation. See DWORKIN, RONALD (1986): 69; DWORKIN, RONALD (2006): 169. we believe that this is an oversimplification, in view of the fact that one of the most controversial dimensions of interpretation is, precisely, the way that the sources (be them principles or rules) are ordered and balanced among themselves.
15 DWORKIN, RONALD, (1986): 404–407.
16 On these critics and Dworkin's response, see DWORKIN, RONALD (2003): 661–663.
17 DWORKIN, RONALD (1986): 65–68; (2011): 130 et sq.

Against this backdrop, our general purpose in what follows is to analyze Argentinian constitutional case law regarding the legal status of unborn human life, under the guidance of the one-step moral reading model and with the aim of revealing its justificatory and semantic margins (or postulates).

3 The Pro-Life Era (2001–2012): *Tanus* and *Portal de Belén*.

In *Tanus* and *Portal de Belén*, the Argentine Supreme Court determined the sense and scope of the fundamental norms that expressively recognize the right to life in relation to prenatal life. Both judicial decisions give rise to the following interpretative rule: unborn human beings are entitled to the right to life, whose scope is equal to the right to life of already born persons, and no differences based on the life's stage of development or on its viability shall be established.

In *Tanus*, the majority of the Court affirmed a previous judicial decision, which had authorized the induction of childbirth labor of an anencephalic fetus in a public hospital. In reaching this decision, the Court pointed out that, even though the authorization to perform the childbirth labor induction had been requested in the 20th week of pregnancy, at the moment the case was to be decided by the Supreme Court, the mother had reached the eighth month of pregnancy. According to the Court, this temporal difference allowed for differentiating childbirth labor induction on the one hand, and an abortion on the other. It was argued that the death of an anencephalic fetus outside the mother's womb, once the stage of extra-uterine viability is reached, is not to be attributed to the anticipated childbirth labor induction, but to the congenital condition.

This noticeable effort to distinguish the facts of the case from those in the case of abortion was grounded in the underlying normative interpretation according to which the fundamental right to life remains enforceable from the moment of conception under the American Convention for Human Rights (Law 23054), Article 4.1, and under Article 2 (Law 23849) that incorporates to Argentine Law, the International Covenant on the Rights of the Child.[18]

---

18 *Tanus (*Cons. 11°). Art. 4th of the American Convention for Human Rights states: "Right to life. 1. Every person has a right to her life being respected. This right shall be granted by Law and, in general, from the moment of conception. Nobody shall be arbitrarily deprived of his life" (the translation is ours). Article 2° of Law 23849 states: "When ratifying the Convention, the following reserves and declarations shall be stated: (. . .) In relation to article 1 of the Convention, the Argentine Republic declares that it shall be interpreted in the sense that the term "child" is understood to refer to all human beings from the moment of conception and until eighteen years old" (The translation is ours). In Spanish: "Al ratificar la Convención, deberán formularse las siguientes reservas y declaraciones: (. . .) Con relación al artículo 1° de la Convención sobre los Derechos del Niño, la República Argentina declara que el mismo debe interpretarse en el sentido que se entiende

In *Portal de Belén*, the Court reaffirmed this normative interpretation, further specifying that conception takes place at the moment of fertilization. In stating this, the Court relied on scientific findings:

> it is a scientific fact that the 'genetic construction' of the person is there, all set and ready to be biologically directed because 'the egg's [zigote] DNA contains the anticipated description of all the ontogenesis in its tiniest details.[19]

From the factual point of view, the Court considered it proven that a contraceptive device, the marketing and distribution of which had been already authorized by the National Ministry of Health and Social Action, would operate under three key guidelines. Firstly, the device would prevent ovulation, or secondly, it would operate as a spermicide. These posed no constitutional objection from the point of view of an embryo's right to life. However, in a third manner, and in order to prevent conception in the event that the two primary means were not successfully activated, the challenged contraceptive would operate by modifying the endometrium and therefore prevent embryo implantation. The Court found that it was this third purpose that violated the embryo's right to life. On the basis of these normative and factual premises, the Supreme Court overturned the appellate court's decision that had permitted the National Ministry of Health and Social Action to authorize the marketing and distribution of the contraceptive in question.

The ruling established in both cases regarding the legal *status* of prenatal life could be, thus, summarized as follows:

➢ Legal personhood is acknowledged since the moment of conception, under both the Argentinian Constitution and International Human Rights Law. Based upon scientific findings, conception is deemed to occur at the moment of fertilization. Therefore, the scientific debate regarding the distinction between pre-embryos and embryos, or between viable embryos and non-viable embryos, lacks any legal basis.

The most relevant, normative roots for the recognition of a right to life from the moment of conception (fertilization) are Article 4.1 of the American Covenant on Human Rights (ACHR) and the declaration introduced by Argentina when ratifying the International Covenant on the Rights of the Child. Although the Court does not explicitly present its own interpretation of Article 4.1 (ACHR), the fact of having used it as a normative premise in the finding indicates that, in its view, the expression "in general" does not exempt Argentina from its international legal duty to refrain from deploying health policies that have an effect of interrupting the embryo's development from the moment of fertilization. In the same vein, by using the declaration made by Argentina when ratifying the International

---

por niño todo ser humano desde el momento de su concepción y hasta los 18 años de edad."
19 Cons. 7°.

Covenant on the Rights of the Child as a source of international human rights law, the Court equated its legal force to that of the main text of the Covenant itself.

Finally, it should be noted that the Court used a declaratory judgment of the Inter-American Court of Human Rights (IACHR) as sufficient normative ground for issuing a writ of mandamus against the executive branch of government. In so doing, it turned what some authors call "soft law" into a valid source of international human rights law.[20]

Summing up, the Court made at least three types of interpretative judgments. Firstly, it performed an underpinning "pre-interpretative" judgment (in Dworkin's terms), according to which the sources of international human rights law include the main text of Conventions, the reservations and declarations introduced by signatory states, and the interpretative practices developed by the IACHR. Secondly, it issued a grammatical interpretative judgment, according to which the expression "in general," stated in Article 4.1 ACHR, does not allow for exceptions to the State obligation to defend unborn human life. Thirdly, it stated a scientific or factual finding, which defines conception as taking place in the moment of fertilization.

Even though the abstract, pre-interpretative judgment concerning the sources of international human rights law would later be reaffirmed in *F.A.L*, this decision drastically changed the criteria used in *Tanus-Portal* for identifying the relevant sources influencing the interpretation of Article 4.1 ACHR and the obligations undertaken by Argentina under this norm and in regards to unborn human life.

4 The Mother's Right to Choose Era Initiated in *F.A.L.*

F.A.L. is the first decision of the Argentine Supreme Court directly concerned with the constitutional interpretation of Article 86, sec. 2 of the federal criminal code. This norm makes it a crime to procure an abortion, "except when pregnancy is the outcome of rape, or of an offense to the honor of an idiot or insane woman."[21] Since its promulgation in 1901, *F.A.L.* has never been constitutionally challenged; however, it has become the object of fierce interpretative debates within the field of criminal law.

Those favoring a pro-abortion position defended an ample interpretation, according to which the comma inserted in between the words "rape" and "or" meant that the exception to the criminalization of abortion was double: it covered both the case of pregnancies that are the outcome of the rape of any woman, and the cases of pregnancies that are the outcome of an "offense to the honor" on insane women. Pro-life positions indorsed a strict interpretation, arguing that pregnancy can never be the result of an "offense to honor." Accordingly, they claimed that the coma had the function of distinguishing between pregnancies that are the effect of

---

20 Portal: cons. 15, citing Consultive Opinion 11/90:23.
21 In Spanish: "si el embarazo proviene de una violación o de un atentado al pudor cometido sobre una mujer idiota o demente."

rape committed on an insane or idiot woman and pregnancies through consensual sexual intercourse between a sane male and an insane woman, whose consent, precisely because of coming from an insane person, is inherently void.[22]

In *F.A.L.*, the Supreme Court decided a final ruling to this historical semantic dispute, not only based on the former grammatical argument, but also and mainly on a strictly constitutional one. The *holding* of the case was stated in the Eighth Consideration, where the Court affirmed "only the ample interpretation of Article 86, sec. 2 is valid, according to Constitutional and international human rights law." This holding was sustained on the following normative and interpretative arguments:

Article 75, sec. 23 of the national constitution does not affirm a state´s obligation to protect unborn human life with the force of criminal penalties, but only to pass on a social security normative framework (cons. 9).

Under the fundamental rights of equality, non-discrimination, and dignity, recognized by Article 16 of the National Constitution, under "diverse" Human Rights Covenants; and under the fundamental principles of legality and *pro homine* recognized by Article Seventeen of the National Constitution (Considerations 8 and 18), women have a right not to be criminally prosecuted for having an abortion in case of rape.

Under these same rules, women that are the victims of rape also have a right to access free, quick, secure, and healthy abortion procedures in public health institutions.

The Court did not straightforwardly deny that the State is obliged to protect the *nasciturus* (unborn) as a subject of rights. Nevertheless, it warned that neither does the *nasciturus* remain entitled to an absolute right to life, nor is the state obliged to use the weight of criminal law in securing this (relative) right.[23] Performing a double leap forward, the Court then jumped from the state´s *faculty* not to turn abortion into a criminal offense, to the state´s *obligation* not to criminalize it in cases of rape and, furthermore, to the positive obligation of the state to facilitate quick, secure, and healthy abortion procedures for any woman who claims to have been raped, her mere assertion being sufficient evidence to allow the procedure.

This triple downgrade of the state´s obligations concerning the protection of unborn human life was sustained on a radically different grammatical judgment from those issued previously in *Tanus* and *Portal*. Thus, the Court argued that the expression "in general" within Article 4.1 ACHR was explicitly intended by its drafters to constrain the obligations undertaken by States with respect to the protection of unborn human life, thus excluding any duty to secure it with the force of criminal law. This "originalist" perspective of the interpretation of Article 4.1

---

22 About this longstanding discussion in Argentine Criminal Law, see Rabbi - Baldi Cabanillas, Renato: 331–378.
23 Cons. 10.

ACHR was, in turn, sustained by a report from the Human Rights Committee of the Convention on the Human Rights of the Children (CHRCH).

Regarding the declaratory judgment introduced by Argentina when signing the CHRCH, the Court found that it was not of a binding nature, for it was not reserved under the terms of Article Two of the Vienna Convention on the Law of Treaties. Finally, the Court cited the reports from different Human Rights Committees as a valid legal source for its decision that Argentina was under the international obligation not to place undue burdens on abortion procedures.[24]

5 A Shared Plain Monist Conception of the International Legal System of Human Rights

As was formulated in the introduction, legal interpretation operates within two margins: a semantic or textual "ground," and a justificatory or teleological horizon of interpretation. The semantic margin is made up of all the relevant legal sources applicable to the case, *plus* the textual, grammatical, and discursive rules that apply to the language of these sources.

Along these lines, the most basic interpretative judgment that any Court is bound to make concerns the choice of the relevant normative sources that make up the semantic margin that is applicable to the case in question. This judgment shouldn´t be expected to be drawn from a "neutral" reading of the sources of international law, as if these were "out there," waiting to be discovered.[25] The question regarding which are the relevant sources of law is perhaps one of the most disputed ones in the field of international law, given the fact of the plurality of factors and practices that converge in its construction[26].

According to Article 75.22 of the National Constitution, the constitutional Bill of Rights is complemented with those rights recognized in all of the Human Rights Conventions signed and ratified by Argentina. Therefore, Courts in Argentina are required to determine whether or not Argentine constitutional law integrates a loose monist system, under which Argentina would only be bound by the texts of the Conventions and by its own interpretative practice of them; or else, a plain monist system, under which Argentina would also be bound by the interpretative practice jointly developed by other relevant officials of international human rights law.

The discursive rules used by both compositions of the Court show that they share a plain monist conception of the system of international human rights law.

---

24 *See* Consideration 6, citing the Final Observations issued by the Committee on Human Rights CCPR/C/Arg/Co /4, of 22/03/2010, and the Final Observations issued by the Committee on the Rights of Children, CRC/C/ARg/Co/3-4, of 21/06/2010.
25 About the impracticability of formalism in the field of international law, *see*, for example, Peat, D., Windsor, M. (2015): 5.
26 *See* VENZKE, I. (2012): 6.

In *Portal* and *Tanus*, the Court extended the formal (textual) frame of international sources of human rights law, incorporating as (new) binding sources some interpretative rules issued by the American Court of Human Rights in cases not involving Argentina. Similarly, in *FAL*, the Court extended the formal textual frame, incorporating as binding, some interpretative rules stated in recommendations and reports that had been issued by different Human Rights Committees.

The Court thus assumed in both stages an underpinning plain monist conception of the international system and practice of human rights, according to which national and international bills of rights should be interpreted and applied in a unique, coherent, and systematic way, by all national and international authorities.

6 Two Different Readings of the Same "Semantic" Margin of Interpretation

The concurrence of both Court's compositions in a plain monist system of international human rights law does not hide a deep disagreement concerning the way of balancing the sources within the system. In effect, the Committees' recommendations and reports that were used in *FAL* as interpretative rules leading to the recognition of a right to abortion in cases of rape already existed at the time that *Tanus* and *Portal* were decided. Nevertheless, the Court did not even discuss their applicability to the interpretation of Article 4.1 ACHR, using instead the (contrary) interpretative declaration introduced by Argentina to the CCHHR.

On the other hand, the Court in *FAL* dismissed the interpretative force of this declaration, altering it in favor of the named recommendations and reports. In view of this deep disagreement, it is pertinent to analyze the extent to which one and the other "pre-interpretative judgments" were actually respectful of the textual, grammatical, and discursive rules that make up the semantic margins of interpretation.

Article 3 of the ACHR asserts the right of every *person* to be recognized as a *legal* person, and Article 6 of the ICCPR states that "every *human person* is entitled to its inherent right to life." Had the Court interpreted these rules in isolation, the Court in *FAL* could have argued that unborn human beings are neither "persons" in the language of the former Convention, nor "human *persons*" in the language of the latter. Nevertheless, at least from a textual point of view, this interpretation is undermined by Article 4.1 ACHR that adjudicates the right to life; not to every person, but to every human being. Thus, it clarifies that the concept of "person" in Article 3 refers to every human being. This co-extensive scope of the concepts of person and human being remains even clearer in the case of UDHR Article 6, which directly recognizes the right of every human being (as well as every person) to be indeed recognized as a person.

Along these lines, it is understandable that the Court in *FAL* did not make any effort to deny the *nasciturus'* wholly legal personhood, as the American Supreme Court had done previously in *Roe v. Wade*.[27] Simply put, the textual frame of

---

27 *Roe v. Wade*, 410 US 113 (1973): 158.

interpretation did not allow this reading. On the contrary and perhaps paradoxically, the Court affirmed both the personal *status* of the *nasciturus* and its right to life, while simultaneously denying the State's obligation to protect it in every case. Here it should be remembered that the Court asserted that the obligation of the state "to legally protect the *nasciturus* as a subject or rights," required by ACHR Article 3, should be interpreted together with Article 4.1 that only requires from States "a limited legal protection to the *nasciturus*' right to life"[28].

Regarding the choice made in *FAL* not to abide by the Argentinian declaration in the CHRCH, neither a textual nor a discursive analysis leads to a *conclusive* denial of its binding force. From a textual point of view, an interpretative declaration is, by definition, a unilateral assertion of the meaning of one's statements. If the statements at stake are part of an International Convention, it necessarily follows that the binding force of the declaration depends on the rules that apply to it. In the context of international conventions, declarations are understood as unilateral expressions of the sense that a certain State bestows to the obligations thereby assumed, that might be useful in case of future interpretative conflicts, but which are not essential conditions either for their acceptance or continuation. Instead, reservations always function as a necessary and exclusionary condition both for becoming and for remaining a part of a Treaty or a Convention. Notwithstanding, it is widely accepted that this difference does not flow from the title under which either declarations or reservations are incorporated in Treaties and Conventions. States rather frequently introduce actual reserves under the name of interpretative declarations (so called "conditional declarations"), whose intended effects are exactly the same as those of the reserves. Under this light, the Court was required to argue (but did not argue) in this case why and how did it come to the conclusion that the interpretative declaration incorporated by Argentina was an actual declaration and not, instead, a "conditional" one.[29]

Neither do the textual and discursive meanings of "recommendations" and "reports" lead to the conclusion that their binding force outweighs that of interpretative declarations. From a textual point of view, a recommendation is, by its very definition, an optional counsel. In respect to reports, nothing in the definition of a "report" includes a binding nature. From a discursive-contextual perspective, it should be added that none of the norms governing the effect of recommendations and reports state that these are binding for the admonished state, let alone third party states.

Sticking to this discursive analysis, it should be added that although the *stare decisis* strictly considered is not incorporated in Argentine constitutional law, there remains an entrenched practice of explicitly justifying brusque shifts in case law.

---

28 Cons. 10.
29 *See* "Report from the UN Committee on International Law," 2011, directives 1.3.2 and 1.4.

Nevertheless, the Court in *FAL* did not say a word regarding the need to overrule the use of *Tanus-Portal* of the interpretative declaration as a valid interpretative rule. At this point, we might conclude that the Court in *FAL* was not respectful of the semantic margin of interpretation. Nevertheless, it may still be argued that this semantic margin left a thin, but real, open window for the named shift. In effect, once the Court in *Tanus-Portal* adopted a plain monist system conception of human rights law, what actually needed to be justified was the substantial conception of justice that led the Court to make such a brusque shift in its understanding of international human rights law. Is this shift sustained by compelling reasons of justice that justify the loss of legal coherence?

7 The Deep Discussion at the Justificatory Level

The Court's decision to give prevalence to the interpretative declaration of the CCHHR in *Tanus-Portal* was explicitly acknowledged as follows:

> The right to life is the chief natural right of the human person, previous to all positive law (. . .). The human being is the central axis of the whole legal system and, as an end in itself—beyond its transcendental nature—its person is inviolable and constitutes a fundamental value respecting which all other values are instrumental. (Cons. 12)

This paragraph contains quite an explicit statement of the justificatory, anthropological, and semantic postulates that sustain the Court's decision to give precedence to the Argentine interpretative declaration over the rest of the sources. Regarding the justificatory postulate, the whole legal practice is justified by its potential to secure respect of pre-existing, natural rights that stem from the inviolable, personal nature of *every* human being. The final value that justifies the existence of legal practices, both in general and in the concrete case of Argentina, therefore acts in its ability to secure the named, natural rights and their root, human dignity.

The anthropological and semantic tenets implied in this final value are in fact two sides of the same coin. From an anthropological perspective, it is understood that all human beings are persons, independently of their physical conditions. Thus, all human beings are dignified, dignity being the name for the "inviolable nature" of each and all persons or human beings. This anthropological view falls within the semantic postulate, according to which neither the legal concept of person nor rights generally are conceived as purely social or institutional constructions. They are, instead, comprehended as intelligible forms, stemming from the intelligible nature of the human being.

The teleological horizon sustaining the Court's decision in *FAL* is not as explicit as it was in *Tanus* and *Portal*. Nevertheless, even if the meanings of the concepts of person and dignity are not defined, they are somewhat made apparent in the way the Court uses them, notably when balancing the right to life of unborn human beings against women's allegedly contradicting rights to dignity and non-discrimination.

In the first place, the Court switches the pivotal role assigned in *Portal* to "previous natural rights" from "principles of equality and non-discrimination," which are now taken as "the axis of both the national and international human legal order."[30] In the second place, the meanings of both principles are determined following (a chosen section of) the international human rights' interpretative practice. This switch reveals a conventional semantic postulate, according to which the meaning of legal concepts is not determined by any intrinsically intelligible reference, but rather by the legal interpretative practices themselves. Using Putnam's distinctions, the meaning of legal concepts is conventionally constructed, and this construction "is prior to reference."[31]

The Court then more deeply analyzes the (conventionally constructed) meaning of "non-discrimination," asserting that decriminalizing abortion only in the case of insane women is an unreasonable discrimination against victims of rape and, furthermore, it entails using women as "means" and thereby affecting their dignity. One may ask at this point why is the Court only concerned with the use of women as a means to protect unborn human beings, and not with the likewise use of unborn human beings as a means to protect women's dignity. The fact that the Court does not even pose this obvious question sufficiently reveals the justificatory horizon it is using in interpreting the legal practice as a whole. That is, a self-conflicted understanding of human rights according to which rights are undetermined spheres of liberty with no other limit than the most probable chance of clashing with others' liberties, and the entrenched way of solving similar clashes in a given legal practice.[32]

"Conflictivism" is actually the other side of the coin of semantic conventionalism. If legal concepts are pure conventional constructions, there are no reasons why they should be constructed in one way or another, nor why the scope of human rights should be traced to one point or another. All we are left with are more or less disguised but polite passing conflicts of interests, where the winning segment is blessed with the language of rights, while the losing segment is stricken from the discursive practice, at least for the time being.

---

30 (Cons. 16).
31 As it is well known, the alternative between giving priority to reference over meaning when determining the sense of concepts was stated and developed in the field of Philosophy of Language by Saul Kripke and Hillary Putnam, in KRIPKE, SAUL (1980), and PUTNAM, HILLARY (1975). These theories were applied to the problem of legal interpretation by MICHAEL MOORE, among many other works, in (2001): 2091 and, with some differences, by Nicos STAVROPOULOS (1996), and DAVID BRINK (2001): 12–65. For a critical revision of these theories, *see* BRIAN BIX (2003): 281–295. About the limitative role of semantics in interpretation out of the English language field *see*, for example, WRÓBLEWSKI, JERZY (2001): 108; and ZAMBRANO, PILAR (2009): 131–152.
32 *See* Cianciardo, J. (2009): 130 sq.

8 A Comparative Synthesis from the Justificatory and Semantic Points of View

The comparative synthesis between both stages of the Court's rulings show the unfolding of a semantic-justificatory debate relating to the most radical, conceptual distinction in the world of law: the one that separates things, on the one hand, and persons, on the other. The substantive question at stake is whom we call the person or subject of the Law, why, and what does it mean to be a person from a legal point of view.

But this justificatory or teleological topic cannot be solved if no viewpoint is previously adopted in relation to the joint, but more abstract, semantic and epistemic debate: how are things generally classified in the world, and, particularly, in the legal field? Are conceptual classifications the result of a reflexive and somewhat explicit social debate that the Law is destined to adopt, as far as there be prior consent? Are concepts the interested impositions of a social group, picked up by the Law and clothed with its coactive force? Or are they something close to the representation of reality, which emerges before us, already classified, if not thoroughly, at least partially?

Regarding the unborn being's legal personhood, these questions could be restated in the following way: Does the constitutional judicial practice here reviewed *find* the personal or un-personal nature of unborn human life as the product of some sort of social construction? Or instead, does it view it as something already given to intelligence, as a self-standing being to be disclosed? Which are the semantic and epistemic theories implied in the interpretative arguments used in one and another judicial stage?

Perhaps aiming for profit from the credibility of scientific discourse, the Argentine Supreme Court in *Portal* based its interpretation concerning the moment of conception almost exclusively on geneticists' findings. Nevertheless, it should be noticed that the Supreme Court in *FAL* managed to rely upon the same normative framework and scientific concepts and findings, and still attributed to them quite different moral and legal consequences. The availability of the same scientific findings and of the same normative framework for both compositions of the Court shows that the decisions in *Tanus, Portal,* and *FAL* were neither grounded in a neutral scientific description of human life nor in an outright legal interpretation of the normative framework. The main question being posed to both compositions of the Court was neither "when do genetics situate the appearance of a new human being?" nor "do valid legal rules grant a right to life to unborn human beings?" The most fundamental question remains whether or not unborn human beings are entitled to the same concern and respect that is due to born human beings and, if so, why.

Along this line, the strongest reason sustaining the *Tanus-Portal* pre-interpretative and interpretative conclusions was an answer to this meta-legal question, according to which in the first place, the reference to the concept of dignity is co-extensive with the reference to the concept of human nature and therefore independent of the factual possibilities of either being actualized. Therefore, all human beings are persons both in an anthropological and legal sense. Secondly, it is this reference that determines the *legal* meaning of "dignity" and of the broad concept of fundamental rights, and not the other way round. Accordingly, the content of the obligations of the Head of the State in order to secure rights is not *only* determined by legal tradition, but *also* and mainly, by the nature of this reference.

Although the deepest reason sustaining *FAL*'s pre-interpretative and interpretative conclusions is not as obvious as it was in *Tanus-Portal*, it is still noticeable. Once it was recognized that unborn human beings were legal persons, what justification was there to assert that women are entitled to a right to receive public health assistance in receiving an abortion? It should be once more remarked that the Court could have only affirmed that women are entitled to a right to not be penalized. In so doing, it might be argued, for example, that criminalizing women in cases of abortion in rape-induced pregnancies is a disproportionate and thus unreasonable policy. Notwithstanding how controversial this line of argument might be, it does not necessarily entail negating all practical measures associated with the recognition of legal personhood of unborn human beings.

On the contrary, the positive obligation of the Head of State to direct government assistance for abortion procedures is nothing more and nothing less than an obligation to sacrifice one holder of rights (the fetus) in favor of another (the mother). This in turn can only be understood through the view of an underlying downgrade of the inherent worth of the former in relation to the latter. The inquiry may still go further, in search of the reasons for this downgrade, where the view of the Court lies only in the discursive dynamics of the legal practice itself: it is the way the concept of "person," as applied to unborn human beings, has been understood in the field of human rights international law.

It is as if Wittgenstein's theory of "language games" had been radically reinterpreted, and the "legal game" had been taken to be completely alien, both to other "language games" and to its own field of reference. This aspiration for a plain autonomy of legal language discloses at least two semantic assumptions. First, the values that justify the legal practice as a whole obtain their justificatory role from the sheer fact of having been endorsed by passing political and/or legal authorities. Second, and consequently, the meaning of legal concepts is absolutely determined by their use within legal practice. Legal concepts would then have no connection at all to any intrinsically intelligible reality and no other point of reference than the sheer will of those who hold the power to authoritatively fix their meaning.

9 Which Semantic and Justificatory Theories Best Fit with Constitutional Law's Final Purpose?

Two semantic postulates that ground the two interpretative stages are here compared: traditional or "criteria" semantics on the one side, and a sort of "light"—with ample space for social construction—realist semantics on the other. The last question to be posed is which of these is more coherent with the categorical and universal nature of fundamental rights?

The discussions regarding which semantic *praxis* better fits these features of fundamental rights are ample and too numerous to be reviewed in this article. However, it seems appropriate to point out that they lead us back to the basic choice that was stated above, that is, that either fundamental rights are social constructions that precede and determine their own reference or else their reference—some basic human good—precedes and determines their meaning.

If the meaning of fundamental rights is exclusively the product of a more or less controlled social construction, and what is more important, if such meaning determines its own field of reference, it would be extremely hard to explain the categorical and universal nature of rights. In effect, rights would be a legitimate and valid source of moral criticism of the law only within those political communities that have previously incorporated them through their legal practice. They would not be, therefore, universal. Secondly, as with their extension, their "trumping force" would hinge on the weight that each legal practice has attached to them, as a matter of fact. In other words, the extension and the categorical force of rights would depend upon the interests of those who handle the power to lead the social construction of their meaning, which is almost impossible to reconcile with the purpose of any constitutional practice, of "making the exercise of public authority accountable neither to the many, nor to the few, but to human dignity of each and every person subject to law´s authority."[33]

Some political philosophers sustaining this constructive approach to fundamental rights principles have openly admitted that the approach is irreconcilable with the categorical and universal nature of such rights. Particularly, when applied to the legal concept of a person.[34] Others are much more reticent to admit this failure openly. For example, Ronald Dworkin has expressly rejected what he deems to be a criterial, semantic approach to Law, according to which all legal concepts—including the concept of Law—are constructed from inside the practice itself, with no grounds other than the sheer fact of convergence about their criteria of use within the practice. Against this claim, Dworkin contends that legal concepts are interpretative and thus there is no need of fundamental convergence in their use.[35] Secondly, he has pointed out that legal and political concepts are the product of a collective, constructive practice in the light of moral and political values and, in the end, reflected in the light of a substantive conception of what counts as a good life. In this sense, he aims at distinguishing himself not only from classical, positivistic approaches to Law which assert a neutral nature to legal concepts´ constructive

---

33 *See* Weinrib, J., (2016): 18.
34 *See*, for example, John Rawls in (2005): 20.
35 *See* DWORKIN, R. (1986): 46, (2006): 12, 151.

process; but also from Rawls' *Theory of Justice*, which aspires to exclude "comprehensive conceptions" from the constructive process of political values.[36]

Ronald Dworkin answers to both of them, explaining that all interpretative concepts are the product of a holistic, constructive practice that synthesizes natural, moral, legal, and political concepts. This holistic account seems much more faithful to legal practice than the "criterial one." In effect, as it has been shown above, both compositions of the Court rely on a holistic approach to the concept of legal personhood, no matter how much both compositions try to disguise this fact.

Now, as we have said above, it is obvious that criterial semantics imply a negative answer to the question of deference to reality. But the opposite is not obvious. For the question is not only how much are legal concepts related to moral, political, or natural concepts, but also, if there is anything prior to the whole conceptual constructive process itself. And to this, Ronald Dworkin would answer "no," or better, "it doesn't matter": the only ground for the whole constructive process is a "reflective equilibrium" between coherence and conviction.[37] However, this mix of conviction and coherence is all that Dworkin claims for moral objectivism.

According to him, there is no place in his theory—nor any need—neither for self-evident or self-justified practical propositions nor, at least, for the claim that these propositions bear any relationship with human nature.[38] Further, it should be noted that although self-justified practical propositions are generally the object of moral and political convictions, this is neither always the case nor, much more important, the epistemic justification.

Now, without a reference to self-justified practical propositions, there is no critical stance with which to confront the whole conceptual constructive process.[39] Instead, if reference leads to the abstraction of meaning, when legal authorities construe intricate and obscure meanings—as, in fact, they have already done in relation to the legal concepts of "person," the reality referred to by these legal and moral concepts would cast light on their abuse in the use of language. For no matter how much *imperium* courts may have to construct and reconstruct concepts in the generic social sphere, and in the world of law in particular, they lack the power to transform and, least of all, to deny the referential frame of this construction. In other words, if reference precedes meaning, then the human or fundamental right

---

36 *See* DWORKIN, R., (2006): 160–161; 225–226.
37 *See* Idem, 162.
38 *See* DWORKIN, R., Idem: 226–227.
39 Both the possibility of grounding moral and legal objectivity in self-evident practical principles, and the possibility of acknowledging a connection between these principles and natural human ends, has constantly be defended by the New Natural Law School and, especially in the field of Law, by John Finnis. *See*, among many other works, FINNIS, J. (2011): chapter 23–24; and FINNIS, J. (1991): xi.

principles and their characteristic universality—for each and every one—and absoluteness—in all cases—would be invulnerable to the abuses of language.[40]

Having reached this stage of the discussion, it is worthwhile asking, one last time, which semantic practice fits better in the conceptual, and, therefore, the necessary characteristics of human rights? A practice that construes concepts from a *vacuum*, or a practice that construes them out with a grasp of reality? In the latter case, how does the reality referred to by the concept of human rights narrow down the construction of the legal concept of person? Is it not by imposing the only condition that its admittance be universal—for every human—and absolute—in each and every situation?

Bibliography

Alexy, Robert, *The Argument from Injustice. A Reply to Legal Positivism*, Litschewski Paulson, B., and Paulson, Stanley, L., (transl.), Oxford University Press, Oxford 2002.

Breen, John M. - Scaperlanda, Michael A., «Never Get out the Boat. *Stenberg vs. Carhart* and the Future of American Law», *Connecticut Law Review*, 39 (2006), 297–323.

Cianciardo, J., *El principio de razonabilidad. Del debido proceso sustantivo al moderno juicio de proporcionalidad*, 2da. Edición, Depalma, 2009.

Dworkin, Ronald, *Justices for Hedgeghos*, Harvard University Press, Cambridge, 2011.

Dworkin, Ronald, *Justice in Robes*, Harvard University Press, Cambridge Mass., 2006.

Dworkin, Ronald, Response to Overseas Commentators», *International Journal of Constitutional Law*, 1 (2003), 651–662.

Dworkin, Ronald *Freedom´s Law. The Moral Reading of the American Constitution*, Harvard University Press, Cambridge, 1996.

Dworkin, Ronald, *Law's Empire*, Harvard University Press, New York, 1986.

Dworkin, Ronald, «My Reply to Stanley Fish (and Walter Benn Michaels): Please Don't Talk about Objectivity Any More», in *The Politics of Interpretation*, (W.J.T. Mitchell ed.), University of Chicago Press Journals, Chicago, 1983.

Dworkin, Ronald, *Taking Rights Seriously*, Duckworth, London 1977.

---

40 An approach to the constructivist semantics that underlies the line of cases following *Roe*, see, BREEN, JOHN M. - SCAPERLANDA, MICHAEL A., «Never Get out the Boat. *Stenberg vs. Carhart* and the Future of American Law», *Connecticut Law Review*, 39 (2006), 304.

Finnis, J., *Natural Law and Natural Rights*, Oxford University Press, New York, 2nd Edition, 2011.

Finnis, J., Introduction, in: (*J. Finnis* comp.), *Natural Law*, Volume I, Darmouth 1991.

Fish,Stanley, «Working on the Chain Gang», *Texas Law Review*, 60 (1982).

Fish,Stanley, «Wrong Again», *Texas Law Review*, 62 (1983).

Marmor, Andrei, *Law and Interpretation: Essays in Legal Philosophy*, Oxford University Press, New York, 1995.

Patterson, Dennis, «Interpretation in Law», *San Diego Law Review*, 42 (2005).

Peat, Daniel, and Windsor, Matthew, «Playing the Game of Interpretation», in *Interpretation in International Law*, Oxford University Press, New York, 2015.

Raz, Jospeh, «About Morality and the Nature of Law», *American Journal of Jurisprudence*, 43 (2003).

Sadowski, M., «Language is Not Life», *Connecticut Law Review*, 33 (2001).

Weinrib, Jacob, *Dimensions of Dignity. The Theory and Practice of Modern Constitutional Law*, Cambridge University Press, 2016.

Wroblewski, Jerzy, «Legal Language and Legal Interpretation», *Law and Philosophy*, 4 (1985).

Wròbleski, Jerzy; Mac Cormick, Neil, «On Justification and Interpretation», *ARSP-Beiheft*, 53 (1994).

Zambrano, Pilar, «Fundamental Principles, Realist Semantics and Human Action», *Rechtstheorie*, 46 (2015), 323.

Zambrano, Pilar; Sacristán, Estela, «Semantics and Legal Interpretation. A Comparative Study of the Value of Embryonic life under Argentine and U.S. Constitutional Case law», Estela Sacristán, *Journal of Civil Law Studies*, Vol. 6, No.1 (2013), 97–140.

Zambrano, Pilar *La inevitable creatividad en la interpretación jurídica. Una aproximación iusfilosófica a la tesis de la discrecionalidad*, Universidad Nacional Autónoma de México (UNAM), México, 2009.´

Zambrano, Pilar «El Derecho como práctica y como discurso. La perspectiva de la persona como garantía de objetividad y razonabilidad en la interpretación», *Dikaion*, Nro. 18 (2009), Colombia, pp. 20–40.

Cases:

Roe v. Wade, 410 US 113 (1973).

T., S. c/ Gobierno de la Ciudad de Buenos Aires s/ amparo, Fallos: 324: 5 (2001);

Portal de Belén – Asociación Civil sin Fines de Lucro c/ Ministerio de Salud y Acción Social de la Nación s/amparo, Fallos: 325: 292 (2002).

Corte Suprema de la Nación, Argentina, F. 259. XLVI; *F., A. L. s/ medida autosatisfactiva*.

Alejandro Miranda and Sebastián Contreras

10 Commentary on the Constitutional Court of Chile's Decision Concerning the So-Called "Morning after Pill"

Abstract: In this chapter we present the main arguments on which the Constitutional Court of Chile based its decision of declaring the morning after pill unconstitutional. We also elaborate the main aspects of the legal case as it was known by the Court, and submit the Court's argument to critical analysis. The chapter is divided into five parts. First, we sketch the due normative and judiciary procedures which precede the declaration of unconstitutionality of the pill. Second, we summarize the legal case. Third, we expound the three controversial questions which the Court considered: the pill's way of acting, the beginning of the human individual, and the unborn as a rights holder. Fourth, we explain the Court's arguments regarding the moment in which human life begins and regarding reasonable doubt. Lastly, we confront the two questions which, in our judgment, would have deserved greater attention from the Court: the question of the raped woman and her right to self-defense, on the one hand, and the question of the value of human life and its bearing on the right to life, on the other.

Keywords: Morning after pill, Right to life, Unborn human being, Constitutional court of Chile

1 Introduction: Antecedent Procedures

The departing point of this juridical discussion may be placed in March of 2001. On March 21st the Public Health Institute, an Office of the Ministry of Health, authorizes the commercialization of the morning after pill, under the name of *Postinal*. The morning after pill, made mostly of levonorgestrel alone or combined with etinilestradiol (which is known as the Yuzpe method), is an emergency contraceptive that can have diverse effects depending on the phase or cycle in which it is taken. It could act by preventing ovulation, by preventing conception, and, presumably, by preventing implantation.

This decision concerning the commercialization of the pill gives rise to the introduction of a constitutional legal action of protection by diverse pro-life organizations. The Appeals Court of Santiago rejects the constitutional action because, allegedly, those organizations were not entitled to introduce it. According to the Court, the individuals which this constitutional action seeks to protect are "not defined and lack the necessary concretion which the Law requires in order to be entitled to introduce the constitutional action of protection."[1] Moreover, in the

---

1 Santiago's Appeals Court, Decision of May 28th, 2001, recital 9.

Court's words, "the scientific briefings and studies [. . .] are alien to this constitutional action of protection, since they would require a long-term civil proceeding in order to be appropriately examined."[2]

Chile's Supreme Court revoked this decision and prevented the commercialization of the pill. In the opinion of the Supreme Court, the authorization for making, selling, and distributing levonorgestrel is contrary to Chilean Constitutional Law because one of the effects of this drug threatens the life of the unborn,[3] which must be protected "in any stage of its prenatal development."[4] The Supreme Court also decides that distributing and selling the pill is contrary to the physical and psychic integrity of women because it could cause an abortion.[5]

On the grounds of a lack of decisive proofs concerning the real effects of levonorgestrel on the endometrium, the Chilean public health authority insists on its decision to authorize the sales and distribution of the morning after pill. Thus, the distribution of a second pharmaceutical product based on the same active principle as *Postinal, Postinor-2,* is authorized. This decision is based on the allegation that the Supreme Court forbade the distribution of *Postinal,* not of levonorgestrel.

In answer to this decision of distributing *Postinor-2,* an action of annulment was brought to court. The plaintiff argued that the authorization of this product violates Chilean Law because it violates the unborn's rights both to life and to not suffering arbitrary discriminations. The action is admitted and the 20th Civil Law Court of Santiago, on June 30th, 2004, decides to annul the act of distribution by the public health authority. An appeal is taken against this decision. The Appeals Court of Santiago revoked the decision arguing that the certitude of the risk run by the unborn's life had not been duly proved by the plaintiff. Against this second decision, a cassation appeal to the Supreme Court was taken. The Supreme Court decided to affirm the Court of Appeals' decision and rejected the cassation appeal in all its parts in November of 2005. Thus, the public health authority was authorized to distribute and sell the so-called morning after pill.

Almost a year later, on September 1st, 2006, the public health authority established the *National Norms Concerning the Regulation of Fertility.* Through them, the State makes mandatory the distribution of the morning after pill in the public health system and to minors, requiring neither their parents' authorization nor knowledge.

The public health authority's decision gave rise to a new constitutional action of protection introduced in the Appeals Court of Santiago. The Court rejected the action and declared that the *National Norms* were neither arbitrary nor illegal, and that they do not violate any personal rights.

---

2   Santiago's Appeals Court, Decision of May 28th, 2001, recital 11.
3   *See* Supreme Court Decision of August 30th, 2001, recital 9.
4   Supreme Court, Decision of August 30th, 2001, recital 17.
5   *See* Supreme Court, Decision of August 30th, 2001, recital 9.

On September 30th, 2006, a group of elected representatives asked the Constitutional Court to declare that the said *National Norms* were unconstitutional. The Constitutional Court accepted the petition and declared that the Norms are unconstitutional due to strictly formal defects. These defects were then corrected by the public health authority. On February 3rd, 2007 the *National Norms Concerning the Regulation of Fertility* were promulgated again by the Health Ministry's Supreme Decree, after revision by the Comptroller General of the Republic.

Since the subsequent petitioners believed that the *National Norms* continued to violate the constitutional rights of the unborn, and since the Constitutional Court had not touched the substance of the matter concerning the abortive action of levonorgestrel, a group of thirty-six representatives introduced a new petition to the Constitutional Court on March 5th, 2007. The petition asked that the Court declare that the *National Norms* are contrary to the Chilean Constitutional System. The Court rejected the petition arguing that "it lacks the required clarity and precision in order for the Court to decide the issue."[6]

On March 24th of the same year, a new more specific petition was introduced to the Constitutional Court. The new petition asked that the Court declare the *National Norms* unconstitutional in regards to what they establish concerning emergency hormonal contraception, non-hormonal contraception, contraception for specific populations, and contraception for teenagers. The Court accepted this petition and in April of 2008 declares that the pill is unconstitutional. This decision is the one upon which we are going to comment in this paper.

2 Introduction to the Case

As stated above, in March of 2007 a group of Congressmen brought a petition to the Constitutional Court asking the Court to declare that some of the norms contained in the Ministry of Health's Supreme Decree Number 48 (*the National Norms Concerning the Regulation of Fertility*) are unconstitutional[7].

The *National Norms* include among their articles, in Section C, heading 3.3, the so-called emergency hormonal contraception. Herein they establish the mandatory distribution of the morning after pill in the establishments which compose the Chain of Assistance of the National System of Health Services.

The petitioners assert that the distribution of the morning after pill violates various articles of the Chilean Constitution. The position of these Congressmen is that the administration of only one pill of pure progestin (normally 0.75 mg of levonorgestrel), or a combination of pills (known as the Yuzpe method), has an abortive effect which is contrary to the Constitution.

---

6   Constitutional Court, Decision of March 20th, 2007, recital 12.
7   To decide on the constitutionality of this kind of norm falls under the competence of the Constitutional Court according to Art. 93, No. 16 of the Chilean Republic's Political Constitution.

Specifically, the Congressmen asserted that the distribution of the morning after pill violates the following articles of the Constitution:

> Article 5, paragraph 2: The exercise of sovereignty recognizes as a limitation the respect for the essential rights originating from human nature. It is the duty of the bodies of the State to respect and promote such rights, guaranteed both by this Constitution and by international treaties ratified by Chile and which are still in force.
> Article 6: The action of the bodies of the State must be subject to the Constitution and to the norms enacted in conformity therewith. Both the incumbent officers of the said bodies or members thereof, as well as all persons, institutions or groups, are bound by the precepts of this Constitution. The breach of this principle shall generate responsibilities and penalties to be determined by the law.
> Article 7: The bodies of the State operate validly within their field of competence, and in the manner prescribed by law, after their members have been properly invested. No judicature, person or group of persons may assume, even on the pretext of extraordinary circumstances, any other authority or rights other than those expressly conferred upon them by the Constitution or by law. Any act contravening this article is null and void and shall give rise to the responsibilities and penalties indicated by law.
> Article 19: The Constitution guarantees to all persons: 1.- The right to life and to the physical and psychological integrity of the person. The law protects the life of the unborn. The death penalty may only be instituted for a crime considered by a law approved by a qualified quorum. Use of all illegitimate pressure is prohibited.
> Article 26: The assurance that the legal precepts which, by mandate of the Constitution, regulate or complement the guarantees established therein or which should limit them in the cases authorized by the Constitution, may not affect the rights in their essence nor impose conditions, taxes or requirements which may prevent their free exercise.

The petitioners asked the Court to declare unconstitutional three classes of norms contained in the Supreme Decree No. 48: (i) those which order the distribution of the morning after pill in the establishments of the public health system; (ii) those which order the implantation of IUDs in the same establishments; and (iii) those which allow the advising of adolescents without their parents´ consent. The Court left aside the issue concerning IUDs. According to its judgment, in this petition there was a contradiction between the arguments and the conclusions in the petition because in its arguments it seems to attempt to annul all norms concerning the use of IUDs, while in its conclusion it seems to attack only those IUDs which use levonorgestrel.[8]

Regarding the problem of the counseling of adolescents, the Court dismissed the petition with a brief statement: "the norms dealing with confidential counseling do

---

8   See Constitutional Court, Decision of April 18th, 2008, recital 12. From now on, references to this decision's recitals will be included in the main body of this text between parentheses.

not prevent the parents from either choosing the school for their daughters or from transmitting to them their knowledge and values concerning the sexual life, which is sufficient to reject the petition on this count" (16). Thus, the bulk of the Court's decision is centered on the constitutionality or unconstitutionality of the distribution of the morning after pill.

3 Controversial Questions

Although the decision does not distinguish the controversial questions with clarity, one can state that the Court focused on three central controversial questions. The first one can be posed thus: whether the morning after pill can prevent the zygote's nesting or implantation in the endometrium. The second concerns the following: at what moment in the reproductive process does a new individual of the human species begin to exist. The third one refers to whether the unborn human individual is a person, that is to say, a holder of rights in general and, specially, of the right to life.

3.1 Causal Mechanism of the Morning after Pill

The *National Norms Concerning the Regulation of Fertility* establish that the goals of emergency contraception are to reduce the number of undesired pregnancies and their consequences, including abortion; and to allow women to use their right to prevent a pregnancy after having been raped. The *Norms* describe emergency hormonal contraception or post-coital contraception as those contraceptive methods which women can use during the first five days following an act of sexual intercourse performed without any contraceptive protection. Regarding its causal mechanisms, the *Norms* point out that the morning after pill can produce two effects: preventing ovulation and preventing conception. The *Norms* explicitly add that levonorgestrel does not prevent implantation, does not interrupt pregnancies, and does not produce abortion.

Clearly, this latter aspect is the relevant one because the main controversial question is whether the morning after pill might have an abortifacient effect. The Constitutional Court received multiple scientific briefings on this subject matter. The examination of such briefings led the Court to realize that the specialists agree on two of the effects of the pill: the pill prevents ovulation and the pill prevents sperm from reaching the egg. But the specialists disagree on its possible prevention of implantation.

Some specialists, indeed, claim that experiments performed on rats and capuchin monkeys permit the rejection of the hypothesis that levonorgestrel interferes with implantation. Other specialists object that the results obtained in experiments with non-human beings cannot necessarily be applied to human beings.

The Court also realized that the US Food and Drug Administration, in describing the mechanism of action of the so-called Plan B (morning after pill), states that one of its possible causal mechanisms consists in preventing the implantation of the zygote in the uterus (32). The same occurs with the information given concerning the pills *Norlevo* and *Postinor-2*, developed, respectively, by HRA-Pharma and Grünenthal Laboratories. On both pharmaceutical products' labels the prevention of implantation of the zygote is indicated as one of their possible effects (38).

From the evaluation of these materials, the Court concluded that the proofs gathered from scientific studies are contradictory and do not allow one to conclude with certainty that the morning after pill does not prevent the implantation of the zygote. Thus, the Court states: "[. . .] this Court can only point out that the scientific evidence gathered in this process does not allow one to exclude with certainty that the administration of the 'morning after pill' [. . .] is capable of affecting a zygote's or an embryo's implantation" (39).

As can be noted, the Court emphasizes that it has not been proved that the morning after pill does not have the effect of preventing implantation. Thus, the Court does not emphasize the contrary statement: that it has not been proved that the morning after pill has such effect. The reason for this will be examined later.

3.2 The Beginning of the Biological Individual of the Human Species

The scientific evidence given in Court during the proceedings led the Court to note the differing opinions of the specialists regarding the nature and the features of the resulting product of conception: "according to some specialists, implantation affects only one 'cell' which, resulting from conception and after some development, could become an embryo; according to other specialists what is implanted is more than just one cell, it is a human being fully identifiable and distinguishable from its parents because of its chromosomal constitution, which has resulted precisely as a consequence of conception" (35).

This divergence of opinion is relevant for the decision of the matter. Indeed, if the product of conception is a human being fully identifiable—an *individual* of the human species—then it could be a person. To the contrary, if the result of conception is not a human being fully identifiable—this is what is connoted when it is stated that it is merely a "cell"—then it is not possible that it is a person. This second position seems to be grounded on the argument according to which the divisibility of the zygote before nesting proves that it lacks individuality.[9]

3.3 The Unborn as a Holder of Rights

The third controversial question considered in the decision has to do with the determination of the question of "who is the right holder of the unborn's right to

---

[9] The argument is stated in: Ford, N., *When Did I Begin? Conception of the Human Individual in History, Philosophy and Science*, Cambridge University Press, Cambridge, 1988, p. 122.

life" (41). More properly one would have to ask whether the unborn is the holder of the right to life. This is equivalent to asking whether the unborn fruit of conception can be placed under the category of *person* because it is to this class of entities to whom the Constitution guarantees the right to life (48).

The way in which the Chilean Constitution's Article 19, No.1, is written has raised differing interpretations. This norm states that the Constitution guarantees all persons the right to life and to physical and psychic integrity, and then adds: "The law protects the life of the unborn."[10] Some understand that this is making a distinction between (i) *persons*, who would be already born human individuals, and (ii) *unborn human individuals*, which would not yet be persons. In this line, the *right* to life would be guaranteed only for persons. Instead, the unborn would not be acknowledged as holder of the right to life, even if its life is acknowledged as deserving protection. Moreover, this interpretation continues, while the person's right to life is guaranteed by the *Constitution*, the protection of the unborn's life is left to the *law*, which indicates an important distinction that the Chilean juridical order makes between the two. This distinction "is concretized in the fact that some degree of discretion is acknowledged to the legislator for the decriminalization of some actions which destroy the life of the *nasciturus* (the unborn), a degree which does not exist when it comes to dealing with actions which threaten the life of the already born."[11] Others, on the contrary, hold that the statement with which Article 19, No. 1, begins ("The right to life and to the physical and psychological integrity of the person") must be understood as inclusive of the other three norms contained in number 1. These three norms deal with the protection of the unborn, the requirements connected with the death penalty, and the prohibition of illegitimate pressure. Otherwise, these interpreters add, one would arrive at the illogical conclusion that also the norm which forbids illegitimate pressure "either would not refer to persons, or at least not only to persons, since it is not explicitly so indicated in the text."[12]

The Court also analyzes the heading of Article 19 of the Chilean Constitution, the one which enumerates the constitutional rights and which states: "The Constitution guarantees to all persons [. . .]". This analysis underscores that by the use of the expression "guarantees," the Constitution seeks to indicate that the enumerated rights and guarantees are not *created* but rather *acknowledged* by the Constitutional Power as inherent to human nature. The Constitution, adds the Court, simply "acknowledges them, regulates their implementation and guarantees them through the juridical institutions which are adequate, so that their protection does

---

10 In Chilean legal system, the law is given by the Congress or the President, under the Constitution.
11 Bascuñán, A., "La píldora del día después ante la jurisprudencia," *Estudios Públicos* 95 (2004), pp. 43–89 [56].
12 *See* Constitutional Court, Decision of April 18th, 2008, concurrent opinion of Justice Mr. Mario Fernández Baeza.

not turn illusory" (47). As some commentators have pointed out, "within the reasoning structure of this decision one can recognize some notions which are equivalent to what classical philosophy has named 'natural law.' "[13]

4 The Arguments of the Constitutional Court

4.1 The Human Person Begins at Conception

Although the Constitutional Court had noted divergences between the scientists' opinions concerning the reproductive process's exact moment in which a new biological individual of the human species begins to exist, the Court considers that their arguments do not have the same force. Actually, the Court takes sides in this case: according to its judgment, the human individual's being starts at the moment of conception or fertilization. Moreover, without specific arguments, the Court equates *human individual* and *person*. Two of the controversial questions are solved in this way.

The argument of the Court is the following: "[. . .] if at the moment of conception an individual is generated which has all the necessary genetic information for its development, and which becomes a distinct being and wholly distinguishable from its father and mother—as has been stated in this proceedings—it is possible to affirm that one is dealing with a person with rights. The singularity of the embryo, from conception, allows one to regard it as an already unique and unrepeatable being which is entitled, from that very moment, to the protection of the Law. Such being cannot be simply subsumed into another entity and may not be manipulated without affecting the essential dignity which it already enjoys as a person" (50).

This paragraph contains one of the main theses which ground the decision of the Constitutional Court. The Court considers that at the time of conception a new individual of the human species is formed because the product of conception is a singular being, distinct from its mother and father, which has all the genetic information needed for its development. Here one can note the echoes of the argument according to which after fertilization, when a new individual of the human species has its origin, the embryonic developmental process is not the scene of any substantial change which would allow one to argue that before there was no person but after there is.

As has been stated, the Court considers as equivalent the concepts of *human individual* and *person*.[14] Although it does not explicate the identity of these concepts,

---

13 Alvear, J., and Cisterna, V., "La sentencia del Tribunal Constitucional sobre la 'píldora del día después': ¿liberalismo posesivo o respeto a la ley natural?" *Revista Actualidad Jurídica* 18 (2008), pp. 23–54 [43].
14 It is worth pointing out that the Court rejects a purely materialist conception of the human person. In its opinion, among the values and principles of the Chilean Constitution implicitly lies a definition of the human person as a being composed of matter and spirit (46).

the Court does show that the Chilean legal system, and especially the Constitution, regards the unborn as a right holder from the moment of conception. Thus, the Court understands the norm "the law protects the life of the unborn" in this sense: "the intention of the Constitutional Power was to leave to the legislator the determination of the concrete ways in which the life of the unborn should be protected, presupposing that one is dealing with a being which exists and is encompassed by the notion of person as right holder referred to in the heading of article 19" (58).

Among the legal norms of which the Constitutional Court makes use, Article 4.1 of the American Convention of Human Rights holds a special place. The text of this precept is the following: "Every person has the right to the respect of its life. This right will be protected by law and, in general, from the moment of conception. No one may be deprived of his or her life arbitrarily." Because it is an international treaty signed and ratified by Chile and remains in force, this Convention is a binding juridical norm for all the organs of the Chilean State and for all its citizens.

4.2 Doubt and the Principle *pro homine*

We have seen that the Court notes contradictory positions among the specialists concerning the possible anti-implantation effect of the morning after pill. In the judgment of the Court, the positions of the doctors are equivalent, because all are held "with identical strength and conviction" (64). For this reason, the Court considers itself, on this matter, in the state of doubt. Gathering the definition from a briefing presented by the Pontifical Catholic University of Chile, the Court points out that "there is doubt when the understanding is unable to assent to or to negate a proposition in the absence of an efficient cause which could determinate it in one direction or the other" (64).

On these grounds, the Court reflects on how it should act *vis à vis* the said doubt. For this, the Court rests on the Pontifical Catholic University's briefing which assumes a common doctrine from the authors of classic natural law theory. According to these writers, there is doubt when the intellect is not inclined to either of the disputing views.[15] In this situation, the classical rule is to choose the safest side (*in dubiis semper tutior pars eligenda est*).[16] This is applicable especially to the judge whose decision, upon ruling on other people's rights, must always follow the most probable opinion, which is another classical rule.[17]

But the Constitutional Court makes use mainly of what are known as the "hermeneutical criteria developed by the fundamental rights theory" (66). In particular, the Court invokes the *pro homine* principle, known as well as the *favor libertatis*

---

15 *See* Aquinas, *Summa theologiae*, II-II, q. 2, a. 1, c.
16 *See* Aquinas, *Super Sent.*, Bk. 4, d. 27, q. 2, a. 3, arg. 2.
17 *See* Soto, D., *De iustitia et iure*, l. III, q. 6, a. 5. Strictly speaking, choosing the safest side is not the same as following the most probable opinion. For a rigorous and updated analysis of conscientious doubts, see Grisez, G., *The Way of the Lord Jesus*. Vol. 1. *Christian Moral Principles*, Franciscan Press, Illinois, 1983, pp. 289–309.

principle. The jurisprudence of the Inter-American Court of Human Rights has formulated such principle thus: "amidst conflicting opinions the norm which is most favorable to the human person must prevail" (66). According to this principle, in the case of doubt one must "give pride of place to such interpretation as favors 'the person's' right to life rather than any other interpretation which could suppress that right" (67). The Constitutional Court holds that "reasoning differently would imply ignoring the essential dignity of all persons" (68). Moreover, with the end of strengthening its position, the Court states that the *pro homine* principle is consistent with Article 1st, paragraph 4, of the Constitution, according to which the State is at the service of the human person (69).

The idea of the Court is, then, that the possible abortifacient effect of levonorgestrel is at odds with the constitutional protection of the unborn's life. If it were allowed to act in case of doubt, the action could result in a violation of the Fundamental Law. Instead, if it were not allowed, no human life would be at risk and no unconstitutional state of affairs could result. Because of its importance, we copy here the entire reasoning of the Court on this point:

"[...] there is an element which, in the view of these justices, neutralizes such equivalence. It has to do with the effect which would follow if we adopt either of the positions. Indeed, if we accept the thesis of those who hold that only after implantation of the embryo in the endometrium a human being and, therefore, a person would exist, and that the morning after pill prevents such implantation, there would not be an attempt against the life of a 'person' according to the way in which the Constitution understands such term. On the contrary, if one follows the thesis according to which life begins at conception because of the union of egg and sperm—which is the way in which the Constitution understands it—the possible effect of the morning after pill of preventing the implantation of a living being—i. e. of a person—would become an abortion absolutely contrary to the constitutional protection of the unborn's life, which the Constitution demands from the legislator and which, along with all other fundamental rights, all organs of the State have the constitutional duty to respect and promote. Thus is broken the stalemate which, according to a first analysis, appears to exist among the views of the scientists who have given their opinions to the court. Indeed, one of those views could result in an unconstitutional state of affairs and the other one cannot" (64).

The perplexity inherent to the state of doubting which renders one unable to incline one's reason to either one or the other side is thus overcome by taking into account both levonorgestrel's abortifacient potential and the opposition between abortion and the unborn's constitutional right to life.

The Court's reasoning has affected the constitutional Law and the philosophy of Law scholars. On the one hand, some of them celebrate "the conceptual precision and the account of the arguments which laid the ground for the decision"[18];

---

18 Alvear, J., y Cisterna, V., "La sentencia del Tribunal Constitucional sobre la 'píldora del día después': ¿liberalismo posesivo o respeto a la ley natural?" p. 43.

and highlight the Court's defense of the metaphysical concept of person and the correct way in which the Court evaluates the scientific data.[19] On the other hand, some attack the decision as a bad decision, contrary to common sense and to the basic rules of logic. The Court, they hold, should have rejected the petition, precisely because it had not proved its position.[20]

5 Some Pending Questions

In the following section we will consider two questions which, in our view, required greater attention from the Court. In the first case is a problem which, although not formulated by the Court, could have led to qualifying the use of the principle *pro homine* in order to solve the doubt regarding the abortifacient effect of the morning after pill. We are referring to the use of the pill by a woman who has been raped. The second case concerns itself with finding the exact extent of the right to life.

5.1 The Morning after Pill and the Raped Woman's Right to Self-Defense

We have already considered that the conflicting views held by the specialists concerning the pill's anti-implantation effect do not allow a settlement of the matter. The arguments of those who assert the pill's possible abortifacient effect are, according to the Constitutional Court, as strong as the arguments of those who deny such possibility. In these circumstances, the Court declares itself to be in a state of doubt. There is doubt, indeed, when the arguments in favor of each conflicting view have the same weight and reason, and so in consequence the intellect cannot adhere to either view.

With the end of overcoming doubt, the Court makes use of a principle of constitutional hermeneutics: the principle known as *pro homine*. In brief, this principle states that one should follow the interpretation which is most favorable to the rights and guarantees inherent to the human being.[21] Specifically, the Court's reasoning is the following: if the pill's administration is allowed despite the doubt concerning its abortifacient effect, this could lead to a violation of the Constitution

---

19 See Zambrano, P., "Una lectura transparente de la constitución," *La Ley, Suplemento de Derecho Constitucional*, Tuesday July 8th, 2008, pp. 43–52.
20 See Figueroa, R., "Comentario relativo a la sentencia del Tribunal Constitucional referida a la píldora del después del año 2008," *Anuario de Derecho Público* 1 (2010), pp. 144–162.
21 See American Convention on Human Rights (San José de Costa Rica Pact), 1969, Art. 29.

through the violation of the unborn's right to life. But if, instead, the distribution of the pill is not allowed, then there could be no violation of the Constitution (64).

Although this is, in general, correct, the issue requires greater reflection. Indeed, the prohibition of the administration of the morning after pill could lead to the violation of another constitutional right, different from the unborn's right to life. The Court's transition from doubt to prohibition is too fast. In case of doubt, the obligation of abstaining from an action (in this case, the administration of the pill) can be reasonably concluded only when it is certain both that the abstention itself does not imply the suppression of a right and that there is no proportionally grave reason to take the risk. Otherwise, the obligation of abstention cannot be concluded from the sole existence of doubt. The common example with which this rule is illustrated is that of a man who is hunting rabbits and sees a small, white object stirring behind a bush; if he does not know whether that object is his prey or a child playing in that place, then he is obliged to abstain from shooting. The reasoning is that the deprivation of a rabbit dinner is a much smaller evil than the killing of a child. But the situation is different if the hunter needs the rabbit to feed his son who is starving to death and knows that in the place where he is hunting the object is very likely not a child. In such case, the right to provide food for his starving son is a proportionately grave reason which justifies running the risk. The Court should have deliberated, then, on whether there is a case in which a woman might have the right to receive and use the morning after pill. If such a case does exist, the *pro homine* principle would not provide enough reason to overcome the doubt, since it could favor either of the two options. In such a case, the Court would have to deliberate on whether the woman's right is a proportionately grave reason to run the risk of the pill preventing the zygote from nesting.

We think that the Court could demonstrate with clear and strong arguments that the use of the morning after pill is not legitimate in order to prevent procreation after an instance of freely consented sexual intercourse. In this case, the pill's possible abortive effect is sufficient reason to forbid its administration. Whoever consents to have sexual intercourse cannot be entitled to the right of preventing its natural effects through an act which endangers the life of a third party. But the situation is different in the case of rape. Clearly, in this other case the woman is entitled to the right of self-defense. Now, this right encompasses not only defense against the act of rape itself, but also defense against the effects of rape which remain in her body. For this reason, after sexual intercourse, the woman has the right to use the morning after pill with the aim of *preventing conception* (although certainly not with the aim of aborting). This right is an aspect of the right to physical and psychological integrity which the Chilean Constitution guarantees to all persons in Article 19, No. 1. The right to physical integrity entitles the woman to prevent the rapist's sperm cells from reaching her eggs and giving rise to conception.

Briefly: a raped woman has the right to use the morning after pill with the intention of preventing the last result of sexual intercourse, that is to say, conception. Therefore, the *pro homine* principle is not sufficient reason to forbid such a pharmaceutical product because of its possible abortifacient effect. Here, another principle of reason must come into play; in particular, a judgment of proportionality. The Court should have asked itself, therefore, whether the raped woman's right to prevent the sperm cells from fertilizing the egg is sufficiently important as to allow some risk to the unborn's life. Concerning this issue, John Finnis writes the following:

> if a procedure such as the administration of the 'post-coital pill' is undertaken for the purpose only of *preventing* conception after rape but involves some *risk* of causing abortion *as a side effect* (because it is not known at what stage in her cycle the woman is), there can be no universal judgment that the adoption of such a procedure is unjust to the unborn. For there are many legitimate activities which foreseeably cause some risk of serious or even fatal harm, a risk which in many cases is rightly accepted by upright and informed people as a possible side-effect of their choices to engage in those activities.[22]

In this same line, Ashley, deBlois, and O'Rourke hold that "when honest *doubt* exists as to whether conception has in fact taken place, the probability should favor the certain rights of the woman. Once it becomes certain or highly probable that conception has occurred, however, she must then recognize the rights of the developing embryo to life and avoid any serious risk of abortion."[23] We are in agreement with these authors. In fact, legal systems allow many actions which imply running the risk of causing some innocent human being's death as a collateral effect, and sometimes for ends which are less important than the preservation of the woman's physical integrity after a rape. Because this is a relevant case, the Court should have offered a specific solution for it. Of course, we realize that a just solution would demand establishing very precise and accurate procedures when there is an allegation of rape with the end of diminishing the risk of the pill acting as an abortifacient. This point might be beyond the scope of a Constitutional Court's decision.[24] The intention of our observation is simply to point out that, in order to avoid unjust results for some complex cases, ruling the unconstitutionality of the morning after pill's administration should be carefully qualified.

Perhaps the categorical judgment of the Court could be explained taking into account its view concerning the right to life, a view which we consider questionable as well. The Court holds that the sovereignty of the State is limited by a limitless respect for the right to life, which is "the most essential right derived from human nature" (69). However, the Court seems to understand that the centrality of

---

22 *See* Finnis, J., "Abortion and Health Care Ethics," en H. Kuhse and P. Singer (eds.), *Bioethics. An Anthology*, Blackwell Publishers, Oxford, 1999, pp. 13–20 [17].
23 Ashley, B.; deBlois, J., and O'Rourke, K., *Health Care Ethics. A Catholic Theological Analysis*, 5th edn., Georgetown University Press, Washington D. C., 2006, p. 84.
24 Concerning these protocols, see Ashley, B.; deBlois, J., and O'Rourke, K., *Health Care Ethics*, pp. 83–86.

the right to life implies that, in the case of an apparent conflict between this and other rights, one must always choose the solution which favors the right to life, so that any other right must yield, even when there is only a risk of affecting the right to life (not a certainty). We think that the Court goes too far in this direction. We will analyze this question in the next section.

5.2 The Value of Human Life and the Right to Life

In recitals 55 and 56 the Court deals with the position of the right to life within the structure of the fundamental rights recognized and guaranteed by the Constitution. On this point, the Court follows a position very widely held by Chilean Constitutional Law scholars, that is to say, that "the right to life is, without a doubt, the right which grounds all others, because without life it hardly makes sense to refer to other fundamental rights" (55). And the Court adds: "as the UN Human Rights Committee has pointed out, in its General Observation concerning Article 6 of the International Pact on Civil and Political Rights, the right to life is 'the supreme right from which no suspension is permitted even in time of public emergency which threatens the life of the nation'" (55).

The Constitutional Court describes the content of the right to life as "the right to maintain and preserve life in front of other humans" (56). But, so described, one must ask, could the right to life really be the supreme right from which no suspension is permitted even in time of public emergency which threatens the life of the nation? The problem of the adequate description or definition of the right to life is a juridical-philosophical question of the highest importance. Controversies regarding the apparent conflicts of rights and/or the reasonableness of proportionality judgments when fundamental rights are at stake must be reduced, in the last analysis, to the problem of the adequate description or definition of rights.

Some critics have pointed out that the definition proposed by the Court is wrong because "to understand the right to life as the right to maintain life would entail that any time someone dies the right to life is violated, which is absurd."[25] We agree with this criticism. But the Court formulates another possible definition: the right to life is the right to having no one take our life from us (55). However, this definition is defective as well. Indeed, the Court seems to want to determine what the Chilean Constitution, in Article 19, No. 26, names as the "essence" of the right; in other words, the core that cannot be affected by legal precepts which are called to regulate and complement each right. Now, nobody has an inviolable right to not be deprived from his or her life, because to kill somebody is justified at least in an act of legitimate self-defense, given that some requirements are met.

Does this mean that the right to life is not an absolute, inviolable right, that is to say, a right which allows for no exception? By no means. The absolute

---

25 Figueroa, R., "Comentario relativo a la sentencia del Tribunal Constitucional referida a la píldora del día después del año 2008," p. 155.

character of a right does not exclude that its definition or description allows for certain qualifications. It only implies that, if the precise definition is found, this right cannot be defeated by considerations of general utility nor by calculus of consequences.[26] According to the natural law tradition, for example, the right to life is absolute or without conditions only if it is understood as the right of an innocent person to not being intentionally killed (that is to say, as an end or as a means to an end).[27] Such right, states the natural law tradition, always exists, independently of any calculus of consequences.

The idea of absolute rights that can be defined and/or described in an abstract way has as its main opponent the consequentialist doctrine.[28] Consequentialism is incompatible with the existence of absolute, inviolable rights because, according to consequentialist principles, any right may be annulled if that were necessary for either achieving the greatest good or avoiding a greater evil. As Jeremy Bentham, one of the main representatives of the consequentialist doctrine, writes, "there is no right which, when the abolition of it is advantageous to society, should not be abolished."[29]

When the Constitutional Court states that it authorizes no suspension of the right to life, not even in situations in which the life of the nation is endangered, it is precisely rejecting the consequentialist thesis according to which all rights are subordinated to utilitarian calculus. This is, of course, remarkable. But the Court's definition must be corrected along the lines defined by the natural law tradition. Indeed, for a subjective right to be absolute, its correlative duty must be negative, that is, of abstention, a duty which is fulfilled only by omissions. No right whose correlative duty requires positive actions can be absolute. There are at least two reasons for this.

---

26 By the way, there are many possible ways of understanding the expression "absolute right." Here we sketch the notion proposed by Alan Gewirth: "A right is absolute when it cannot be overridden in any circumstances, so that it can never be justifiably infringed and it must be fulfilled without any exceptions" (Gewirth, A., "Are There Any Absolute Rights?" *The Philosophical Quarterly* 31.122 (1981), pp. 1–16 [2]).
27 For an exhaustive treatment of this subject, even if slightly different form the traditional one, *see* Finnis, J.; Boyle, J., and Grisez, G., *Nuclear Deterrence, Morality and Realism*, Oxford University Press, Oxford, 1987, pp. 297–319.
28 This has been noted by authors from different perspectives: see Hart, H. L. A., "Utilitarianism and Natural Rights," *Tulane Law Review* 53.3 (1979), reprinted in Hart, H. L. A., *Essays in Jurisprudence and Philosophy*, Clarendon Press, Oxford, 1983, pp. 181–197 [188]; Finnis, J., *Natural Law and Natural Rights*, 2nd edn., Oxford University Press, Oxford, 2011, p. 224; Gewirth, A., "Are There Any Absolute Rights?" *The Philosophical Quarterly* 31.122 (1981), pp. 1–16 [6].
29 Bentham, J., *Anarchical Fallacies* (1823), in J. Bowring (ed.), *The Works of Jeremy Bentham*, II, Simpkin, Marshall, and Co., London, 1843, p. 501.

First, in many cases it can be physically impossible to realize the positive actions required for the fulfillment of the duty. When this is the case, the right ceases to be enforceable. Suppose that the right to life is conceived as the right to receive whatever is necessary for the preservation of life. Thus understood, the right to life cannot be absolute since giving what is necessary for the preservation of life could prove impossible for other people. Think of medical treatments which demand technological resources which cannot be made available in time. In extreme situations even the supply of water and food could become physically impossible. Now, because no one is obliged to do the impossible, in such cases, the holder of this supposed right cannot require anyone to fulfill it. But a right that in some cases is unable to require the correlative obligation is not an absolute right.

Unlike positive actions, omissions are always physically possible. One can always abstain from a voluntary act. For this reason, a right whose fulfillment requires only omissions can be absolute. Hence, bestowing an absolute character to the innocent person's right to not be intentionally deprived of his or her life is logically consistent. Indeed, it is always physically possible to abstain from intentionally killing an innocent person.

Second, there is an even more fundamental reason that explains why a right whose correlative duty demands positive actions cannot be absolute: for a right of this class to be absolute, the good protected by such right would have to be of such importance as to include and surpass the goodness of all other goods. Indeed, only in this case there would be an obligation to give always preference to the action directed to acquire and/or promote such good when that action is incompatible with another one directed to acquire and/or promote a different good. Instead, if the first good did not have such importance, the incompatibility could be solved in favor of the action protective of a different good and there would be no right to demand an action protective of the first good. Now, there is no reality whose goodness includes and surpasses all other goods, because the diverse realizations of the fundamental human goods are incommensurable.[30]

To begin with, there could be an incompatibility between actions needed to preserve the life of two different persons, and no one could legitimately demand that his or her own life be preferred, in all circumstances, to those of others. Think, for example, of two sick people who simultaneously and with the same urgency need the only mechanical ventilator available. Obviously, it is impossible for both of them to have an absolute right to be provided with the ventilator. But the problem also arises when the preservation of life appears as incompatible with achieving other goods, because the good of life does not contain and surpass all other goods. It is true that in some sense the good of life has priority over all other goods,

---

30 See Grisez, G., and Shaw, R., *Beyond the New Morality. The Responsibilities of Freedom*, 3rd edn., University of Notre Dame Press, Notre Dame, 1988, pp. 132–133.

because without being alive one could not enjoy any other good. And this also could be stated regarding the right to life in comparison with other rights. But this is not equivalent to life containing and surpassing the goodness of all other goods. For this reason, everyone acknowledges that to seek other goods might be legitimate and even mandatory, even if the action required to obtain such goods entails one to suffer death. Thus, to state and to defend an important truth is legitimate even if one knows with certainty that doing so will entail being killed by a tyrant. Refusing to cooperate with a criminal action (e.g., a rape) is equally legitimate even if the criminal threatens us with killing an innocent person if we do not cooperate. This is why neither the State nor particular people are obliged to prefer in all circumstances actions directed to preserve life. The State may dedicate a part of its resources to education and the arts and culture, even if this implies that less life support machines would be purchased or less medical treatments for sick people would be afforded.

Rights correlative to negative duties do not pose the described problem, because an omission or abstention is never incompatible with another abstention: all of them can be fulfilled simultaneously. The existence of absolute rights of this class, therefore, is consistent with the incommensurability of differing realization of basic human goods.

The Court, in consequence, has not succeeded in offering an adequate definition of the right to life as an absolute right. This is probably why it did not see the difference between intentionally killing an innocent person and accepting the risk of affecting his or her life when a proportionately grave or morally serious reason makes taking such a risk legitimate.

6 Conclusions

If the protection of human life fails, a society's whole politico-juridical system fails. This seems to be the idea that the Constitutional Court of Chile had in mind when it solved the question concerning the unconstitutionality of the morning after pill. Assessing data drawn from medical science and appealing to juridical principles of general application, such as the principle *pro homine*, the Court determined that the distribution of the levonorgestrel pill is not compatible with the protection of the constitutional right to life and of the human person's dignity. In this paper we have scrutinized the main arguments of the Constitutional Court and have identified some of the problems which the Court could have considered in a more exhaustive way.

Even if we find the Court's decision to be in general correct, some points could have been grounded in a more solid way. In matters such as those considered by this decision, philosophical argument cannot be avoided. We think that in this aspect the said decision is not as sound as it could have been. A greater development of philosophical arguments would have turned this decision into an even more valuable contribution for the current discussion concerning the protection of the unborn's life.

Bibiliography

Alvear, J., and Cisterna, V., "La sentencia del Tribunal Constitucional sobre la 'píldora del día después': ¿liberalismo posesivo o respeto a la ley natural?" *Revista Actualidad Jurídica* 18 (2008), pp. 23–54.

Aquinas, *Summa theologiae* and *Super Sentiarum*, available in http://www.corpusthomisticum.org/iopera.html

Ashley, B., deBlois, J., and O'Rourke, K., *Health Care Ethics. A Catholic Theological Analysis*, 5th edn., Georgetown University Press, Washington D.C., 2006.

Bascuñán, A., "La píldora del día después ante la jurisprudencia," *Estudios Públicos* 95 (2004), pp. 43–89.

Bentham, J., *Anarchical Fallacies* (1823), in J. Bowring (ed.), *The Works of Jeremy Bentham*, II, Simpkin, Marshall, and Co., London, 1843.

Figueroa, R., "Comentario relativo a la sentencia del Tribunal Constitucional referida a la píldora del después del año 2008," *Anuario de Derecho Público* 1 (2010), pp. 144–162.

Finnis, J., *Natural Law and Natural Rights*, 2nd edn., Oxford University Press, Oxford, 2011.

Finnis, J., "Abortion and Health Care Ethics," in H. Kuhse and P. Singer (eds.), *Bioethics. An Anthology*, Blackwell Publishers, Oxford, 1999, pp. 13–20.

Finnis, J.; Boyle, J., and Grisez, G., *Nuclear Deterrence, Morality and Realism*, Oxford University Press, Oxford, 1987.

Ford, N., *When Did I Begin? Conception of the Human Individual in History, Philosophy and Science*, Cambridge University Press, Cambridge, 1988.

Gewirth, A., "Are There Any Absolute Rights?" *The Philosophical Quarterly* 31 (1981), pp. 1–16.

Grisez, G., *The Way of the Lord Jesus. Vol. 1. Christian Moral Principles*, Franciscan Press, Illinois, 1983.

Grisez, G., and Shaw, R., *Beyond the New Morality. The Responsibilities of Freedom*, 3rd edn., University of Notre Dame Press, Notre Dame, 1988.

Hart, H. L. A., "Utilitarianism and Natural Rights," *Tulane Law Review* 53 (1979), reprinted in Hart, H. L. A., *Essays in Jurisprudence and Philosophy*, Clarendon Press, Oxford, 1983, pp. 181–197.

Soto, D., *De iustitia et iure*, Instituto de Estudios Políticos, Madrid, 1967–1968.

Zambrano, P., "Una lectura transparente de la constitución," *La Ley, Suplemento de Derecho Constitucional*, Tuesday July 8th, 2008, pp. 43–52.

Hugo S. Ramírez García and José María Soberanes Díez

11 The Right to Life in the Context of Mexican Legal Experience: From the Constitution to the Jurisprudence

Abstract: This chapter describes and discusses the path that the human right to life has experienced in Mexican legal practice, by focusing mainly on the problems associated with the definition and qualification of *who* is in fact entitled thereto. This analysis is performed from the point of view of the Mexican Constitution and the Mexican Supreme Court of Justice leading decisions.

Keywords: Human right to life, Right holder, Judicial precedents, Mexican Constitution, Legal certainty

1 Introduction

§ 1. This article follows a thesis proposed by Professor Marta Albert according to which biolaw has two developmental routes which do not necessarily coincide. On one hand, a set of general and abstract norms, *biolaw in books*, and on the other hand, the application of those rules in the decisions which judges issue, *biolaw in action*.[1] This distinction is helpful to point out that the normative discourse and the practical effects of adjudication act may be inconsistent: while the general norms seek a certain result, adjudication in a specific case does not necessarily pursue this purpose.

§ 2. This idea reflects what we want to communicate in this chapter: the protection of human life in Mexico has not been limited to the production of general statutory rules, especially constitutional norms, but it has been further shaped by the creative action of judges, who interpret and apply them.

§ 3. In this context, this chapter describes the path that the human right to life has experienced in the Mexican legal practice, by focusing mainly on the problems associated with the definition and qualification of who is in fact entitled thereto. The objects of study, chosen to undertake this description, were, especially, decisions of the Mexican Supreme Court of Justice (hereafter Supreme Court). However, it additionally includes a brief reference to the content of the Political Constitution of the United Mexican States (hereafter Constitution), precisely the norm mainly interpreted by the Supreme Court.

---

1 Marta Albert, "¿Hacia un bioderecho universal? Bioderecho en acción y funcionalización del valor de la vida humana," en *Cuadernos de Bioética*, núm. 26 (2013), pp. 223–224.

2 The Right to Life in Mexico. Recent Constitutional Amendments

§ 4. The original text of the 1917 Constitution does not specifically recognize the right to life. However, as a part of due process, it forbade extrajudicial executions, noting that nobody should be deprived of life without prior trial.

§ 5. So, for several decades, human life protection in Mexico was indirect, since it was not considered as a value in itself: as a good of utmost importance and priority for human beings. Instead, in its original text, the Constitution seeks to prohibit the arbitrariness, that is to say, the grounding of public decisions depriving one of goods and rights, such as life, privacy, property, freedom, etcetera, on the mere will of the public officers: *Hoc volo, sic iubeo, sit pro ratione voluntas*.

§ 6. Years later, the model of indirect legal protection of life was changed drastically. An amendment to the Constitution abolished the already restricted possibility of death penalty in 2005 (article 22), and the word "life" was deleted from the list of rights that a person may be deprived of (insofar as the appropriate authority had fulfilled all of the requirements of due process).

§ 7. In the context of the most important constitutional amendment in the field of human rights in Mexico, carried out in 2011, the right to life was recognized, at least indirectly, by stating that decrees authorizing the suspension of the exercise of some human rights cannot restrict such a right (article 29). In this reform, it was recognized that human rights have a constitutional and international source, and that both have the same normative importance and direct effectiveness. Therefore, through this broadening of sources recognizing human rights, international treaties that explicitly recognize the right to life are incorporated into the Mexican constitutional system.

§ 7 bis. Concerning specifically unborn human life, the American Convention on Human Rights (article 4.1) to which Mexico is a party, provides that this right shall be protected by law and, in general, as of the moment of conception. However, when signing this international treaty, Mexico included an interpretative reserve, stating that the expression "in general" does not constitute an obligation to maintain in force legislation that protects human life "as of the moment of conception," as it was judged that this decision belongs to the signatory States.

§ 8. The path followed by the original Constitution text and its successive amendments in terms of the right to life raises two considerations. On the one hand, with the abolition of the death penalty and the exclusion of the right to life from the set of rights whose enjoyment can be suspended due to an emergency, the current Mexican constitutional regime does not recognize any legal reason that justifies the deprivation of the life of anyone. Consequently, it could be argued that at the present time there is a system of constitutional norms in Mexico, which recognizes the right to the inviolability of human life. In other words, from the practical perspective, we are not facing a *prima facie* right, whose deprivation through a judicial process could be justified occasionally, but an absolute and unexceptional right. On the other hand, the constitutional norms do not indicate the moment in which the protection of life turns into a human right, and therefore, that determination must be made by means of interpretation. This was the reason for important controversies since the beginning of this century, as we will see below.

3 Protection of the Right to Life as of the Moment of Conception in Recent Mexican Constitutional Jurisprudence

§ 9. Provided that the beginning of the protection of human life, as a human right, is an issue that must be determined by means of interpretation, jurisprudence is, respecting this particular issue, a fundamental source of law. That is why we are going to analyze the issues in which the foremost Mexican judicial authority has been able to address on the subject.

3.1 Constitutional Action 10/2000, the "Robles Amendment"

§ 10. The first time that the Supreme Court determined the moment when the protection to human life begins was in the decision concerning the constitutional action 10/2000, during the sessions held on 29 and 30 January, 2002.

§ 11. This issue came up due to an amendment to the Criminal Code for the Federal District (since 2016 referred to as Mexico City), which established that the existence of genetic abnormalities diagnosed by two physicians was an absolving excuse of the crime of abortion. This reform was called the "Ley Robles" after Rosario Robles, the Head of Government of the Federal District in those days. A minority of representatives of the local Congress that approved it challenged this amendment through a constitutional action before the Supreme Court.

§ 12. The first issue that the Supreme Court had to determine was if the human right to life was or was not protected by the Constitution, since neither it nor other legal texts expressly recognize this right. In that regard, with a majority of 10 votes, the Court stated that the right to life may be deduced from several precepts, just as may be the prohibition of extrajudicial executions. So, it was considered as a fundamental right, without which there is no existence and enjoyment of other rights.[2]

§ 13. Next, they had to specify the moment of human existence as from which the right to life is protected. To resolve this problem, the justices noted that the Constitution protects pregnant workers; that the Convention on the Rights of the Child provides the protection of the child's life, both before and after birth; that

---

2   Case Law P./J. 13/2002, published on *Semanario Judicial de la Federación y su Gaceta*, ninth period, volume XV, February 2002, p. 589. In Mexico the binding force of a precedent can be limited to its legal interpretative directives, as in this case; or it can also attain the whole judicial decision.

civil law considers the *nasciturus* (the unborn) as a holder of rights; and that criminal law punishes those who cause his/her death. Based on these norms, a majority of nine justices concluded that "the protection of the right to life of the product of conception derives from both the Political Constitution of the United Mexican States, international treaties and federal and local laws."[3]

§ 14. Once it was settled that the right to life is constitutionally protected as of the moment of conception, the Supreme Court had to rule whether the impugned norm of the Federal District Criminal Code, which established an absolving excuse in the case of genetic abnormalities, was or was not contrary to the right to life. They considered that the impugned norm did not provide that "the product of conception should be deprived of his/her life, but only that, if death occurred in these circumstances and with the requirements filled, it is not appropriate to impose penalty."[4] For that reason, a majority of seven votes considered that the impugned norm did not violate the right to life protected as of the moment of conception, and recognized the constitutionality of the amendment undertaken to the Criminal Code.

§ 15. The deliberative process that gave rise to resolution 10/2000 highlights the Court's effort to integrate a sufficient legal protection for human life. It is based on a systematic approach that emphasizes the relative importance of the right to life with respect to other rights. This, in turn, allowed the Court to build an argument regarding the holder of the right to life as extensively as possible, that is, including the *nasciturus* as of the moment of his or her conception. This interpretative exercise can be qualified as an application of the *pro personae* principle, as several justices strove to apply norms so as to ensure the maximum benefit for the unborn human being.

§ 16. On the other hand, we maintain that the conclusions of the judgment are weak in relation to the extent of the protection of the right to life. The Court made a distinction between "liberal" and "state" eugenics, disapproving only the latter. State eugenics implies, among other things, a public decision to penalize those parents who refuse to perform abortion, in spite of having accurate data about a congenital malformation on their unborn child. Only this kind of decision would be unconstitutional for the Court. Liberal eugenics, on the other hand, means that the decision to perform the so-called "therapeutic abortion" is freely assumed by the parents. In our opinion, making an unjustified distinction between "state eugenics" and "liberal eugenics" involves a sophism that minimizes the practical effect of the abstention to penalize the so-called "therapeutic abortion." It is clear that if the unborn child has congenital malformation, the public or private nature of the decision to abort does not affect in any way the fact of the elimination of the

---

3 Case Law P./J. 14/2002, published on *Semanario Judicial de la Federación y su gaceta*, ninth period, volume XV, February 2002, p. 588.
4 Sentence for the constitutional action 10/2000, published on *Semanario Judicial de la Federación y su Gaceta*, ninth period, volume XV, March 2002, p. 793.

nasciturus.[5] In short, the decision moved towards eugenic approaches because, in fact, it assumed that the value of a human being rests on genotypic features or on his/her health. Moreover, it encourages the paradoxical practice that eliminates an ill individual in order to overcome the disease; instead of considering an ill unborn child as a patient, the judgment criteria may lead to the conclusion that he is an individual unfit to live.

3.2 Constitutional Action 145/2007. The Decriminalization of Abortion in the Federal District

§ 17. The second time the Supreme Court stated the moment in which the protection of life starts was by means of the constitutional action 145/2007 and its additional ruling in action 146/2007. This issue was raised on occasion of the amendment dated 26 April 2007 to the Criminal Code that modified the definition of abortion, stating that "it is the termination of pregnancy after the 12th week of gestation." This change in the legal text legalizes abortion prior to the 12th week of pregnancy. The amendment was challenged through a constitutional action by the National Human Rights Commission and the Attorney General of Mexico.

§ 18. After the composition of the Supreme Court was changed by the replacement of four members in the years after the prior case was decided, the Court had to analyze once again if the right to life was or was not constitutionally protected. In that regard, a majority of eight justices considered that the Constitution does not recognize a right to life in a normative sense. However, the Court stated that once life exists, there is a positive obligation for the State to protect it as a legal good,[6] but not as a human right.

§ 19. By accepting that human life is a legally protected good, the Court faced the need to determine if there is any obligation to establish or maintain criminal standards of conduct that protect this good. The Supreme Court did not find a constitutional mandate to penalize behaviors causing deprivation of human life. Based on this, it concluded that the legislator has total freedom to determine "the behaviors that must be or not be sanctioned in the criminal field. Given the lack of a specific constitutional obligation, it is its prerogative to balance the facts, problems and rights that may be in conflict."[7]

§ 20. For these reasons, it was resolved that the amendment to the criminal definition of abortion was constitutional by a majority of eight votes during the session held on 28 August 2008. However, one clarification should be made. In Mexico,

---

5 For more about state and liberal eugenics, *see* Habermas, Jürgen, *The Future of Human Nature*, Polity Press, 2003.
6 Sentence for the constitutional action 145/2007 and its aditional 146/2007, published on *Semanario Judicial de la Federación y su Gaceta*, ninth period, volume XXIX, March 2009, p. 1421.
7 Idem.

the vote of at least eight Supreme Court justices is required so that the ruling of a constitutional action becomes a forceful binding precedent. And although there were eight votes on behalf of the constitutional validity of the legal reform, there are eight different opinions concerning the reasons for this conclusion. Therefore, although there is a common resolution, it does not have the status of a required legal source for future cases: it does not produce a *stare decisis* with normative force.[8]

§ 21. The positivist-normativist nature of the resolution of this case (i.e., that the legislator is free to define the actions that will be treated as criminally infringing the right to life) is noticeable. Its effect is to consider the right to life as a subjective right whose content and scope are defined totally by a normative statement from the legislator and thus by the will of a majority. To paraphrase Robert Spaemann, the right to life, in the context of this judicial decision, is a revocable edict of tolerance.[9]

§ 22. We need to focus on the fact that the decision that we are discussing is nowadays obsolete and anachronic. In effect, this decision is based on the premise that there is no norm in the Mexican legal context which explicitly recognizes the right to life, but this is no longer the case after the constitutional reform of 2011. Let us keep in mind that this amendment incorporates the expression "right to life," meaning that it is a human right. Moreover, as it is ordered after the 2011 amendment, all Mexican authorities must promote, respect, protect, and guarantee all human rights.

4 Protection of Human Life from Conception in Local Constitutions

§ 23. Mexico is a federation of states, so it has a federal Constitution; each of the 31 states has a local Constitution; and its capital Mexico City will be obtaining its own Constitution in the near future. Within this constitutional frame, 18 states decided to recognize in their own constitutions the right to life as of the moment of conception. This legislative movement was challenged before the Supreme Court, as the amendments were considered by those filing actions, as being contrary to women's reproductive rights. The Supreme Court decided cases where these arguments were discussed twice.

---

8 According to Article 43 of the Regulation Act for the Sections I and II of Article 105 of the Constitution, the reasons contained in a sentence passed by the vote of at least eight justices will be a binding precedent for all Mexican judges. In this case, although eight justices vote in favor of the sentence, they did not concur with the reasons to approve it; therefore those reasons are not a binding precedent.
9 Robert Spaemann, *Lo natural y lo racional*, Madrid, Rialp, 1989, p. 90.

4.1 Constitutional Actions against Pro-Life Amendments

§ 24. Against the amendment introduced by the state of Baja California, stating the protection of human life from conception, the local human rights commissioner promoted constitutional action 11/2009. Likewise, a minority of local congressmen filed constitutional action 62/2009 against the amendment introduced by the state of San Luis de Potosí. The Supreme Court *en banc* discussed these cases during the 28 and 29 September 2011 sessions.

§ 25. Following the normal procedure of decision in Mexico, Justice Fernando Franco González-Salas was designed as drafter of the preliminary decision that would then be submitted to the vote of the remaining 10 members of the Court. He proposed a decision draft declaring the unconstitutionality of the protection of the right to life as of the moment of conception for two reasons. First, providing that neither the Constitution nor the international instruments deem the product of gestation to be "an individual," local Constitutions have no authority to recognize any right to a "group of subjects" that are not recognized as rights holders by the former norms of higher hierarchy. Secondly, because the absolute and unconditional protection of human life as of the moment of conception was contrary to the reproductive rights of women, they could not abort under any circumstances.

§ 26. Seven of the 11 justices, who attended such Supreme Court sessions, voted in favor of this proposed draft. However, this vote was not enough to declare unconstitutional and to invalidate the impugned local constitutional norms, since the vote of at least 8 justices is required to have such effects. Given the fact that the qualified voting was not reached, the Supreme Court dismissed the constitutional actions. This means that there is no pronouncement, neither in favor nor against the challenged norms; and according to the principle of presumption of constitutionality of laws, they keep their legal validity. In other words, it is a neutral judicial decision, which does not annul the local constitutional norms.[10]

§ 27. As we see it, the thesis sustained in the ruling draft according to which the identification of the subjects-holders of human rights is not based on their common human nature but on textual constitutional rules counteracts the universality of human rights. The Preamble of the Universal Declaration of Human Rights is clear as it states that: "Whereas recognition of the inherent dignity and of the equal and inalienable rights of all members of the human family is the foundation of freedom, justice and peace in the world." Thus, any attempt to establish a legal source as the limit of human kind, threatens human dignity "of all members of the human family" and its inherent rights.

---

10 Sentence for the constitutional action 11/2009, *Semanario Judicial de la Federaciòn y su Gaceta*, ninth period, volume IV, January 2012, t. 1, p. 615; and sentence of the constitutional action 62/2009, *Semanario Judicial de la Federación y su Gaceta*, ninth period, volume IV, February 2012, t.1, p. 789.

§ 28 From a more ample, conceptual and anthropological perspective, the conclusion about the content and scope of the right to reproductive freedom is also questionable for two reasons. First, contrary to scientific evidence, it denies the biological and ontological identity of the *nasciturus*, reducing it to a part of the body of the pregnant woman.[11] This is, at most, a legal fiction, that is, a necessary condition of a further legal fiction, according to which abortion causes no legal or moral damage to the *nasciturus*. Secondly, in affirming woman's reproductive freedom against the protection of the right to life as of the moment of conception, the ruling draft performs an unjustified discrimination against men, who take equal part in the event of conception. Men are denied their own right to reproductive freedom in view of becoming a father, for their choice is totally subordinated to the women's unilateral decision to choose termination of pregnancy.

4.2 Constitutional Controversies against Pro-Life Amendments

§ 29. Against the local constitutional amendment which declares the right to life fully enforceable as of the moment of conception in the state of Guanajuato, the municipality of Uriangato filed a procedure before the Supreme Court, referred to as a constitutional controversy. So did the municipality of Asunción Ixtaltepec against the amendment to the Constitution of the state of Oaxaca. Unlike constitutional actions where all kind of constitutional violations can be exposed, in the constitutional controversies only violations in the sphere of competence of the promoter can be claimed. That is, constitutional controversies are directed to uphold the competence bestowed by Constitutional law to different authorities, when these are disavowed by other authorities.

§ 30. In the controversy pertaining to the state of Guanajuato (62/2009), Justice Arturo Zaldívar Lelo de Larrea was appointed drafter of the preliminary decision that would then be submitted to the vote of the remaining members of the Court. He proposed to annul the constitutional reform based on the argument that the protection of the right to life from the moment of conception infringes

---

11 Indeed, by means of embryology we know that the human embryo is, since the beginning, different to any mother's or father's cell. We also know that the human embryo has a genetic constitution that is characteristic of human beings. Accordingly, it can be concluded that the human embryo is a complete living *Homo sapiens* individual, at the first stages of his natural development, and who will be the same being from that moment until his adulthood, regardless of the biological changes that he will experience. The scientific articles included in the link below concur in showing evidence that proves the existence of a new individual of the human species at the moment of conception. https://www.princeton.edu/~prolife/articles/embryoquotes2.html. (Accessed: March 30th, 2016). More references about the scientific literature of the zygote, the human embryo, and its moral interpretation in: Robert George and Christopher Tollefsen, *Embryo. A Defense of Human Life*, Knopf Doubleday Publishing Group, 2008.

women's fundamental right to abort. On the other hand, in the controversy of Oaxaca (104/2009), the appointed drafter Justice José Fernando Franco González-Salas followed the same line of reasoning of justice Zaldívar Lelo de Larrea, arguing that it is unconstitutional to consider an unborn child to be an "individual," and that by proclaiming the right to prenatal life in an absolute way, women's reproductive rights were violated.

§ 31. In both cases, the decision drafts were rejected by a majority of five of the nine justices who attended the sessions. In the corresponding Supreme Court decisions, the majority considered that it was not the task of the Supreme Court to analyze if the protection of the right to life as of the moment of conception was or was not contrary to the woman's human rights because these issues were not within its jurisdiction in the scope of a constitutional controversy.[12]

§ 32. The Supreme Court *en banc* decided a third constitutional controversy filed against the protection of the right to life as of the moment of conception promoted by the municipality of Arroyo Seco *versus* the corresponding amendment made to the Constitution of Querétaro. However, the debate alluded to a violation of the legislative process only.[13]

5 Conclusions

§ 33. The recent historical trend regarding the protection of the right to life in Mexico generates the following scenarios which, in turn, constitute an ambiguous situation.

§ 34. In the textual level of constitutional and conventional norms (*law in books*), the right to the inviolability of human life is clearly recognized. Moreover, according to these norms, there are good reasons to maintain that it is a truly universal right: that includes all members of human kind, regardless of their condition or stage of biological development. In order to confirm our assumption, it must be recalled that the justices of the Supreme Court reached the same conclusion in a judgment previously analyzed in this chapter, v. gr. the Supreme Court decision pertaining to the "Robles amendment."

§ 35. On the other hand, the indeterminacy of the entitlement to the right to life in judicial interpretative practice (*law in action*) contrasts with the clarity of the

---

12 Sentence for the constitutional controversy 62/2009, published on *Semanario Judicial de la Federación y su Gaceta*, tenth period, volume XXV, October 2013, t. 1, p. 644; and sentence of the constitutional controversy 104/2009, published on *Semanario Judicial de la Federación y su Gaceta*, tenth period, volume XXV, October 2013, t. 1, p. 739.

13 The sentence invalidated, only for the territory of Arroyo Seco, the right to life from the conception because the reform is not approved by the majority of municipalities, as the Constitution of Querétaro indicates. Sentence for the constitutional controversy 104/2009, published on *Semanario Judicial de la Federación y su Gaceta*, tenth period, volume XXIV, September 2013, t. 1, p. 464.

interpreted rules. Actually, this lack of decision shows that the Supreme Court is inclined to deny the recognition of the entitlement of the right to life in *nasciturus* favor. As a result of this bias, the country is legally divided towards this relevant issue. In some local legal spaces, the protection of the right to life is broader and more inclusive, while in other spaces it is extremely limited and precarious. This division causes uncertainty and insecurity regarding a right of paramount importance. At the same time, it is clearly contrary to the obligations assumed by Mexico in diverse international treaties to respect, protect, guarantee, and promote all humans rights.

Bibiliography

Albert, Marta, "¿Hacia un bioderecho universal? Bioderecho en acción y funcionalización del valor de la vida humana," en *Cuadernos de Bioética*, núm. 26, (2013), 475-498.

Habermas, Jürgen, *The Future of Human Nature*, Polity Press, Cambridge, 2003.

Spaemann, Robert, *Lo natural y lo racional*, Rialp, Madrid, 1989.

George, Robert, and Tollefsen, Christopher, *Embrio. A Defense of Human Life*, Knop Doubleday, New York, 2008.

Cases:

Case Law P./J. 13/2002, published on *Semanario Judicial de la Federación y su Gaceta*, ninth period, volume XV, February 2002.

Case Law P./J. 14/2002, published on *Semanario Judicial de la Federación y su gaceta*, ninth period, volume XV, February 2002.

Sentence of the constitutional action 10/2000, published on *Semanario Judicial de la Federación y su Gaceta*, ninth period, volume XV, March 2002

Sentence of the constitutional action 145/2007 and its additional 146/2007, published on *Semanario Judicial de la Federación y su Gaceta*, ninth period, volume XXIX, March 2009.

Sentence of the constitutional action 11/2009, *Semanario Judicial de la Federaciòn y su Gaceta*, ninth period, volume IV, January 2012.

Sentence of the constitutional action 62/2009, *Semanario Judicial de la Federación y su Gaceta*, ninth period, volume IV, February 2012.

Sentence of the constitutional controversy 104/2009, published on *Semanario Judicial de la Federación y su Gaceta*, tenth period, volume XXV, October 2013.

Sentence of the constitutional controversy 104/2009, published on *Semanario Judicial de la Federación y su Gaceta*, tenth period, volume XXIV, September 2013.

Luis Castillo Córdova

12 Legal Status of Unborn Human Life: A Case from Peru

Abstract: One of the main questions concerning human rights' interpretation today is related to their constitutional protected content. This question can be stated in the abstract, or in relation to a specific legal problem. Taking the latter alternative, we explore the extent to which the Peruvian Constitution secures the right to life of unborn human beings, and whether it compels the State to restrict the free distribution of the "morning after pill." This issue is discussed from the point of view of the leading decision issued in the matter by the Peruvian Constitutional Court in case STC N° 02005-2009-PA/TC.

Keywords: Right to life of the unborn, Morning after pill, Constitutional interpretation Validity.

1 Introduction

This chapter analyzes the position of the Peruvian Constitutional Court with regard to the legal status of unborn human life. It does this through exploring judgment EXP. N° 02005-2009-PA/TC, a Constitutional appeal demanding "the Health Department to pause the programme to distribute the 'After Day Pill' (known in Europe as the 'morning after pill') in all public and care organizations, hospitals, and other health centers where it is dispensed without charge."[1] The analysis is focused on this judgment and on the legal problems relating to the right to life, specifically whether the distribution of the "morning after pill"[2] by public entities concerns the constitutionally protected right to life.

The chapter will first establish the conceptual framework by which we can understand the nature of the judgments of the Constitutional Court on the Peruvian Constitution.

---

1 STC N.° 02005-2009-PA/TC, # 1.
2 Also named the Emergency Contraception Pill and henceforth referred to by the initials ECP.

2 Constitutional Framework. Directly Established Constitutional Norms and Indirectly Established Constitutional Norms

It is nowadays well accepted that judges[3] and especially constitutional court judges[4] play an active role in the creation of law inside the constitutional system of law. This chapter will not contest this role but instead will use it as the basis for a discussion of comments on the rights of the embryo by the Peruvian Constitutional Court in case STC N° 02005-2009-PA/TC.

Taking for granted the classic difference between texts and norms derived therefrom,[5] and considering interpretation as the mechanism to transform texts into norms,[6] it is possible to accept the distinction among constitutional norms made by the well-known philosopher R. Alexy. According to Alexy, constitutional norms can be directly established or derivatives (also called, indirectly established norms)[7]. Established constitutional norms are found literally from the text of the norm considered. However when related to a directly established constitutional norm, it is necessary to include not only the norm to be explained but also all related norms as well.[8] This approach is a particularly important one as will be explained later.

Derivative constitutional norms have been explained by Alexy in the following way: "a derivative norm is valid and is a correct constitutional norm when it is possible to provide a correct constitutional justification for it under a directly established norm."[9] Using this definition, it is possible to develop a more general definition, that is, a derivative norm is a valid constitutional norm when it is possible to provide the correct constitutional justification for it under a directly established norm. This is the definition of an indirectly established, derivative constitutional norm and is valid not only for constitutional norms on fundamental rights.

---

3   Judges are also known as "law lords." See ZAGREBELSKY, G. *El Derecho ductile*. Trotta. Madrid. 2007, p. 150.
4   Specifically, the Peruvian Constitutional Court has said of itself that: "Constitutional judgments, as far as they represent Constitutional interpretation from the highest court of the country, become sources of law binding all the powers of the State." EXP. N° 3741-2004-PA/TC, #42.
5   GUASTINI, R., "Disposición vs. Norma," in POZZOLO, S. and ESCUDERO, R., *Disposición vs. Norma*, Palestra, Lima, 2011, pp. 133–156.
6   GUASTINI, Riccardo, *Estudios sobre la interpretación jurídica*, Porrúa – UNAM, México 2008, pp. 3–6.
7   ALEXY, Robert, *A Theory of Constitutional Rights*. Oxford University Press. Oxford. 2010, p. 36.
8   CASTILLO CÓRDOVA, Luis, *Los derechos constitucionales. Elementos para una teoría general*, 3ª edición, Palestra, Lima, 2007, pp. 238–240.
9   ALEXY, R. *A Theory of Constitutional. . . .*, op.cit., p. 36.

2.1 The Constitutional Court as a Creator of Constitutional Norms

Directly established constitutional norms are created by the constituent power as a legal text. Its creation as a legal text is sufficient to ground their validity. Indirectly established constitutional norms are not an accomplishment of the citizen, but a binding interpretation of the directly established constitutional norms by those with decision-making authority.[10] Even if the man on the street were able to make an interpretation of the constitution, it would not be binding.[11] Among the public bodies with public functions that include making binding interpretations of the Constitution, the authority of the Constitutional Court should be highlighted.[12]

Constitutional interpretation of constitutional texts by the Constitutional Court will always end with the formulation of an indirectly established constitutional norm. Although the preciseness of the indirectly established constitutional norm will vary, it will always define the directly established norm more precisely and will share its binding force.

There are different reasons why constitutional interpretations by the Constitutional Court result in constitutional norms: first because the interpretation is binding, which is a singular effect of any norm[13]; and second because these interpretations share the same nature with directly established constitutional norms. This is the way Constitutional Court creates norms: by means of interpreting. Norms created by the Constitutional Court carry, therefore, the same authority as directly established constitutional norms for two reasons: first, the normative hierarchy assigned to the derivative norm is equal to that of the corresponding directly established constitutional norm; and second, because if the Constitutional Court is the highest interpreter and upholder of the Constitution, its decisions should have constitutional relevance. In this way it must be accepted that the Constitutional Court has a role as a creator of constitutional law.

2.2 The Derivative Character of the Constitutional Norms Created by the Constitutional Court

Those constitutional norms created by the Constitutional Court must be understood as derivative norms from a directly established constitutional norm. Once

---

10 CASTILLO CÓRDOVA, Luis, *Los precedentes vinculantes del Tribunal Constitucional*, Gaceta Jurídica, 2014, p. 574.
11 *See* HÄBERLE, Peter, *El Estado Constitucional*, UNAM, México 2003, pp. 149–162.
12 *See* CASTILLO CÓRDOVA, Luis, "Análisis de algunas recientes normas procesales constitucionales creadas por el Tribunal Constitucional", in *Gaceta Constitucional*, # 37, enero 2011, pp. 23–25.
13 *See* BERNAL PULIDO, Carlos, *El principio de proporcionalidad y los derechos fundamentales*, 3ª edición, Centro de Estudios Políticos y Constitucionales, Madrid, 2007, p. 127.

created by the Constitutional Court they join the legal system at the level of the Constitution. From this moment, they become directly established, concrete, constitutional norms. These concrete norms are either in accord with the directly established norm, or they conflict with it; and this is also the case for derived constitutional norms in relation to directly established constitutional norms. In the paragraphs below, I shall analyze both situations of accord and of conflict.

If the derivative norm is formulated in agreement with the directly established constitutional norm, then there are good reasons to sustain and justify the interpretation by the Constitutional Court, and this is congruent with Alexy's concept of indirectly established constitutional norms.

But if this is not the case, the situation is quite different. If the interpretation included in the indirectly established constitutional norm contradicts the legal content of the directly established norm that means there are no reasons for the former norm to be sustained. If the concept of derivative norm is understood according to Alexy's interpretation, then if there are no good constitutional reasons to sustain the interpretation, the derived constitutional norm cannot exist at all. On another interpretation, however, due to the force of the constitutional interpretation made by the Constitutional Court, these interpretations will always concur with the directly established norm. They remain as real derivative norms because of the two aforementioned reasons, that is, the binding character of the interpretation, and the normative character of the product summarized by means of the interpretation.[14]

This observation leads to a closer examination of Alexy's concept of indirectly established constitutional norms. Any constitutional interpretation by the Constitutional Court will always create a constitutional norm that, by the legal force of the creator, will be linked to the directly established constitutional norm interpreted. A norm born in this way will always be constitutional from a formal point of view because the criteria to define its constitutional nature are formal: the binding force of the Constitutional Court's decisions is strong enough to link the interpretation with the directly established norm.

However, a derivative norm, formally constitutional, could be unconstitutional from a material point of view if it is in contradiction with the directly established constitutional norm. In this case, the reasons given by the Constitutional Court would be necessarily incorrect because they would justify the violation of a directly established norm. So, the incorrect reasons supporting a formally constitutional derivative norm transform this norm into a materially unconstitutional one. This is a type of unconstitutional constitutional norm.[15] In this way it must be concluded

---

14 This point was recently confirmed by the judgment, EXP. N° 04293-2012-PA/TC that cancels the stare decisis created by the Constitutional Court itself at the EXP. N° 3741-2004-PA/TC.
15 See BACHOF, Otto, ¿Normas constitucionales inconstitucionales?, Palestra editores, Lima, 2008, p. 65 y ss.

that the formula, whilst fitting a materially constitutional derivative norm, does not fit a derivative constitutional norm and Alexy's definition neither includes formally constitutional derivative norms nor materially unconstitutional norms.

2.3 The Binding Force of Materially Unconstitutional Derivative Norms Created by the Constitutional Court

The existence of formally constitutional but materially unconstitutional derivative norms compels us to explore the binding nature of these norms. Two different rules apply. The first concerns their validity: any formally constitutional derivative norm (any summarized directly established norm) must be considered valid until changed by the Constitutional Court. The exception to this rule is if the reasons that sustain such an interpretation are shown to be demonstrably wrong; for example, in the situation when it is not possible to give any reason to accept the explanation made by the Constitutional Court, the norm should be taken as invalid.

The second rule refers to efficacy and is a formal or procedural rule: a formally constitutional derivative and materially unconstitutional norm has a general binding power. The exception is when a judge revokes in a specific case the derivative constitutional norm created by the Constitutional Court because he is able to give a more grounded reason than the Constitutional Court.[16]

In the context of the constitutional framework already presented the following questions shall be considered with regard to STC. N° 02005-2009-PA/TC.

a. What are the interpretations of derivative constitutional norms created by the Constitutional Court?
b. Which is the directly established constitutional norm tied to these interpretations?
c. What reasons are offered by the Constitutional Court to sustain these derivative norms?
d. Are these reasons sufficient to materially sustain the constitutionality of the derivative norms created?

3 The Interpretation of Constitutional Norms Created by the Constitutional Court

The Constitutional Court has offered interpretations of STC. N° 02005-2009-PA/TC on a number of occasions, of which this chapter is interested in two in particular. The first can be found in paragraph 8 of the aforementioned judgment:

---

16 See CASTILLO CÓRDOVA, Luis, "Las exigencias de racionalidad del Tribunal Constitucional como controlador de la Constitución," in *Gaceta Constitucional*, # 39, March 2011, p. 27.

38. In face of the quandry of having to choose one of the above developed interpretative constitutional principles governing the understanding of conception, this Court leans towards considering that the conception of a new human being occurs with the fusion of the mother´s and the father´s cells, which fusion brings a new cell that, according to the present state of science, is the beginning of a new being´s life. A unique and unrepeatable being, with its own complete genetic configuration and individuality, that may, if the living process is not interrupted, continue its way towards an independent life. Anidation or implantation is a part of this vital process, but it is not its starting point.

Considering this statement it is possible to conclude the following derivative constitutional norm:

N38: It is commanded that the conception of a new human being shall be considered as the combination of the mother's cells with those of the father thus creating new cells that, according to science, represent the beginning of a new life.

Another way to express norm N38 could be:

N38: It is commanded to consider that new human being's life starts with the fertilization.

In the aforementioned judgment the Constitutional Court talks about the principle of caution, expressing the following idea:

50. b) The principle of caution (...) is strictly linked to the principle of prevention. The latter requires that protective measures be undertaken to stop actual environmental damage from occurring. It ... operates in face of both the risk of damage to health or the environment, and the lack of scientific certainty regarding its causes and effects The Court then added that c) even if the core element of the principle of caution is the lack of scientific certainty, ..., its application requires that there be reasonable and sufficient hints of the existence of the risk, and that its seriousness justifies the need to take urgent, proportionate and reasonable measures.

It is possible to conclude from the above a derivative constitutional norm expressed using deontic logic as follows:

N50: It is commanded that if there is no scientific certainty but sufficient reasonable evidence to put at risk a fundamental right or a constitutionally protected good, then urgent, balancing and reasonable measures must be adopted to prevent the risk from occurring.[17]

---

17 STC. 02005-2009-PA/TC, #50, repeats the constitutional interpretation in STC 3510-2003-PA/TC, #4. So in fact, it should be said that the derivative norm must be link to STC 3510-2003-PA/TC, #4; to link both derivative norms with the same judgement.

So it is possible to recognize the existence of the derivative constitutional norms N38 and N50 on judgment STC N° 02005-2009-PA/TC.

4 The Link to the Directly Established Constitutional Norm

At this juncture it is important to decide which directly established constitutional norm is linked to the derived constitutional norm created in this case. We shall begin with N38. It is possible to maintain that this norm is derived from the directly established norm emerging from Article 2.1 of the Constitution concerning the right to life. Two reasons uphold this conclusion. The first is that STC N° 02005-2009-PA/TC is the answer to a constitutional appeal in favor of the right to life of the unborn child; and the second is that the legal grounds (to sustain N38) are mainly connected to the right to life[18].

Article 2.1 of the Peruvian Constitution, referring to the right to life has the following wording:

> D2.1: Every person has the right to life (...). The unborn child is a holder of rights, in any event which is beneficial for him.

From Article 2.1 a directly established norm can be formulated using deontic logic as following:

> N2.1: It is commanded that the right to life shall be respected and the unborn child considered as a holder of rights in any event which is beneficial for him.

N38 from STC 02005-2009-PA/TC can be linked to N2.1 of the Constitution, which can be formulated in the following way:

> N2.1: It is commanded that the right to life shall be respected and the unborn child considered as a holder of rights in any event which is beneficial for him. It is commanded that a new human life shall be considered as beginning with fertilization.[19]

On the other hand, N50 on STC 02005-2009-PA/TC has a normative content that could link the directly established norm by a disposition that recognizes a fundamental right (a fundamental disposition). So N50 could be a link to the directly

---

18 The legal grounds of STC N° 02005-2009-PA/TC before N38 are named: § 3. Life as a fundamental right (#7 to 12); § 4. Human being onthogenesis from a scientific point of view (#13-14); § 5. The legal protection of the embryo (# 15 to 24); § 6. Constitutional interpretation standards. Position of the Constitutional Court on the conception (# 25 to 38).
19 A norm like this may have the following wording:

> D 2, 1: Every person has the right: To life (...) the unborn child is a holder of rights in any event which is beneficial for him. Conception starts with the fertilization.

established norm which recognizes the right to life. That norm would be expressed as following:

> N2.1: It is commanded that the right to life be respected. It is commanded that even if there is no scientific certainty but sufficient reasonable evidence to put at risk the fundamental right to life, then urgent, balancing and reasonable measures must be adopted to prevent the risk from occurring.

5 Constitutional Court Reasons to Sustain the Derivative Norms

I shall now move to an examination of the reasons presented by the Constitutional Court as justification for N38 and N50 in STC 02005-2012-PA/TC.

A. Reason to explain N38

With regards to N38 an important group of arguments come from the paragraph "Life as a fundamental right," where three main justificatory reasons can be found. Reason one (R1), it can be said that fundamental rights are binding not because of their inclusion in the law but because of the dignity of their owner[20]; and a second reason can immediately be added (R2) that because of the dignity of human beings, human life must be considered as a supreme value, requiring for its essential protection as an ontological concept[21] defense and protection by the State[22]. R3 is that the Constitutional Court has referred to an important number of international documents signed by Peru that include protection of the right to life.[23]

---

20 The Constitutional Court has said that: "the enforceability [of fundamental rights] is not only grounded in their recognition by the law but also, and even more, in the ethical and axiological connotation of fundamental rights, that are ... positive concretizations of the rights-principle of human dignity, which is previous to the State and is the supreme end of both society and the State." STC N° 02005-2009-PA/TC, #8.

21 The Constitutional Court has said that: "the person is recognized as a supreme value, and the State is obliged to protect her. The fulfillment of this supreme value entails the unrestricted enforcement of the right to life, because this right is both its projection and ... the ontological presupposition of the enjoyment of the rest of rights." STC N.° 02005-2009-PA/TC, #9.

22 According to the Constitutional Court: "life cannot therefore be only understood as a limit to the exercise of power, but also, and fundamentally, as a public goal that guides the positive action of the State, which is required to fulfill the social assignment of ensuring, among others, the right to life and security." STC N.° 02005-2009-PA/TC, #10.

23 American Declaration of the Rights and Duties of Man, Article 1; Universal Declaration of Human Rights, Article 3; International Pact of Civil and Political Rights, Article 6; American Convention on Human Rights, Article 4,1, and 5; Declaration of the Rights of the Child, Preamble.

The second group of legal grounds is linked with the concept of "human ontogenesis from the scientific point of view," and here in fact it is possible to recognize a single reason (R4) which warns that even if in science there exist different answers to the question about when human life begins, there are two main ones: *The theory of fertilization*, which concerns the existence of a new and self-directing living organism of the human species with its own individual DNA; and *the implantation theory*, based on the viability of the embryo in pregnancy.[24]

The third group of legal grounds, named "*conceptus* as a legally protected being," is related to norms at the infra-constitutional level. Reason 5 (R5) clearly expresses that even if the Peruvian legal system protects life from the point of conception through international,[25] constitutional[26] or legal[27] norms, none of these norms have established the precise moment when human life begins, except for an internal regulation applying the concept "unborn child" from fertilization till birth.[28] So it is essential for the Constitutional Court to give a legal (not scientific) meaning to the conception.

At this point the Constitutional Court uses the idea that it is divided by the two aforementioned theories, that is, *fertilization* and *implantation*, to create a complementary reason (R6) based on medical science according to which the lawyer should be ready to solve this controversy using the constitutional interpretative principles *pro homine* and *favor debilis*.[29]

Finally the fourth group of legal grounds is named: "Applying the constitutional interpretation: the position of the Constitutional Court on conception." At this

---

24 STC N.° 02005-2009-PA/TC, # 14.
25 According to the American Convention on Human Rights, Article 4.1: "Every person has the right to have his life respected. This right shall be protected by law and, in general, from the moment of conception. No one shall be arbitrarily deprived of his life."
26 Article 2.1: "Every person has the right: (. . .) to life, his identity, his moral, psychic and physical integrity and his free development and well-being. The unborn child is a holder of rights, in any event which is beneficial for him."
27 Article 1 of the Civil Code: "The human person is a holder of rights from the moment of conception. The conceived is a holder of rights for all that benefits him/her. The adjudication of patrimonial rights is subject to the condition of having been born alive."
28 "La Salud Integral; Compromiso de Todos—Modelo de Atención Integral de Salud," approved by Ministerial Resolution N.° 729-2009-SA/DM, on the 20 of June 2003. This document orders the implementation of an "Integral Health Assistance Programme for Children," from the moment of fertilization until the age of nine.
29 STC N.° 02005-2009-PA/TC, # 24.

level the Constitutional Court describes the *pro homine*[30] and the *favor debilis* principles,[31] the definitions of which may be used as reasons (R7).[32]

5.1 Reasons to Justify N50

The second derivative norm made by the Constitutional Court can be validated in the following way. The first reason (R8) is that "producers and distributors of the 'morning after pill' operating in Peru have made a description of their product."[33] The High Court mentioned the advice provided in the packaging of Glanique, Tibex, Postinor 2, Nortrel and Post Day, commercial names for the ECP in Peru, to conclude that: "in all cases there is a reference to the 'third effect' (. . .). It is (. . .) explicitly stated that, on top of preventing ovulation or thickening the cervical mucus, they prevent, interfere or impede implantation."[34] Then the Constitutional Court said that this notice is accepted as certain by the Peruvian Health authorities through the act of authorizing their commerce.[35]

In order to complete this reasoning, the Constitutional Court has also included in R9: "reference is made to what is indicated by the U.S. Food and Drug Administration—FDA—respecting emergency contraceptives and, specifically, the product 'Plan B´, (one of the ways in which this product is presented in the U.S.A)[36]." This clearly points out that according to the FDA, "if fertilization occurs, Plan B can impede the fertilized ovum from adhering to the uterus (implantation)."[37] In addition, the FDA has included as an ECP the pill named One-Step, whose prescription advice says that: "Additionally, it can inhibit implantation (through alteration of the endometrium)."[38]

---

30 "This is an interpretative principle that states that, when more than one rule is applicable to a case, courts should apply that *fundamental* norm which results in the most effective and extensive enforcement of fundamental rights. Conversely, it implies that the most restrictive norm (or interpretation) should be preferred, when the matter at stake involves either permanent or extraordinary restrictions to the exercise of rights. STC N.° 02005-2009-PA/TC, Argument 33.
31 Such a principle: "commands that, in cases of conflict between fundamental rights, the weakest part be afforded a special consideration." STC N.° 02005-2009-PA/TC, Argument 34.
32 The Constitutional Court also mentions the principle of institutional interpretation (# 27 to 32), but it is unclear whether this principle helps to justify N38. (Not sure that it would help to justify N38.)
33 STC N.° 02005-2009-PA/TC, # 40.
34 Idem, # 41.
35 Idem, # 43.
36 Idem, # 45.
37 Idem, # 45.c.
38 Idem, # 46.

And as a final reason (R10), the Constitutional Court has described the caution principle, pointing out a number of its elements: "a) the existence of menace, danger or risk of damage; b) the existence of scientific uncertainty due to ignorance, or the lack of convincing evidence, regarding the innocuousness of the product or activity, even when the cause-effect relation between this and prospective damage is not absolutely established, or there is an important contest within science about those effects; c) the need to take positive actions to prevent any danger or damage from taking place, or to secure a legal value such as health, environment, ecology, etc."[39]

5.2 Analysis of the Reasons

It is important now to ask whether the reasons offered by Constitutional Court are sufficient to sustain the constitutional derivative norms N38 and N50 from STC 02005-2009-PA/TC. The legal problem to be solved by the Constitutional Court is to decide whether or not the decision taken by the executive to dispense for free the ECP affects the right to life. Posed in this way, the argument to solve the problem can take two routes. The first has a legal nature and directly deals with the constitutionally protected content of the right to life. In this channel the following question must be answered: At which point does a human being have an autonomous right to life? The second has a factual nature and is related to the consequences that ECP has on human life. In this channel, the relevant legal question to be answered is whether it has any negative effect on life. The Constitutional Court answered both questions: the first one is by N38, and the second one by N50, offering acceptable arguments to sustain both norms.

5.3 Analyzing the Accurate Reasons to Justify N38

The first thing to do to verify the accuracy of reasons sustaining N38 is to ask if the Constitutional Court has done a correct job in exploring the origins of life. The Court has been criticized for closing a scientific debate by deciding that life starts with fertilization.[40] Nevertheless, doing so was specifically necessary to solve the legal problem set out in the case and besides this solved only the legal and not the scientific side of the problem.

The legal problem to be solved is linked with Article 2.1 of the Constitution where it is established that, "the unborn child is a holder of rights." The directly established norm related to this article has some open elements which need to be examined. The

---

39 Idem, # 49.
40 *See* LLAJA, Jeannette, "Comentarios a la última sentencia del Tribunal Constitucional sobre la AOE," in *Gaceta Constitucional*, # 23, p. 28.

first is the concept of "the unborn child." If every person has the right to life, and the unborn child is a holder of rights in any event which is beneficial for him, the unborn child will be a holder of the right to life.

It is fair that the Constitutional Court should give legal meaning to concepts such as fertilization and implantation but in doing so the Court does not terminate scientific discussion of these points because science cannot give legal meanings to the facts; it can only describe them.[41] If law cannot explain the development of the embryo, it is not the task of science to point out that the embryo is a holder of rights or to discuss at what moment the embryo should be protected. Both questions must be answered by law. So if law, by rule or by judgment, decides where in the process of fertilization/birth the concept of "rights holder" should arise, it is doing nothing but its job.

Law, then, has the right to ask when conception occurs. This is the reason to sustain the validity of R5.

In endeavoring to specify the legal (not scientific) meaning of conception, the Constitutional Court has correctly determined that medical science has two answers to the same question about the origin of life: fertilization or implantation. Both are the best evidenced scientific theories and they comprise reason R4.

The embryo as a person seems not to be at issue in so far as the Constitution has established that the unborn child is a holder of rights (in any event which is beneficial for him), since a person carries a value recognized—not created—by the constitutional power in the following terms: "The defense of the human person and respect for his dignity are the supreme purpose of society and the State" (Article 1 of the Constitution). The person, as a goal, has a supreme value. If the person is a goal, it is commanded by the Constitutional Court to establish the means to promote her development; from a legal point of view this should be done by promoting the conditions that enable her to fulfill her potential by enforcing the human goods inside the constitutional human rights, that is, by the complete fulfillment of fundamental rights,[42] particularly by promoting the right to life as a precondition for the existence of every being.[43] And this is the way to explain the correctness of reasons R1 and R2[44].

In this way, once it has been verified that the unborn child is a holder of rights who must thus be considered as a person, who—by his value—obliges public

---

41 ZAMBRANO, Pilar; CASTRO VIDELA, Santiago, "Reflexiones en torno al derecho a la vida y la 'píldora del día después' a la luz de tres precedentes judiciales," pp. 13–14, (Accessed on 28th June 2014) in:
http://www.usergioarboleda.edu.co/lumen/biblioteca/Pilar%20Zambrano/pildora%20del%20dia%20despues.pdf
42 CASTILLO Córdova, Luis, "El contenido constitucional de los derechos fundamentales como objeto de protección del amparo," in *Anuario Iberoamericano de Justicia Constitucional*, # 14, 2010, pp. 93–95.
43 PEREIRA MENAUT, Antonio Carlos, *En defensa de la Constitución*, Palestra, Lima, 2011, pp. 593–594.
44 R3 is also correct (here), however it is not relevant to this argument.

powers to protect his rights and enable him to fulfill his potential,[45] the case should be decided in view of the effectiveness for one particular right, that is, the right to life. It may thus be maintained that it is compulsory that the unborn child be enabled to exercise his right to life in the most effective way possible, and thus as an expression of justice, it is important to legally determine when life begins. This forces those responsible for interpreting the law to give legal content to a scientific concept, using interpretative criteria which in a situation of doubt will better protect the right to life.

Consequently, it is legally relevant to know when life begins in order to afford it the maximum possible protection, and if there exists a scientific doubt about this point (doubt created by the coexistence of two scientific theories giving two different answers to the same question) then, the unborn child as supreme value requires that in case of doubt the more protective theory for the right to life has to be chosen. In this case, the fertilization theory does the better job. If it is an acceptable view that life begins with fertilization, and fertilization is a previous stage to implantation, then to promote effectively the right to life, we must adopt the fertilization theory. This is more directly connected with the principle of *pro homine* than with *favor debilis* because the first one forces us to understand the facts of science in the best way to protect life. In this way the correctness of R6 and R7 can be sustained.[46]

Using this methodology it is possible to pinpoint the reasons that sustain the constitutional derivative norm N38, and accepting this, it is commanded by the Constitutional Court that it should be recognized as a formal—because it is linked to Article 2,1 of the Constitution—and material constitutional norm.[47]

5.4 Analyzing the Accurate Reasons to Justify N50

Only one of the three reasons mentioned by the Constitutional Court to sustain the accuracy of N50 is directly related to R10. To help the interpretation, the same reasons presented by the Court to explain N38 can be used. If it is possible to maintain that the person is a goal, and that this value is recognized by the constitutional power, which does its utmost to protect the human person; then we are justified in using the precaution principle because with this principle, as established in R10, the person and his rights are best assured.

The efficacy and implementation of the precaution principle has a formal and material explanation. With regards to efficacy, the principle commands us to take

---

45 See MARTÍNEZ-PUJALTE, Antonio Luis, "El art. 9.2 y su significación en el sistema constitucional de derechos fundamentals," in *Revista de las Cortes Generales*, # 40, Madrid, 1997, pp. 118–119.
46 Again see, ZAMBRANO, Pilar y CASTRO VIDELA, Santiago, op. cit., pp. 17–21.
47 Some other strong reason could be given to sustain the material constitutionality in N38, but in this paper the only reasons referred to are the ones deriving from STC 02005-2009-PA/TC.

measures to prevent damage, even if there is no scientific certainty that damage would occur. Considering its implementation and extension, the Constitutional Court has specifically mentioned the human goods of health, environment and ecology that require protection.

Therefore, if the precaution principle works in this way, we are justified in applying it to protect a wide range of legal goods, including fundamental rights.[48] As far as its focus is to prevent damage it generates better and wider protection, and it is a principle that should be materially linked with the sanctity of the person; in this way, it should be used to achieve better protection of fundamental rights and constitutional goods.

This explanation proves the accuracy of reason R10.

6 Reference to the Case

6.1 Validity of Normative and Factual Premises

STC 02005-2009-PA/TC presents a complex legal problem. Justification for the final solution is taken—through constitutional interpretation—by creating two derivative norms. By their correctness both derivative norms must be considered as formal and material constitutional norms. In other words, both norms will be linked to some other directly established constitutional norms. Both derivative norms have summarized, directly established fundamental norms, and it is necessary for them to work together to solve the present case. So, N38 and N50 provide the normative premises for this case.

In addition to the normative premise, there exists a factual premise which is as follows: the ECP carries a risk to the right to life, a risk with no scientific certitude but with reasonable and sufficient evidence. The validity of the factual premise is sustained by reasons R8 and R9 above and the risk consists of the fertilized ovum (or oocyte) being prevented from implanting in the endometrium.

These reasons, even if they come before the creation of rule N50, justify the factual premise. The Constitutional Court has recognized a reasonable doubt concerning the existence of this risk[49]; first because the instructions included in all commercial ECP packs in Peru, approved and authorized by the Health Department,

---

48 Fundamental rights can be described as human goods due to the human person. See CASTILLO CÓRDOVA, Luis, "La interpretación iusfundamental en el marco de la persona como inicio y fin del derecho," in SOSA SACIO, Juan Manuel (Coordinator), *Pautas para interpretar la Constitución y los derechos fundamentales*, Gaceta Jurídica, Lima, 2009, p. 42.

49 Specific reference in N50 to the right to life of the unborn child is expressed by Constitutional Court as follows: "This Court considers that there are sufficient elements raising a reasonable doubt regarding the way in which the AOE acts upon the endometrium, and its possible anti-implantation effects, which would fatally affect the continuity of the conceived being's vital processes." STC N.° 02005-2009-PA/TC, #51.

mention the existence of such a risk; and second, because in the other case, Plan B, the existence of the risk is sustained by the FDA (Food and Drug Administration) of the USA.

The warning made by these public (national and foreign) authorities about the risks to the unborn child is relevant and sufficient to sustain the existence of a risk. Of course, R8 and R9 are not strong enough reasons to sustain the certitude of the risk, but they do not have to demonstrate certitude but need only to create a reasonable doubt. So the accuracy of R8 and R9 has to be recognized as demonstrating the validity of the factual premise.

6.2 The Inference

Normative premise (built with N38 and N50) can be expressed in the following terms:

NP: It is commanded to consider that life begins with fertilization and from this moment the right to life exists, justifying reasonable measures to prevent the risk of danger to life, even if there is no scientific certitude but reasonable evidence.

At the same time the factual premise can be expressed in the following terms:

FP: The ECP generates a risk to the life of the embryo a risk about which there is no scientific certitude but reasonable evidence thereof.

Using both premises, an inference can be expressed in the following terms:

I: Reasonable measures must be taken to prevent the risk to the right to life of the unborn child by the ECP.

Expressed in this way, we must consider whether the cancellation by the Health Department of free distribution of the ECP represents a reasonable measure to avoid the risk to the unborn life.

STC 02005-2009-PA/TC made this inference in the following terms: "considering that, on the one hand, conception takes place with fertilization, when a new being is created with the union of the female and the male pronucleus, which occurs before implantation; and, on the other hand, that there are reasonable doubts regarding the way and scale in which the so called "After-Morning Pill" affects the endometrium and, consequently, the implantation process, it should be declared that the right to life of the conceived is affected by the named product. Therefore, the claim of the plaintiff that its distribution be cancelled is found valid."[50]

As can be seen, the Constitutional Court ordered the suspension of the free distribution of the ECP without affording a complete explanation of the logical connection between this order, the normative premises and the findings of fact of the

---

50 Idem, # 53.

case.[51] This lack of an explanation does not necessarily invalidate the constitutional answer provided because reasons might be found to sustain the correctness of the judicial measure. Therefore, it is necessary to see if those reasons can be found.

6.3 Explaining the Reasonableness of Suspending Free Distribution of the ECP

6.3.1 Arguments According to the Doctrine of Norm Conflict Doctrine

Some reasons could emerge through taking into consideration other fundamental rights related to the right of the unborn child to life and, in particular, the "right to reproductive self-determination," using the same concept as used by the Constitutional Court in this case.[52] Analyzing this fundamental right, the reasoning could take two different paths.

The first path could be inspired by the conflicts doctrine, according to which a real and effective conflict between the right of the unborn child life and his mother's right to reproductive self-determination is present in the case. A conflict like this can be solved by considering the weight of each right[53] using the equation proposed by Alexy, represented by:

$$GPi,jC = IPiC. GPiA.SPiC$$

$$WPjC.GPjA. SPjC$$

In this case the following variables should be applied:

Pi the right of the unborn child to life
Pj women's right to reproductive self-determination

Considering both variables, the equation could be translated as follows: on the one side, the value of the specific right of the unborn child to life as against the woman's right to reproductive self-determination, is equal to the quotient obtained if this value were divided by (i) the damage to the unborn child's right to life, (ii)

---

51 See ALVITES ALVITES, Elena, "Los límites de la jurisdicción constitucional a propósito del proceso de amparo sobre la anticoncepción oral de emergencia," in *Gaceta Constitucional*, # 23, p. 25; and MORALES LUNA, Félix, "El debate en torno a la anticoncepción oral de emergencia y al aborto desde una perspectiva argumentative," in *Gaceta Constitucional*, # 23, p. 49.
52 According to the Constitutional Court: "the right to reproductive self-determination is entailed in the more generic right to the free development of personality. It consists of the autonomy to decide those issues that only affect the person herself. But it could also be said that the right to reproductive self-determination stems from the recognition of the dignity of the human person and the general right to liberty that is inherent in it." STC N.° 02005-2009-PA/TC # 6.
53 MORALES LUNA, Félix, op. cit., p. 48.

the specific weight of the unborn child's abstract right to life, and (iii) the level of certainty regarding the findings about the right to life in the specific case. On the other side of the equation, the product obtained by (i) the level of fulfillment of the woman's right to reproductive self-determination in the specific case, (ii) the specific weight of the abstract right of women's right to reproductive self-determination, and (iii) the level of certainty regarding the findings concerning the right of women to reproductive self-determination.

In addition, the restrictive measure to be balanced:

M: free distribution of the ECP by the Health Department.

Using Alexy's values for the different variables, it will be concluded that M will be:

IPiC: possible damage to the right to life is serious because of the threat to implantation, without which fertilization unborn life will cease. The arithmetic value of this damage is 2^2, i.e., 4.

GPiA: the weight of the abstract right to life is always the highest possible because, as a fundamental right, it is indispensable to all other rights, such as the right of reproductive self-determination. This variable also has the value of 2^2.

SPiC: in this case there is no certainty over the third effect of the ECP, so the value should be not "sure" but "probable", (that is, 2^{-1}), or "not obviously false", (that would be a 2^{-2}). The lower possible value should be chosen to give the equation a higher margin of efficacy. So in the specific case, if the ECP affects implantation it would be "not obviously false," and this will give it a value of 2^{-2}, which is ¼.

WPjC: effective realization of women reproductive self-determination rights cannot be slight, as far as the ECP aims to avert unwanted pregnancies. To give the equation a higher effectiveness this concept has the assigned value of 2^2, i.e., 4.

GPjA: the abstract value of women's right to reproductive self-determination cannot be equal with the right to life; if life has a high damage value, then the right of women to reproductive self-determination should have a medium value, which could be 2^1, i.e., 2.

SPjC: the certitude level that use of the ECP can avert pregnancy is not "sure" as far as it is not completely scientifically proven that the ECP prevents implantation. To support the equation, the highest possible of the remaining values will be assigned: that is 2^{-1}, i.e., ½.

If written variables are replaced by the numeric values we get.

$$GPi,jC = 4.4.1/ 4 = 4 = 1$$

$$4.2.1/2\,2$$

Even though, in the case of doubt, the lowest possible value has been assigned to those variables relating to the right to life, to fulfill the efficacy of the equation to solve the conflict, the result is 1. That means that in this specific case both rights, that is, that of the unborn child to life and that of women to reproductive self-determination, have the same weight. Nevertheless, if a higher value is assigned to the variables relating to the right to life in SPiC, it is shown that the right to life weighs more than women's right to reproductive self-determination.

Applying a balancing test to this case will thus, either result in a technical tie between both rights, or in a slight victory for the right to life of the unborn child. With regards to the main question of this paper, the balancing test offers a fuzzy result. It concludes that there are not enough reasons either for declaring M constitutional or unconstitutional, nor for or against the reasonability of the judicial rule suspending the free distribution of the ECP.

6.3.2 Reasoning from a Non-Conflict Perspective

A different way to see the picture is by rejecting the idea that constitutional content or the essential content of the right to life has ever been in contradiction with the constitutional content or with the essential content of the right of women to reproductive self-determination, understanding that human goods justifying and describing the scope of any fundamental right cannot justify at the same time two different and competing notions.[54] Therefore the court is not actually required to choose between rights, but, rather, to clarify which of the clashing claims is truly grounded in a protected exercise of the alleged fundamental right. To do this it is necessary to discover which party has constitutionally and correctly exercised its fundamental right, interpreting the constitutions in a teleological and systematic perspective.[55]

From a systematic point of view, it can be maintained that no constitutional content of a fundamental right includes the liberty to damage other fundamental rights because, amongst other reasons, the Constitution must be interpreted according to the principles of unity[56] and systematic norm.[57] If the Constitution is seen, not as a set of unrelated norms, but as a unique norm (principle of unity) with different coherent, non-contradictory sections (principle of systematicity), this means that if the essential or constitutional content of the right to life has been sufficiently explained, the constitutional or essential content of the right of women to reproductive self-determination cannot logically be in contradiction with the right to life.

Using a teleological point of view, the final purpose of the Constitution is framing the social conditions for the Good, which is perfection for the human being[58] or, what is the same, the satisfaction of all her essential needs (i.e., those

---

54 SERNA, Pedro; TOLLER, Fernando, *La interpretación constitucional de los derechos fundamentales*, La Ley, Buenos Aires, 2000, pp. 37–75.
55 CASTILLO CÓRDOVA, Luis, "Algunas pautas para la determinación del contenido constitucional de los derechos fundamentales," in *Actualidad Jurídica* (Gaceta Jurídica), # 139, June 2005, pp. 144–149.
56 On this regard, *see*, Constitutional Court, Exp. N.° 5854–2005-Pa/TC, # 12a.
57 *See* Idem, # 12e.
58 ARISTOTLE. *Nicomachean Etichs*. I, 1094a-1103a.

that spring from her essence). If this is so, the Constitution is ordained to satisfy in the very first place the needs of human life, the most basic of all human needs, which in turn entails, in the very first place, recognizing that all human beings, as ends in themselves, are entitled to the right to be secure against any damage to their life

It could thus be concluded that the constitutional or essential content of the right to life includes the duty—of the public powers as previously mentioned—not to promote access to any device that could be used to deny the prerequisite (factual and normative) represented by life, that means, that could cause death. The constitutional content of the right of women to reproductive self-determination cannot give public powers the right to ignore this obligation in such a manner that it would be obliged to promote the use of means to cause the death of a human being. If, as has been shown, the ECP could cause the death of an unborn child, then the right of women to reproductive self-determination does not allow the promotion of means that could cause the embryo's death by preventing implantation in the endometrium. It is precisely for this reason that it is not possible to ask the State to promote use of the ECP through its free distribution.[59] It is possible, thus, to give reasons to sustain the request for the cancellation of the decision by the Health Department to promote the use of ECP by their free distribution.

7 Conclusion

Analyzing this judgment it is possible to conclude that the Constitutional Court has created two formal and material constitutional norms linked to Article 2.1 of the Constitution. According to the first one, it is required to hold that life begins with fertilization; and according to the second, it is required to take reasonable measures to avoid possible risks to the right of the unborn child to life. These derivative constitutional norms define the normative premise in this case; the factual premise is placed in the assertion that ECP pills could create a risk to the unborn because there is a reasonable doubt that one of their effects is to prevent the implantation. Taking into account both premises it can be said that it is necessary to take reasonable measures to avoid the risk to unborn life represented by the ECP.

With the inference expressed in this way, the question is whether there are reasons to hold that forbidding the free distribution of the ECP by the Health Department is not a reasonable measure. An approach based on the conflict among rights could give two possible answers: the right to life prevails over the right of women to reproductive self-determination; or results in a technical tie between

---

59 It should be pointed out that constitutional content of the right to life does not force the State to forbid those means that could cause death. For example, to protect the right to life it is not justified to forbid the sale of guns, but it is justified to forbid their promotion (by specific regulations to restrict the sale and use of guns), or to forbid their free distribution.

both rights (the balancing test was not useful to solve this conflict). Using another doctrine, no conflict among rights, reasons could be given to hold that included in the constitutional content of the right to life is the duty of the State to avoid any kind of restriction or damage to life, since this is the requirement for the existence of human beings. These reasons allow us to conclude that creating any kind of risk to unborn life is beyond the proper limits of the right of women to reproductive self-determination.

In this way it is established that the measure forbidding free distribution of the ECP by Health Department is a justified measure. Therefore it is a fair and well-founded answer by the Peruvian Constitutional Court.

Bibliography

Alexy, Robert, *A Theory of Constitutional Rights*. Oxford University Press. Oxford. 2010.

Alvites Alvites, Elena, "Los límites de la jurisdicción constitucional a propósito del proceso de amparo sobre la anticoncepción oral de emergencia," in *Gaceta Constitucional*, 23 ps. 15–26, 2009.

Bachof, Otto, *¿Normas constitucionales inconstitucionales?*, Palestra editores, Lima, 2008.

Bernal Pulido, Carlos, *El principio de proporcionalidad y los derechos fundamentales*, 3ª edición, Centro de Estudios Políticos y Constitucionales, Madrid 2007.

Castillo Córdova, Luis, *Los derechos constitucionales. Elementos para una teoría general*, 3ª edición, Palestra, Lima, 2007.

Castillo Córdova, Luis, "La interpretación iusfundamental en el marco de la persona como inicio y fin del derecho," in Sosa Sacio, Juan Manuel (Coordinator), *Pautas para interpretar la Constitución y los derechos fundamentales*, Gaceta Jurídica, Lima, 2009.

Castillo Córdova, Luis, "El contenido constitucional de los derechos fundamentales como objeto de protección del amparo," in *Anuario Iberoamericano de Justicia Constitucional*, 14, ps 89–118, 2010.

Castillo Córdova, Luis, *Los precedentes vinculantes del Tribunal Constitucional*, Gaceta Jurídica, Lima, 2014.

Guastini, Riccardo, *Estudios sobre la interpretación jurídica*, Porrúa – UNAM, México, 2008.

Guastini, Riccardo, "Disposición vs. Norma," in Pozzolo, Susanna. and Escudero, Rafael, *Disposición vs. Norma*, Palestra, Lima, 2011.

Häberle, Peter, *El Estado Constitucional*, UNAM, México, 2003.

Llaja, Jeannette, "Comentarios a la última sentencia del Tribunal Constitucional sobre la AOE," in *Gaceta Constitucional*, 23, ps, 27–34, 2009.

Martínez-Pujalte, Antonio Luis, "El art. 9.2 y su significación en el sistema constitucional de derechos fundamentales," in *Revista de las Cortes Generales*, 40, Madrid, 1997.

Morales Luna, Félix, "El debate en torno a la anticoncepción oral de emergencia y al aborto desde una perspectiva argumentativa" in *Gaceta Constitucional*, 23, ps. 43–56, 2009..

Pereira Menaut, Antonio Carlos, *En defensa de la Constitución*, Palestra, Lima, 2011.

Serna, Pedro; Toller, Fernando, *La interpretación constitucional de los derechos fundamentales*, La Ley, Buenos Aires, 2000.

Zagrebelsky, G. *El Derecho dúctil*. Trotta. Madrid, 2007.

Zambrano, Pilar; Castro Videla, Santiago, "Reflexiones en torno al derecho a la vida y la 'píldora del día después' a la luz de tres precedentes judiciales," http://www.usergioarboleda.edu.co/lumen/biblioteca/Pilar%20Zambrano/pildora%20del%20dia%20despues.pdf. Accessed on 28th June 2014.

Cases:

EXP. N.° 3510-2003-PA/TC

EXP. N.° 3741-2004-PA/TC

Exp. N.° 5854-2005-Pa/TC

EXP. N.° 02005-2009-PA/TC

EXP. N.° 04293-2012-PA/TC

John Finnis

Unborn Human Life and Fundamental Rights: Concluding Reflections

As its title signals, this timely and significant book informs and invites reflection on two broad themes: (1) the place of unborn children in the human family and the extent of their human rights; (2) the place of judicial power and adjudication in the political and legal order for defending and promoting human rights. As most of the book's chapters demonstrate, the entrusting of human rights to the judicial branch of constitutional order has—over the past 50 years—turned out to be at best a thoroughly inadequate means of protecting those rights against popular or legislative abuse or neglect, and at worst has *eased* the way for strong persons to exercise an abusive dominance over the weakest.

I

The place of the unborn in the human family has never been as widely obvious as it now is. Everyone now knows that at six or seven weeks, ultrasound can normally allow you to see that your baby has a beating heart and is properly within the gestational sac, and before halfway through prenatal gestation can allow you to see whether you have a boy or a girl. And everyone can easily find out in five minutes on the Internet what are all the prior stages of gestation involved, from the decisive minutes of conception onwards. Truths that became securely clear to embryologists and medical practitioners only in the late 18th century, and that persuaded so many medical practitioners in the early and mid-19th century to campaign for new laws protecting unborn life—better put: unborn human persons—from assault and extinction even in earliest gestation, are truths now available to all and palpable to anyone who is willing to contemplate the evidence in good faith for a few minutes.

But we need a language with which to think clearly about the similarities and differences between human existence before and after birth, and between before and after self-consciousness, between before and after "the age of reason," and between before and after senility or dementia *or coma*—all of these important *states* or conditions in which one may be in the course of one's single unbroken existence between conception and death. The key idea we need is *capacity*, with its implied counterpart, *actualization* of capacity, and the further implied counterpart, unactualized (not-yet-actualized), that is to say, *radical* (= root) *capacity*. And right from the start we need to be clear that a radical, not yet actualized, capacity is nonetheless a real (in that sense actual, though not yet actualized) capacity.

Consider. Everyone is devoid of self-reflective consciousness at times, indeed for hours each day and many hours each week. So it cannot be a precondition of one's personhood or one's human rights that one be actually conscious, let alone self-reflectively conscious. Capacity, real capacity, is what counts. But real (not merely potential) capacity for self-consciousness (including experience and awareness) is present in the unborn human from a very early stage in its (his or her) existence as a distinct individual—the one who traverses the single, continuous span from conception to death as a continuous, self-identical individual.

Provided the product of a fertilizing of human gametes has the epigenetic primordia for development of the kind characteristic of humans, that conceptus then and there already has the real capacities—in their earliest form, which I am suggesting can helpfully be called radical capacities—to laugh, be conscious of failure and frustration, and in general to live the life of a human person in the way appropriate to its (his or her) age. Already he or she—should (as a matter of coherent respect for data) be judged to be a subject of rights—for example, of the right not to be killed by a technician or gynecologist who wants to kill members, including the youngest members, of a certain race or sex he hates. *Compared with a mouse embryo in an adjacent petri dish*, the human embryo is already in a condition to have aims, experience disappointment, regret having been harmed in early life, and so forth—though, unlike a six- or sixty-year-old, the embryo's condition requires that the having of such experiences be postponed quite a lot longer than a normal period of sleep.

In thinking, judging, and talking like this, we are of course contesting the prime philosophical assumption of much post-modern discourse, which is that rights (and status as a subject, "moral status," and personhood) are matters of attribution or ascription, rather than of truths to be acknowledged. The relevant truth and reality is that, despite their manifold differences between each other, human beings are each other's equals in a fundamental respect, namely in each possessing the *radical capacities* for understanding, for self-conscious reasoning, and for choosing between alternatives. These are capacities that, in the relevant sense of understanding (and of self-conscious reasoning, and of choosing), are evidently not shared by animals of any other species known to us but are, as radical capacities, shared by all of us human beings (possessing the aforementioned epigenetic primordia) even when the exercise of that capacity is prevented by sleep, illness, disability, decay, *or immaturity*—forms of overlaying, blocking, or *delaying* of the radical capacity's exercise which do not negate the individual's dynamic, constitutive orientation towards such exercise, an orientation and dynamic structure which enables many forms of therapy to alleviate or overcome the overlay or block and allow the individual's nature to actualize its capacities.

The line of thought sketched in the preceding four paragraphs has nothing arbitrary about it. It is not dependent on convention, or on any religious faith or tenet; nor is it a speciesism (giving preference to the *us* or the *ours* because us and ours). It is a matter of understanding and acknowledgment, of each reader of these words understanding and acknowledging what it is to exist as a human kind of being.

And equally it is a matter of understanding and acknowledgment when one—each reader—goes a step further and acknowledges that one's own existence and knowledge—the reader's own existence and knowledge—are intelligible and deep *goods* opposable to any claim to trash them, and that the existence and knowledge of other human beings is of the same kind, and so, similarly, is opposable to such a claim. There is something mysterious about the depth of personal goods such as these, and therefore about personal reality in all its stages of immaturity and maturity, and all its vicissitudes. One has no accurate understanding of the ethical, the moral ought— moral right and wrong—unless one has some sense of, and tension towards, this mysterious *depth* (which can, and perhaps should, be referred to in other ways, without the metaphor, depth, that I am for brevity using here).[1]

One legitimate way of conveying the significance of this depth is the theological doctrine that each human being is at conception specifically ensouled by a specific act of divine creative power. But everyone, even those unwilling to affirm that proposition, can grasp the substantially empirical evidence that neither birth (having been born) nor even "viability" (having acquired the present ability to survive outside the womb more or less without medical support), constitutes a reasonable "line" or precondition for moral entitlement to human rights. Each nascent human being *in utero* (or indeed *in vitro*)— provided it has the epigenetic primordia (the basic constitution needed) for development substantially of the kind characteristic of humans—is morally entitled to sustenance, care, and protection by virtue of the human constitution and radical capacities he or she *first acquired* at conception. Even if there is still some sort of case for treating birth as decisive for purposes of property law, neither the law of criminal protection nor the morality and law of human and fundamental rights can any longer treat birth as a rationally sustainable precondition for equal protection of the law; and "viability" fares no better. The agnosticism professed by judges such as the majority in *Roe v Wade* was and is willfully inattentive to admissible evidence and rigorous philosophical and common-sense inference.

It follows that a just legal order will proceed on a principle (whether given constitutional status or not) such as was articulated from 1973 to 2018 by the Constitution of Eire: "The State acknowledges the right to life of the unborn and, with due regard to the equal right to life of the mother, guarantees in its laws to respect, and, as far as practicable, by its laws to defend and vindicate that right." Such "due regard" for the life of each is not properly maintained by a law that prohibits

---

1 On the "depth" and "mysteriousness" or "strangeness" of commonplace, everyday life as a person engaging in acts of understanding (and misunderstanding), communication (and miscommunication) of abstract ideas and arguments, regrets and aspirations, etc., *see* my "Nature and Freedom in Personal Identity," *Collected Essays of John Finnis* [*CEJF*] vol. II *Intention and Identity* (Oxford: Oxford University Press, 2011), 1–10; "Human Rights and Common Good: General Theory," *CEJF* III *Human Rights and Common Good*, 4–9.

killing the unborn "except to save the life of the mother." For even though the law of many Christian nations has been framed in that sort of way, the formula implies that it is sometimes right to choose precisely to kill as a means to a (good) end. And when one chooses something (e.g., to kill) as a means, one is intending that (e.g., intending to kill).

So if the mother is threatening to commit suicide (or if her relatives or others are threatening to kill her) unless her baby is aborted, authorizing the abortion is authorizing the killing of someone (the unborn baby) as a means, albeit to a good end—an end that ought instead to be pursued by other means such as guarding or restraining her (or protecting her from her relatives or others). The majority of the Irish Supreme Court, in line (as William Binchy shows in chapter 7) with misguided concessions of counsel for the Attorney General, erred gravely in *Attorney-General v X* [1992] IESC 1, [1992] 1 IR 1 in holding that the above-quoted constitutional provision made lawful an abortion performed to avert the mother's threat to kill herself unless she could get an abortion; the dissenting judge rightly said:

> If there is a suicidal tendency then this is something which has to be guarded against. If this young person without being pregnant had suicidal tendencies due to some other cause then nobody would doubt that the proper course would be to put her in such care and under such supervision as would counteract such tendency and do everything possible to prevent suicide. I do not think the terms of the Eighth Amendment or indeed the terms of the Constitution before amendment would absolve the State from its obligation to vindicate, and protect the life of a person who had expressed the intention of self-destruction. This young girl clearly requires loving and sympathetic care and professional counselling and all the protection which the State agencies can provide or furnish.
>
> 129. There could be no question whatsoever of permitting another life to be taken to deal with the situation even if the intent to self-destruct could be traced directly to the activities or the existence of another person.

Means of protecting the life of the mother are proper when they are means *inherently suited* to protecting life and intended to preserve both lives *as far as possible*. Abortion for the purpose treated by the majority judges as legitimating abortion— to forestall suicide—satisfied neither of the preconditions, and involved intending and using means to get the baby dead.

The preconditions are satisfied most obviously when (i) some pathology threatens the life of the mother and consequently the life also of the unborn child, (ii) waiting will probably result in the death of both, (iii) there is no way to save the life of the child alone, and (iv) an operation likely or certain to result in the death of the child can save the life of the mother. Thus it is just and not homicidal to terminate ectopic pregnancies (where the embryo cannot be successfully transplanted from the fallopian tube to the uterus) either by removing the tube containing the embryo (salpingectomy) or, where medically indicated, by removing the embryo leaving the tube in place (salpingostomy). On the same principles and criteria, it is neither homicidal not unjust to perform a craniotomy in order to make it possible to remove an unborn child from the birth canal to save the life of the mother, even if the procedure immediately kills the child by crushing and emptying its skull. For, accurately judged, such a procedure can and should be performed without any intent to kill, and without any inadequacy of regard for the child's right to life.[2]

In this volume, Gerard Bradley's chapter 2 provides significant illumination on the failure of the Supreme Court of the United States, and some other judges, to engage even plausibly, let alone seriously and soundly, with the realities of the existence of the unborn. Binchy's chapter 7 shows that the European Court of Human Rights has—quite openly since *Vo v France* (2004)—made the same unblushing refusal to consider the facts and even the question. Judicial failure of this kind is shown up as the abject default it is by Bradley's chapter's study of the extensive and ongoing efforts (all too rarely studied, analyzed, and discussed as Bradley does) by state and federal legislatures to acknowledge and give proper juridical effect to the relevant human realities within the constraints of the Supreme Court's rationally indefensible but constitutionally governing decisions in *Roe v Wade* (1973) and *Planned Parenthood v Casey* (1992).

II

The earlier of those two US decisions (decided along with its equally or more destructive twin, *Doe v Bolton* (1973)), was accurately described by one of the two dissenting justices as an exercise of "raw judicial power"—raw because lacking any sufficient basis in reason or law. The later decision, *Casey*, tacitly acknowledged *Roe*'s juridical inadequacy, explicitly overruled it in part, but upheld its "central holding" because of its "rare precedential force." The *Casey* quasi-majority alleged, extravagantly, that *Roe* had that force because in it "the Court's interpretation of the Constitution calls the contending sides of a national controversy to end their national division by accepting a common mandate rooted in the Constitution," something the Court had done "only twice in our lifetimes."[3] In truth, *Roe* had aborted a "national controversy" that had only just begun, and did so on grounds almost universally regarded by constitutional scholars (even the many who favored overturning laws restricting abortion) as unrooted in the Constitution. And much more solidly rooted in the doctrine and practice of the US Supreme Court is the opposite doctrine, that the Court's decisions overturning legislation on constitutional grounds should have less rather than more precedential weight than its other decisions.[4]

---

2 *See CEJF* vol. III essay 19 ("Justice for Mother and Child"); vol. II essay 19 (" 'Direct' and 'Indirect' in Action").
3 *Casey* 505 United States Reports 833 at 867.
4 *See* Paul Yowell, *Constitutional Rights and Constitutional Design: Moral and Empirical Reasoning in Judicial Review* (Oxford: Hart, 2018), 138–140.

In considering the place of judicial power and adjudication in the political and legal order for defending and promoting human rights, the question when a supreme court should overrule its own previous decisions is, of course, less important than the question whether and on what bases and with what (if any) freedom it should, or can legitimately, overrule legislation. And that more important question arises in specially acute form when the legislation proposed to be overruled or set aside is legislation that was *in force at the time of the adoption of the constitutional provisions* that the court is now treating as invalidating the legislation. And the question arises most acutely of all when that legislation was not merely in force at the time of the adoption of the constitution or charter of rights, but peacefully and uncontroversially in force, in such a way that all or substantially all of those who drafted and approved the Constitution or charter either assumed or would if asked have assumed that it was compatible with the Constitution or charter. This, albeit in differing ways, is true of the rules of criminal law prohibiting suicide, assisting suicide, and euthanasia that were overthrown by the Supreme Court of Canada in *Carter* (2015), and the rules restricting abortion overthrown by the same court in *Morgenthaler* (1988)—decisions prominent among those discussed, always rewardingly, in Dwight Newman's chapter 3.

The proper function and authority of courts and judiciary is to declare, apply, and order the enforcement of *the law that existed at the time when the dispute arose* that has been brought before the court by the disputing persons (the parties to the litigation). It is not the courts' function or proper authority to introduce *new rules or propositions of law*, except perhaps within certain fields of private law that have traditionally been left to "common law," substantially without the initiative or enactment of constitutional provisions or legislative enactments by the legislature. (Luis Córdova in chapter 12 may seem to contradict this by saying it is "well accepted that judges and especially constitutional court judges play an active role in the creation of law inside the constitutional system of law," but the conflict between us may be more apparent than real, since he accepts that judicial "creation of norms" is "materially unconstitutional" unless it is effected by an *interpretation* (of a directly established constitutional norm) for which there is "good constitutional reason." I think his quasi-Kelsenian framework for considering the juridical propriety of judicial interpretation is inconvenient, but this is not the place to conduct an argument about that. Suffice it to say that even apart from considerations of democratic legitimacy, the case for a separation of judicial from legislative power is very strong, in view of the need for a constitutional organ or institution that is dedicated to upholding and enforcing the law in force at the time (past) when a dispute arose. And nothing confers on court proceedings an aptitude for the sort of polyvalent moral and factual investigations, considerations, assessments, and provisions needed to settle just law for the future of the whole community.)

This being so, it ought to have been axiomatic that legislation *in force at the time of the adoption of the constitution or charter of rights* is to be treated by the courts as—or at least as if—consistent and compliant with the Constitution or charter. The purposes of the adoption of the Constitution or charter should have been assumed to include no purpose of conferring on the courts the new role of being a roving law reform commission or unelected legislature activated by the concerns and claims of litigants. Rather, the purpose of adopting a judicially enforceable charter or Constitution should have been assumed to be help preserve the political community from *backsliding* and regression by the executive or legislature. Deliberate change in the law is for the legislature and/or for constitutional amendment by referendum or other established procedures, not for the courts under the guise of applying the vague terms of a Constitution or charter adopted partly because those terms were taken by their makers to have left intact the existing law they had been content to leave in force.

So for the last half-century and more, the record of courts in many English-speaking countries, like for 40 years, the record of the European Court of Human Rights has been a record of accelerating *usurpation* of legislative authority to introduce and push through, by raw judicial power, the reforms desired by pluralities among elites unable or unwilling to effect such reforms by legislation or constitutional amendment. Juan Cianciardo's chapter 8 describes the conduct of the Inter-American Court of Human Rights in 2012, conduct that we can see amounted to legislation and juridical error in so far as it involved declaring a "human right" to procreate by *in vitro* fertilization. For this result was achieved by extrapolating from the Convention right to "private life," an extrapolation made *before and without* considering whether elevating this *interest* (desire to resort to IVF) to the status of a human or Convention *right* is compatible or instead incompatible with the indubitable Convention right of human beings to life. And Salvatore Amato's chapter 4 finishes by outlining somewhat similar misconduct by the Italian Constitutional Court in its decisions of 2009 and 2014, weakening further some of the (admittedly flawed and compromise) provisions of the Italian legislature that protected interests and rights of "unborn" children conceived by IVF, and doing so on the basis of a postulated "right to procreate" that in philosophical and moral truth is a pseudo-right to *produce* or manufacture a product—a human child but one thereby doomed in most cases to an utterly enslaved and inhuman condition mid-way between life and annihilation. This abject judicially confected result only works out further the incoherent position adopted (as that chapter recounts) by the same court in 1975, preferring a trade-off of values to rigorous truth about the reality of a human being's existing and moral claim to acknowledgement and protection.

It goes without saying that legislatures and constitutional referenda, though in many ways their public deliberations are more likely to illuminate the moral and related social issues at stake in such "reforms," are capable —like courts—of introducing and imposing morally repugnant or inept rules of law. Having in 1983 introduced the sound constitutional guarantee of the unborn child's equal right to life, quoted and discussed in part I above, the people of Eire 35 years later repealed it (again by 2:1 majority) so as to allow the introduction of an abortion law on its face widely permissive (though in truth, despite many false assurances by political leaders, much more widely permissive still). The debate included some claims even less rational than those that have been visible in the often compressed and conclusory judgments of "liberalising" courts and judges. On the day of the referendum, the *London Times* urged Irish voters to approve repeal because "To place the rights of the unborn on a par with those of the mother is iniquitous. It strikes at the very foundations of family life. . . . It is no prerogative of government to dictate when and to how many a mother will give birth." And so on.

But at least such inaccurate and illogical rhetoric is visible for all to see and assess. The deliberations of judges all too often conceal the moral premises and trains of reasoning or fallacy that have in fact moved the judges to their conclusions. And the judges conceal them because they know that, presumptively, it is not their business or professional competence as judges to consider such matters, but rather to identify and apply settled law.

Of course, where the makers of the Constitution or charter are uncertain or substantially divided about the moral soundness of the law existing at the time of their work, and therefore devise rights provisions vague enough for them to hope that the matter will be taken up and resolved by the courts or the constitutional court, the presumption I have just articulated does not hold securely. The court must then do its best, at least in relation to *new* legislation. And doing its best will, or should, include acknowledging that ontological truth which *Roe* and *Casey* refused to acknowledge, a truth so basic that it provides a basis for judicial reasoning and decision even deeper than the principle that judges are to apply law, not make it.[5] This in turn provides the right criterion for evaluating, for example, the decision STC 53/1985 of Spain's Constitutional Court in face of the Spanish Constitution of 1978. Chapter 5 traces the inglorious actions of the legislature, and the inglorious silence of the Court, in the aftermath of the Court's equivocal and divided 1985 decision and judgment(s), now by-passed on many fronts. The Spanish courts and the Constitution alike have proved a weak barrier to backsliding and civilizational regression.

The Constitutional Chamber of Costa Rica, in a reasoned decision of 15 March 2000, erected such a barrier by a judgment that—as is recounted by Cianciardo in chapter 8— admirably sets out the alternative views about the reality of embryonic human beings generated by IVF and then correctly identifies and upholds the rationally sound and correct view. For this, Costa Rica was treated as a violator of the Inter-American Convention on Human Rights by the above-mentioned 2012 decision of the Inter-American Court of Human Rights, a decision markedly inferior to the decision of the Costa Rica Constitutional Chamber in logic, juridical science and philosophical and natural-scientific judgment. Again, the Argentine Supreme Court, in reasoned decisions of 2001 and 2002, upheld the reality and personal status and equal right (legal right) to life of anencephalic

---

5   *See* "The Priority of Persons" in *CEJF* II, pp. 19–35 at 27–28; "The Priority of Persons Revisited," *American Journal of Jurisprudence* 58 (2013) 45–62 at 46–51.

children and of even pre-implantation human embryos. But, as is further recounted and analyzed (with critical commentary) by Pilar Zambrano in chapter 9, the basis of these two decisions has been eviscerated or circumvented by a 2012 decision of the same court, holding that the state has no obligation to give any legal effect to the reality and personhood of the unborn at any stage.

Still, chapter 10 shows us the Constitutional Court of Chile functioning in 2008 with admirable (if not quite complete) success as a forum for examining biological and ontological realities, and their juridically appropriate implications, in relation to even pre-implantation embryonic human existence and life (in the context of certain kinds of contraceptive). But in 2017 a closely divided Constitutional Court upheld the constitutionality of legislation permitting abortion in three kinds of limited circumstance. And chapter 12 indicates that the Peruvian Constitutional Court in 2009 was able to reach appropriate results similar to those of the 2008 Chilean judgment, and in a similar context. But Peruvian law has long permitted abortion in the interest of the mother's health.

The emergence of IVF (not to mention the stem cell research and cloning discussed in William Saunders' chapter 1) has made it easier to grasp something that juridical science ought to have understood long ago: If there is to be a legal sub-category of homicide to deal with the violation of the right to life of the unborn, that category should not be framed (as it typically has been) in terms such as "abortion," or "inducing a miscarriage." Instead, the proper description of the *actus reus* (the prohibited behavior) is *destruction of the life of the unborn child*, or, in the case of children generated *in vitro*, a category such as *destruction of a developing human embryo*. The *mens rea* (state of mind making the *actus reus* criminally punishable) of the relevant criminal offenses would then be specified in terms of intent to destroy, so as to leave room for the cases where the destruction of the child (or termination of its development) is a side effect (unintended effect) of fair measures to preserve the life of the mother (or of a conjoined twin) as discussed briefly in part I above.

But in English-speaking countries, even conservative judges willing to defend laws restricting abortion (inducing miscarriage, etc.) have been all but universally unwilling to do so on the basis of a proper juridical assessment of the boundaries of the key juridical category *person*. Instead, they have relied on arguments about the usurpation of judicial power, or about the impropriety of overriding the authority of state/provincial legislatures. This has been a notable failure of judicial nerve and technique, and has left the field open for legislatures or "living constitution" and "living instrument" judges to introduce legally progressive but civilizationally and morally regressive laws authorizing the relatively powerful to exercise untrammelled power of life and death over the relatively powerless, the unborn, by unprincipled "liberty to choose"—that is, to choose, for any reason or none, to impose death on the unborn child or the embryo summoned into life for destruction.

The wholesale failure of courts in English-speaking countries to consider these matters on reality-based principle, and the by now predictable overwhelming or bypassing of the efforts to do so made by some national courts in some (not in all: see Mexico in chapter 11) Spanish-speaking countries show up the hollowness of Ronald Dworkin's primary slogan: "the courts are *the* forum of principle." As is shown and illustrated in detail in the important recent collective work *Legislated Rights*,[6] the slogan always underrated and demeaned legislatures and spoke untruly not only of their capacity to vindicate human and constitutional rights and the corresponding principles, but also untruly of their record of effectively doing so. To say this is not, of course, to deny that legislatures have also failed (and not rarely) to do so. But when a realistic account of the legislative record is aligned with a realistic account of the corresponding judicial record, the relative or comparative failure of the courts is all too apparent. (The Polish experience recounted in chapter 6 provides a sort of exception, of the kind that tends to "prove the rule": for thought the Constitutional Tribunal's beneficent decision of May 1997 overrode bad legislation of 1996, it did so with the encouragement of sounder 1993 legislation and, above all, of the explicit constitutionalizing of the right of the unborn to life, a constitutional right that technically was operative only from October 1997 but was fully and authoritatively enacted during the month *before* the Constitutional Tribunal's decision. And the technical, "legal" grounds deployed by the Tribunal to warrant its decision were, to be frank, rather lame, and scarcely models for judicial reasoning: defective if not bad means to an admittedly good end.)

III

The past 50 years have seen a collapse of fundamental civility and humanity: widespread abandonment of the sense of obligation to give legal protection to the unborn in face of maternal and paternal desires to avert the inconvenience of caring for a child for years, even decades. This has involved the abandonment of the principle that innocent human life is not to be made the object of an *intent* to extinguish it. That principle has been a bright line, and abandoning that bright line has predictably led or is leading fairly promptly to the introduction of state sanctioned or state sponsored euthanasia and assisted suicide even for people who are not terminally ill and/or not autonomous.

The fish rots from the top, and for elites it has been a matter partly of chance circumstance whether the desired changes in fundamental law are effected by judicial action (as in the United States and Canada), police inaction (as in Australia), legislative action (as in England), or carefully managed referendum (as in Ireland). But most widely corrupting and regrettable is judicial activism in the service of such fundamental and unprincipled violations of equality.

---

6   Grégoire Webber, Paul Yowell, Richard Ekins, Maris Köpcke, Bradley W. Miller, and Francisco J. Urbina, *Legislated Rights: Securing Human Rights through Legislation* (Cambridge University Press, 2018)

Ad Fontes

Schriften zur Philosophie

Herausgegeben von Tadeusz Guz

Band 1 Dominik Lusser: Individua Substantia. Interpretation und Umdeutung des Aristotelischen ουσια-Begriffs bei Thomas von Aquin und Johannes Duns Scotus. 2006.

Band 2 Magdalena Börsig-Hover: Zur Ontologie und Metaphysik der Wahrheit. Der Wahrheitsbegriff Edith Steins in Auseinandersetzung mit Aristoteles, Thomas von Aquin und Edmund Husserl. 2006.

Band 3 Tadeusz Guz (Hrsg.): Das Naturrecht und Europa. 2007.

Band 4 Erik M. Mørstad: Der Tod und die Erinnerung. Eine kulturphilosophische und theologische Auseinandersetzung mit der Erinnerung an Jesus von Nazaret und an den Menschen. 2007.

Band 5 Magdalena Börsig-Hover: Romano Guardini (1885-1968). Wegbereiter des 21. Jahrhunderts. 2009.

Band 6 Tadeusz Guz / Elżbieta Szczurko / Leszek Bruśniak (Hrsg./eds.): Metaphysik heute / Metaphysics today. 2009.

Band 7 Anton Hilckman: Gesammelte Werke. Schriften zur Kulturwissenschaft. Teil 1: Die Wissenschaft von den Kulturen. Bearbeitet, kommentiert und herausgegeben von Tomasz Stępień. 2011.

Band 8 Anton Hilckman: Gesammelte Werke. Schriften zur Kulturwissenschaft. Teil 2: Grundlagen des Abendlandes. Bearbeitet, kommentiert und herausgegeben von Tomasz Stępień. 2011.

Band 9 Manfred Balkenohl: Plädoyer für das Leben. Philosophisch und theologisch. 2011.

Band 10 Aleksander Stępkowski (ed.): Protection of Human Life in Its Early Stage. Intellectual Foundations and Legal Means. 2014.

Band 11 Igor Nowikow: Der Freiheitsbegriff bei Kant. Eine philosophische Untersuchung im Rückblick auf das christliche Freiheitsverständnis. 2014.

Band 12 Heinz-Georg Kuttner: Paradoxien der soziologischen Vernunft und ihre Überwindung. 2015.

Band 13 Kateryna Vaskivska / Oksana Khymych / Paweł Marzec: Planning and Regulation of Investment Operations at Meso Level. Management, Intensification, Mechanisms. 2016.

Band 14 Aleksander Stępkowski (ed.): Contemporary Challenges to Conscience. Legal and Ethical Frameworks for Professional Conduct. 2019.

Band 15 Pilar Zambrano / William L. Saunders (eds.): Unborn Human Life and Fundamental Rights. Leading Constitutional Cases under Scrutiny. Concluding Reflections by John Finnis. 2019.

www.peterlang.com